SIMPLE FORMAL LOGIC

Perfect for students with no background in logic or philosophy, *Simple Formal Logic* provides a full system of logic adequate to handle everyday and philosophical reasoning. By keeping out artificial techniques that aren't natural to our everyday thinking process, *Simple Formal Logic* trains students to think through formal logical arguments for themselves, ingraining in them the habits of sound reasoning.

Simple Formal Logic features:

- A companion website with abundant exercise worksheets, study supplements (including flashcards for symbolizations and for deduction rules), and instructor's manual
- Two levels of exercises for beginning and more advanced students
- A glossary of terms, abbreviations and symbols

This book arose out of a popular course that the author has taught to all types of undergraduate students at Loyola University Chicago. He teaches formal logic without the artificial methods—methods that often seek to solve far-fetched logical problems without any connection to everyday and philosophical argumentation. The result is a book that teaches easy and more intuitive ways of grappling with formal logic—and is intended as a rigorous yet easy-to-follow first course in logical thinking for philosophy majors and non-philosophy majors alike.

Arnold vander Nat is Associate Professor of Philosophy at Loyola University Chicago. He has taught courses at the introductory, intermediate, and advanced levels in logic, epistemology, and early modern philosophy.

SIMPLE FORMAL LOGIC

with Common-Sense Symbolic Techniques

Arnold vander Nat
Loyola University Chicago

Routledge
Taylor & Francis Group

NEW YORK AND LONDON

First published 2010
by Routledge
270 Madison Avenue, New York, NY 10016

Simultaneously published in the UK
by Routledge
2 Park Square, Milton Park, Abingdon, Oxon OX14 4RN

Routledge is an imprint of the Taylor & Francis Group, an informa business

© 2010 Taylor & Francis

Typeset in Stone by
RefineCatch Limited, Bungay, Suffolk
Printed and bound in United States of America on acid-free paper by
Edwards Brothers, Inc.

Library of Congress Cataloging in Publication Data
Vander Nat, Arnold.
  Simple formal logic : with commn-sense symbolic techniques / Arnold
  vander Nat.
    p. cm.
  Includes index.
  1. Logic.   I. Title.
  BC71.V36 2009
  160–dc22   2009001506

ISBN10: 0–415–99745–3 (hbk)
ISBN13: 978–0–415–99745–4 (hbk)

CONTENTS

PREFACE

This logic book is designed for a first course in logic, and as the title suggests, a course in formal logic. Teachers often find themselves in a quandary about what logic text to use for their introductory course. They want to teach a real course in logic, that treats the laws and the methods of logic, to ordinary students across the curriculum, but they do not want to teach a more advanced course in formal logic. This is precisely the objective that this logic book is designed to achieve.

The purpose of this logic course is to give students a comprehensive knowledge of *the laws of logic*, together with *the method of logical deduction* that uses these laws, in such a manner that people can make use of this knowledge in their *ordinary reasoning*. Of course, many other interesting and useful topics are covered as well (as the Table of Contents shows), but the focus is on the laws and method of logic. This focus, by itself, makes this course a course in formal logic (in contrast to what is normally called informal logic), but naturally, it is formal logic in another sense as well. Logic is presented as a precise *symbolic system*, divided into the three areas of Propositional Logic, Traditional Logic, and Quantificational Logic. The nature of this symbolic system, is, of course, the very issue that creates the educational quandary. Our purpose requires that the symbolic system be formulated to correspond to the patterns and methods of *ordinary reasoning*. This may sound like a truism that hardly needs to be stated, but that is not so. Many introductory logic texts present logic systems that use special rules and formal techniques that do not correspond to ordinary reasoning, such as the now commonly presented method of semantic (truth) trees with open or closed branches to determine logical validity, which is an elegant and efficient technique, and an important tool for solving system-related theoretical questions, but which is artificial and unnatural, and ironically, incapable of being used in ordinary reasoning. By contrast, our presentation of logic gives students exact formal tools that are readily used in ordinary reasoning. The symbolic techniques will be natural, and the rules of logic will be ample, familiar, and readily usable.

This book, then, presents logic as a formal, symbolic system, and includes a comprehensive presentation of the laws of logic and the method of logical deduction, all such as correspond to patterns of ordinary reasoning. The three areas of Propositional Logic, Traditional Logic, and Quantificational Logic are presented, and treated in a standard way, except for Traditional Logic. Traditional Logic is standardly treated with much archaic detail and as an unserviceable *truncated system*, that has some rules but no method of deduction. Our treatment of Traditional Logic trims off all the *archaic* detail and replaces it with a simple, comprehensive, and commonsense method of syllogistic deduction identical to the deductive methods of the other areas of logic. This new treatment integrates Traditional Logic into the deductive framework of modern logic as a partner on an equal footing with the other areas, which is something that many teachers of logic will find to be a very satisfying result.

The book has been designed to make good use of many *exercises* spaced throughout the book. All of the sections of the chapters include various sets of exercises, typically of varying degrees of difficulty. To achieve the pedagogical goals of the book, the students should be required to do many of these exercises on a *daily basis*. There are specially designed *worksheets* on the Routledge Companion Website (see information below) for these exercises that facilitate the completion, as well as the correction, of these exercises. It is also recommended that the daily lectures review the exercise material to some extent.

There is more material in this book than what is needed to have a good introductory course in logic. The material has been arranged so that the instructor can selectively choose various parts to achieve the desired content, the desired level of difficulty, and the desired pace of the course. The book has the following main divisions:

Chapter 1. Basic logical concepts
Chapter 2. Propositional Logic
Chapter 2. More advanced topics in Propositional Logic
Chapter 3. Traditional Logic
Chapter 4. Modern Quantificational Logic
Chapter 4. More advanced topics in Quantificational Logic
Chapter 5. Logical Fallacies

The order of the chapters is flexible. In particular, the chapters on Propositional Logic and Traditional Logic are independent of each other, and one may therefore reverse their order if desired. As a further alternative, since the chapters on Propositional Logic and Quantificational Logic are complete treatments of logic, one may simply opt not to do the chapter on Traditional Logic. But our treatment of that material is a much improved and useful version, and from the viewpoint of application, this chapter is highly recommended. The chapter on Logical Fallacies is a stand-alone chapter, and one may take it at any point after Chapter 1, or not at all. There is, then, significant flexibility in how one may use this book. Here are some examples:

(1) For a more *moderate* course, do all the chapters 1 through 5, but skip the advanced sections of both chapters 2 and 4.

(2) For a more *relaxed* course, do the material suggested for (1), except, also skip section 2.6 (additional uses of truth tables), section 3.8 (combined deductions of Propositional and Traditional Logic), and section 4.4 (quantificational deductions).

(3) For a more *intense* course, do the entire book, chapters 1 through 4, including the advanced sections, but with Chapter 5 optional.

(4) For a course in *formal logic*, do chapters 1, 2, and 4, including the advanced sections, with Chapter 3 optional, and skipping Chapter 5.

(5) For a course in *applied logic*, do chapters 1, 2, 3, and 5, with the advanced sections of Chapter 2 optional, and skipping Chapter 4.

Enjoy the book.
Arnold vander Nat

Routledge Companion Website

The Routledge companion website for this book contains important supplemental materials to aid students in their study of logic. It is located at:

http://www.routledge.com/textbooks/9780415997454

Its key features are:

1. The website contains all the Exercise Worksheets for each of the exercises in the book. Throughout the book, the student is asked to use these Exercise Worksheets, which are a great convenience for both the students and the teacher. These worksheets are printable PDF files, and the student may download them one at a time, or in entire chapter batches.

2. In addition, this website contains a special Deduction Strategy Module that helps students learn effective strategy techniques in building deductions for arguments in both Propositional and Traditional Logic. This module also provides students with practice in learning the rules of deduction. The program tabulates a score for each problem as well as a score for the whole session.

3. The website also contains printable study supplements, such as flashcards for symbolizations, flashcards for the deduction rules, and summary rule sheets. All of these are downloadable PDF files.

4. Finally, this website contains the Instructor's Manual for this book. Verified teachers with authorized passwords will be able to access the Instructor's Manual from the website.

CHAPTER 1

BASIC LOGICAL CONCEPTS

Section 1.1 Introduction

> Logic is the study of correct reasoning.
>
> The study of correct reasoning is the most important study there can be.
>
> Therefore, logic is the most important study there can be.

There. What a fine piece of reasoning. Aren't you glad you chose logic? Of course you are, but *should* this argument give you a reason for such gladness? That will depend on whether the argument is correct. If the argument *is* correct, then the conclusion must be true, and indeed you are now engaged in the most important study that human beings can undertake. What glory! And this argument has shown this to you. But, if the argument is *not* correct, then the argument does *not* provide a reason for such gladness, and we will have to look elsewhere for such a reason.

There is a question that can be raised about the second premiss of the argument. What kind of importance are we talking about? How do areas of knowledge gain their importance? Clearly, importance is a relation. Things are never just important by themselves. Things are important *to* someone, and even more, are important *to* someone *for* some goal. Things are important only in relation to the goals that people have. This applies also to areas of knowledge. The study of physics is important for the achievement of such goals as flying to the Moon. The study of physics is not important for the baking of pastry cakes. It is clear now that the above argument is not stated as precisely as it should be. The argument should make clear the kind of importance that is intended. We propose that the intended importance is an *epistemic* importance, for which the goal at issue is the attainment of *truth*, the acquisition of *knowledge*. We also propose that the purpose of logic is to be an instrument in the achievement of that goal. What field of study is better suited to the attainment of that goal? What about physics? It is true that physics produces truths about our universe, but it also produces, as a goal, tentative hypotheses, many of which are later rejected by physics. Here is a more telling consideration: one can do logic without doing physics, but one cannot do physics without doing logic. The same is true for *any* field of study. Claims of knowledge in any field of study depends on correct reasoning—on a knowledge of logic. Logic is a foundation of physics, of all science, of all fields of knowledge. With this new understanding of the second premiss, we can restate the argument as follows, and it should now be apparent that the argument is entirely correct.

1. Logic is the study of correct reasoning.
2. The study of correct reasoning is the most important study there can be, for the purpose of attaining truth.
3. Therefore, logic is the most important study there can be, for the purpose of attaining truth.

A Definition of Logic

Logic is indeed the study of correct reasoning, but this definition can be made more precise. Reasoning is a somewhat wide-ranging activity, and logic does not really deal with everything that is involved in that activity. Logic has a natural focus on a part of reasoning that can be called *argumentation*, the making of *arguments*. The advantage of identifying logic with this focus is that we know exactly what arguments are, and what the standards are for their correctness. There is also a second issue regarding the focus of logic: whether this focus will be organized as a *formal system*, specifying techniques, rules, laws, and applied to reasoning in general, or whether it will *not* be organized as a formal system, applied always to concrete cases of reasoning. The former kind of study is called *formal logic* and involves great precision and abstraction, and the latter kind of study is called *informal logic* and involves a lack of such precision and abstraction, but addresses real cases more effectively. These considerations lead us to the following definitions:

- *Logic* is the study of the methods and principles of correct argumentation.
- *Formal logic* is logic organized as a formal system.
- *Informal logic* is logic not organized as a formal system.

The logic that we will study in this course will be *formal* logic. That is, we will study the methods and the principles (these are two different things) of correct argumentation, as these methods and principles are part of a formal system. This definition assumes that the reader has some knowledge of what a formal system is, and for now we can leave it at that, except to say that an *excellent* example of a formal system is one that most of us are already familiar with, namely, the system of *Euclidean Geometry*. We can even temporarily define a formal system as a system that resembles Euclidean Geometry in its arrangement, apart from its content. Later, we will *construct* the formal system of logic, slowly, one step at a time.

The Strange Argument

Let's start our study with a big bang. Let's start with a *complicated* argument, and let's go through this argument step by step, to see whether or not it is any *good*. We will use methods and rules here that we won't introduce until later in the course, and you may not understand very much of what is going on. But that is OK. This is *only* an example to give you some idea of what we will be doing later on.

You may have heard about *The Tooth Fairy*, the magical creature that collects the lost teeth of little children and gives them money under their pillows while they sleep.

Is this just a fairy tale, or does the Tooth Fairy really exist? Well, here's an argument that claims to prove that it is not a fairy tale, but that the Tooth Fairy *really* exists.

1. If John is in the house, then John came in through the front door.
2. If John came in through the front door, then someone saw John come in.
3. It is not the case that someone saw John come in.
4. Yet, John is in the house.

So, there really is a Tooth Fairy.

The first question that must always be answered is whether the argument before us is *correct*. One thing is clear: *emotional* responses, like "Oh, I don't believe in Tooth Fairies," are *worthless*, since there is an actual argument here that claims to have proved the exact opposite. We have an intellectual *obligation* to evaluate arguments that affect our views. We have to *show* either where such arguments go wrong, or how they are correct. We must conduct a test.

We note at the outset that whether the conclusion *follows* from the premisses does not depend on the *content* of the sentences but only on the *abstract pattern* that the argument has. The reason for this is simple: the laws of logic are themselves abstract patterns with a total disregard for particular content.

In logic, it is customary to use capital letters both to abbreviate sentences and also to represent the patterns that sentences have. We can thus represent the argument as follows. (You will soon become experts in generating such symbolic representations, even ones more complicated and more symbolic than this.)

1. if H then D

2. if D then S

3. not S

4. H

———————————

So, T

We will *test* this argument pattern. (Later in the course we can return to this argument to confirm that our method is correct, and that it conforms to the rules and procedures of established logical theory. Again, don't worry if you feel a bit confused at this point.)

1. if H then D   first premiss

2. if D then S   second premiss

3. not S   third premiss

4. H   fourth premiss

———————————

5. D   lines 1 and 4 correctly produce line 5

6. S   lines 2 and 5 correctly produce line 6

Let's assess where we are in the test. We were able to derive steps 5 and 6 with great ease. We have "if H then D," and H is also available; so, this produces D.

And we have "if D then S," and D is now available; so, this produces S. But how can one derive something T from items that use only H, D, S? Hmm, this does seem to be a problem. How can there be a connection? It seems, then, that we cannot derive the Tooth Fairy conclusion after all, as all of you believed right from the start. Hmm.

Wait a minute. We can at least bring T into the picture. One can always bring *anything* into *any* picture. All one has to do is say "or." For example, you say "George scored 100 percent." You must now also say "yes" to the question "Did either George or Queen Elizabeth score 100 percent?" You must say "yes" because that is the way "or" works. Of course, this introduction is harmless, because when you agree to an "or" sentence, you don't have to agree with both choices. So, there is a harmless way of bringing the Tooth Fairy into the picture. Just say "or."

7. S or T   line 6 correctly produces line 7. *Amazing!* (but harmless)

Where are we now in our test? We have gotten as far as "S or T." This is harmless, because line 6 asserts S. Well, it seems that we are no closer to getting the conclusion than before, because all we have is "or." Hmm.

Wait a minute. We have "S or T," but line 3 says "not S," S is the wrong one. Still, "S or T" is right. So, that means that T must be the right one! *The test is finished*. We derived T from the premisses.

    8.   T   lines 7 and 3 correctly produce line 8. *Holy Cow!*

So, we *must* conclude, from our premisses, that the Tooth Fairy *really* does exist. Surprise. Surprise. Of course, the test did not *prove* that the Tooth Fairy really does exist. The test only proved that this *follows from* our four premisses. So, everything depends on whether the four premisses are OK. But that is another story, one we will tell at a later time.

Main Areas of Logic

We will finish this section with a brief review of the different areas of logic, to better understand what logic is, and also to better understand how much of logic we will cover in this course. We also present a chart illustrating the relationships.

Logic, in a broad sense, is the study of correct reasoning. Logic has a number of subdivisions, and they all call themselves *logic*. These various subdivisions all belong to two main divisions of logic: *Formal Logic* and *Informal Logic*.

Formal Logic studies reasoning by organizing logic as a formal system that is characterized by items such as laws of logic, rules of inference, techniques of argumentation, deductions. Formal logic is often characterized as *deductive logic* and is contrasted with another area of informal logic called *Inductive Logic*.

Informal Logic studies concrete cases of reasoning directly, without presenting a formal system of laws, rules, and techniques. There are two important areas of Informal Logic. One used to be called "Informal Logic," but it is now generally known in college curricula as *Critical Thinking*. The other area is *Inductive Logic*.

Critical Thinking is an area of Informal Logic that studies the reasoning process by addressing concrete cases of reasoning in terms of their content, purpose, effect; there is also an emphasis on mistakes in reasoning, known as logical fallacies. We will not be studying this area of informal logic, since our approach is a formal one. An example of a topic taken up in Critical Thinking is something like this: "The type of reasoning known as *argumentum ad hominem* is a logical error, but it is so effective psychologically that it has always been a standard form of popular reasoning."

Inductive Logic is a study of arguments whose conclusions are based not on laws of logic but on relations of probability in the real world. Inductive Logic is usually contrasted with

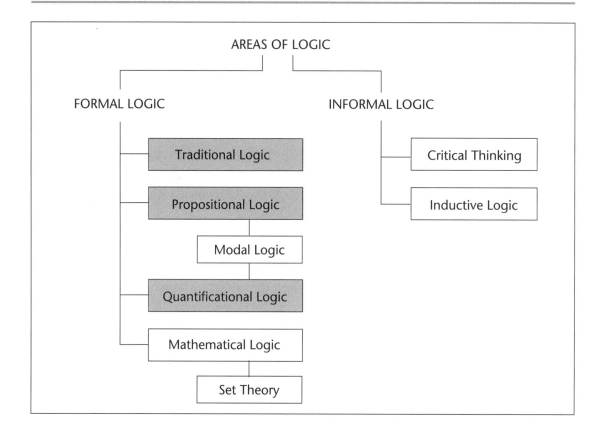

deductive logic, also known as Formal Logic. Again, we will not be studying this area of informal logic. An example of an inductive argument is: "George is picking a card from a well-shuffled, ordinary deck of playing cards. So, most likely, he will pick a card that is not a face card."

Traditional Logic is the first main division of Formal Logic. We will study this logic in *Chapter 3*. This area of logic was developed by the ancient Greek philosopher, Aristotle, and has continued from ancient times to the present. Since about 1950 Traditional Logic has been in competition with Modern Symbolic Logic in college curricula. *Traditional Logic* is also known by other names, including *Aristotelian Logic*, *Categorical Logic*, and *Syllogistic Logic*. Because of the natural and commonsense formulation of Traditional Logic, it is often incorporated to some extent in courses on Critical Thinking. The type of problems studied in Traditional Logic always involve subject–predicate sentences that compare classes of things. An example of a principle of this logic is: "All A are B, all B are C, so, all A are C."

Propositional Logic is the second main division of Formal Logic. We will study this logic in *Chapter 2*. Some parts of this logic were studied in earlier times, but it was not until about 1900 that this study was developed into a formal system of logic. This area of logic studies external relations of sentences (propositions) apart from their internal subject–predicate patterns. An example of a principle of this logic is: "Either P or Q, not P, so, Q;" or symbolically, "P ∨ Q, ~P /∴ Q."

Modal Logic is a formal system that *extends* systems of formal logic to include the ideas of *necessity* and *possibility*. This area of logic lies outside the scope of topics selected for this course. An example of a principle of this logic is: "Necessarily if P then Q, possibly P, so, possibly Q;" or symbolically, "□(P ⊃ Q) , ◇P /∴ ◇Q."

Quantificational Logic is the third main division of Formal Logic, and is an extention of Traditional Logic and Propositional Logic. We will study this logic in *Chapter 4*. This logic was developed about 1900 as an improvement to Traditional Logic, but it was not taught regularly until about 1950. This logic is heavily symbolic and abandons any resemblance to commonsense language. An example of a principle of this logic is: "For all things x, x is F; so, *m* is F;" or symbolically, "(∀x)Fx /∴ F*m*."

Mathematical Logic is a study in which mathematical systems are reformulated as special systems of formal logic. Mathematical Logic is an advanced study of logic, and lies outside the scope of our course. An example of a principle of this logic is: "0 has φ; whenever n has φ, n+1 has φ; so, all numbers have φ"; or symbolically, "φ(0), (∀n)[φ(n) → φ(n+1)] /∴ (∀n)φ(n)."

Set Theory is a component of Mathematical Logic, and studies the existence and characteristics of special sets of things. This is an advanced study of logic, and lies outside the scope of this course. An example of a principle of this logic is: "If K is a subset of L, then the set of all subsets of K is a subset of the set of all subsets of L;" or symbolically, "K ⊆ L → {N: N ⊆ K} ⊆ {N: N ⊆ L}."

Exercise 1.1 Logic Questions

Study questions. These question do not have easy answers. (But that doesn't mean that they have no answers.) Just think about these issues. There is no particular order here. Start where you like. Use the available **Exercise Work Sheet** to submit your work.

1. Will the study of logic make you more logical?
2. What are some advantanges of making things formal (symbolic)?
3. What are some disadvantanges of making things formal (symbolic)?
4. Is it true that logic is the most important study there can be for the purpose of attaining truth?

5. True or false? "Some things are settled issues. So, further arguments about them are pointless."

6. Is it true that people have an intellectual obligation to evaluate all arguments related to their beliefs?

7. True or false? "If there is a completely correct argument for a position, then it is true."

8. True or false? "If there is a completely correct argument for a position, then all right-thinking people will accept that position."

Section 1.2 Arguments

When someone makes a *claim* about some item that is being considered, people who are part of that discussion and wonder about the *truth* of that claim will certainly want to hear some *reasons* for thinking that the claim is true. People are, in this sense, *rational creatures*: they want to hear *arguments* that *support* the claims that are being made.

What is an Argument?

The idea of *argument* is the most central idea of logic, much like in the way that the idea of *number* is the most central idea of mathematics. The fact that logic is one of the oldest systems of knowledge shows that people have always placed great importance on the science of reasoning. We must begin, then, with a definition of what an argument is.

> An *argument* is a group of given sentences such that:
>
> (1) Some of these sentences are being *offered* as *reasons* for *one* other of these sentences.
>
> (2) The sentences being offered as reasons are called the *premisses* of the argument.
>
> (3) The one sentence for which the reasons are given is called the *conclusion* of the argument.

A simple example of an argument is:

Unicorns are magical creatures, because unicorns have a single horn on their forehead, and such horns possess magical powers.

We must analyze this argument as follows: two reasons are being offered for the acceptance of some claim. We label these reasons as "Premiss 1" and "Premiss 2," and we label the claim as "Conclusion," and we arrange them as:

Premiss 1:	Unicorns have a single horn on their forehead. (Reason)
Premiss 2:	Such horns possess magical powers. (Reason)
Conclusion:	So, unicorns are magical creatures.

Another example is:

The earth is a large flat material body. Careless people can fall off large flat material bodies. You are a careless person. So, you can fall off the earth.

We may analyze this argument as follows:

Premiss 1:	The earth is a large flat material body. (Reason)
Premiss 2:	Careless people can fall off large flat material bodies. (Reason)
Premiss 3:	You are a careless person. (Reason)
Conclusion:	So, you can fall off the earth.

It is important to notice that the definition of what an argument is does *not* require that the premisses *really are* reasons for the conclusion. The definition allows that the premisses, as well as the conclusion, are in fact ridiculous inventions, and even ones that have no relationship to each other. What the definition *does* require is that the premisses must be *offered* or *claimed to be* reasons for the conclusion. And, of course, anyone can always *offer* anything as anything. Here is an example: "Dear reader, listen carefully. I want to tell you something. The famous city of Paris is located in Italy." You heard me say it; I made the claim. Of course, I am wrong about it, but I *did* claim it. So, what do we have, then, when we have an alleged argument with ridiculous premisses? The answer is, we have something that is indeed an *argument*, and in addition, it is a *bad* argument. Some arguments are *good* arguments, and some arguments are *bad* arguments. The study of Logic will enable us to better distinguish the two.

We may pause here to emphasize the difference between passages that are *mere groups of sentences*, and passages that are *arguments*. Consider the following:

The weather is unusual lately. Colleges have good enrollments. Most people love music. Law school is so hard to get into.

Not a very interesting passage, nothing controversial, just a list of facts. But now compare it to the next passage. It will upset you. You will feel compelled to object:

The weather is unusual lately. Colleges have good enrollments. Most people love music. Therefore, Law school is so hard to get into.

Most of us cannot tolerate that kind of irrational thinking. The addition of that *one* word, "therefore," takes a passage that was a mere list of sentences, and turns it into a special construction of *premisses* and *conclusion*, and this has the additional effect of imposing on the audience a new *obligation to evaluate* that construction. A very remarkable process, indeed.

A Formally Stated Argument

Before we can *evaluate* an argument, we must be sure that we have correctly *understood* the argument. It would surely be a strategic blunder on our part to spend much time in criticizing an argument, only to discover later that it was all a waste of time, because we had *misunderstood* the original argument. "Ooops. Sorry. Never mind." The evaluation process requires, then, that one begins by carefully stating the argument, in clear and unambiguous language, omitting nothing that the argument proposes, and, of course, adding nothing that the argument does not propose. That is what we shall mean by the notion of a formally stated argument.

An argument is a *formally stated argument* if and only if

    (1)   all its sentences are *statements* (i.e., sentences that are *true* or *false*),

    (2)   all and only *intended* parts of the argument are explicitly stated,

    (3)   it has the *format*:
- all the premisses are listed first,
- next, an inference indicator ("therefore"),
- next, the conclusion is listed last.

    (4)   A formally stated argument may sometimes also be accompanied by a full or partial demonstration that provides a number of *intermediate* conclusions showing how the premisses are connected to the final conclusion.

Let us consider the four elements of this definition. (1) All the sentences of a formally stated argument must be *statements*. A statement is a *declarative* sentence, and hence a sentence that is *true or false*. This rules out questions, commands, and interjections of feelings, because these do not declare anything to be the case. For example, the (declarative) sentence "The earth is round" is a true statement, and the (declarative) sentence "The Sun is green" is a false statement, but the question "How could you say that ghosts exist?" is not true, and it is not false. It is literally neither true nor false, because no declaration has been made. In logic it is customary to say that a statement has the *truth-value* **true**, or has the *truth-value* **false**, instead of saying that the statement *is true*, or *is false*. There are thus two truth-values that all statements have: **true**, T, or **false**, F. Having made the distinction between sentences and statements, we can now mention that in regular logic one deals only with sentences that are statements, and with this restriction in place, we can now use the terms "sentence" and "statement" inter-changeably.

The Correspondence Theory of Truth is the view that the truth-value of *simple, basic* sentences is determined solely by the situation of the real world. The truth-value of *complex* sentences then depends in a *functional* way on the truth-value of the relevant simple, basic sentences, as we will study later on. (Such correspondence with the real world applies *only* to the basic sentences, because it is wrong to say that *grammatical complexity*, such as "not," or "if . . . then," or "either . . . or," somehow has a correspondence with the real world. For example, "The Earth is round" is **T**, because that corresponds to the real world, and "The Great Pyramid at Giza is round" is **F**, because that does not correspond to the real world. Based on these values, the complex sentence, with its four abstract grammatical operators, "*Some*thing is round, *and not every*thing is round," acquires the value **T**.) The Correspond-ence Theory has the benefit of explaining in a *simple* way how sentences *acquire* their truth-values.

(2) The next condition for a formally stated argument is that nothing may be left unstated. Everything that is *intended* to be part of the argument must be *explicitly stated* in the argu-ment. It is important to keep this in mind, because in our everyday conversations we usually *suppress* a great deal of information, primarily because we assume, and rightly so, that the people we are talking to already know those things. We do not tell people "Well, pennies are money, you know," or "Well, grandmothers are people, you know," or "Well, walls are rigid, you know," or "Well, sandwiches are food, you know," and so on, and so on. But a formally stated argument must explicitly say these tedious things, because the connection of the premises to the conclusion will depend on those details. Consider the following argument:

> Every person makes mistakes.
>
> So, Abe Lincoln makes mistakes.

Looks like a good argument, doesn't it? Well, that depends on whether this a formally stated argument or an informally stated argument. If this is the informal version, then it is a fine argument, because then we are allowed to "fix it up" in the formal version. But if this argument is already in its formal form, then it is an *awful* argument. Why? Because the following argument is logically identical to the first one:

Every person makes mistakes.

So, the Moon makes mistakes.

These two arguments have the same logical pattern, a pattern that is *invalid*:

all P are M.

so, thing X is M.

This is a terrible way to reason, as the Moon argument shows, and if this is what the first argument has in mind, it really is a *terrible* argument. But wait, everything is becoming clear now. This is *not* the pattern *intended* in the first argument. We forgot to state the *intended* premiss "Abe Lincoln is a person." This extra premiss was certainly intended by the arguer, and so, we *must* add it to the formal version.

Every person makes mistakes.

Abe Lincoln is a person.

So, Abe Lincoln makes mistakes.

Great. Nothing wrong with this argument. When it is stated in this manner, the logical connection is crystal clear, and both premisses are true.

(3) The third requirement for formally stated arguments is that it must have the arrangement in which all the premisses are stated *first* and the conclusion is stated *last*. Why? This is just the most direct and the most simple way to represent arguments. You start with the starting point, and you end with the ending point. This is just a superior way to present an argument for further analysis.

(4) The fourth element for formally stated arguments is not so much a requirement as an observation, that sometimes the arguer not only presents the argument in a formal manner, the arguer also provides the audience with a step-by-step demonstration of how the premisses are connected to the conclusion. This is something *extra*. This demonstration is not required for the mere identification of what the argument is. But neither does it interfere with that identification, and in fact, it begins the further process of evaluating the argument, which must eventually be completed. So, such additional information at the outset is certainly acceptable.

Inference Indicators

Inference indicators are words that indicate that an inference is being made, that an argument is being given. The most common inference indicators are the words "so," "therefore," "since," and "because." But these words do not all have the same function. The word "so" always introduces a *conclusion*, and the word "since" always introduces a *premiss*, and in general, all inference indicators fall into one of those two categories. So, when we analyze an argument, some care must be taken to give each part of the argument its proper function.

conclusion indicators	premiss indicators
so, *conclusion*	since *premiss*
therefore, *conclusion*	because *premiss*
ergo, *conclusion* [Latin, "so"]	for *premiss*
thus, *conclusion*	as *premiss*
hence, *conclusion*	given that *premiss*
consequently, *conclusion*	it follows from *premiss*
it follows that *conclusion*	in consequence of *premiss*
we conclude that *conclusion*	in light of the fact that *premiss*
from this we infer that *conclusion*	due to the fact that *premiss*

Our everyday arguments use *both* kinds of inference indicators. But above, we required of *formally* stated arguments that a *conclusion* indicator must always be used in the *last* line of the argument. So, when an argument uses a premiss indicator, it will be our task to *rearrange* the argument into its formally stated form.

The earth is a big flat thing. And since big flat things are made flat by powerful flatteners, it must have been God who flattened the earth. God is, as we all know, very powerful.

The original argument here has the following order of parts:

The earth is a big flat thing. *Premiss*
Since big flat things are made flat by powerful flatteners, *Premiss*
it must have been God who flattened the earth. *Conclusion*
God is, as we all know, very powerful. *Premiss*

This argument is not arranged properly, since the conclusion is in the *middle*! We must rearrange the argument into a formally stated form:

1. The earth is a big flat thing.   *Premiss*
2. Big flat things are made flat by powerful flatteners.   *Premiss*

3. God is very powerful.   *Premiss*

So, it was God who flattened the earth.   *Conclusion*

Now, that's a nicely arranged argument!

Deductive and Inductive Arguments

When we reason, we make an inference from premisses to a conclusion. In making such an inference, we *claim* that there is a relationship, a connection, leading from the premisses to the conclusion, and this claimed connection is one of two possible kinds. Either we *claim* that the connection is *based on the laws of logic*, or we *claim* that the connection is based on *empirical relationships* that we have learned by experience to hold generally among things in the world, relationships of *probability*. If we claim that the connection is a logical connection, then the argument is a *deductive argument*, and if we claim that the connection is an empirical connection, then the argument is an *inductive* argument. Strictly speaking then, only the arguer, the maker of the argument, can say whether the argument is deductive or inductive. Nevertheless, the arguer's choice of words usually reveals what the arguer has in mind, and we can then simply report the argument to be deductive, or inductive.

> An argument is a *deductive* argument if and only if
>
> - the maker of the argument *intends* the connection to be based on the *laws of logic*.
>
> An argument is an *inductive* argument if and only if
>
> - the maker of the argument *intends* the connection to be based on *probabilities*.

We have already given examples of deductive arguments. Here is an example of an inductive argument.

1. Very often, when a candidate runs for public office and makes a promise to do something, the candidate does not have a strong commitment to fulfill that promise.
2. This candidate for office has made a promise to fight gangs and drugs.
3. So, more than likely, this candidate for office does not have a strong commitment to fight gangs and drugs.

It is obvious that the maker of this argument is not basing the inference here on laws of logic. The conclusion is prefaced by the phrase "more than likely," and that shows that the arguer does not claim a connection of logic but only one of probability.

The study of logic usually focuses on *deductive* arguments and deductive reasoning, and has much less to say about inductive reasoning. The reason for this is that there are *no formal laws* for inductive reasoning. Correct inductive reasoning does not depend primarily on laws of reasoning but rather depends primarily on a broad knowledge of the empirical facts pertaining to the topic of inquiry. Let's look more closely at inductive argument patterns. Compare the following:

Pattern I	*Pattern II*	*Pattern III*
all A are B	most A are B	most A are B
thing x is A	thing x is A	thing x is A
so, thing x is B	so, thing x is B	so, thing x is probably B

Pattern I is a deductive pattern, and it is a law of logic. Each instance makes a correct inference, and this pattern has no exceptions. Pattern II is also a deductive pattern, and it is an incorrect deductive pattern, so that *each* instance makes a mistake, because in *each* instance the premisses do *not* guarantee the conclusion—the quantity "most" just does not provide the required connection. But Pattern II presents no problem, because it is *recognizably defective*. Pattern III, on the other hand, is not defective in this way. The conclusion is stated in a guarded way: the pattern claims a *probable* connection. That qualification makes a world of difference. Pattern III does not claim that the conclusion follows from the premisses. It claims that there is a relationship of "probability," of "likelihood," of "good chance." It is this qualification that makes the above stated argument about the politician (which has the form of Pattern III) a reasonable inference. Still, there is a problem with Pattern III. Let's take a closer look. Consider a simpler argument, that also uses Pattern III:

Most people live in a moderate climate.

Boris is a person.

So, Boris probably lives in a moderate climate.

Looks pretty good, doesn't it? The premiss says "most," and the conclusion says "probably," and so the inference seems to have the right proportion of connection. This inference from the *deductive* point of view is, of course, incorrect. But what about from the *inductive* point of view? There is not an easy answer. The inference "So, probably" makes a claim about relationships of probability in the real world, and so, the *relevant* relationships in the real world must be taken into account in evaluating the inference. In this example, the place where people live relates to various *special factors*, and the inference must take those factors into account. Suppose that Boris is a tax accountant. That makes a difference (a plus). Suppose he is an Eskimo seal hunter. That *really* makes a difference (a big minus). Consider:

Case 1: Boris is an Eskimo seal hunter	*Case 2: Boris is a tax accountant*
Most people live in a moderate climate	Most people live in a moderate climate
Boris is a person	Boris is a person
So, Boris prob. lives in a mod. climate	So, Boris prob. lives in a mod. climate

The case where Boris is an Eskimo seal hunter makes the item of inquiry (Boris) a *poor match* for inclusion in the stated generalization. So, in Case 1 the inference is unacceptable. The case where Boris is a tax accountant makes Boris a *good match* for inclusion in the stated generalization. In Case 2 the inference is much stronger.

These examples make it clear that the correctness of an inductive inference depends not so much on the *pattern* used, but in a very strong way on the *other factual evidence* that is available regarding the item of inquiry. And this means that, unlike in deductive reasoning, there can be no valid *patterns* in inductive reasoning. The claimed connection of inductive arguments must always be evaluated in conjunction with the empirical facts surrounding the case at issue. One can see now why the study of formal logic cannot include inductive reasoning. Inductive reasoning is very important, both in everyday thought and in the sciences, and a number of important rules have been formulated for the making of proper inductive inferences. But these rules are not rules of logic, and one must always place the greatest weight on the available empirical evidence related to the topic of inquiry. For this reason, then, we will not devote our attention to the topic of inductive inferences. Throughout our discussions, deductive arguments will simply be referred to as "arguments." If on some occasion we want to refer to inductive arguments, we will explicitly refer to them as such. In this convenient way we can preserve the distinction between these two modes of inference.

Informally Stated Arguments

Our discourses are characterized by a wide *variety* of styles of expression, and the arguments that are part of them are equally varied. The conclusion of an argument can come first, or last, or somewhere in the middle of a passage, and likewise the premises can have any location. There is also no restriction on the type of language used: We argue by means of assertions, questions, exclamations, hints, ridicule, praise, exaggeration, understatement, and so on. Most troublesome of all, we argue by *omitting* to say what is taken for granted by the speaker or the audience. An evaluation of an argument, therefore, requires that we first spend a fair amount of time presenting the argument in a complete and orderly fashion, presenting what we have called a *formal statement* of it. This means that passages that are arguments must have the following features, and if these are not originally present, as is usually the case, then the analyzer must *reconstruct* the argument so that these features are clearly displayed:

- all the sentences of the argument are true/false statements
- all the intended parts are included among the sentences
- the order of the argument is: premises first, conclusion last

Let's consider some examples. *First example.* McX and McY are having a back and forth discussion, and it goes like this:

"Holy cow, Jones is strange! Of course. Of course? Yes, everybody is mentally weird, to some extent. Oh, and I suppose, then, that those people that we know to be perfectly normal are mentally weird too? Of course. You're strange too. Of course."

This discussion contains several arguments (six, in fact). We will look at the *first* of these, and the readers can attempt the remaining ones on their own.

Sentence 1.	McX:	Holy cow, Jones is strange!
Sentence 2.	McY:	Of course.
Sentence 3.	McX:	Of course?
Sentence 4.	McY:	Yes, everybody is mentally weird, to some extent.

Sentence 1. McX makes a simple observation, in the form of an interjection and an exclamation. Perhaps this is a conclusion on McX's part, but the passage doesn't say, and so we leave it as an observation. *Sentence 2.* McY seizes on the moment not only to express his agreement, but also to express a *conclusion*. "Of course," when so asserted, is always a phrase that indicates that some proposal *follows* in an obvious way *from* something obvious. And so, McY has begun to state his argument, by confiscating McX's observation as his own conclusion: ". . ., therefore, Jones is strange." The interjection "Holy cow" is simply deleted, because there is no true/false assertion associated with that phrase. With *Sentence 3*, a question, McX challenges McY to actually state the reasons for this unexpected argument. As such, Sentence 3 is not itself part of the argument, and it is therefore deleted. Accepting the challange, McY supplies the premiss through *Sentence 4*. Here, then, is a reconstruction of the sentences listed:

Every person is mentally weird

So, Jones is strange

But this is not the whole of McY's argument. Sentences 1–4 contain something else. Even McX understands that and agrees with it. McY certainly *intended* that the mentioned weirdness accounts for the strangeness, and McY also certainly *intended* that Jones is a person, to whom these generalizations apply. And therefore, we must *add* these *unstated intentions* as extra premisses alongside the stated premiss. We should always use a *principle of logical charity* in presenting arguments: If the original statement of an argument *permits* a more favorable interpretation, then one should select that interpretation, because no one derives any worthwhile benefit from defeating a weak version of an argument, when the stronger version will automatically emerge to take its place.

> Every person is mentally weird
>
> Jones is a person
>
> Every person who is mentally weird is strange
>
> So, Jones is strange

It must be admitted that this reconstruction is actually a surprisingly substantial piece of argumentation, surprising because the initial wording given in the above sentences does not appear, at first glance, to have much going on.

Here is the *second example*. Some people are talking, and someone mentions that Bill, who is known to them, is a bachelor. Someone then responds with the following outburst:

> "How could you say that Bill is a bachelor? We all know that he's a married man, and has been for a long time. What were you thinking?"

First of all, this *is* an argument. A premiss has been given, and a conclusion has been drawn. Admittedly, the conclusion is in disguised form, in the form of a question, but the meaning is clear. The function of this question is to make a *denial*: Bill is *not* a bachelor. And this denial must be taken as a *conclusion*, because a *reason* is being given for the denial, namely, that Bill is a married man. Notice, secondly, that the argument order is inverted: conclusion first, premisses last. In a formal presentation, that order should be, premisses first, conclusion last. So, the orginal argument must be reconstructed as the following argument, whose presentation is clearly superior:

> Bill is a married man
>
> So, Bill is not a bachelor

This much comes directly from the initial wording of the argument. But there's more. This argument is *intentionally* relying on an obvious relationship between the premiss and the conclusion. If someone is a married man, then he can't be a bachelor, *because* all bachelors are, by definition, *not* married. This additional relationship must be taken as an *unstated but intended* premiss, and this relationship must therefore be added to the final reconstruction of the argument:

> Bill is a married man
>
> All bachelors are not married
>
> So, Bill is not a bachelor

Notice how these two examples of informally stated arguments, like a great many informally stated arguments, violate *all three* of the requirements for being formally stated: some sentences were questions, some intended premises were unstated, and the argument order was listed in inverted form.

These examples also illustrate how our ordinary discussions are stuffed full of arguments. We are constantly trying to prove things to others and trying to convert others to our points of view. For the most part, this is beneficial for us all, because we need the knowledge that others have to help us in our own lives. There can be a downside to this: because our discussions contain arguments, our discussions can easily *turn into* arguments—of the nasty kind. (Take that, you idiot! Kapow!)

Exercise 1.2. A,B Detecting Arguments

Part A. As you read the following passages, interpret each in the ordinary way. For each passage, determine whether or not it is an argument. If it is an argument, then identity the premises and conclusion of the argument; if it is not an argument, write "Not an argument." For this exercise, do *not* try to add any missing premisses. Use the available **Exercise Work Sheet** to submit your work.

1. If you lie to a parrot, it will bite you. George has never lied to his parrot. So, his parrot has never bitten him.

2. Earthworms are not carnivorous, because carnivores have teeth, and no earthworms do.

3. Dogs always like bones. Susan's dog will therefore like these items I have brought. They are bones.

4. Dogs always like bones. I have brought some items to Susan. They are bones.

5. Your Honor, the traffic light was not red when I went through it. Please believe me. I am telling the truth.

6. You have a good deal here. The item is not too expensive, and you can make good use of it.

7. If inflation increases, then the price of gold will increase. We have observed this matter.

8. Since inflation is increasing, the price of gold is increasing too. We have observed this matter.

9. The lecture was very boring. Everybody fell asleep. No one listened to anything that was said.

10. Everybody fell asleep. No one listened to anything that was said. So, it's fair to say the lecture was boring.

Part B. These following problems are all arguments, and they are more difficult. For each of them, identify the premises and the conclusion (you may shorten them). For this exercise, do *not* try to add any missing parts, unless the problem requests it. Use the available **Exercise Work Sheet** to submit your work.

1. That is definitely not my book. My book had my name on it, and that book does not, and that wouldn't be so if it were my book.

2. Since people should learn logic, they should learn the basics and learn logic, because if they don't learn the basics, then they won't learn logic and won't learn the basics. Logic is so important.

3. This position on human nature is impossible, because this position is based on the idea that people can never be trusted. And yet, it claims that on rare occasions certain people can be trusted. But there is no way to reconcile these two points, and that's why this position is impossible.

4. Life is short. [Supply the missing parts.]

5. Since our candidate has a commanding lead in the polls, and in as much as her opponent advocates unpopular views, she will surely win the election. And no one can minimize her considerable administrative experience. No one can lose with advantages like that.

6. Liz really wants to meet Bill. And we know she is not shy. So, I think she is coming to the party, because she said that she was free then, and she also knows that Bill will be there. After all, people generally do what they want to do, if they are in a position to do it. She'll be there. You can rely on it.

7. It may appear that people's minds are sometimes completely inactive, but it must be true that our minds are really always active. Otherwise, it would be impossible for an alarm to waken us from such inactivity. But, as we all know, alarms *do* actually work. (Don't forget to set your alarm clock.)

8. Since Bill went to the party in order to meet Liz, and given that the party was a small one, Liz will certainly meet Bill if she goes there, because two people in those circumstances will meet each other, if they want to, and Liz does.

9. You have to watch out for sneak attacks. They will make them, you can count on

that. They agreed to have an open debate, but instead they only attacked us. You see, it's true.

10. The bigger the burger, the better the burger. The burgers are bigger at Burger Barn. [Supply what is missing.]

Section 1.3 Evaluating Arguments

Now that we have a good understanding of what arguments are *made of*, we are ready to begin the different process of *evaluating* arguments. Here is a simple but unappreciated statistic: Most people do *not* know what it means to *evaluate an argument*. When asked to evaluate an argument, most people turn their attention to the *conclusion* of the argument, and they then explain that they agreed with the conclusion, or that they disagreed with the conclusion, and they might even give some reasons. But agreeing or disagreeing with the conclusion is completely *irrelevant* to the evaluation of a given argument. It is easy to see why. Without a previous evaluation of the argument, one does not know whether the argument is a good one or a bad one. And if one does not know whether the argument is a good one or a bad one, then one does not know whether agreement or disagreement with the conclusion is even *allowed*. Let's start from the beginning to see what is involved in the evaluation process. Consider the following three arguments:

Some cats are green	All pigs are chess players	All persons are born
The Earth is round	All chess players can fly	You are a person
So, all pigs can fly	So, all pigs can fly	So, you were born

It is *very* obvious that argument #1 is a *very* bad argument. The premisses are completely ridiculous, and the conclusion comes out of nowhere. But not all bad arguments are *that* bad. Argument #2, for example, is *much better*. The argument has a certain feel to it: it has the feel of a "very logical" argument. Of course, the premisses are still ridiculous, but it is nevertheless *logical*. And then there's argument #3. This argument is *perfect*: The premisses are simple facts, and these facts lead us to the conclusion. Interestingly, there are no better, obvious arguments that we can appeal to. Do we ourselves remember that we were born? (No.) Should we ask our parents whether we were born? (Suppose they say no.) Should we check some hospital archives to see whether it happened? (Suppose the records say no.) Wait, there is a better way: we can figure it out for ourselves. There's a perfect argument for it. You guessed it, argument #3.

These three examples illustrate that there are two criteria for evaluating arguments. The first criterion is *the connection criterion*, namely: There must be a correct connection leading from the premisses to the conclusion. The second criterion is *the truth criterion*, namely: All the premisses must be true to begin with. These two criteria are incorporated into the two definitions that follow.

Valid and Invalid Arguments (Preliminary Version)

The first step in the evaluation of an argument is to see whether the conclusion is correctly based on the premisses. If there is *no* connnection, then the conclusion is just a wild, groundless claim, and of course, no one is obligated to pay any attention to a wild, ground-less claim. Your response should be, "Sorry, there is no connection to your conclusion. Your premisses are completely irrelevant: they aren't connected to the conclusion. No connection—no support. Sorry, start over." So, do *not* continue with an argument that has an *unconnected* conclusion. That is a pointless activity. The first step is always to see whether the argument is *valid*:

An argument is a *valid* argument if and only if

  • there is a *conclusive connection* leading from the premisses to the conclusion.

Otherwise, the argument is *invalid*.

We will give a more precise definition of *conclusive* connection later, but we can rely here on the intuitive idea that the premisses *guarantee* the conclusion: if the premisses are true, then the conclusion has to be true as well—no exception of any kind. The matter is settled. Consider again the three arguments given above, but this time look at their respective argument patterns:

invalid pattern	*valid pattern*	*valid pattern*
some C are G	all P are C	all P are B
thing X is R	all C are F	thing X is P
so, all P are F	so, all P are F	so, thing X is B

The first pattern has no connection at all. The conclusion comes out of nowhere. It's not even close. So, that argument pattern is *invalid*, and so is the argument that used it. The second pattern, on the other hand, has a wonderful connection. It's perfect. So, the argu-ment pattern and the argument that uses it are *valid*. Likewise, the third pattern has the right connection, and the pattern and the argument that uses it are valid. Later we will see that there are *very many* valid argument patterns that we use on a regular basis, and we will learn various techniques to prove that they are valid, and we will also learn how to spot the invalid patterns.

Truth is not Validity. Falsehood is not Invalidity

It is important to stress that the truth of the premisses (true in the real world) or their falseness (false in the real world) does *not* determine the validity or invalidity of the argument. Validity is a matter of having the right *pattern*, and patterns transcend the truth-values that exist in the real world. There are invalid patterns with all true sentences, and there are valid arguments with all false sentences. These combinations of truth-values may seem surprising, but the next examples prove the matter.

All cats have tails	= T		All cats are sailors	= F
All dogs have tails	= T		All sailors are artists	= F
So, no cats are dogs	= T		So, all cats are artists	= F

- no connection
- invalid pattern
- invalid argument

- nice connection
- valid pattern
- valid argument

When you *ask* people who have not been trained in logic to do some explicit logical analysis, they often begin to *invent* little rules, because they think those things *sound* logical when spoken. (Luckily, people don't do such silly things in ordinary circumstances.) One of those invented "logical" rules is:

A valid argument is an argument that contains all true sentences. [Wrong!]

(a) If an argument contains all true sentences, it is a valid argument. [Wrong!]

(b) If an argument contains false sentences, it is an invalid argument. [Wrong!]

These inventions are *completely wrong*. The first of the two examples listed right above proves that (a) is wrong. There is no such rule as (a). Merely having all true sentences is *not* a criterion for there being a correct connection. Also, the second of the two examples proves that (b) is wrong. There is no such rule as (b). Merely having false sentences is *not* a criterion for there being an incorrect connection. And this is important: If something is not a rule, then it is wrong to use it as a rule. So, don't do it.

Sound and Unsound Arguments

The second example above shows that a good argument requires more than just a pretty pattern. Not only must the connection criterion be satisfied, but the truth criterion must be satisfied too. No conclusion is ever proven to be true by using false premisses. One must always begin with all true premisses and then continue with a valid pattern. And then a *wonderful* thing happens: there is an *absolute guarantee* that the conclusion is true as well. This is the gift that is given by a sound argument.

An argument is a *sound* argument if and only if

    both   (1)   the argument is valid,

    and   (2)   all the premisses are true.

Otherwise, the argument is *unsound*. Comment: A sound argument guarantees that the conclusion is true. An unsound argument leaves the matter undecided.

We will make four important comments about soundness.

(1) First of all, the idea of soundness, as here presented, is the *official* version of the intuitive idea of what it means for an argument to be "perfectly good." Nothing more is contained in the intuitive idea of a "good" argument than that the "therefore" connection is correct and that the premisses are in fact true. So, no other criterion is relevant for the goodness of an argument.

(2) Secondly, this definition provides us with a *test* for testing whether an argument is good, and there are exactly two parts to this test: part one, test the connection; part two, test the truth of the premisses. When this two-part test is done, the test for goodness is finished. There is nothing left to do. In particular, after doing part one and part two, do *not* go to a part three in which you try to test the truth of the conclusion. An independent test of the truth of the conclusion is *never* part of testing the goodness of an argument.

(3) The third comment continues the suggestion introduced in the previous one. People sometimes ask, "What about the conclusion? Shouldn't we test the truth of the conclusion?" The answer is: Of course. *That* is why the argument was given in the first place! The whole point of giving the argument was to present a *method* (an argument) for showing that the conclusion is true; and that *method* itself is tested for correctness by the two-part soundness test. The matter becomes clearer when one considers what "conclusive connection" means. We must wait till later for a *full* treatment of this matter, but in the meantime we can say that it means, "If the premisses are true, then the conclusion must also be true, no exceptions." And so, if there is a correct, conclusive connection, and if the premisses are in fact true, then, clearly, the conclusion must also be true. *Q.E.D.* And here is where the argument patterns come into play: *some* special argument patterns, because of their special arrangement, inherently guarantee that if the premisses are true, then the conclusion must also be true. These patterns are instruments of conclusive connection. But *which* patterns they are, and *how* they are shown to be conclusive, must wait till later

chapters. By the way, *Q.E.D.* (pronounced by spelling the three letters) is the abbreviation of a nice Latin phrase, *quod erat demonstrandum*, which means "[which is] what was to be proved." You use this to proclaim *success* at the end of a complex proof of some kind, as we just did.

(4) Finally, we want to emphasize a consequence of the fact that soundness has a two-part requirement. In general, there are *three* ways that one can violate any two-part requirement. Suppose the parts are A and B. One can violate part A and satisfy part B, or one can satisfy part A and violate part B, or one can violate part A and violate part B. Suppose the terms of an agreement specify that you must write a letter of apology and also pay $10,000 in reparations, or else you will be fired. There are three ways that you can violate that agreement:

Make the apology?	Pay the $10,000?		Result:
no	yes	⟶	You're fired!
yes	no	⟶	You're fired!
no	no	⟶	You're fired!
yes	yes	⟶	Success!

The moral of this story is that there are three different ways for an argument to be *unsound*, and only one way to be *sound*.

arg valid?	all prems true?		arg is . . .?	
no	yes	⟶	unsound	bad
yes	no	⟶	unsound	bad
no	no	⟶	unsound	bad
yes	yes	⟶	sound	BINGO!!

With all these offical ideas at our disposal, we are now able to give decisive evaluations of arguments. We will consider a few more examples of arguments, and this time we will give them a *complete* evaluation.

All cats are dancers	All cats are dancers	All persons are born
All dogs are dancers	All dancers are furry	You are a person
So, all cats are dogs	So, all cats are furry	So, you were born

We will first evaluate the pattern of the arguments. The respective patterns are:

all C are D	all C are D	all P are B
all O are D	all D are F	thing X is P
so, all C are O	so, all C are F	so, thing X is B
invalid pattern	*valid* pattern	*valid* pattern

Next, we evaluate the truth-value of the premisses of the arguments. We record their values right next to the premisses.

All cats are dancers = **F**	All cats are dancers = **F**	All persons are born = **T**
All dogs are dancers = **F**	All dancers are furry = **F**	You are a person = **T**
So, all cats are dogs	So, all cats are furry	So, you were born

We now have available all the information that we need to give the status of each of the three arguments.

Summary:	*Summary*:	*Summary*:
• invalid pattern	• valid pattern	• valid pattern
• not all prems are **T**	• not all prems are **T**	• all prems are **T**
• so, arg is UNSOUND	• so, arg is UNSOUND	• so, arg is SOUND
• so, DUMP IT	• so, DUMP IT	• so, KEEP IT

Chart of the Types of Arguments and their Relationships

We can make a chart of the relationships of all the different types of arguments that we have discussed. You should understand these ideas well enough to be able to give examples of arguments that fit into the displayed slots.

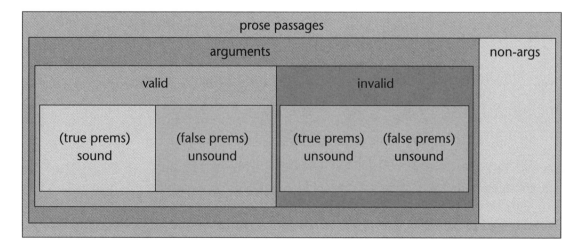

Exercise 1.3 Evaluating Arguments

Instructions. Write the following arguments as abstract patterns. Use the obvious capital letters to abbreviate the regional groups. Also, for the purposes of *this* exercise, let us stipulate that a person is said to be a member of a certain regional group just in case that person was *born* in the specified region, e.g., an Italian is only someone who was *born* in Italy. Then, answer the following three questions with *yes* or *no*. Use the available **Exercise Work Sheet** to submit your work.

Question 1. Is the argument valid?   (base this on the *pattern* used)

Question 2. Are all of the premisses true?   (base this on the *real* world)

Question 3. Is the argument sound?   (base this on Q.1 and Q.2)

Ex. All Athenians are Europeans.	1.	all A are E	Is the arg valid?	*no*
All Greeks are Europeans.	2.	all G are E	Are all prems true?	*yes*
So, all Athenians are Greeks.	So,	all A are G	Is the arg sound?	*no*

1. All Romans are Italians. All Italians are Europeans. So, all Romans are Europeans.

2. All Greeks are Russians. All Russians are Spaniards. So, all Greeks are Spaniards.

3. All Hollanders are Greeks. All Europeans are Greeks. So, all Hollanders are Europeans.

4. All Egyptians are Africans. All Chinese are Africans. So, all Chinese are Egyptians.

5. All Egyptians are Chinese. All Chinese are Africans. So, all Egyptians are Africans.

6. All Moscovites are Russians. All Moscovites are Europeans. So, all Europeans are Russians.

7. All Londoners are Britons. No Britons are Russians. So, no Londoners are Russians.

8. No Greeks are Russians. No Athenians are Russians. So, no Greeks are Athenians.

Section 1.4 Classification of Sentences

We learned earlier that a key part of evaluating arguments is evaluating the premisses. While it is true that logic has a strong emphasis on the study of logical connection, it is also true that the practical value of arguments consists in the conclusions that are derived from the premisses. So, unless we can ascertain the truth of the premisses, the conclusions based on them remain unestablished and are subject to doubt. We will devote this section to one part of the process of evaluating premisses, namely, determining what *kinds* of sentences the premisses are. As we will see later, these different *kinds* of sentences are evaluated in different ways. The four main classifications of sentences are: *necessary truths*, *empirical truths*, *empirical falsehoods*, and *necessary falsehoods*. But first a story about possibilities.

Possible Truths and Possible Falsehoods

There is a fundamental distinction in logic between sentences that *must* be true and sentences that *can* be true. But in what sense of "must" and "can"? In our everyday speech the word "can" is used in various ways.

- I *can* listen to that all day!   = I really like hearing it.   (feelings)
- You *can* have that, if you like.   = You are permitted to.   (permission)
- It *could* be true.   = For all we know, it is.   (evidence)
- Gray clouds. It *could* rain.   = There's a probability.   (probability)
- The sofa *can* fit through the door.   = It's physically possible.   (physics)

The reason for listing these different sorts of possibilities is to distinguish all of them from the *only* kind of possibility recognized by logic, namely, *logical* possibility. In logic almost everything is logically possible. The only thing that is *not* logically possible is a *contradiction*. We already possess a fairly robust understanding of what a contradiction is. We can rely on that understanding here. A contradiction is a sentence that asserts that two exactly opposite situations are both true. This is one: "Yes, some dog bit me really hard, and boy did that hurt, but that's OK, it didn't bite me." Try this one: "Good news, every single one of you got an A, congratulations; unfortunately, some of you did not get an A." What characterizes a contradiction is that it simultaneously asserts, regarding something X, both that X is true and that X is false. Contradictions are not logically possible, but *everything else is* logically possible. By the way, the different sorts of possibility listed above *all* fall into the category of being logically possible, because none of those are contradictions. So, one can honestly say that there is really only *one* kind of possibility: logical possibility (and sub-distinctions are not useful).

Here is a rather interesting fact about our minds: We have a built-in possibility-or-contradiction detector, namely, our *imagination*. Logical possibility is the same as imaginability. If something *is* imaginable then it *is* logically possible, and if something is *not* imaginable, then it is *not* logically possible. Philosophers sometimes debate this point, but the bottom line is that it's true. And, it's also a *very* useful circumstance. We all have very active imaginations, and we can put them to good use, to decide logical possibilities.

There are several comments we should make about imaginable situations. (1) First of all, people sometimes say that they have a poor imagination, and that they can't imagine things like pigs playing chess. Here it seems that people are *misanalyzing* the situation. It is true that one can't imagine a world in which the laws of nature (biology, neurophysiology, etc.) are exactly the same as they are now, and in which pigs have exactly the same brains, etc., as they have now, and in which pigs are nevertheless playing chess. But that's not what it means to *imagine* pigs playing chess. To imagine pigs playing chess one has to imagine a world that is *different* from the present world, a world in which pigs are *different* from what they are now, one in which pigs are more like people in their mental abilities. We are certainly able to imagine that. (Weren't the three little pigs playing chess when the big bad wolf came to blow their house down? Oh, maybe it was the day before. Didn't you imagine that just now?)

(2) The second comment is that "imaginable" and "imaginary" are not the same idea. This is not a big point, but there might be some confusion about it. An *imaginary* situation is one that is imagined, and which is false in the real world. It is *imaginable* that pigs can play chess, simply because we can imagine that they can, and in addition it is an *imaginary* situation, because in the real world it is false that they can. On the other hand, Christopher Columbus *imagined* that the Earth was round, and his thought was *not* imaginary, because in reality it was true. All together now, let's imagine that elephants exist on planet Earth. There. We imagined something that was not imaginary. We imagined something that was also true.

(3) The third comment concerns our ability to imagine that some things are *not* true. We can imagine that elephants do not exist on Earth; that human beings are not able to speak; that unicorns are not unreal; that the Moon is not round. Here's the point: to imagine that a situation is not true is the same as imagining that the situation is false. We can imagine that it's false that elephants exist, and so on. So, these kinds of cases are examples of *possible falsehoods*. More generally, we say that a sentence is a possible falsehood (is possibly false) if we can imagine that the sentence is false. So, the sentence "Elephants exist" is a possible falsehood because we can imagine that it is false that elephants exist: we can imagine that elephants don't exist.

(4) The last comment is related to the previous comment. Many sentences are *both* possibly true and possibly false. The sentence "Elephants exist" is possibly true and it is possibly false. It is possibly true because we can imagine that elephants do exist, and it is possibly false because we can imagine that elephants do not exist. If we can imagine something to be true and also imagine it to be false—if we can imagine it both ways—then the sentence in question is possibly true and also possibly false. This is not unusual. Most of the things we have said in our lives have this double status. "Oh, I love that movie!"—possibly true, and possibly false, and true in the real world; unless you lied, and then it is possibly true, and possibly false, and false in the real world. By the way, don't confuse this double status with something that is impossible: "possibly both true and false." Don't say that the sentence "Elephants exist" is possibly true and false, because that means that one can imagine *one* situation in which that sentence is simultaneously true and false. Say instead that the sentence is possibly true and possibly false.

A sentence p is *possibly true* (is *logically possible*, is *possible*) if and only if

- one can imagine a situation in which p is true, which equals:
- p does not contain a contradiction within it.

A sentence p is *possibly false* if and only if

- one can imagine a situation in which p is false.

A sentence p is both *possibly true* and *possibly false* if and only if

- one can imagine a situation in which p is true, and one can also imagine a different situation in which p is false.

Here are some sentences that are possible truths:

- The Moon exploded   possibly true; and false in the real world
- Clinton ate 25 bananas for lunch   possibly true; and false in the real world
- Elephants exist on the Earth   possibly true; and true in the real world
- Unicorns don't exist on the Earth   possibly true; and true in the real world
- Some square has 5 sides   *not* possibly true; but necessarily false

Here are some sentences that are possible falsehoods:

- The Moon is round   possibly false; and true in the real world
- Clinton ate a hamburger   possibly false; and true in the real world
- Unicorns exist on the Earth   possibly false; and false in the real world
- Elephants don't exist on the Earth   possibly false; and false in the real world
- All squares have 4 sides   *not* possibly false; but necessarily true

Here are some sentences that are possible truths as well as possible falsehoods:

- The Earth is round   possibly true; possibly false; really true
- The Moon exploded   possibly true; possibly false; really false
- Elephants exist   possibly true; possibly false; really true
- Unicorns exist   possibly true; possibly false; really false

Necessary Truths and Necessary Falsehoods

Some sentences are such that they *must* be true, no matter what. These sentences are *necessarily true*. The qualifier "no matter what" means "no matter what the world is like." Here, again, the imagination test comes into play. Necessarily true sentences are sentences that are true in *every imaginable* situation, or, as we say in logic, "true in every possible world." But how can there be something that is constant in that way? How can there be something that is true in no matter what we imagine? Aren't our powers of imagination boundless? Can't we imagine anything we want? Actually, there are limits to our imagination, and these limits give rise to necessary truths.

Consider, for example, "Every triangle has three sides." Let's imagine the world to be anything whatsoever; say, dogs all meow, trees never lose their leaves, elephants don't exist, and so on. Now, also imagine a triangle. In order to imagine a triangle, you have to imagine a figure with three sides. If you imagine something with four sides, you would be imagining, say, a square, or a rectangle, but it would not be a triangle. So, no matter what you imagine the world to be like, when you imagine a triangle, you are imagining a figure with three sides. That means the sentence, "Every triangle has three sides," is a necessary truth (is true in every possible world).

Now consider the similar sentence, "Every dog has four legs." Again, let's imagine the world to be anything whatsoever. Now imagine a dog. Can you imagine the dog to have five legs, say it was born that way? Of course, you can. Notice the difference with the triangle case. Triangles *must* have three sides in order to be triangles, but dogs don't have to have four legs in order to be dogs. So, the sentence, "Every dog has four legs," is not a necessary truth.

A survey of necessary truths reveals that they fall into three main groups:

(1)   mathematical truths $2 + 3 = 5, \ (a + b)^2 = a^2 + 2ab + b^2$

(2)   logical truths   Everything is red or not red; All horses are horses

(3)   definitional truths   All triangles have three sides; All books have pages

(Philosophers sometimes also distinguish a fourth group of necessary truths, called *synthetic apriori* truths, such as "All material bodies exist in space," or "Every event has a cause.")

In addition to necessary truths, there are *necessary falsehoods*. These are sentences that *must* be false, no matter what. Necessarily false sentences are sentences that are false in every imaginable situation, or as we say, "false in every possible world." Consider, for example, "Some person is a happily married bachelor." Now pick any imagined world, arrange it any way you like. The sentence in question has to be false in that world, because "married bachelor" is a self-contradictory idea, forcing the sentence to be false. Because necessarily false sentences always contain a self-contradictory idea, they must always be imagined to be false.

There is a nice relationship between necessary truths and necessary falsehoods. The *negation* of a necessary truth is a necessary falsehood, and the *negation* of a necessary falsehood is a necessary truth. If you negate the one, you get the other. One can prove that by using the definitions we have given for these two ideas, but one can also see that relationship in particular examples. "All triangles have three sides" is a necessary truth. Let's negate it. Then we get, "Not all triangles have three sides," which means that some triangle does not have three sides, but *that* is false in all imaginable worlds. So, "Not all triangles have three sides" is a necessary falsehood.

There is also a relationship between necessary falsehoods and impossibilities. They are one and the same thing. Whatever is necessarily false is impossible, and vice versa, whatever is impossible is necessarily false. We can actually prove this using our definitions. A necessary falsehood is a sentence that is false in every possible world. That means that there is *not* some possible world in which it is true. So, it is *not* a possible truth, that is, it is an *impossibility*.

A sentence p is *necessarily true* (is *necessary*) if and only if

- in every imaginable situation, p is true, which equals:
- one cannot imagine a situation in which p is false.

A sentence p is *necessarily false* (is *impossible*) if and only if

- in every imaginable situation, p is false, which equals:
- one cannot imagine a situation in which p is true.

Here are some sentences that are necessary truths:

- All bachelors are unmarried   necessarily true (by definition)
- All squares have four sides   necessarily true (by definition)
- Four is two times two   necessarily true (mathematics)
- Two points fix a straight line   necessarily true (mathematics)
- All green horses on Mars are green   necessarily true (logic)
- Either God exists or God does not exist   necessarily true (logic)
- The Sun is the center of our solar system   *not* neces. true; true in real world
- All bananas are blue   *not* neces. true; false in real world

Here are some sentences that are necessary falsehoods (impossibilities):

- Some bachelor is married   necessarily false (by definition)
- Some square doesn't have four sides   necessarily false (by definition)
- Four is two times three   necessarily false (mathematics)
- Two straight lines cross twice   necessarily false (mathematics)
- Some green horse on Mars is not green   necessarily false (logic)
- God exists, but God does not exist   necessarily false (logic)
- Earth is the center of our solar system   *not* neces. false; false in real world
- Some bananas are yellow   *not* neces. false; true in real world

Empirical Truths and Empirical Falsehoods

Here is a really neat division. Sentences are necessary truths, or they are necessary falsehoods, or they are whatever is left over (neither necessary truths nor necessary falsehoods). This is airtight. Each sentence belongs to one of those three categories. It is the third category that we focus on next. Sentences in this left-over group have two names. Since they are not in the two "necessity" groups, they are called *contingent* sentences, indicating thereby their non-necessity status. Their second name is *empirical* sentences, and for a good reason. It turns out that these left-over sentences have a special character all of their own. They are more than just the left-overs. Consider a necessary truth, say, "All green horses are green." There is a clear *lack of content* in this sentence. What does the world have to be like in order for this sentence to be true, or false? This sentence makes no claims regarding the world. The world can be what it wants, and the sentence will still be true, regardless. You see, there is no content. Or, consider a necessary falsehood, say, "Some angry elephants are not elephants." Again, this sentence makes no claims regarding the world. The world can be what it wants, and the sentence will still be false, regardless. Again, there is no content. But the left-overs, the empirical sentences, they *do* have a content. And it is this content that is responsible for their truth-value. By means of this content, empirical sentences make their claims about the world, and depending on what the real world is like, they are assigned their rightful value. It is because of the relationship between their content and the real world that the name "empirical" has been given to these sentences. Some empirical sentences will turn out to be true, and others will turn out to be false, depending on what the real world is like. Accordingly, the group of empirical sentences is divided into two subgroups: empirical sentences that are true and empirical sentences that are false. And so the three-fold division with which we began has expanded into a four-fold division: necessary truths, empirical truths, empirical falsehoods, and necessary falsehoods. The chart on p. 35 displays this division.

A point about imaginability. Empirical sentences are ones that are neither necessarily true nor necessarily false. That means something special in terms of imaginability. Since they are not necessarily false, one can imagine situations in which they are true; and since they are not necessarily true, one can imagine situations in which they are false. *That* is their special mark. Empirical sentences are sentences that you can imagine *both* ways. Above, when we discussed possibility, we mentioned that *most* of the sentences we have said in our lives have the double status of being both possibly true and possibly false. That's exactly what empirical sentences are like. You can imagine them both ways, so they are both possibly true and possibly false.

A sentence p is *empirical* (is *contingent*) if and only if

- p is not necessarily true, *and* p is not necessarily false, which equals:
- one can imagine p to be true, *and* one can imagine p to be false

A sentence p is *empirically true* if and only if

- p is empirical, and p is true in the real world

A sentence p is *empirically false* if and only if

- p is empirical, and p is false in the real world

Here are some sentences that are empirical truths or falsehoods:

• The Moon has exploded	empirically false
• The Moon has not exploded	empirically true
• Clinton ate 25 bananas for lunch	empirically false
• Clinton did not eat 25 bananas for lunch	empirically true
• The Sun is the center of our solar system	empirically true
• Some square has 5 sides	*not* empirical, but neces. false
• All squares have 4 sides	*not* empirical, but neces. true

We have introduced a lot of categories in the above discussion. The following chart summarizes how all these different ideas relate to one another:

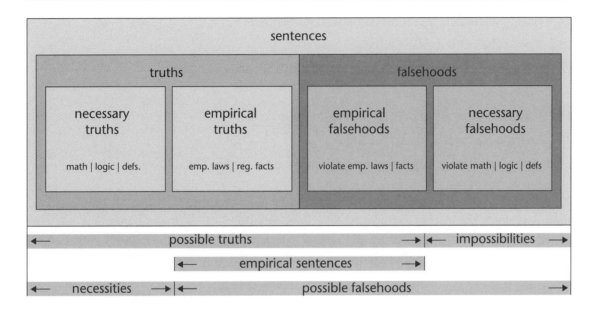

Exercise 1.4. A,B Classifying Sentences

Part A. Classify each of the following sentences as being *one* of the following: necessarily true (nec. T), necessarily false (nec. F), empirically true (emp. T), empirically false (emp. F). Interpret these sentences according to their ordinary meaning. Use the available **Exercise Work Sheet** to submit your work.

1. The Earth is round.
2. The Earth is flat.
3. All cats are animals.
4. All cats have tails.
5. There are people that live on the Moon.
6. There are people that own round cubes.
7. Wherever you go, you are there.
8. Past events occur at some time before the present.
9. Every banana on the Moon is located on the Moon.
10. Loyola U. Chicago is the world's largest university.
11. One pear, one peach, and one plum add to six fruits.
12. Either all cats have green tails, or some cats do not.
13. TVs did not exist before the 20th century.

14. Boiling water (212°F) causes damage to human skin.

15. Every cube has 8 corners, 12 edges, and 6 faces.

16. A figure's perimeter is longer than any of its diagonals.

17. Cows moo.

18. Water is composed of oxygen and hydrogen.

19. There are lakes of water on the Moon.

20. All bachelors who are married are both married and unmarried.

Part B. Give an example of each of the following kinds of arguments. You don't have to make these examples fascinating arguments. Silly ones will do. Each of these arguments has two premisses. Start with a valid or invalid abstract pattern, then fill in the pattern with English sentences. Use the available **Exercise Work Sheet** to submit your work.

Ex. An invalid argument with all the premisses and conclusion empirically false.

prem1:   Some P are B :   Some persons are banana-shaped things

prem2:   All B are G   :   All banana-shaped things are residents of Chicago

concl :   All P are G   :   All persons are residents of Chicago

1. A valid argument with all the premisses and conclusion empirically false.

2. A valid argument with all the premisses and conclusion empirically true.

3. A valid argument with all the premisses false and the conclusion true.

4. A valid argument with all the premisses and conclusion necessarily true.

5. A valid argument with one of the premisses necessarily false.

6. A valid argument with the conclusion necessarily false.

Section 1.5 Proofs, Inconclusive and Erroneous Arguments

We have already discussed the important distinctions between valid and invalid arguments as well as between sound and unsound arguments. But there is a practical problem here, one that arises from our *lack of knowledge*, that is, our ignorance.

The aim of argumentation is to produce a sound argument, since that is the only kind of argument that guarantees the truth of the conclusion. So, the evaluation of an argument always has two separate parts: (1) we must determine whether the inference is valid, and (2) we must determine whether the premisses are true. The first part of the evaluation is usually *not* a problem. If we are careful in our investigation, armed with a modest knowledge of logical technique, we *will* be able to determine whether or not any argument placed before us is valid. Of course, in this part, *practice makes perfect*. This is what a logic course is all about. But the second part of the evaluation, to determine the truth of the premises, usually presents a problem.

The problem is that often we cannot determine whether the premises are true or false. We simply do not have enough knowledge. So in these cases, what should our *verdict* be regarding the soundness of the argument? Consider the situation: Since all arguments must be either sound or unsound, there are many cases where the argument *is in fact sound*, but we don't know that; and likewise there are many cases where the argument *is in fact unsound*, and we don't know that either.

We introduce three new ideas into the evaluation process to make the process more clearly defined. These new ideas handle the matter of our knowledge and ignorance.

> An argument is a *proof* (of its conclusion) if and only if
>
> > the argument is *known* to be sound, that is,
> >
> > (1)   the argument is *known* to be valid, and
> >
> > (2)   all the premises are *known* to be true.

The notion of *proof* is well known to us, especially from *mathematics*. To know that an argument is sound we must know two things: (a) we must know that the argument is valid and (b) we must know that all the premises are true.

Consequently, if an argument is invalid, then of course, we do not know that it is valid, so that the argument is not a proof. Also, if we do not have sufficient knowledge to know that all the premises are true, then, again, the argument is not a proof. (A comment here. Whose knowledge are we talking about here? An argument has an audience, and it is the knowledge of the audience that counts here. Also, various groups of people are in fact the official experts on various matters, and we may rely on their knowledge in these matters.)

It is also important to *know* which arguments make *mistakes*, and there are two possible sources of error here: incorrect connection or incorrect premises.

> An argument is an *erroneous* (or *false*) argument if and only if
>
> > the argument is *known* to be unsound, that is,

> (1)   the argument is *known* to be invalid, OR
>
> (2)   some premiss is *known* to be false.

So, if we know that an argument is invalid, then we know it is unsound, and the argument is erroneous. If we know that some premiss is false, then again, we know the argument is unsound, and the argument is erroneous. When the only defect is a known false premiss, we may justly call the erroneous argument a *false* argument.

Unfortunately, most arguments do not yield an easy solution. Our limited knowledge in most matters affects the outcome of the evaluation process. We do not have the knowledge to prove the matter, but we also do not know that a mistake has been made. The argument has an unsettled status.

> An argument is an *inconclusive* argument if and only if
>
> the argument is *not* known to be sound, and *also*
>
> the argument is *not* known to be unsound; that is,
>
> (1)   the argument is known to be *valid*; but
>
> (2)   *not all* the premisses are *known* to be true, although
>
> (3)   none of the premisses are known to be false,
>
> that is, at least one of the premisses is *questionable*.

Since the matter of validity can normally be determined, an inconclusive argument turns out to be one that is correct in all respects, except that there is a *premiss* that we are *ignorant* about. This premiss we do not know to be true, but we do not know it to be false either. The premiss is *questionable*, it is *debatable*, it is *undecided*, it is *unresolved*. Sad to say, most of the significant arguments that people propose have this unresolved status: we just don't know enough.

Let's turn to some examples to illustrate our three new classifications.

Argument #1 You Cannot Know That You Are Not Real

1.   If you know that you are not real, then you are *not* real.

2.   If you know that you are not real, then you *are* real.

So, you cannot know that you are not real.

- *Evaluation of the argument pattern*. The argument has the form

1. if K then not R
2. if K then R

So, not K

In Chapter 3 we will demonstrate that this pattern of reasoning is logically correct. Hence, the argument is *valid*. But even now it is intuitively clear that the two premises combine to give the result "if K is true, then a contradiction follows." Since contradictions are impossible, we must conclude that K can't be true.

- *Determination of the truth-status of the premisses*. The first premiss is true. In fact, it is necessarily true. This follows from the very *idea* of what knowledge is: whatever is *known* to be so, in *fact* has to be so. Could George *know* that the Earth is a cube? Of course not. Knowledge requires truth. So, if you know that you are not real, then *that* has to be so: you are not real.

The second premiss is also true. In fact, it too is necessarily true. Again, the very idea of knowing something requires that there *exists* some kind of agent that *has* that kind of mental activity. Action requires agency. In other words, if you know something, then you thereby act, and if you act, you must exist, you must be real.

- *Summary*. We have demonstrated both that the argument is valid and that the premisses are true. So, we have demonstrated that the argument is sound. And since this was a demonstration, we all now *know* that the argument is sound. So, this argument is a *proof* of the conclusion: No person can know that he is not real.

Argument #2 God Does Not Exist

1. If God exists, then God is omnipotent, omniscient, and omnibenevolent.
2. If God is omnipotent, then God can do everything that is possible.
3. If God is omniscient, then God knows everything that can possibly occur.
4. If God is omnibenevolent, then God acts as good as anything can possibly act.
5. If God can do everything that is possible and knows everything that can possibly occur, and acts as good as anything can possibly act, then evil things do *not* happen.
6. But, evil things *do* happen.

So, God does *not* exist.

- *Evaluation of the argument pattern.* The argument has the pattern

1. if G then (P & S & B)
2. if P then D
3. if S then K
4. if B then A
5. if (D & K & A) then not E
6. E

So, not G

This pattern is a *valid* one, as we will learn later. But even now we can reason this out as follows: Premisses 2, 3, and 4 produce the *intermediate conclusion* "if (P & S & B) then (D & K & A)," and when we combine that result that with premisses 1 and 5, we get the intermediate conclusion "if G then not E." But Premiss 6 rejects "not E," and so we are forced to reject G as well, and that is the final conclusion.

- *Determination of the truth-status of the premisses.* The first premiss is a *necessary truth*, since the indicated attributes are part of the very idea of "God." [This argument deals only with what may be called the *traditional* view. This argument has no relevance at all to positions that hold a different view of God. This sort of qualification is important in debates. Keep it in mind.]

Likewise, premisses 2, 3, and 4 are *necessary truths*, since they merely state what each of the attributes means.

Premiss 6 is a report of an empirical fact: some really bad things do happen every now and then; for example, a baby is killed, or a plane crashes, or innocent people undergo great suffering, and so forth. So, Premiss 6 is *empirically true*.

The whole matter rests, then, on the status of the remaining premiss, Premiss 5, which says that if God is so perfect in all these ways, then he would see to it that evil does not occur. So, what can we say about *its* status? Is it true, or is it false? Well, as it turns out, there has been considerable *debate* about the matter. For example, the early twentieth-century philosopher Bertrand Russell argued for its truth (focusing on a commonsense understanding of God's goodness), whereas the contemporary philosopher Alvin Plantinga argues that it is false (focusing on the fact that human beings have free will). But *all* sides agree on the following: no one claims that *it is known* that Premiss 5 is true, or that *it is known* that Premiss 5 is false. In other words, Premiss 5 has the status of an *undecided proposition*.

• *Summary*. The argument has been shown to be valid, and five of the six premisses are known to be true. But Premiss 5 is *not* known to be true, and *not* known to be false. So, not all of the premisses are known to be true, and the argument is not a proof, but rather an *inconclusive argument*.

Argument #3a Columbus, You'll Fall Off The Earth!

1.   The Earth is a large, flat, material body.
2.   Any large material body is such that one can fall off it.

So, one can fall off the Earth.

• *Evaluation of the argument pattern*. The argument has the pattern

1. x is A
2.   all A are B
   _____

So, x is B

It is intuitively clear that this argument pattern is valid. In fact, it is one of the simplest valid argument patterns there is. Perhaps another example will help: "Harry is an inhabitant of Tomonia, and all inhabitants of Tomonia (no exceptions) drink banana beer. Therefore, _____ ?" You know what to add here.

• *Determination of the truth-status of the premisses*. Premiss 1 is false. Columbus also believed Premiss 1 to be false, but he was not sure. (After all, how could he have been sure?) But, *we* have seen pictures of the Earth from outer space, and these picture show the Earth to be round, not flat. So, Premiss 1 is known to be false.

• *Summary*. So, the argument is not a proof, and the argument is not an inconclusive argument. Rather, as we have defined these terms, the argument is an *erroneous argument*; in fact, we call it a *false argument*, because it uses a premiss that is known to be false.

What is the point of a false argument? Well, sometimes people want to deceive others, or, perhaps they intend such an argument to be rhetorical. But many arguments are false arguments because the makers of the arguments *thought* they had knowledge when in fact they were dead wrong. All of us have made many inferences based on false premisses, without knowing at the time that the premisses were false! But as we learn more, we recognize the errors, and we *stop* using those false arguments.

So, now that we know that the Earth is not flat, let's give it *another* try.

Argument #3b Columbus, You'll Fall Off The Earth! (Again)

1. The Earth is a large, round, material body.
2. Any large material body is such that one can fall off it.

So, one can fall off the Earth.

• *Evaluation of the argument.* This argument has the same pattern as the other one, so this argument is also *valid*. And, we have removed the false part about the flatness of the Earth, so this time Premiss 1 is known to be true.

Question: Is the present argument a proof? No. The problem was actually never the alleged flatness of the Earth, since that part played no role in the production of the conclusion. The real problem is, and was, Premiss 2. It is not true that one can fall off just any large material body—only off *some* of them, the ones that have a humongously large gravitational body *near* them, so that something falls *from* the smaller body *towards* the center of gravity of the very large one. That is what falling is. And since we know that there is no humongously large gravitational body near the Earth, we know that nothing can fall off the Earth. So, the case of the Earth, then, is a counter-example to Premiss 2. It turns out, then, that the new argument is also a *false argument*, since it also uses a premiss that is known to be false.

Chart of the Types Of Arguments and their Relationships

We can make a chart of the relationships of all the different types of arguments that we have discussed. You should understand these ideas well enough to be able to give examples of arguments that fit into the displayed slots.

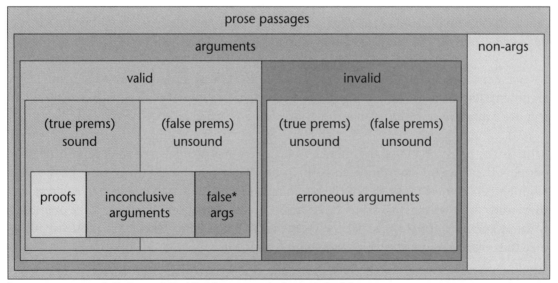

* erroneous arguments that are valid but that have a premiss *known* to be false

Exercise 1.5. A,B Review of Terms

Part A. Determine whether the following assertions are true or false (use **T** or **F**). Remember, when these assertions mention true or false premisses or conclusions, that means premisses and conclusions that are true or false *in the real world*. Use the available **Exercise Work Sheet** to submit your work.

1.   All valid arguments have a correct connection.
2.   All valid arguments have only true premisses.
3.   All valid arguments have a true conclusion.
4.   All invalid arguments do not have a correct connection.
5.   All invalid arguments have some false premisses.
6.   All invalid arguments have a false conclusion.
7.   All sound arguments are valid.
8.   All sound arguments have only true premisses.
9.   All sound arguments have a true conclusion.
10.   All unsound arguments are invalid.
11.   All unsound arguments have some false premisses.
12.   All unsound arguments have a false conclusion.
13.   All proofs are known to be sound.
14.   All proofs have true premisses.
15.   All proofs are valid.
16.   All proofs have a conclusion that is true.
17.   All proofs have a conclusion that is a proven truth.
18.   All non-proofs are invalid.
19.   All non-proofs have some false premisses.
20.   All inconclusive arguments are not known to be sound.
21.   All inconclusive arguments are not known to be unsound.
22.   All inconclusive arguments are not proofs.
23.   All inconclusive arguments are invalid.
24.   All inconclusive arguments have some false premisses.

Part B. For your consideration. You should be able to back up your answers to Part A with examples. Also, if an assertion is false (**F**), consider whether changing the word "all" to "some" would make a difference.

Section 1.6 Deductive and Inductive Validity

We have so far relied on an *intuitive* notion of "correct connection." On the one hand, it is important that we have such an intuitive idea at our disposal, since it is by means of it that we make many of our daily, simpler inferences. On the other hand, this intuitive notion is effective *only* for inferences that are simple, leaving us without a proper means to engage in more complicated reasoning. Moreover, the notion is imprecise, and even at the simpler level it sometimes leads us to make mistakes. This is why the study of logic is important. We will enlarge and improve our understanding of "correct connection" by studying the laws of logic as well as a number of special techniques, and we will begin this study with a precise, technical characterization of this idea of connection. It turns out that there are two different kinds of connection.

Deductive Connection

What makes an argument a *deductive argument*, we have already said, is that the person making the argument *claims* that the connection from premises to conclusion is a necessary one. This claim is often signaled by the use of special words when the conclusion is introduced, such as, "So, it *necessarily* follows that . . .," or "So, it *must* be that . . .," or some phrase to that effect. But sometimes, special wording is not used, and the reader is expected to know that a deductive connection is intended. Thus, we give the following definition:

> An argument is *deductively valid* if and only if
>
> - it is *not logically possible* that
>
>   (all the premises are true *and* the conclusion is false)
> - it is *not imaginable* that
>
>   (all the premises are true and the conclusion is false)

There are *two* definitions here for deductive validity, one in terms of logical possibility and the other in terms of imaginability. We have given both because we want to emphasize that these two definitions are the *same*: what is logically possible is imaginable, and vice versa: what is imaginable is logically possible, and so too for their negations. The definition says that an argument is deductively valid when the connection between the premises and the conclusion is so strong that the connection cannot be broken, not even in the imagination. An argument is valid when one can't even *imagine* a situation in which the premises are true and the conclusion is false. That is a powerful connection, indeed. An important consequence of this definition is that we now have a *concrete method* for testing whether an argument is valid. We need only consider what is and what is not *imaginable* about the argument.

Consider the following example:

> All horses are green
>
> Sam is a horse
>
> So, Sam is green

To test whether this argument is valid, we need to find out whether it is possible (imaginable) for the premises to be true while the conclusion is false. If that "bad" combination (true premises, false conclusion) is *not* possible, then the argument is valid, for that would show that the connection cannot be broken in the imagination. On the other hand, if that "bad" combination *is* possible, then the argument is invalid, because that shows that the connection *can* be broken in the imagination.

bad combo poss ?

All horses are green	T
Sam is a horse	T
So, Sam is green	F

if **not**, then arg is **deductively valid**
if **yes**, then arg is **deductively invalid**

To test this, let's enter some possible (imaginary) world, say, **World #233**, and let's see whether we can actually imagine all the premises to be true and yet imagine the conclusion to be *false*. We will attempt this in stages. Let's *first* imagine Premiss 1 to be true: We line up all the horses, and we make each of them green. OK, that was easy. No problem imagining that. Next, we *also* imagine Premiss 2 to be true: We pick one of the horses, and we call him "Sam." OK, that worked too. So, all the horses have been imagined to be green, and we imagined Sam to be one of those green horses. Up to this point we have had no problem imagining all this. Now comes the last step. We have to *try* to imagine the conclusion to be false. Question: Can we actually imagine this?

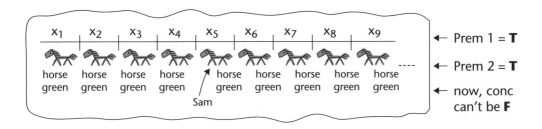

In other words, can we now, at the same time, in **World #233**, imagine Sam *not* to be green? No, of course not. That's because, *while* we imagined all horses to be green, and then imagined Sam to be one of those horses, the conclusion turned out to be automatically included: it turned out that we automatically, without intending to, imagined Sam to be green! That kind of automatic inclusion is the very *mark* of a valid argument. We conclude that our *attempt* to break the connection with our imagination *failed*. Consequently, the argument is deductively valid.

On the other hand, consider a different argument.

<table>
<tr><td></td><td align="center">bad combo poss ?</td><td></td></tr>
<tr><td>All horses are green</td><td align="center">T</td><td rowspan="3">if not, then arg is deductively valid
if yes, then arg is deductively invalid</td></tr>
<tr><td>Sam is green</td><td align="center">T</td></tr>
<tr><td>So, Sam is a horse</td><td align="center">F</td></tr>
</table>

Again, to test this, let's enter some other possible world, say, **World #5012**, and let's see whether we can imagine the premisses to be true and yet the conclusion to be false. So, let's *first* imagine Premiss 1 to be true: we line up all the horses, and we make them green. *Next*, we also imagine Premiss 2 to be true, and this time, we pick another thing, a green leaf, and we call it "Sam." So, we have successfully imagined both premisses to be true.

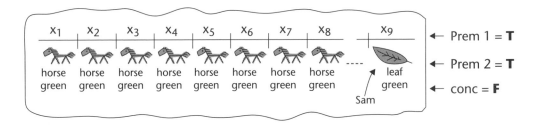

Question: Can we now, in this **World #5012**, imagine the conclusion to be *false*? Yes, indeed. When we imagined Sam to be a green leaf, we also imagined Sam *not* to be a horse. So this time, our *attempt* to break the connection of the argument with our imagination was *successful*. Consequently, this argument is deductively invalid.

Inductive Connection

What makes an argument an *inductive argument*, we have said, is that the person making the argument *claims* that the connection from the premisses to the conclusion is not a connection of logic, but rather a connection that is based on matters of *fact* or *probability*.

Such a claim is often signaled by using special words when the conclusion is introduced, such as, "So, we can *reliably* conclude that . . .," or "So, in all *likelihood* . . .," or some wording to that effect. But sometimes, a regular inference indicator, such as "So, . . .," is used, and the reader is expected to know that an inductive connection is intended. Thus, we have the definition:

> An inductive argument has a *connection* whose *degree of strength* is defined by the *degree of probability* (%) that the conclusion has relative to the premises:
>
> > a *very weak* inference (5%)
> >
> > a *weak* inference (25%)
> >
> > a *somewhat strong* inference (51%)
> >
> > a *medium strong* inference (75%)
> >
> > a *very strong* inference (99%)
> >
> > a *conclusive* inference (100%)

Of course, the possible degrees of inductive strength cover the entire range of probabilities from 0 percent to 100 percent, but the qualitative labels indicated are useful for ordinary purposes. Here are some examples.

> Swimming after eating a meal often leads to cramps.
>
> Alex just ate a sandwich and went swimming.
>
> So, Alex will probably get cramps.

The conclusion has some merit. If Alex got cramps, then we would not be surprised. But there is no guarantee that he will get cramps, nor would we expect that he would. Given the information in the premises, we might put the probability of getting cramps at 51 percent. The inference is therefore inductively *somewhat strong*.

Our inferences are often much stronger than somewhat strong.

> We heard laughing voices coming from the classroom across the hall.
>
> So, in all likelihood, there are people in that room

The probability of this conclusion is extremely high—99 percent would be a good estimate—but it falls short of 100 percent, since the voices could come from some device, say a VCR. So, we would say that the inference is inductively *very strong*.

Sometimes inferences are even stronger than that. Sometimes the inductive connection is *fool proof*, in the sense that it allows of *no exceptions*. This happens when the connection is based on proven *laws of nature*. In these cases it is appropriate to say that the argument is *inductively valid*, because the conclusion is conclusively established (relative to the premisses), in virtue of that fact that there are no exceptions to the connection. This is what the following definition says.

> An inference is *inductively valid* if and only if
>
>> the conclusion has a 100% probability relative to the premisses.

For example, the next two arguments are inductively valid:

> There is a city on the Moon
>
> So, it was built by some intelligent beings

> Bill Clinton jumped off the top of the John Hancock Building, furiously flapping his arms. (He was normally dressed, had no ropes on him, no attached jets, etc.)
>
> So, Bill Clinton fell helplessly towards the ground.

There is an additional, useful label to describe inductive arguments. The purpose of this label is to capture the commonsense idea of *good reasoning* when inductive relationships are involved, especially when those relationships are less than *conclusive*. We all make many inductive inferences that are cases of *good* reasoning, and we all like to be rewarded for doing so with some official label of praise. The label in question is that of *cogent argument* (with its opposite, *uncogent argument*), and as it turns out, this label agrees very well with the ordinary meaning of the word.

> An inductive argument is *cogent* if and only if
>
>> (1)   all the premisses are known to be true, and
>>
>> (2)   the conclusion has a *strong* degree of probability (51% or greater) relative to the premisses.
>
> Otherwise, the argument is *uncogent.*

The following argument, for example, is a *cogent* argument:

Up to now I have always been able to buy food from my grocery store.

My grocery store has given no notice that it is closing down soon.

So, I will be able to buy food from my grocery store next week.

Excellent reasoning. The premisses are known to be true, and the conclusion has a very strong probability (95%) relative to the premisses. This is a cogent argument, just like so many other arguments we give every day. But, when an argument uses false information, or when the connection is inductively weak, the argument is *uncogent*, as in the following example.

All the logic quizzes in the course have been very easy so far.

The teacher announced that the next quiz will be extremely difficult.

Therefore, the next quiz will be very easy as well.

This is really bad reasoning. The probability of the conclusion is very low (5%) given the information of the premisses (because, generally, teachers do *not* lie to their students). So, this is an uncogent argument.

A final terminological point. It must be said that there is not a consensus among philosophers and logicians about what *labels* one should use for the various inductive relationships that characterize inductive arguments. For example, we may plausibly restrict the lablel "valid" to apply *only* to *deductive* arguments, so that the arguments that we have here called "inductively valid arguments" must then be re-labeled as "inductively conclusive arguments." And various logic books take that very approach. Semantic issues like this often arise in any discipline, but they are unimportant, provided one is always clear about *how* labels are used *when* they are used.

Exercise 1.6. A,B Testing Validity

Part A. Use the possible world test to determine whether the following arguments are deductively valid. In each test give an itemized description of the relevant items such that: (a) for the invalid arguments, the description must show the premisses to be true and the conclusion to be false, and (b) for the valid arguments, the description must show that having true premisses then means that you *can't* have a false conclusion (annotate "= **F**?" with "can't"). Use the given capital letters to make the descriptions, and use the available **Exercise Work Sheet** to submit your work.

1. Arg is *invalid*

	poss. values	possible world description:					
		x1	x2	x3	x4	x5	x6
All Democrats want gun control.	= T ? *yes*	D	D	D	R	R	R
George wants gun control.	= T ? *yes*						
So, George must be a Democrat.	= F ? *yes*	C	C	C	F	F	C
							George

(D = Democrat, C = gun control, F = gun freedom, R = Republican)

2. All ants are blue. No blue things are square. So, no ants are square. (A, B, S, R = round)

3. All Democrats want gun control. George is not a Democrat. So, he doesn't want gun control. (D, C, F, R = Republican)

4. No ants are blue. All blue things are square. So, no ants are square. (A, B, S, G = green)

5. Some ants are round. Some ants are blue. Some round things are blue. (A, R, B, S = square, G = green)

6. No Democrats are bald. Some Democrats are tall. So, some tall things are not bald. (D, B, T, H = has hair, R = Republican, S = short)

Part B. The following are all inductive arguments. Determine whether these arguments are *cogent* by answering the three indicated questions with *yes* or *no*. Use the available **Exercise Work Sheet** to submit your work.

Question 1. Are all the premisses true? (Use your best judgment.)

Question 2. Is the inductive connection a strong one? (Use your best judgment.)

Question 3. Is the argument cogent? (Base this on Q.1 and Q.2.)

1. College tuition is much more expensive now than two generations ago. So, fewer students are able to attend college now than two generations ago.

2. Most college students today have a strong sense of social responsibility. Most people think that Senator Obama has a platform that represents social responsibility and that Senator McCain has a platform that represents national security. People generally vote for candidates that agree with their view of things. So, most college students today will vote for Senator Obama.

3. Despite some gloomy prospects, the younger generation still seeks the "American dream," and they realize that achieving it will be more difficult than it was for the previous generations. But they also have a hopeful outlook about the possibility of their own success. So, the younger generation will succeed in achieving the "American dream."

4. Many people nowadays are aware of the various health hazards that exist in their everyday lives, such as cigarette smoking, substance abuse, processed foods, environmental pollution,

lack of exercise, and they also know how best to avoid such hazards and have changed their lives accordingly. So, these people will enjoy healthier lives.

5. Some people have jobs that actually require them to meet specific goals, and if they do not meet those goals, they will lose their jobs. One of your friends has a job with specific performance recommendations. So, your friend will lose his job, if he does not meet those recommendations.

6. When people begin to consider their retirement, they usually worry more about the market performance of their retirement funds. Some of your acquaintances have mentioned their concern about the poor performance of the stock market. So, they are probably thinking about retiring soon.

7. Americans now find European vacations to be very expensive, because the price of everything in euros when converted to dollars costs much more than in the U.S. A number of American families are planning vacations in Europe next year. So, they must be expecting that the value of the euro will go down substantially against the dollar next year.

8. Most people are confident about their present state of health, and yet, they buy health insurance, if they are able to do so. Now, people wouldn't do that, if they didn't think that they needed health insurance. So, while most people think that they will not *actually* undergo costly medical procedures in the near future, most people *do* think that this is a real *possibility*.

CHAPTER 2

PROPOSITIONAL LOGIC

Section 2.1 Introduction to Propositional Logic

Propositional Logic is the study of the argument patterns that are made by the various arrangements of *simple sentences* and *sentential operators*. In this part of our study we will ignore, for the time being, the internal structure that the simple sentences themselves have. An example can illustrate this point.

> If George has a soul, then some people have souls.
> If some people have souls, then all people have souls.
> So, if George has a soul, then all people have souls.

This argument is constructed out of the three simple sentences "George has a soul," "some people have souls," and "all people have souls." Presently, we *ignore* the fact that these sentences will later be analyzed as having the patterns "g is H," "some P are H," and "all P are H." Instead, we now consider these three sentences to be *basic units* that can in their entirety be represented by individual capital letters, so that we can represent the argument in the following way:

If G then S	G = "George has a soul"
If S then A	S = "some people have souls"
So, if G then A	A = "all people have souls"

This pattern is easily recognized to be valid from a commonsense point of view. This chapter will introduce various techniques for evaluating these kinds of patterns.

Simple and Compound Sentences

A *simple* sentence is one that is *not* grammatically constructed out of other sentences by means of *sentential operators*, and a *compound* sentence is a sentence that *is* grammatically constructed out of other sentences by means of *sentential operators*.

Symbolization Rule #1:

All simple sentences are symbolized by a unique capital letter: A, B, C, . . . , Z.
And *only* simple sentences are symbolized in this way.

Examples of simple sentences:	*Symbolization*
Sue likes to dance.	S
Some old books are made of solid gold.	M
No pigs can fly.	P
All schools in Chicago have few students.	C

Note that each of these sentences is *not* constructed out of any *part* that by itself is another sentence. Therefore, each of these sentences is a simple sentence.

Symbolization Rule #2:

Sentential operators are symbolized in the following way:

Type	*Example*	*Symbolization*
negative operators	not p	~p
conjunctive operators	both p and q	p & q
disjunctive operators	either p or q	p ∨ q
conditional operators	if p then q	p ⊃ q
biconditional operators	p if and only if q	p ≡ q

Examples of compound sentences:	*Partial symbolization*	*Symbolization*
Sue likes to dance, and Bob likes to sing.	S and B	S & B
Not all pigs can fly.	not F	~F
Everyone has a soul, or no one does.	P or Q	P ∨ Q
If Bob sings, then the party is over.	If B then O	B ⊃ O

Negations

A *negative* sentence is a sentence that is the explicit *denial* of another sentence. Such a sentence is formed by applying a *negative operator* to the sentence that is being denied.

English negative operators	Examples	Symb.
not p	Chicago is not an exciting city.	~ C
not p	Not everyone is a sinner.	~ S
it is not the case that p	It is not the case that all pigs can fly.	~ P
it is not true that p	It is not true that some houses are red.	~ H
it is false that p	It is false that the Moon is inhabited.	~ M
that p is not the case	That unicorns exist is not the case.	~ U
that p is false	That frogs can sing is false.	~ F
no way that p	No way that Joe is that smart.	~ J
p. Not.	Someone likes you. Not.	~ L

Conjunctions

A *conjunctive* sentence is a sentence that makes a *double assertion*. Such a sentence is formed by applying a *conjunctive operator* to the two sentences being asserted.

English conjunctive operators	Examples	Symb.
p and q	Chicago is large and windy.	L & W
p and q	Chicago is large, and Chicago is windy.	L & W
both p and q	Both Sue and Bob are exhausted.	S & B
not only p but also q	Not only is it hot, but it is also muggy.	H & M
p, but q	Loyola U. is good, but it is expensive.	G & E
p, moreover q	I am tired; moreover, I want food.	T & F
p, although q	Cats are cute, although they are selfish.	C & S
p, yet q	You have eyes, yet you see nothing.	E & S
p; q	Liz was smiling; she knew what to do.	S & K

Disjunctions

A *disjunctive* sentence is a sentence that asserts *two alternatives*. Such a sentence is formed by applying a *disjunctive operator* to the two sentences at issue.

English disjunctive operators	Examples	Symb.
p or q	The box contains books or old records.	B ∨ O
either p or q	Either God exists or things have an end.	G ∨ E
p, or else q	Sue is at school, or else she is at home.	S ∨ H
p, but maybe q	The test was easy, but maybe it was hard.	E ∨ H
p; alternatively, q	We will sail; alternatively, we will fly.	S ∨ F

Conditionals

A *conditional* sentence is a sentence that asserts that *if* one situation occurs [the *condition*], *then* another situation also occurs [the *result*, or *consequent*]. Such a sentence is formed by applying a *conditional operator* to the condition part and the result part. In English, there are many diffent kinds of conditional expressions, but they are all equivalent to the standard form: "if p then q." When a conditional sentence is symbolized, the condition is always listed on the *left-hand side*.

English conditional operators	*Examples*	*Symb.*
if p then q	If Sue went out, then she took a taxi.	O ⊃ T
if p, q	If Sue went out, she took a taxi.	O ⊃ T
q, if p	Sue took a taxi, if she went out.	O ⊃ T
provided p, q. [sometimes]	Provided Sue went out, she took a taxi.	O ⊃ T
q, provided p. [sometimes]	Sue took a taxi, provided she went out.	O ⊃ T
in the event that p, q	In the event Sue went, she took a taxi.	O ⊃ T
q, in the event that p	Sue took a taxi, in the event she went.	O ⊃ T
not p unless q	Sue didn't go out unless she took a taxi.	O ⊃ T
not p without q	Sue didn't go out without taking a taxi.	O ⊃ T
p only if q	Sue went out only if she took a taxi.	O ⊃ T
p requires q	Sue's going requires that she take a taxi.	O ⊃ T

The last four conditional forms are somewhat complicated and require expanations, but we won't give them right now. We will discuss these later in Section 2.3. For the moment, just accept these translation rules *exactly* as stated, without variation.

Biconditionals

A *biconditional* sentence is a sentence that asserts that two sentences are *equal conditions* for each other. The two sides are equal in the sense that each side produces the other. Such a sentence is formed by applying a *biconditional operator* to the two sentences at issue.

Biconditional sentences are especially important in mathematics, science, and law, and in any situation that requires spelling out in *complete detail* under what conditions some item under consideration will obtain or occur. Think of theorems of algebra, or engineering projects, or complex inheritance situations, or what it takes to graduate and get a diploma.

Eng. biconditional operators	*Examples*	*Symb.*
p if and only if q	It snows if and only if it is real-cold-and-wet.	S ≡ W
p when q, and only when q	It moves when and only when it is touched.	M ≡ T
p in case q, and only then	We fight if we are attacked, and only then.	F ≡ A
p exactly when q	George smokes exactly when he is bored.	S ≡ B
p if q, but not otherwise	He get an A if he studies, but not otherwise.	A ≡ S

Symbolization Rule #3:

> If a compound sentence is a *part* of a larger sentence, then that compound part must be enclosed in *parentheses* (except, if the part is a negative sentence ~p , then such parentheses are optional).

The normal sentences of our discourses are more complex than the examples we have given so far. Usually the *parts* of our sentences themselves have *sub-parts*, and those in turn have their parts. Consider this example:

Either both Bob and Sue will go, or neither will go.

The sentence as a whole is a disjunction, but each of the two choices is a conjunction. We can approach the symbolization in successive stages:

(Bob will go and Sue will go) or (Bob will not go and Sue will not go)

(B and S) or (not B and not S)

(B & S) ∨ (~B & ~S)

Here is another example:

George will go if Alice goes, yet it is false that Sue isn't going.

(G if A) and not (not S)

(A ⊃ G) & ~(~S)

Why don't you try some. Check the symbolizations of the following sentences. One of them is *wrong*. Can you find it?

1. If either David or Alice works tonight, then the work order will be finished on time and the contract will be honored.   (D ∨ A) ⊃ (W & C)   Is it OK? _____

2. If the dog is sleeping and not a person is home, then either $(S \ \& \sim H) \supset ((D \ \& \ W) \lor K)$
   the doors are locked and the windows too, or the killer cat   Is it OK? _____
   is on the alert.

3. Both the dog goes, and the cat goes, and the mouse goes $((D \ \& \ C) \ \& \ M) \supset Y$
   too, and, if they all go, then so do you.   Is it OK? _____

Let's do some more of this, but now we are going to start using *your* money. You will be glad that you are taking logic, because you have been ordered by the Donations Committee to give donations to Liz, Dave, Sue, and Joe in any amount, but it must be in accordance with the *donation rule* that the Donations Committee has assigned to you. Here is the donation rule that you are required to follow:

> "Liz gets $100, and Dave gets $100, and Sue gets $100, or Joe gets nothing."
>
> "..., and ..., and ..., or ..."   ← That is the pattern that the rule specified.
>
> L & D & S ∨ ~J   ← Oops, is that a legal formula?

Well, luckily for you, this donation rule was *badly written*, and you certainly cannot be blamed for interpreting that stated rule in the way that is most advantageous to you—as long as the money you donate agrees with the rule as it is *worded*. If only someone on that committee had taken some logic! However, they didn't, but you did.

First, some general observations. Ordinary language has special *tools* of grammar and style for representing exact logical relationships.

(1) Ordinary language has various grammatical operators that have duplicate *auxiliary* words, written to the left, separated from the main operator word, to indicate the *word range* of the operators. These auxiliary words help to indicate word groupings:

> both.... and...., either.... or...., neither.... nor...., if.... then....

(2) Another device that ordinary language has is to *collapse* duplicated grammatical forms into single ones. For example, longer, double sentences can be collapsed into shorter, single sentences that, as a result of the contraction, contain a grouping:

> "Liz *is happy*, and Dave *is happy*" = "Liz and Dave *are happy*"

(3) Ordinary language has special *punctuation marks*, to separate the words of a written passage into smaller self-contained meaningful groups. These are periods, commas, semi-colons, colons, dashes, and quotation marks.

Of course, our new logical language does not have any of these tools. Those tools belong only to natural languages. The one and only tool that the language of logic has is the use of *parentheses* to create the groupings that are intended.

So, let's continue with the previous example about your financial donations. There are three possible interpretations that we can give to the badly written donation rule, and we can write these in an exact manner by using any of the three above-mentioned tools (but the words "both" and "either" are especially helpful here):

1. Both Liz gets $100, and Dave gets $100; and, either Sue gets $100, or Joe gets $0.
    = Liz and Dave each get $100, and, either Sue gets $100, or Joe gets $0.
    = (L & D) & (S ∨ ~J)   Ouch! That will cost you $200.

2. Liz gets $100, and either both Dave gets $100 and Sue gets $100, or Joe gets $0.
    = Liz gets $100, and either Dave and Sue each get $100, or Joe gets $0.
    = L & ((D & S) ∨ ~J)   Ouch! That will still cost you $100.

3. Either Liz gets $100, and Dave gets $100, and Sue gets $100, or Joe gets $0.
    = Either Liz, Dave, and Sue each get $100, or Joe gets $0.
    = (L & (D & S)) ∨ ~J   Yes! That will cost you nothing. *Take that one!*

The Language of Propositional Logic

Let's review what we have presented so far and put it into a more focused form. The following expressions make up the language of Propositional Logic. First, there is a list of the individual symbols that may be used in the language. These symbols are:

simple sentence symbols:	A , B , C , D , . . . , Z
operator symbols:	~ , & , ∨ , ⊃ , ≡
grouping symbols:	(,) , [,] , { , }
the inference symbol:	∴

(The commas used here are not symbols of the logical language but are used only as visual separators for the convenience of the reader.) Secondly, these symbols may be combined into meaningful sequences called *sentences* and *arguments*. Sentences are divided into certain types, which we list separately below. In this description the *variables* p and q represent all sentences, of any degree of complexity:

simple sentences:	A , B , C , D , . . . , Z
negations:	~p
conjunctions:	p & q
disjunctions:	p ∨ q
conditionals:	p ⊃ q
biconditionals:	p ≡ q

The only punctuation used in the symbolic language is parentheses. If a compound sentence occurs as a part of a larger sentence, then that compound part must be written as a unit by enclosing it in parentheses. But, negative sentences ~p are an exception: the parentheses are *optional*. A & ~B and A & (~B) are both correct.

According to these grammar rules, expressions such as the following are *well-formed*, and thus qualify as sentences,

~~B

~(~B)

D & ~G

(S & Q) ∨ (R & W)

but the following expressions are *ill-formed*, and thus may not be written:

M, K & B   – was the intention to write: M & (K & B) ?

⊃ D ⊃ G   – was the intention to write: D ⊃ G ?

A & B ∨ R & W   – was the intention to write: A & [B ∨ (R & W)] ?

An *argument* is a list of sentences (called the *premises* of the argument) followed by the inference indicator, followed by another sentence (called the *conclusion* of the argument). Arguments may be written in two ways, depending on the circumstance of their use. One may write them as a *vertical* list, using no punctuation to separate the sentences. This is usually done when an argument is being presented for analysis or demonstration:

p_1 A ⊃ B

.   B ⊃ C

.   A ∨ M

p_n ~M

――――   ――――

∴ q   ∴ C

One may also write arguments as a *horizontal* list. This is usually done when one only wants to identify an argument, without devoting special attention to it at that point:

p1 , p2 , . . . , p_n ∴ q

A ⊃ B , B ⊃ C , C ⊃ D , A ∨ M , ~M   ∴ D

When an argument is written in English, it is typically written as a horizontal list, using normal punctuation, so that sentences are separated by periods. When an argument is symbolized and written as a horizontal list, then no punctuation is used, except that as a *visual aid*, the premises are separated by commas, as shown here.

There is an *optional convention* regarding the use of parentheses when they are *nested* within other parentheses. Nested parentheses use brackets and braces in place of parentheses in the following manner: innermost are parentheses, next outermost are brackets, next are braces; next are large parentheses, next are large brackets, next are large braces; next are very large parentheses, etc.

$$\ldots\{\,.\,.[\,.\,.(\,.\,.\{\,.\,.[\,.\,.(\,.\,.)\,.\,.]\,.\,.\}\,.\,.)\,.\,.]\,.\,.\}\ldots$$

The following far-fetched example illustrates this convention. (Wait. Please don't worry right now about being able (unable) to symbolize sentences as complex as the one that will now appear before your very eyes. That sort of ability is an unintended by-product, not a goal. The only purpose here is to illustrate the method of *nesting* parentheses, as it is called.)

> If animals exist, but, either neither horses nor cows exist or chickens don't, then, if pigs don't exist, then farms exist if and only if both sheep and goats exist or cows don't.

> If A but either neither H nor K or not C, then, if not P, then F if and only if either both S and G or not K.

> $\{\,A\ \&\ [\,(\sim H\ \&\ \sim K)\ \vee\ \sim C\,]\,\} \supset (\,\sim P \supset \{\,F \equiv [(S\ \&\ G)\ \vee\ \sim K]\,\}\,)$

Of course, using just regular parentheses is also correct, but it is harder to read:

> $(A\ \&\ ((\sim H\ \&\ \sim K)\ \vee\ \sim C)) \supset (\sim P \supset (F \equiv ((S\ \&\ G)\ \vee\ \sim K)))$

Incidentally, we will soon introduce a *truth-value calculation method* by which we can *easily* show that this last sentence is actually true. Imagine that!

Exercise 2.1. A,B Symbolizing basic sentences

Part A. Symbolize the following sentences. First, give a *partial symbolization* with capital letters and the *original* English operator expressions. Secondly, give a *complete* symbolization. Write the sentences and the two results side by side for comparison. Use the available **Exercise Work Sheet** to submit your work.

1. If there is no noise, the parrot will bite.   if not N, B $\sim N \supset B$
2. Although there was noise, the parrot bit.   although N, B   N & B
3. The parrot won't bite, if there is noise.
4. The parrot will bite, or there will be noise.
5. It is false that the parrot will not bite.
6. Either there is noise, or there is no noise.

7. There was noise, but the parrot didn't bite.
8. The parrot didn't bite; yet, there was noise.
9. There was noise, and the parrot did bite.
10. There was no noise; the parrot did not bite.
11. The parrot does not bite, if there is no noise.
12. That the parrot didn't bite is definitely true.
13. That the parrot did bite is definitely false.
14. Not only was there noise, the parrot also bit.
15. The parrot did bite, even though it didn't.
16. It bites if and only if there is noise.
17. If the parrot didn't bite, there was no noise.
18. It doesn't bite if and only if there's no noise.
19. The choices are noise and a biting parrot.
20. Yay, though it noised, it bit thee not.

Part B. Just some practice. Each of the following expressions is intended to be a single, compound symbolic sentence, but some of them are incorrectly written. Figure out which of these is a *well-formed* sentence. Write "YES" or "NO." (Of course, don't worry about whether any of these are true or false.) It may help here, if you try to read these in English. There is an available **Exercise Work Sheet.**

A = Apples are red
B = Bananas are yellow
C = Carrots are crunchy

K = Kangaroos are jumpy
M = Monkeys are funny
P = Parrots are noisy

1. A & ~M
2. ~A ⊃ ~C
3. K (& ~M)
4. ⊃ A, B
5. ~P & M
6. ~A & B
7. A ⊃ B C
8. K ∨ (~M)
9. A & B ∨ C
10. (~A) & B

11. A, B, & C
12. ~(A & B)
13. (~A)(& B)
14. (K ∨ M) ∨ ~P
15. K ∨ (M ∨ ~P)
16. M & (~P & ~M) ∨ P
17. (M & ~P) & (~M ∨ P)
18. ~(~A) & ((~B) & (~C))
19. ~(~(~M)) & ~~~P
20. ~(B ∨ ~C) ⊃ (~B & C)

Section 2.2 Details about Negations

So far we have looked at five fundamental types of English sentences, and we have shown how to represent them in our language of logic. There are, of course, very many English sentences that are *complex cases* of these five general patterns. For the most part, we handle these complex sentences quite well, but there are difficulties here, and we do on occasion get confused and make mistakes.

Details about Negative Combinations
(Not both, both not, not either, either not, neither)

There is a difference between *not both* and *both not*, as the following examples show:

Not both Ken and Sue went.	Both Ken and Sue did not go.
Not both Ken went and Sue went.	Both Ken didn't go and Sue didn't go.
not both K and S	both not K and not S
~(K & S)	(~K & ~S)

Who went to the party? Did Ken? Maybe. Did Sue? Maybe. We can't tell who did and who didn't. Did *both* go? No! That much we know. *Not both* of them went. At least one of them didn't.	Who went to the party? Did Ken? Definitely not. Did Sue? Definitely not. So, there! We know what happened. Ken did not go, and Sue did not go. *Neither* of them went.

There is also a difference between *not either* and *either not*, as the next examples show:

Not either Ken or Sue went.	Either Ken or Sue did not go.
Not either Ken went or Sue went.	Either Ken didn't go or Sue didn't go.
not either K or S	either not K or not S
~(K ∨ S)	(~K ∨ ~S)

Who went to the party? Did Ken? Definitely not. Did Sue? Definitely not. Well, that's it then. We know what happened. *Not either* of them went. *Neither* of them went.	Who went to the party? Did Ken? Maybe, maybe not. Did Sue? Maybe, maybe not. *Somebody* didn't go, but we can't tell who. Well, since somebody didn't, it was *either* Ken who did *not*, or it was Sue who did *not*.

We can see now what the logical relationships are. On the one hand, if *not both* Ken and Sue went, then *either* Ken did *not* go, or Sue did *not* go (and vice versa). On the other hand, if *not either* Ken or Sue went, then *both* Ken did *not* go, and Sue did *not* go (and vice versa). And thrown into the mix is the operator "neither," which means "not either" as well as "both not." All these relationships are called *De Morgan's Laws*.

not both p and q ≠ both not p and not q
not either p or q ≠ either not p or not q

$$\sim(p \ \& \ q) \ \neq \ \sim p \ \& \ \sim q$$
$$\sim(p \lor q) \ \neq \ \sim p \lor \sim q$$

BAD:
One can *never* just distribute negations (or collect them).

not both p and q = either not p or not q
not either p or q = both not p and not q

$$\sim(p \ \& \ q) \ = \ \sim p \lor \sim q$$
$$\sim(p \lor q) \ = \ \sim p \ \& \ \sim q$$

GOOD:
De Morgan's Laws

Details about Multiple Negations

There are all sorts of patterns that involve more than one negation. People tend to think, when they try to do formal analysis, that multiple negatives, somehow, just *cancel out*. And there is indeed one special rule to that effect—but it applies only to *one* special case. We must have a closer look. Just always remember the following rule (that has only one exception):

> General Rule: Multiple negatives do *not* just cancel out—with one exception.

Double Negation

The exception to the general rule is the case of *double negation*. Somebody (Bob) says, "Chicago is not an exciting city," and offended, someone (Sue) replies, "That's not true." Whereupon Bob says, "How can you say that? You're wrong." And the argument continues. So, what are they saying?

Bob:	not C	~C
Sue:	not (not C)	~(~C)
Bob:	not (not (not C))	~(~(~C))

This looks like complicated stuff, but Bob and Sue don't give it an extra thought, because they are each employing the *Law of Double Negation*. The thoughts are complex, but they reduce to something very simple. Notice, this law applies only to the *denial* of a *denial*: When one denies the denial of a sentence, then one affirms the sentence:

$$\sim(\sim p) = p$$

Bob was thinking that Chicago is *not* exciting, ~C, and he said so. Sue denied that Chicago is not exciting, ~(~C), because she thinks Chicago is exciting, C. Bob then questions Sue's denial, ~(~(~C)), because he knows that denying her denial of his denial keeps things as *he* said them, ~C. Phew! Good thing that we do these things on auto-pilot, otherwise, we might actually get them wrong.

Emphatic Negation

People are often criticized for not speaking proper English, especially when it comes to negations. It is actually incorrect to say, "And don't talk to no strangers," because if one does *not* talk to *no* strangers, then one *does* talk to *some* strangers. Or, so it would be, *if* the speaker were intending to negate a negation. But in the realm of informal, popular speech, that is not the intention. In informal speech, negation can be *emphatic*, in the sense that any number of negative expressions can be used to express the meaning of a *single* denial. The next sentence is somewhat theatrical, but the intention is clear.

I don't never give no peddlers no money.

What this sentence (with four negatives, count them) literally says is:

Not at all times do I *not* to all peddlers *not* all the money *not*-give,

and what that means is not so easy to figure out. But in any event, that meaning is not the intention. Instead, the original assertion means the simple, *single* denial:

not (I do sometimes give some peddlers some money).

Negations of Negative Conjunctions (Not both not)

Consider the sentence:

It is not the case that both Bob does not go and Sue does not go.

not both not B and not S

~(~B & ~S)

It would be wrong to *cancel* out the negatives

~(~B & ~S)   . . . .
B & S   DEAD WRONG

Rather, the correct analysis proceeds as follows:

~(~B & ~S)   . . . .
~(~B) ∨ ~(~S)   by De Morgan's Law
B ∨ S   by the Double Negation Law

You can see that the correct answer is quite different from the "cancellation" answer.

Negations of Negative Disjunctions (Not either not)

Consider the sentence:

It is not the case that either Bob does not go or Sue does not go.

not either not B or not S

~(~B ∨ ~S)   (to cancel to B ∨ S would be DEAD WRONG)
~(~B) & ~(~S)   yes, by De Morgan's Law
B & S   yes, by the Double Negation Law

Again, the correct answer is altogether different from the "cancellation" answer.

Exclusionary Disjunction (Either but not both)

Normally when we assert alternatives, we do not have anything special in mind: Do you drink coffee or tea? Do you have a brother or a sister? If you own either a dog or a cat then you are prohibited from renting the apartment. And so on. All these alternatives employ the *weak* sense of "p or q," also called the *inclusive* sense. In the weak sense, "p or q" is true if *at least one* of the choices is true; and it is false if both choices are false. The inclusive sense is the ordinary sense of "or," and it is the default interpretation.

But sometimes we have something special in mind when we say "or." In this special sense we *mean* to limit the alternatives to the cases where *exactly one* of the two choices is true. This is known as the *strong* sense of "or," also called the *exclusive* sense. We already know how to deal with the weak sense of "or": use the symbol "∨". So, what about the strong sense? Should we introduce a *new* logical symbol to represent this different sense of "or"? No. The simplest way to symbolize sentences that use the strong sense of "or" is to explicitly write out the full form of what is *intended* (one should always make intentions explicit):

p or q, but not both p and q.
(p ∨ q) & ~(p & q)

In spoken English, the word "or" will receive a special intonation as well as a special emphasis. In written English, all we can do is to underline or bold-face the expression at issue:

> Bob *either* went with Sue, *or* he went drinking. (She hates it when he drinks.)
>
> S or D, but not both S and D
>
> (S ∨ D) & ~(S & D)

Please notice, the presence or absence of the word "either" does *not* determine whether the strong or weak sense of "or" is intended. Only the presence or absence of *special emphasis* on "either . . . or" determines what sense is meant. And the same is true when the word "or" is used by itself.

Negative Conditionals (If not, then not)

Consider the negative conditonal sentence:

> If Bob did not go, then Sue did not go.
>
> If not B then not S
>
> ~B ⊃ ~S

What shall we do with these two negatives? First of all, note that there are many examples that show it is DEAD WRONG to just cancel out the negatives. Consider,

> If Bob does *not* have a penny to his name, then he is *not* a millionaire.
>
> ~P ⊃ ~M

This sentence is a necessary truth. But, see what happens when one just cancels the two negatives. The necessary truth is turned into a ridiculous falsehood:

> If Bob *does* have a penny to his name, then he *is* a millionaire.
>
> P ⊃ M

The second thing to notice is that there is an important law that governs how negations behave inside conditional sentences. This law is known as the *Law of Contraposition*. But, let us also state what is *not* permitted.

- ~p ⊃ ~q ≠ p ⊃ q   CANCELLATION is DEAD WRONG
- ~p ⊃ ~q ≠ ~q ⊃ ~p   CONVERSION is DEAD WRONG
- ~p ⊃ ~q = q ⊃ p   YES, the *Law of Contraposition*

The Law of Contraposition is actually very general, and it applies to *all* conditional sentences, regardless of whether any part is originally negated. The law says that, for a given conditional sentence, *if* the *result* part is *wrong*, then the *condition* part is also *wrong*. (Be careful, don't reverse what was just said.) Since the starting conditional sentence can already contain a negative, up front or in back, there are four forms that the Law of Contraposition can take.

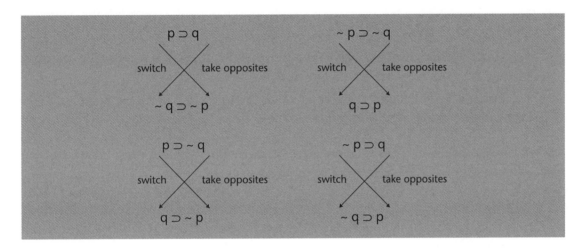

Exercise 2.2. A,B Symbolizing Arguments

Part A. Analyze each of the following arguments in two stages. (1) First, use the suggested capital letters to abbreviate the *simple* sentences of the argument. This results in a *partial symbolization* consisting of capital letters connected by English operator expressions. (2) Next, finish symbolizing the arguments by replacing the English operator expressions by the symbolic connectives. Write the results side by side for comparison. (3) *Optional*: In your *opinion*, is the argument valid or invalid? Use the available **Exercise Work Sheet** to submit your work.

1. Either this painting is by Rembrandt or it is   either R or M   R ∨ M
   by Vermeer. It isn't by Rembrandt. So, it   not R   ~R
   must be by Vermeer. (R, M) Argument   So, M   ∴ M
   is: valid

2. Coffee and tea both contain the drug caffeine. So, tea contains the drug caffeine. (C, T)

3. If the premium was paid, then the insurance is in force. But the premium was not paid. So, the insurance is not in force. (P, I)

4. If people can live on Venus, then they can live on Mars. If they can live on Mars, then they can live on Jupiter. Therefore, if people can live on Venus, then they can live on Jupiter. (V, M, J)

5. The house will be sold by August, or it won't be sold this year. It won't be sold by August. So, it won't be sold this year. (A, Y)

6. If George is not late for the meeting, then he will introduce the speaker. But, George was late for the meeting. So, he did not introduce the speaker. (L, I)

7. Rotterdam is in Holland or in Europe. Rotterdam is in Holland. So, Rotterdam is not in Europe. (H, E)

8. The dog won't bark, if the child won't scare it. The child won't scare it. So, the dog won't bark. (D, C)

9. If it rains, then the streets are wet. If it freezes, then the streets are slippery. It is raining or freezing. So, the streets are wet or slippery. (R, W, F, S)

10. If it rains and freezes, then the streets are wet and slippery. It is raining or freezing. So, the streets are wet or slippery. (R, F, W, S)

Part B. Use exactly the same instructions as for Part A above. These sentences are a little more difficult. Use the available **Exercise Work Sheet** to submit your work.

1. If George or Liz went to the party, then Tom and Susan were upset. Liz, as it turned out, didn't go, but Tom and Susan were still upset. Therefore, George did indeed go to the party. (G, L, T, S)

2. If Al isn't singing then Bo isn't dancing. Either Bo or Clyde is dancing. So, if Clyde is not dancing then Al is singing. (A, B, C)

3. The orchestra won't play both Stravinski and Mozart tonight. They will, as we know, play Mozart tonight. We must conclude, therefore, that they will not play Stravinski tonight. (M, S)

4. It is not true that both you can't go on the kiddie rides and also you can't go on the adult rides. You, naturally, can't go on the kiddie rides. Therefore, you can go on the adult rides. (K, A)

5. His driving license won't have been revoked if he hasn't violated the law. But he must have violated the law, because his license has been revoked. (R, V) [Note: "because"]

6. If this school is to survive, it must increase its tuition (in order to offset expenses). But, if this school is to survive, it can't increase its tuition (so as to remain competitive). So, this school is definitely not going to survive. (S, I)

7. If this creature doesn't have teeth, then it does not bite. Ouch! Well, it is not the case that it doesn't bite. So, it is not the case that it doesn't have teeth. (T, B)

8. They won the battle, and it is false that they did not win the war. So, they did win the war, and it is not true that they didn't win the battle. (B, W)

9. If some number N is the largest possible number, then both N is the largest possible number (by hypothesis) and N is not the largest possible number (since you can add 1 to it). So, it's false that some number N is the largest possible number. (L)

10. Paris, London, or Rome will host the wine convention this year. If Paris does, then French wines will win. If London does, then British wines will win. If Rome does, then Italian wines will win. British wines will not win this year. So, either French wines or Italian wines will win this year. (P, L, R, F, B, I)

Section 2.3 Details about Conditional Sentences

We continue our analysis of the complex cases of the five basic types of English sentences. At this point we turn to conditional sentences together with the various pitfalls that they pose.

Details about Doubly Conditional Sentences

One large group of conditional sentences contains *two* conditional sentences. The English form of these sentences can be analyzed in different, but equivalent ways, resulting in different, but equivalent symbolizations. There are three subgroups here.

Biconditional Sentences (If and only if)

We have already introduced biconditional sentences, so we will not say much more about them. A biconditional sentence is a sentence composed of two conditional sentences with the one being the converse of the other: the condition of the one is the result of the other, and vice versa.

Bob will go if and only if Sue will go

Bob will go *if* Sue will go, *and* Bob will go *only if* Sue will go

$(B \supset S) \ \& \ (S \supset B)$

$B \equiv S$

Since we have introduced the triple-bar symbol to abbreviate the longer version, we have at our disposal the *Law of Biconditionals*:

$$p \equiv q \ = \ (p \supset q) \ \& \ (q \supset p)$$

Later, when we do deductions, we will give two separate rules for this law.

Double Thens [Double Consequents]

Some conditional sentences express a double *result*.

If Bob goes, then Sue will go, and Liz will go too.

This sentence may plausibly be analyzed in either of the following two ways:

(B ⊃ S) & (B ⊃ L)

B ⊃ (S & L)

What makes this possible is that both sentences have the same condition part, B, and both sentences have the same double result, S and L. These sentences mean the same thing, and the fact that these two sentences mean the same thing is recorded in the *Law of Double Thens* (we may also call it the *Law of Double Consequents*):

p ⊃ (q & r) = (p ⊃ q) & (p ⊃ r)

Again, later, when we do deductions, we will give two separate rules for this law.

Double Ifs [Double Antecedents]

When we want to say something, not just conditionally, but on a *double* condition, we have a variety of ways to say that.

If Bob went, and Sue went, then Liz also went.

(B & S) ⊃ L

If Bob went, then, if Sue went, then Liz also went.

B ⊃ (S ⊃ L)

Both these sentences have *each* of B and S as a *condition* part, and both these sentences have L as the *result* part. These sentences mean the same thing, as the *Law of Double Ifs* indicates (this law is better known as the Law of *Exportation*):

(p & q) ⊃ r = p ⊃ (q ⊃ r)

There is yet a third way to say all this in English:

if Bob went, and if Sue went, then Liz also went.

B ⊃ & (S ⊃ . . . . Ooops! *Nonsense*

This third English pattern, "if p, and if q, then r," has no independent counterpart in the formal language, because it is a *grammatical mixture* of the two preceding sentences. So, the proper way to symbolize this third sentence is to pick *one* of the two preceding ways.

Details about Two Functions of Conditional Sentences

All conditional sentences are the same. They all have a condition part, and they all have a result part. And they all share the same function: if the condition part is true, then the result part is being asserted; otherwise, there is no commitment, and nothing is asserted to be true or false. Still, there are *two* different *purposes* that one can have in mind when one utters a conditional sentence: the purpose of stating a sufficiency or the purpose of stating a requirement.

The Purpose of Stating a Sufficiency

When a speaker intends that something is sufficient, a predetermined *end result* is the focus of the discussion. Here, the speaker is trying to express that, of all the different *conditions* that are sufficient for him to be able to assert this one result, he is proposing one stated condition. This could be important, for example, if someone is trying to explain something that happened.

   If ____what?____, then Sue did not go to the party.

   If Bob went with Liz, (that is sufficient for that) Sue did not go to the party.

   If it was cancelled, (that is sufficient for that) Sue did not go to the party.

   If Sue had to work, (that is sufficient for that) Sue did not go to the party.

When sufficiency is at stake, the kinds of English expressions that the speaker often uses are any of the following:

   If p then q

   If p, q

   q, if p

   In the case that p, q

   In the event that p, q

   When p, q

   Provided p, q

The Purpose of Stating a Requirement

When requirement is the purpose, the speaker has fixed on a predetermined *condition*, and he is asserting that that condition has certain *requirements*, that is, *required consequences*, and in particular the requirement that he states.

If Bob went to the party, then _____what?_____ .

If Bob went to the party, then (it is required that) Sue gave him permission.

If Bob went to the party, then (it is required that) he took Liz along.

If Bob went to the party, then (it is required that) he did not have to work.

If Bob went to the party, then (it is required that) he dressed up for it.

If Bob went to the party, then (it is required that) he had transportation.

(Logic and mathematics texts usually call these types of sentences "statements of necessary condition". And one must keep that in mind. But, to refer to *required consequences* as being "conditions" creates confusion in ordinary speech. Much better to use the idea of *requirements*, which everyone understands very well.)

One can certainly express a sense of requirement by using the conditional expression "if . . . then . . .," if one *adds* the phrase "it is required that," as we have just done above. But without such further qualification, the expression "if . . . then . . ." is used mostly to express sufficiency. By contrast, there are special, *dedicated* forms of expression that *always* express the meaning of something that is *required*. Speakers mostly use these special forms to accomplish this purpose:

1a.	Not p unless q	Bob did not go unless Sue gave him permission.	B ⊃ S
2a.	Not p without q	Bob did not go without taking Liz along.	B ⊃ L
3a.	p only if q	Bob went only if he did not have to work.	B ⊃ ~W
4a.	p requires q	To go to the party, Bob was required to dress up.	B ⊃ D
5a.	if p, q *must* be so.	If Bob went, he must have had transportation.	B ⊃ T

An important feature of requirement talk is that it lets you know what will happen if the requirement is *not satisfied*. That kind of negative thinking is generally the only point of using requirement talk. And when that is indeed the case, it is quite appropriate to *symbolize* the original sentence in terms of the negative meanings. So, the five previous sentences may also be symbolized, correctly, by making the intended negations *explicit*. These two versions, the affirmative one and the negative one, are logically equivalent.

1b.	If Sue did not give him permission, then Bob did not go to the party.	~S ⊃ ~B
2b.	If Liz did not come along, then Bob did not go to the party.	~L ⊃ ~B
3b.	If Bob had to work, then he did not go to the party.	W ⊃ ~B
4b.	If Bob did not dress up, then he did not go to the party.	~D ⊃ ~B
5b.	If Bob did not have transportation, then he did not go to the party.	~T ⊃ ~B

Admittedly, all of the above requirement expressions have an independent existence in ordinary speech, and we are rarely, if ever, asked to re-express any of them as affirmative conditional sentences. Nevertheless, it is very important that we be able to do this rare thing. Logical clarity is always important. In this regard, we note that the above-listed correlations can be efficiently summarized by means of the following *general recipes*:

1. | not p unless q = p "then" q | "not. . .unless" is a COMBO, entire COMBO becomes "then"

2. | not p without q = p "then" q | "not. . .without" is a COMBO, entire COMBO becomes "then"

3. | p only if q = p "then" q | ". . .only if. . ." is a COMBO, entire COMBO becomes "then"

4. | p unless q = p , "if not" q = "if not" q , p | left-hand side is AFFIRMATIVE, "unless" is replaced by "if not"

5. | The alternative "negative versions" agree with 1, 2, 3, by Contraposition

We should observe that the word "without" can be used in a second way, not as a conditional operation, but as "and not," a *conjunction* with a *negation* on the right-hand side. If the without clause has the meaning of an *accomplished* negative fact, then "without" means "and not," but if the without clause has the meaning of a *potential* negative outcome, then "without" means "if not."

George can't keep the store, without having the money.	$K \supset M = {\sim}M \supset {\sim}K$
We cannot improve the situation, without their help.	$I \supset H = {\sim}H \supset {\sim}I$
George ordered the dinner, without having the money.	$D \mathbin{\&} {\sim}M$
We have success, without their help.	$S \mathbin{\&} {\sim}H$

Meaning Change Through Special Emphasis

It is a plain fact about the spoken language, that two people can speak the *same* worded sentence and yet mean two *different* things. And to everyone around it is perfectly plain what each uttered sentence means. One linguistic tool that achieves this effect is *spoken emphasis*. Throughout this course we will have several occasions to note specific cases of this, and we have already examined this device in the case of *exclusionary disjunction*. Here are some additional cases where the meaning of an English operator is changed by means of emphasis.

Different Meanings of "provided"

The word "provided" is also capable of different meanings. Without special emphasis the word means a mere "if," something that is *sufficient*. But with special emphasis, the word "if" means "if . . . but not otherwise," so that with special emphasis it has the meaning of the biconditional operator "if and only if." Here are some examples illustrating the difference:

#1. Bob will get an A, provided he studied a bit.

A, if S = if S then A

S ⊃ A

In example #1, "provided" has the meaning of sufficiency; studying a bit is enough to get the A. There is no hint here that "provided" also means requirement. If Bob didn't study a bit, who knows what he'd get. Maybe he'd luck out and still get the A.

#2. The function $f(x) > 0$, provided the number $x > 1$.

if N then F

N ⊃ F

In example #2, "provided" means that the condition is sufficient to produce the result. If the number x is greater than 1, then the function has a value greater than 0. But, that is just one of the listed solutions. Maybe there are other values for x for which it has not yet been proven that the same relationship holds. The intention is *not* to state a necessary and sufficient condition for the function. But, the next example is different.

#3. Bob will get an A, *provided* he has studied hard.

A if S, but not otherwise.

(S ⊃ A) & (~S ⊃ ~A)

S ≡ A

In example #3, "provided" has the strong meaning of both sufficiency and necessity. This is indicated by the *emphasis* that is applied to the word "provided" by putting it in italics. This emphasis signals that the speaker intends to say that studying is not only sufficient, but it is also required.

#4. Yes, *I* will pay your expenses, *provided* that *you* go back to school.

E if S, but not otherwise.

(S ⊃ E) & (~S ⊃ ~E)

S ≡ E

Again, in example #4, "provided" has the strong meaning of sufficiency and necessity. The two conditions are equal. They stand together or they fall together.

It is probably fair to say that this double meaning of the word "provided" is so ingrained in ordinary speech, that it is not possible to dismiss the stronger uses as "sloppy" speech.

Misusing the Word "if"

It is worth mentioning that even the simple connective "if" *can* be used by some people, on some occasions, to mean "if and only if," with the right kind of emphasis and intonation. But for formal, public speech this is not acceptable, and we should strive not to use such imprecise language. Even in colloquial speech this use is very *misleading*, as the next example shows.

Joey: Mom, may I go out and play?

Mom: Yes, you may go and play, *if* you clean your room.

Joey: Gee thanks, Mom. Good thing you didn't require it. Bye.

Mom: Wait. I said *"if* you clean your room!"

Joey: I know. And thanks. You proposed sufficiency. You need to take some logic, Mom. Bye.

Mom: Wait. I *did* take logic. I *did* require it. I emphasized the word "if". So, you're grounded.

In some sense they are both right. Thank goodness that nothing important was at issue, like who inherits what, and under what conditions, in a last will and testament.

A Closing Note about Determining Meaning

With the possibility of sentences having alternative meanings, how should one analyze and symbolize such sentences? The answer lies in distinguishing written sentences from spoken sentences. First of all, *written* sentences have a *default* meaning. (This makes written books and written articles possible, and libraries for them useful.) But, when written sentences are *spoken*, the speaker can, on such occasion, *create* different meanings for them by using special *intonation* and *emphasis*. By contrast, sentences that are not spoken but written, the ones we find in articles and books, lack those very tools that create the alternative meanings (with some exception), and because of that, written sentences have only their *default* meaning (again, with some exception). Consequently, when we analyze sentences and symbolize them, we may only consider this default meaning, and questions about possible alternative meanings when spoken in some special way, must be dismissed as irrelevant. The exception mentioned is this. There are writing devices such as italicizing, underlining, and scare-quoting, whose purpose is to introduce some special meaning that the reader must determine. But that effect is very limited, and for the rest, written sentences have only their default meaning. Of course, there is a different kind of case, one in which some written passage is a *transcript* of some *conversation*. Such sentences were originally spoken with possible special meanings that we cannot now know with certainty. In this type of case, the default meaning is available, but possible alternative meanings must also be allowed.

Reference Sheet for Conditional Sentences

Statements of sufficient condition		
if *what?* then q if p, then q if p, q q, if p in the event that p, q in the case that p, q provided p, q (sometimes)	p is sufficient for q if p then q	p ⊃ q

Statements of requirement (a.k.a. statements of necessary condition)		
if p then *what?* p requires q if p then it must be that q not p unless q not p without q p only if q	q is necessary for p if not q then not p if p then q	~q ⊃ ~p p ⊃ q

Statements of equal condition (a.k.a. statements of necessary condition and sufficient condition)		
p if and only if q p if q, and p only if q if p then q, and if q then p p when and only when q p in case and only in case that q p just in the case that q p, provided q (sometimes) p, but only if q p equals q	p and q are equal conditions p is a nec. and suf. cond. for q p if and only if q	$(p \supset q) \,\&\, (q \supset p)$ $p \equiv q$

Statements qualified by condition (here p is often affirmative)		
definitely p, unless q unless q, p p, except if q	if the qualification q does not occur, then p is true	$\sim q \supset p$

Exercise 2.3. A,B,C,D Complex Symbolizations

Part A. Analyze each of the following arguments in two stages. (1) First, give a *partial* symbolization, consisting of the capital letters suggested and the original English operator expressions. (2) Give a *complete* symbolization, consisting only of the capital letters and the symbolic connectives. Write the results side by side for comparison. (3) *Optional*: Say whether you think the argument is valid or invalid. Use the available **Exercise Work Sheet** to submit your work.

1. Robert knows Latin if and only if he doesn't know Greek. He does know Greek. So, Robert doesn't know Latin. (L, G) Arg. is: __valid__

   L if and only if not G   L ≡ ~G
   G   G
   So, not L   ∴ ~L

2. Beth will go, if James asks her. If Matthew asks her, Beth will go also. If James doesn't ask her, Matthew will. So, Beth will go. (B, J, M)

3. The music isn't by Vivaldi unless the style is baroque. If the style is romantic then it is not baroque. So, if the music is by Vivaldi, then it is not romantic. (V, B, R)

4. Matthew will have eaten, if Beth cooked. Matthew did not eat unless James ate too. So, James ate only if Beth cooked. (M, B, J)

5. Laura will give the lecture unless no one shows up. Luckily, people did show up. So, she did give the lecture. (G, S)

6. If the host knows the senator, then the senator will be invited. If the hostess likes the senator, then he will also be invited. But neither does the host know him nor does the hostess like him. So, the senator won't be invited. (K, I, I)

7. They won't sell the house only if they can pay the mortgage. But they are selling the house. So, they can't pay the mortage. (S, P)

8. Samantha will not run unless the weather isn't hot. Thus, that she will run while the weather is hot isn't going to happen. (R, H)

9. This cylinder is square only if it isn't round. But, even if the cylinder is square, it still has to be round. But any fool knows it can't be both round and not round. So, this cylinder can't be square. (S, R)

10. If the demand for these products goes up, then the price will go up. Also, the demand for these products will go up only if employment goes up. However, the demand hasn't gone up at all. So, either the price or the employment is not going up. (D, P, E)

11. Some employees must be let go, if the budget is reduced. There won't be a pay increase unless the budget is not frozen. The budget will be either reduced or frozen. So, some employees must be let go, or there won't be a pay increase. (L, R, P, F)

12. Unless clubs were not led, I can take this trick. I have a good hand, if spades are trump. Either clubs were led or spades are trump. So, either I can take this trick, or I have a good hand. (C, T, G, S)

13. If the pressure is too low, the engine won't run. And, if the pressure is too high, the engine won't run. So, if the engine runs, the presssure is neither too low nor too high. (L, R, H)

14. The landlord may evict the tenant only if the tenant has not satisfied the terms of the lease. The tenant has not satisfied the terms of the lease unless the rent is paid. So, if the rent is not paid, the landlord may evict the tenant. (E, S, P)

15. Provided Albert knows calculus, he knows algebra. But he doesn't know calculus if he doesn't know trigonometry. So, he doesn't know trigonometry unless he doesn't know algebra. (C, A, T)

16. Joe does not know calculus, but he does know algebra. But, he doesn't know trigonometry without knowing calculus. So, Joe knows algebra, but he doesn't know trigonometry. (C, A, T)

Part B. Symbolize the following sentences. First, give a *partial symbolization* with capital letters and the original English operator expressions. Then, give a *complete* symbolization. Write the results side by side for comparison. Pay special attention to what symbolization recipe you use for each of the conditional sentences. Use the available **Exercise Work Sheet** to submit your work.

1. If this is a platypus, then it lays eggs.   if P, then E   P ⊃ E
2. This doesn't lay eggs, if it is a platypus.

3. If this is not a platypus, it doesn't lay eggs.

4. This is a platypus only if it lays eggs.

5. It isn't a platypus only if it doesn't lay eggs.

6. It lays eggs if and only if this isn't a platypus.

7. This is not a platypus unless it lays eggs.

8. This lays eggs unless it is not a platypus.

9. Unless it lays eggs, this is not a platypus.

10. Only if this is a platypus does it lay eggs.

11. It doesn't lay eggs without being a platypus.

12. This lays eggs without it being a platypus.

13. Without it laying eggs, it isn't a platypus.

14. Being a platypus requires that it lay eggs.

15. This is a platypus, but only if it lays eggs.

16. Provided this lays eggs, it is not a platypus.

Part C. Symbolize the following constructions. Use the available **Exercise Work Sheet** to submit your work.

1. A, B, so C
2. A, since B and C
3. A, so B, since C
4. A and B
5. A but B
6. A but not B
7. A even though not B
8. A or B
9. either A or B
10. not not A
11. that not A is not true
12. it is not false that not A
13. not both A and B
14. not both A and not B
15. both not A and not B
16. neither A nor B
17. not either A or B
18. either not A or not B
19. not either not A or not B
20. A, B, and C
21. A, B, or C
22. one of A, B, and C
23. not all of A, B, and C
24. not any of A, B, and C
25. not one of A, B, and C
26. if A then B
27. B, if A
28. if not A then not B
29. not B if not A
30. not A unless B
31. not A unless not B
32. A unless B
33. A unless not B
34. A only if B
35. not A only if B
36. A only if not B
37. not A without B
38. A without B
39. A if and only if B
40. A but only if B
41. Only if B, A
42. if and only if A, B
43. A exactly when B
44. if A and B then C
45. if A and if B then C
46. if A then if B then C
47. if A then both B and C
48. if A then either B or C
49. if A or B then C
50. not if A, then not B
51. unless B, not A

Part D. These are difficult. Symbolize the following sentences. Hint: first of all, write a partial symbolization with capital letters that keeps the English operators as stated and that also adds parentheses as an additional tool for grouping; after that, symbolize it all. Use the available **Exercise Work Sheet** to submit your work.

1. Unless Liz or Mandy goes, neither George nor Sam will go, provided Bill goes but Alice doesn't.

2. Unless Liz or Mandy goes, not both George and Sam will go; but regardless, either Bill or Alice won't go.

3. If either neither Liz nor Mandy goes or neither George nor Sam go, then Bill won't go only if Alice does go.

4. If Bill and Alice go, then if George or Sam goes, and if Liz doesn't go, then Mandy will go without Liz going.

5. While both Liz and Mandy won't go only if either George or Sam do go, that Bill and Alice will go while both Liz will and George won't, is not true.

6. Either Bill will go and not both Liz and George will, or either Bill will go and both Sam and Mandy won't, or Alice will.

7. Only if not both George and Sam won't go, will Liz and Mandy go, even though Bill and Alice will not go without George and Sam not going.

8. It is false that both neither both Liz won't go and either George won't go or Mandy won't go, nor Sam won't go, and also Alice won't go.

9. Unless Liz goes, unless George goes, Mandy goes, unless Sam goes; unless Alice goes, unless Bill goes. *

10. If and only if Liz goes is it true that if George goes, then, Mandy goes only if Alice goes, if Bill goes.

* A very weird sentence! Some logic books rightly recommend always treating "X unless Y" as "X or Y." That approach would work very nicely here. But replacing "unless X" by "if not X" works as well.

Section 2.4 Determining the Truth-Value of Sentences

Statements are sentences that have a *truth-value*, that is, sentences that are true, or that are false. So, we can say that there are *two* truth-values: "being true," or **T**, and "being false," or **F**. We will discuss here *how* we determine what the truth-value of a sentence is.

CASE 1. The Case of Simple Sentences

We have spent a great deal of our lives observing what things are like and learning from other people things that we did not or could not observe ourselves. That means that we *know* a great many things to be *true*, and we *know* a great many things to be *false*, and we are *ignorant* about everything else. It is in *this* manner that we determine the truth-value of simple sentences. Because of our present knowledge, we could say that the truth-value of simple sentences is a *given starting point*. Thus, we *start* with the following (agreed upon) truth-values for the indicated sentences:

Horses exist	T (known by observation)
Some people own Jeeps	T (known by observation)
All roses are red	F (known by observation)
The Moon has lakes of water	F (known by education)
$(5 + 5) - (15 - 5) = 0$	T (known by arithmetic)
Christopher Columbus once talked to the Beatles	F (known by education)
Christopher Columbus collected sea shells	**unknown**
An earthquake will hit Los Angeles next year	**unknown**

CASE 2. The Case of Compound Sentences

The case is altogether different when it comes to compound sentences. It would be wrong to say that we have observed or learned all the truth-values of all the compound sentences. Consider,

Some people own Jeeps, and some people own castles.

This sentence, we all know, has the truth-value T. But, we have *never* in our lives considered this sentence before, so it is wrong to say that we observed or learned before that the sentence is true. Rather, the truth-value of this sentence, and all compound sentences, is *calculated* by us, as we say, *on the fly*. We *calculate* the value *while* we encounter the sentence. In the case at issue, the sentence "Some people own Jeeps" has the truth-value T, and the sentence "Some people own castles" has the truth-value T, and there is a *rule* for calculating truth-values that says that if two sentences have the truth-value T, then the *conjunction* of the two sentences also has the truth-value T. Consequently, the conjunctive sentence "Some people own Jeeps, *and* some people own castles" has the truth-value T.

In general, we use *precise rules* to make all such calculations. That means there are five such rules, one for each operator. These rules can be conveniently displayed here in the form of *tables*.

negations "not"		conjunctions "and"			disjunctions "or"			conditionals "if then"			biconditionals "if and only if"		

p	~p
T	F
F	T

p	q	p & q
T	T	T
T	F	F
F	T	F
F	F	F

p	q	p ∨ q
T	T	T
T	F	T
F	T	T
F	F	F

p	q	p ⊃ q
T	T	T
T	F	F
F	T	T
F	F	T

p	q	p ≡ q
T	T	T
T	F	F
F	T	F
F	F	T

MEMORIZE THESE TABLES CAREFULLY. MEMORIZE. MEMORIZE.

Each of these tables displays the rule for calculating the truth-value of a given type of compound sentence. We will illustrate these rules in turn.

Negations. A negated sentence has the *opposite* value of the unnegated sentence.

calculated value	basis	
pigs do **not** exist = F	pigs do exist = T	[need opposite value]
not all dogs bark = F	all dogs bark = T	[need opposite value]
not no cats purr = T	no cats purr = F	[need opposite value]

Conjuctions. A conjunctive sentence is T when *both* parts (the conjuncts) are T; otherwise, the sentence is F.

calculated value	basis		
cats **and** dogs eat = T	cats eat = T	dogs eat = T	[need two T's]
cats **and** dogs purr = F	cats purr = T	dogs purr = F	[Oops!]
cats **and** dogs bark = F	cats bark = F	dogs bark = T	[Oops!]
cats **and** dogs sing = F	cats sing = F	dogs sing = F	[Oops!]

Disjunction. A disjunctive sentence is T when *at least one* of the two parts (the disjuncts) is T; otherwise, the sentence is F.

calculated value	basis		
cats **or** dogs eat = T	cats eat = T	dogs eat = T	[need one T]
cats **or** dogs purr = T	cats purr = T	dogs purr = F	[need one T]
cats **or** dogs bark = T	cats bark = F	dogs bark = T	[need one T]
cats **or** dogs sing = F	cats sing = F	dogs sing = F	[Oops!]

Conditionals. A conditional sentence is *always* T—*except*, when the condition part is T and the result part is F, then the conditional is F.

calculated value	basis		
if cats eat **then** dogs do = T	cats eat = T	dogs eat = T	[avoid T — F]
if cats purr **then** dogs do = F	cats purr = T	dogs purr = F	[Oops!]
if cats bark **then** dogs do = T	cats bark = F	dogs bark = T	[avoid T — F]
if cats sing **then** dogs do = T	cats sing = F	dogs sing = F	[avoid T — F]

Biconditionals. A biconditional sentence is T when the two parts have the *same* value (2 T's or 2 F's); otherwise, the sentence is F.

calculated value	basis		
cats eat **if and only if** dogs do = T	cats eat = T	dogs eat = T	[same values]
cats purr **if and only if** dogs do = F	cats purr = T	dogs purr = F	[Oops!]
cats bark **if and only if** dogs do = F	cats bark = F	dogs bark = T	[Oops!]
cats sing **if and only if** dogs do = T	cats sing = F	dogs sing = F	[same values]

Using the Tree Method to Calculate Truth-Values

Let us introduce a *uniform procedure* for determining the value of any compound sentence. There are several recognized methods, and the reader may already be familiar with one or another of them. But the method that one uses in logic must be absolutely foolproof, because a single error in any part of the process completely invalidates the entire process. Methods of logic must be 100 percent right, and anything less than that is 100 percent wrong. So, we will adopt a single method to eliminate the possibility of a *confused mixture* of methods when several methods are allowed. We call our method the "Tree Method" because the finished product has the appearance of a branched tree. This tree is constructed in small pieces, and when these small pieces are done according to the rules, the end result has the character of an absolute proof.

Here is the procedure:

Stage 1. Write the sentence to be evaluated, and just beneath each of the simple components, write the *given* truth-value of that component. For example, suppose that each of the simple components A and K happens to have the value T, and that each of the simple components M and W happens to have the value F. Write these values directly beneath those simple sentences, as illustrated here:

Stage 1:   ~(A & M) ∨ (K & ~W)
                  T   F   T   F

Remaining stages. Use the truth function *rules* to calculate the values of all the many sub-parts of the sentence. First, calculate the innermost sub-parts. Then, working outwards, calculate the value of the next outermost sub-part(s), then the next ones, continuing until one has calculated the final value of the sentence itself. In the present example, one must progressively calculate the value of the entire left-hand side, which is T, and also the value of the entire right-hand side, which is T. The whole sentence ~(A & M) ∨ (K & ~W) then receives the final value T. Here are the steps that were taken:

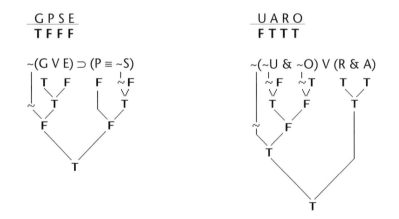

Of course, each step is added *on top of* the previous steps, so that throughout the entire process there is only *one* growing tree. Here are a few more finished examples.

Exercise 2.4. A,B Calculating Truth-Values

Part A. This is just some practice to help you learn your **T**'s and **F**'s. You should know the results here without looking at the rules. So, learn the rules *first*.

T & F	F ⊃ F	F ⊃ T	F & T
F ∨ T	F & T	F ∨ T	T ≡ T
F ≡ F	T ∨ F	F ⊃ F	T & F
F ⊃ F	T ⊃ F	F ≡ F	T ∨ F
F ∨ F	F ≡ T	F & F	F & F
T & T	T ∨ T	F ∨ F	T ≡ F
F ⊃ T	T ≡ T	T ⊃ T	T ⊃ F

Part B. Use the Tree Method to determine the values of the following compound sentences. Do not skip any steps: show your work for *every* sub-calculation that you make. You are not allowed to use any rules other than the rules for calculating truth-values. The capital letters have the indicated meanings and the indicated real-world values. Use the available **Exercise Work Sheet** to submit your work.

A = Amsterdam is a city   C = Cairo is a city

M = Morocco is a city   R = Russia is a city

A	C	M	R
T	T	F	F

1. ~A ∨ M
2. R & ~M
3. C ≡ ~M
4. C & (A ∨ R)
5. C ⊃ (R ∨ M)
6. (A & R) ⊃ M
7. ~A ∨ ~M
8. ~R ⊃ ~C
9. R ≡ ~(~C)
10. (M ⊃ ~R) & A
11. A ∨ (M & ~R)
12. (C ∨ R) ≡ ~M
13. (M & A) ∨ (C ∨ ~R)
14. (A ⊃ R) ∨ (A ⊃ ~R)
15. ~(A & R) ⊃ (C & M)
16. ~A ∨ [(M ⊃ C) ∨ R]
17. (~A ∨ ~R) ⊃ (A ∨ ~M)
18. ~(A ∨ (M ⊃ (C ∨ R)))
19. ~((A ≡ ~A) & C) ⊃ (~M & ~(M & R))
20. ((~A ⊃ M) ⊃ (A ⊃ R)) ⊃ ((C ≡ M) ⊃ ~C)
21. ~(~A & ~(~M & ~C)) ≡ (A ∨ (M ∨ C))
22. (((C ≡ M) ≡ R) ≡ ~R) ≡ (C ≡ ~M)

Section 2.5 Truth-Tables to Test the Validity of Arguments

Earlier, in Chapter 1, we introduced a precise definition for the notion of validity. Recall that this definition was:

An argument is *valid* if and only if:

the following combination is not a logical possibility –

> all the premisses are true and the conclusion is false.

We will now develop a special method for using this definition, called the *truth-table method.* At the heart of this method is the idea that all the many possibilities regarding the simple components of an argument can be *itemized* in a *list of possibilities*, so that we can actually scrutinize what happens in each possible case. Consider the following argument:

> If these bananas are fresh, then these grapes should be fresh too.
>
> But these grapes are not fresh.
>
> So, neither the bananas nor grapes are fresh.

This argument is symbolized as:

> B ⊃ G
>
> ~G
>
> ∴ ~(B ∨ G)

To test this argument for validity, we have to build a truth-table for it. First of all, we have to determine what the *simple sentences* are that make up this argument. We *scan* the argument from left to right, and from top to bottom, and we *record* the simple sentences that we encounter in the following manner:

B G	

Next, we want to consider how many *possible situations* there are regarding the truth or falsity of these two simple sentences. What are the situations that we can *imagine* regarding the freshness of the bananas and the grapes? We can imagine *four possible situations*: that both are fresh; that the bananas are fresh, but the grapes are not; that the bananas are not fresh, but the grapes are; and finally, that neither are fresh. These four situations can be added to the table, in the following way:

B G	
T T	
T F	
F T	
F F	

Our purpose is to determine the validity of the argument. So, we must find out whether or not it is logically possible that the premisses are true while the conclusion is false. Since we already know what the four possible situations are, our task is simply to calculate the values of the premisses and the conclusion in *each* of these situations, to see whether the *invalid combination* of true premisses and false conclusion can exist. So, we continue building the table we have just started, by constructing *main columns* for each of the premisses and the conclusion, and by also introducing *auxiliary columns* that display the compound parts whose values will be *used* to calculate the values in the main columns. Notice how each column has been *labeled*.

B G	prem B ⊃ G	prem ~G	aux B ∨ G	concl ~(B ∨ G)
T T				
T F				
F T				
F F				

So, our task is to calculate the value of the expressions in *each* of the columns in *each* of the rows. *Every spot needs a value*. This is a tedious task, but somebody has to do it. Now, it turns out that it is *far* more efficient to calculate values column-by-column than row-by-row. So, let us proceed in that manner.

The values in the two premisses columns can be calculated directly from the simple columns on the left:

premiss 1: row 1: T ⊃ T = T, row 2: T ⊃ F = F, row 3: F ⊃ T = T, row 4: F ⊃ F = T

premiss 2: row 1: ~T = F,   row 2: ~F = T,   row 3: ~T = F,   row 4: ~F = T

B G	prem B ⊃ G	prem ~G	aux B ∨ G	concl ~(B ∨ G)
T T	T	F		
T F	F	T		
F T	T	F		
F F	T	T		

The values for the conclusion column cannot be determined immediately from the simple columns on the left. The value of ~(B ∨ G) must be calculated from the value of (B ∨ G). So, we must first calculate all the possible values in the auxiliary column.

Aux. column: row 1: T ∨ T = T, row 2: T ∨ F = T, row 3: F ∨ T = T, row 4: F ∨ F = F

Conclusion: row 1: ~T = F, row 2: ~T = F, row 3: ~T = F, row 4: ~F = T

B G	prem B ⊃ G	prem ~G	aux B ∨ G	concl ~(B ∨ G)
T T	T	F	T	F
T F	F	T	T	F
F T	T	F	T	F
F F	T	T	F	T

It remains now to apply the test for validity. Notice how we will *cross out* the auxiliary column. The values in the auxiliary column were needed only to calculate the values in a main column. But now that that part is done, we have no further need for the auxiliary values. We also want to eliminate the auxiliary values from the test we are about to perform because they get in the way and cause confusion. The test is to see whether there is an *invalid combination* (all true premisses and a false conclusion) amongst all the possible situations. If such a combination *does* exist, then that proves that the argument is *invalid*; but if such a combination does *not* exist, then that proves that the argument is *valid*. Here she goes:

		T	T		F	invalid combo	?
		prem	prem	aux	concl		
	B G	B ⊃ G	~G	B ∨ G	~(B ∨ G)		
B ⊃ G	T T	T	F	T	F	– ok	
~G	T F	F	T	T	F	– ok	
――――――	F T	T	F	T	F	– ok	
∴ ~(B ∨ G)	F F	T	T	F	T	– ok	

This table shows the argument to be *valid*, because there is no invalid combination [T T F] in any row.

Let's try another argument, a slight variation on the previous one.

If these bananas are fresh, then these grapes are fresh.

But these bananas are not fresh.

So, neither the bananas nor grapes are fresh.

Here is the symbolization of this argument, the truth-table, and the validity test:

		T	T		F	invalid combo	?
		prem	prem	aux	concl		
	B G	B ⊃ G	~B	B ∨ G	~(B ∨ G)		
B ⊃ G	T T	T	F	T	F		
~B	T F	F	F	T	F		
―――――――	F T	T	T	T	F	– bad comb	
∴ ~(B ∨ G)	F F	T	T	F	T		

This table shows the argument to be *invalid*, because there is an invalid combination [T T F] in row 3.

More Complicated Cases

We must now generalize the method. How does this method work for more complicated kinds of arguments? For example, if an argument is built up from three, or four, simple components, then *how many* possible situations must we write out for these simple components in order to test the argument for validity? The answer relies on a rule:

For 2 simple components, there are $2^2 = 2{\times}2 = 4$ possible situations.

For 3 simple components, there are $2^3 = 2{\times}2{\times}2 = 8$ possible situations.

For 4 simple components, there are $2^4 = 2{\times}2{\times}2{\times}2 = 16$ possible situations.

In general, for k simple components, there are $\mathbf{N} = 2^k$ possible situations.

To *automatically* generate all of the possible cases for a given problem, perform the following steps:

Step 1. First of all, begin the top line of a table, and list on the left side of the table all the simple sentences that occur in the problem.

Step 2. There will be $\mathbf{N} = 2^k$ rows in the table, when there are k such simple sentences.

Step 3. In the first column, write half a column of **T**'s and half a column of **F**'s, using up all **N** rows.

Step 4. Move one column to the right, and cut the size of the blocks of **T**'s and **F**'s in half, and alternate such halved blocks, using up all **N** rows.

Step 5. Repeat Step 4, each time *cutting in half* the size of the alternating blocks of **T**'s and of **F**'s, until the last column has been filled in. (When you get to the last column, there will be a perfect alternation of one **T** by one **F** throughout the entire column.)

Let's consider the following argument:

S ⊃ ~L

L ≡ ~B

∴ S ⊃ B

This argument contains 3 simple sentences, and so there must be 8 possible cases (rows). We must list these simple sentences in their *natural order* as they occur in the argument (left to right, top to bottom). To generate the complete list of possible cases for the argument, we first write the column TTTTFFFF under S, then we write the column TTFFTTFF under L, and then we write the column TFTFTFTF under B.

S L B	
T T T	
T T F	
T F T	
T F F	
F T T	
F T F	
F F T	
F F F	

As before, we now add the main columns and the auxiliary columns in the top of the table, and we then calculate all the values in every column and every row.

S ⊃ ~L	S L B	aux ~L	prem S ⊃ ~L	aux ~B	prem L ≡ ~B	concl S ⊃ B	
L ≡ ~B	T T T	F	F	F	F	T	– ok
	T T F	F	F	T	T	F	– ok
∴ S ⊃ B	T F T	T	T	F	T	T	– ok
	T F F	T	T	T	F	F	– ok
	F T T	F	T	F	F	T	– ok
	F T F	F	T	T	T	T	– ok
	F F T	T	T	F	T	T	– ok
	F F F	T	T	T	F	T	– ok

This table shows the argument to be *valid*, because there is *no* invalid combination [T T F] in any row.

Verifying the Laws of Logic

The truth-table method just presented has an important application to the verification of the *laws of propositional logic*. We will study these laws in detail in Section 2.7 below, but we take the opportunity here to illustrate the *theoretical* importance of the truth-table method with regard to these laws. By using this method, we are able to *prove* in a comprehensive way that all these laws are in fact *valid inferences*. This is significant, because without this method, we would have to rely on *mere intuition* to determine whether some principle is a law of logic. We need not worry right now about *learning* these laws. That will come later. We only want to *test* them now with the truth-table method. One group of laws belong to a *type* that are *argument* forms, and they are nowadays usually presented as the following group:

(1) p ⊃ q , p   /∴ q   Modus Ponens
(2) p ⊃ q , ~q   /∴ ~p   Modus Tollens
(3) p ⊃ q , q ⊃ r   /∴ p ⊃ r   Hypothetical Syllogism
(4) p & q   /∴ p   Simplification
(5) p , q   /∴ p & q   Conjunction
(6) p ∨ q , ~p   /∴ q   Disjunctive Syllogism
(7) p   /∴ p ∨ q   Disjunctive Addition
(8) p ⊃ q , p ⊃ ~q   /∴ ~p   Reductio ad Absurdum
(9) p ∨ q , p ⊃ r , q ⊃ s   /∴ r ∨ s   Complex Dilemma

We illustrate how the proof is done for the Hypothetical Syllogism, and we leave it as an exercise for the reader to give the proofs for the others. They are all very easy.

To prove: The Hypothetical Syllogism is a valid argument pattern.

Proof: We construct a complete truth-table for the argument form in question. We then show that an invalid combination of values does not exist. From this it follows that the argument form in question is *valid*.

p q r	prem p ⊃ q	prem q ⊃ r	concl p ⊃ r	invalid comb.?
T T T	T	T	T	– ok
T T F	T	F	F	– ok
T F T	F	T	T	– ok
T F F	F	T	F	– ok
F T T	T	T	T	– ok
F T F	T	F	T	– ok
F F T	T	T	T	– ok
F F F	T	T	T	– ok

We conclude that this argument form is valid. Q.E.D.

All the proofs for the remaining argument forms proceed in a similar fashion. So, they too are valid. In addition to this group of argument forms, there is another group of laws of a different *type*. These laws are *equivalence forms*, a few of which we have already met, such as the Law of Double Negation and De Morgan's Laws. We will have an opportunity to continue the needed proofs for these additional laws in the very next section.

Exercise 2.5. A,B,C Truth-Tables to Test Validity

Part A. Give complete truth-tables for these arguments to determine whether they are valid. Label the columns as "aux," "prem," or "concl." Use the available **Exercise Work Sheet** to submit your work.

1.	2.	3.	4.	5.
~(A & B)	K ∨ M	~R ∨ ~S	G ⊃ (G & H)	A ∨ W
~A	~M	~R ∨ S	~G	~A ∨ ~W
———	———	———	———	———
∴ B	∴ K ≡ ~M	∴ ~R	∴ ~H	∴ ~W ≡ A

6.	7.	8.	9.	10.
~(Q & ~P)	~D ⊃ ~T	F ⊃ (G & A)	F ⊃ (G ∨ A)	S ≡ ~K
Q	D ⊃ T	~G	~G	K
———	———	———	———	~B ⊃ S
∴ Q & P	∴ T ∨ D	∴ ~F	∴ ~F	———
				∴ ~B ∨ S

Part B. These are the laws of logic that we discussed above. Give complete truth-tables for them to show that they are valid. Label the columns as "aux," "prem," or "concl." Use the available **Exercise Work Sheet** to submit your work.

1. p ⊃ q , p	/∴ q	Modus Ponens
2. p ⊃ q , ~q	/∴ ~p	Modus Tollens
3. p ⊃ q , q ⊃ r	/∴ p ⊃ r	Hypothetical Syllogism
4. p & q	/∴ p	Simplification
5. p , q	/∴ p & q	Conjunction
6. p ∨ q , ~p	/∴ q	Disjunctive Syllogism
7. p	/∴ p ∨ q	Disjunctive Addition
8. p ⊃ q , p ⊃ ~q	/∴ ~p	Reductio ad Absurdum
9. p ∨ q , p ⊃ r , q ⊃ s	/∴ r ∨ s	Complex Dilemma
10. p ≡ q	/∴ (p ⊃ q) & (q ⊃ p)	Bicondition
11. p ⊃ (q & r)	/∴ (p ⊃ q) & (p ⊃ r)	Double Consequents

Part C. Give complete truth-tables for these arguments to determine whether they are valid. Label the columns as "aux," "prem," or "concl." Use the available **Exercise Work Sheet** to submit your work.

1. A ⊃ (B & C) , ~C ⊃ ~B , ~A /∴ ~B

2. E ∨ ~P , U ∨ ~E , ~U ∨ ~E /∴ ~(P & E)

3. ~(A ≡ B) , B ≡ ~C /∴ ~(A ≡ C)

4. A ≡ (B & C) , ~(A ∨ ~C) /∴ ~B

5. P ⊃ T , ~T ⊃ ~Q , ~(~P & ~Q) /∴ T

6. (A ∨ ~B) ≡ (C & B) , C ⊃ ~A /∴ ~A & B

7. F ⊃ (G & A) , ~G ∨ M /∴ M ∨ ~F

8. (M ⊃ S) ⊃ (N & O) , ~S , O ⊃ S /∴ ~M

Section 2.6 Truth-Table Tests for Other Logical Concerns

We have just seen how the truth-table method can be used to test (1) the *validity* of arguments. There are several other matters that are the proper concern of logic and that can be tested by the truth-table method. These are: (2) the *equivalence* of two sentences; (3) the *logical status* of one sentence, which is either *logical truth* (tautology), or *logical falsehood* (contradiction), or *logical contingency* (neither of the above); and finally, (4) the *consistency* of a set of sentences. Let's turn to these other concerns.

The Equivalence of Two Sentences

We have already used the idea that certain kinds of sentences are equivalent to each other; for example, earlier we introduced *De Morgan's Laws*, the *Law of Double Negation*, the *Law of Contraposition*, the *Law of Bicondition*, the *Law of Double Ifs*, and the *Law of Double Thens*.

Intuitively, two sentences are equivalent if they *mean* the same thing. And if they mean the same thing, then the one sentence *may take the place of* the other one in any process of inference. For example, sometimes we make an inference from P to Q, by showing first that P produces R and secondly that R means the same thing as Q. Or, to give another example, sometimes we can clarify the meaning of some complex assertion P by showing through a series of equivalent substitutions that P means the same thing as some simpler assertion S. Let's develop this idea of sameness a bit.

If two sentences mean the same thing, then:

- one cannot imagine any cases in which the two sentences have different truth-values, which in terms of possibilities means that,

- it is not logically possible for the two sentences to have different values, or to put the matter affirmatively,

- in every possible situation, the two sentences have the same truth-value.

This suggests, then, the following criterion for determining whether two sentences are equivalent.

> Two sentences are *equivalent* (in virtue of their connective structure) if and only if, in the truth-table for the two sentences,
>
> - the truth-table *columns* for the two sentences are identical.

The criterion can be put to work in the following way. First, we make a list of all the possible situations regarding the two sentences. We have shown in the preceding section how we can always do this for sentences that have a structure defined by propositional operators. Secondly, we test each of those possible situations to see whether the two sentences have the same truth-value.

As an example, let us test the two sentences:

If Sue does not go, then Bob will go = ~S ⊃ B

Either Bob or Sue will go = B ∨ S.

We first set up a truth-table for the two sentences, as given below. Next, we apply the *equivalence test*: Do the two sentences have the *same* value in *each* row of the truth-table? The table indicates that, yes, in each row the two sentences do have the same truth-value. (The values are always both true or both false.) So, the answer is yes:

The two sentences ~S ⊃ B , B ∨ S are equivalent.

	aux	sent 1	sent 2	
S B	~S	~S ⊃ B	B ∨ S	□ ←— □ ←— same values?
T T	F	T	T	same? – yes
T F	F	T	T	same? – yes
F T	T	T	T	same? – yes
F F	T	F	F	same? – yes

The Logical Status of a Sentence

In Chapter 1 we discussed three types of sentences: necessary truths, necessary falsehoods, and empirical sentences. We also noted there that necessary truths fall into three subgroups: definitional truths, mathematical truths, and logical truths. Similarly, there are three kinds of necessary falsehoods, namely, the violations of the just mentioned necessary truths. And then there are all the other sentences, the ones that are neither necessary truths nor necessary falsehoods. We will now have a closer look at just those sentences that are what they are in virtue of their logical form.

Logical Truths

Logical truths are sentences that are *necessarily true* in virtue of their logical form. In our earlier discussion we characterized them as sentences that are *true* in *all* possible (imaginable) situations. This characterization is the basis for the following criterion:

> A sentence is a *logical truth* (in virtue of its connective structure) if and only if, in the truth-table for the sentence
>
> • the truth-table *column* for the sentence contains only **T**'s.

Logical truths are also called *tautologies*. There are logical truths that are well-known laws of logic:

The Law of Excluded Middle:	p ∨ ~p
The Law of Contradiction:	~(p & ~p)
Laws of Implication	
Iteration:	p ⊃ p
Simplification:	(p & q) ⊃ p
Addition:	p ⊃ (p ∨ q)

These particular logical truths are relatively simple ones, and one can easily understand that these patterns *must* be true in all cases. But there is no limit on the possible complexity of logical truths, and, more often than not, one needs a testing mechanism to tell whether a given sentence is a logical truth. The criterion that we have proposed above can be put to work as follows. As before, we make a list of all the possible situations regarding the sentence in question. We do this by writing a list of the simple component sentences that make up the sentence, and by enumerating all the combinations of values that these simple sentences can have. Next, we check to see whether the original sentence has the value **T** in each of these possible situations. Let us test the sentence:

If Sue will go, then both Bob and Sue will go; or else, Bob won't go at all.

[S ⊃ (B & S)] ∨ ~B

We first set up a truth-table for the sentence, as given below. Next, we apply the *logical truth test*: Does the sentence have the value **T** in *every* row of its truth-table? The table indicates that, yes, in each row the sentence has the value **T**. So, the answer is yes:

The sentence [S ⊃ (B & S)] ∨ ~B is a logical truth.

				$\boxed{\text{T}}$ ← only T's?	
	aux	aux	aux	sent	
S B	B & S	S ⊃ (B & S)	~B	[S ⊃ (B & S)] ∨ ~B	
T T	T	T	F	T	T? – yes
T F	F	F	T	T	T? – yes
F T	F	T	F	T	T? – yes
F F	F	T	T	T	T? – yes

Logical Falsehoods

Logical falsehoods are sentences that are *necessarily false* in virtue of their logical form. In Chapter 1 we characterized them as sentences that are *false* in *all* possible (imaginable) situations. This characterization is the basis for the following criterion:

> A sentence is a *logical falsehood* (in virtue of its connective structure) if and only if, in the truth-table for the sentence
>
> • the truth-table *column* for the sentence contains only **F**'s.

Logical falsehoods are also called *contradictions*. There is one group of sentences that can immediately be recognized to be necessary falsehoods, for example, "Horses do exist, and yet they do not exist," "Sue went to the party tonight, but she did not go to the party tonight," "Abraham Lincoln was the Emperor of Rome in the year 238 C.E., and he was not the Emperor of Rome in the year 238 C.E." These sentences have the form:

p & ~p

and because of this form, they are called *explicit contradictions*. These sentences are conjunctions that assert two parts—the one part affirms something and the other part denies that very thing. That is why it is impossible for contradictions to be true. On the other hand, there are other contradictions that are not explicit in this way. Even though they also make two contradictory assertions, their logical form does not immediately reveal that this is so. We can call such sentences *implicit contradictions*.

The criterion that we have proposed above can be put to work as follows. As before, we make a list of all the possible situations regarding the sentence in question. We do this by writing a list of the simple component sentences that make up the sentence, and by enumerating all the combinations of values that these simple sentences can have. Next, we check to see whether the original sentence has the value **F** in each of these possible situations. Consider the example:

> The grapes are fresh, and the bananas are not; but in spite of that, either the bananas are fresh or the grapes are not.
>
> (G & ~B) & (B ∨ ~G)

We first set up a truth-table for the sentence, as given below. Next, we apply the *contradiction test*: Does the sentence have the value **F** in *every* row of its truth-table? The table indicates that, yes, in each row the sentence has the value **F**. So, the answer is yes:

> The sentence (G & ~B) & (B ∨ ~G) is a contradiction.

					$\boxed{F}$ ⟵——— only F's?	
	aux	aux	aux	aux	sent	
G B	~B	G & ~B	~G	B ∨ ~G	(G & ~B) & (B ∨ ~G)	
T T	F	F	F	T	F	F? – yes
T F	T	T	F	F	F	F? – yes
F T	F	F	T	T	F	F? – yes
F F	F	F	T	T	F	F? – yes

Logical Contingency

Sentences are *logically contingent* when they are not logical truths and also not contradictions. In terms of possibilities, it is logically possible that they be true and also logically possible that they be false. These are sentences that one can imagine to be true, and one can also imagine them to be false. This characterization is the basis for the following criterion:

> A sentence is a *logically contingent* (in virtue of its connective structure) if and only if, in the truth-table for the sentence
>
> • the truth-table *column* for the sentence contains both **T**'s and **F**'s.

It is easy to see that most of the sentences that we encounter in our daily affairs are neither logical truths nor logical falsehoods. Most concern empirical matters, and are therefore logical contingencies. So, if we tested such sentences, their truth-table column must contain both **T**'s and **F**'s. Consider the following example:

We ordered green beans, and fish, but maybe it was chicken.

B & (F ∨ C)

As the table shows, the sentence B & (F ∨ C) is a logical contingency.

		□ ←		what values?
	aux	sent		
B F C	F ∨ C	B & (F ∨ C)		
T T T	T	T		
T T F	T	T		
T F T	T	T	←	value = T, so,
T F F	F	F		not a contrad.
F T T	T	F		
F T F	T	F	←	value = F, so,
F F T	T	F		not a log. truth
F F F	F	F		

The Consistency of a Set of Sentences

Certainly, an important logical concern is whether people are *consistent*, or *inconsistent*, in what they say. First of all, if someone is inconsistent, and says one thing S, and, somewhat later, also says the direct opposite, not-S, then we must puzzle about what, if anything, that person actually asserted. We would surely conclude that the person was confused or made some mistake, and we would not allow our discussion to continue until the matter was resolved. Notice, incidentally, that all assertions "p and not-p" are cases of inconsistency, but not all cases of inconsistency need take that form. The sentences P, Q, R, S, if Q then not-P, form an inconsistent set.

But contradictions, when explicit, do not only generate utter incoherence, they also have the deductive power to validly introduce arbitrary conclusions (that can through subtlety destroy reasonable discourse and action). It is important, therefore, for us to be able to detect contradictions, so that we may eliminate them and their consequences from our discussions.

A set of sentences, taken together, is *consistent* if the set does not contain a contradiction. But contradictions are false in all possible situations. So, any set of sentences is consistent if the entire set is *true* in *some* possible (imaginable) situation. This characterization is the basis for the following criterion:

A set of sentences is *consistent* (in virtue of its connective structure) if and only if, in the truth-table for the set of sentences,

- *one row* of the truth-table has *all* the sentences of the set as **T**.

The negative side of this criterion takes the following form:

A set of sentences is *inconsistent* (in virtue of its connective structure) if and only if, in the truth-table for the set of sentences,

- *no* row in the truth-table has *all* the sentences of the set as **T**.

Consider again the Strange Argument we introduced in Chapter 1.

1. If John is in the house, then John came in through the front door.
2. If John came in through the front door, then someone saw John come in.
3. It is not the case that someone saw John come in.
4. Yet, John is in the house.

So, there really is a Tooth Fairy.

We showed in Chapter 1 that this argument is valid, but not sound. The problem with the argument is not that it has an obviously false conclusion. Nor is the problem that we cannot deduce the conclusion from the premisses (because we did deduce it). The problem lies with the premisses. Taken individually, each premiss is plausible enough. But taken *together*, they form an inconsistent set. Let us consider the four premisses by themselves:

H ⊃ D , D ⊃ S , ~S , H

We first construct a truth-table for these four sentences, as given below. Next, we apply the *consistency test*: Is there one row in the table such that in that row all four sentences have the value **T**? The table indicates that there is *no* row that has all four sentences as **T**. So, the answer is:

The four sentences H ⊃ D , D ⊃ S , ~S , H form an *inconsistent* set.

	☐	☐	☐	☐	← ── one whole row has all T's?
	sent 1	sent 2	sent 3	sent 4	
H D S	H ⊃ D	D ⊃ S	~S	H	
T T T	T	T	F	T	← ── row all T's? – no
T T F	T	F	T	T	← ── row all T's? – no
T F T	F	T	F	T	← ── row all T's? – no
T F F	F	T	T	T	← ── row all T's? – no
F T T	T	T	F	F	← ── row all T's? – no
F T F	T	F	T	F	← ── row all T's? – no
F F T	T	T	F	F	← ── row all T's? – no
F F F	T	T	T	F	← ── row all T's? – no

It is worth mentioning that even though *inconsistency* is a very bad thing and must be avoided at all costs, *mere consistency* is also *not good enough* when it falls short of truth. Silly and false sentences easily combine to form consistent sets, as:

> Elephants can fly. The Moon is a cube. If apples are blue then fire is cold. George Bush cannot play golf.
>
> E , M , A ⊃ F , ~G

Even though these four sentences are all *false* in the real world, nevertheless the set is *consistent*, because no contradiction is produced by the set! There is certainly an *imaginable* situation in which all four sentences are true together, and we can describe this situation in detail, as in the table below. Without presenting the entire 32-row truth-table needed for the five simple components of these four sentences, we can easily identify one row, row #2, in which all four sentences are true:

	sent 1	sent 2	sent 3	sent 4	
E M A F G	E	M	A ⊃ F	~G	row #2
T T T T F	T	T	T	T	← has all T's

Verifying the Laws of Logic

In the previous section we showed how the truth-table method can be used to prove that the laws of logic that are argument forms are *valid* inferences. Now that we have explained how this method can also be used to show that two sentences are equivalent, we can use this method to *prove* that those proposed laws of logic that are equivalence forms are indeed equivalences in the defined sense. Again, we need not worry about learning these laws right now, since our only objective is to show that the proposed equivalence forms are really equivalences. The laws in question are usually presented as the following group:

(1) ~(~p)	= p		Double Negation
(2) ~(p & q)	= ~p ∨ ~q		De Morgan's Laws
(2) ~(p ∨ q)	= ~p & ~q		De Morgan's Laws
(3) p ⊃ q	= ~q ⊃ ~p		Contraposition
(4) p ⊃ q	= ~p ∨ q		Conditional Relation
(5) p ≡ q	= (p ⊃ q) & (q ⊃ p)		Bicondition
(6) (p & q) ⊃ r	= p ⊃ (q ⊃ r)		Exportation
(7) p & p	= p		Duplication
(7) p ∨ p	= p		Duplication
(8) p & q	= q & p		Commutation
(8) p ∨ q	= q ∨ p		Commutation
(9) p & (q & r)	= (p & q) & r		Association
(9) p ∨ (q ∨ r)	= (p ∨ q) ∨ r		Association
(10) p & (q v r)	= (p & q) ∨ (p & r)		Distribution
(10) p ∨ (q & r)	= (p ∨ q) & (p ∨ r)		Distribution

As before, we illustrate how the proof works for one law, the Law of Exportation, as it is called, and we leave it as an exercise for the reader to give the proofs for the others. They are all very easy. *To prove*: The two sides of the Exportation law are equivalent in the defined sense.

Proof: We construct a complete truth-table for the two sentence forms in question. We then show that the two sentence forms have the same truth-value in all of the possible cases. From this it follows that the two sentence forms are *equivalent*.

	aux	sent 1	aux	sent 2	same
p q r	p & q	(p & q) ⊃ r	q ⊃ r	p ⊃ (q ⊃ r)	value?
T T T	T	T	T	T	– yes
T T F	T	F	F	F	– yes
T F T	F	T	T	T	– yes
T F F	F	T	T	T	– yes
F T T	F	T	T	T	– yes
F T F	F	T	F	T	– yes
F F T	F	T	T	T	– yes
F F F	F	T	T	T	– yes

We conclude that these sentence forms are equivalent in the defined sense. Q.E.D. All the proofs for the remaining equivalence forms proceed in a similar fashion. So, they too are equivalences in the defined sense. Q.E.D. Now that we have verified all the proposed laws of logic (that is, the ones that are usually presented), we may proceed to use these laws in any context, without being required to again provide a justification for them.

Exercise 2.6. A,B,C,D Other Uses for Truth-Tables

Part A Use complete truth-tables to determine whether the following equivalence forms are equivalent in the defined sense. Be sure to label the columns as "sent 1," "sent 2," or "aux." Use the available **Exercise Work Sheet** to submit your work.

1. ~(~(~p)) , ~p
2. p ∨ ~q , ~p ∨ q
3. p ⊃ ~q , ~p ⊃ q
4. p ⊃ ~q , q ⊃ ~p
5. ~(p & q) , ~p & ~q
6. ~(p & q) , p ⊃ ~q
7. ~(p ∨ q) , ~p & ~q

8. p ∨ q , ~p ⊃ q
9. p ≡ q , ~p ≡ ~q
10. p ≡ q , (p ⊃ q) & (~p ⊃ q)
11. p ⊃ (q ∨ r) , (p ⊃ q) ∨ (p ⊃ r)
12. (p & q) ⊃ r , (p ⊃ r) & (q ⊃ r)
13. (p ∨ q) ⊃ r , (p ⊃ r) & (q ⊃ r)
14. p , (p & q & r) ∨ ((p & ~q) ∨ (p & ~r))

Part B. Use complete truth-tables to determine the *logical status* of the following sentence forms. Be sure to label the columns as "main sent" or "aux." Use the available **Exercise Work Sheet** to submit your work.

1. p ∨ ~p
2. ~(p & q) ∨ p
3. ~p ∨ (p & q)
4. (p & q) & ~p
5. p ⊃ (q ⊃ q)
6. (p ⊃ p) ⊃ (q & ~q)
7. (p & q) ∨ (~p & ~q)

8. (p ∨ q) ∨ (p ∨ ~q)
9. (p & q) & (p & ~q)
10. (p & q) ⊃ q
11. (p ≡ q) ≡ (~p ≡ ~q)
12. [p & (~p ∨ q)] ⊃ (q ∨ r)
13. ((p ⊃ q) & (r ⊃ q)) ∨ (p ∨ r)
14. ((p ⊃ q) & (q ⊃ r)) & (p & (r ⊃ ~p))

Part C. Use complete truth-tables to determine whether the following sets of sentence forms are *consistent*. Be sure to label the columns as "sentence" or "aux." Use the available **Exercise Work Sheet** to submit your work.

1. p , p ⊃ q , ~q
2. ~p , p ⊃ q , q
3. ~p , p ∨ q , p ≡ q
4. p , p & ~q , q ∨ p
5. p ≡ q, p ≡ ~q

6. p & ~q , (p & r) ≡ q , p ∨ r
7. ~(p & q) , ~(q & r) , ~(p & r)
8. ~(p ∨ q) , ~(q ∨ r) , ~(p ∨ r)
9. ~(p ≡ q) , ~(q ≡ r) , ~(p ≡ r)
10. ((p & q) & ~(q & r)) & (p ⊃ r)

Part D. These are the laws of logic we discussed above. Give complete truth-tables for these equivalence forms to show that they are equivalent in the defined sense. Be sure to label the columns as "sent 1," "sent 2," or "aux." Use the available **Exercise Work Sheet** to submit your work.

1. ~(~p)	= p	Double Negation
2a. ~(p & q)	= ~p ∨ ~q	De Morgan's Laws
2b. ~(p ∨ q)	= ~p & ~q	De Morgan's Laws
3. p ⊃ q	= ~q ⊃ ~p	Contraposition
4. p ⊃ q	= ~p ∨ q	Conditional Relation
5. p ≡ q	= (p ⊃ q) & (q ⊃ p)	Bicondition
6. (p & q) ⊃ r	= p ⊃ (q ⊃ r)	Exportation
7a. p & p	= p	Duplication
7b. p ∨ p	= p	Duplication
8a. p & q	= q & p	Commutation
8b. p ∨ q	= q ∨ p	Commutation
9a. p & (q & r)	= (p & q) & r	Association
9b. p ∨ (q ∨ r)	= (p ∨ q) ∨ r	Association
10a. p & (q v r)	= (p & q) ∨ (p & r)	Distribution
10b. p ∨ (q & r)	= (p ∨ q) & (p ∨ r)	Distribution

Section 2.7 Presentation of the Rules of Deduction

We have arrived, now, at the point where we can begin to study the real process of argumentation. This process consists of a series of step by step inferences that begin with stated premises and end with a conclusion, but in such a way that all the inferences are carried out by the laws of logic. We will explain the deduction process in great detail in the following sections, but right now we will spend some time looking at each of the laws individually. We will introduce the laws one by one, stating them both in regular English and in symbolic form. We also give conceptual explanations and provide key examples. As you learn each law, take time to learn its English form, its symbolic form, its concept, and key examples.

Modus Ponens (MP)

The most basic rule for conditional sentences is the rule Modus Ponens. The whole point of a conditional sentence is to infer the result part when the condition part has been satisfied. It is convenient to illustrate these laws by means of *events* taking place.

if p then q	p ⊃ q	P will result in Q;
p	p	and, P is occurring.
———	———	———
so, q	∴ q	So, result Q must occur as well.

1. If the White Sox won the World Series, Chicago had a great celebration.

2. Hey, the White Sox won the World Series.

So, Chicago had a great celebration.

Modus Tollens (MT)

The rule Modus Tollens is also a fundamental law for conditional sentences. Again, since a conditional sentence states that a given condition *will* have a result, we can immediately see that when the predicted result does not occur, then the condition could not have occured either.

if p then q	p ⊃ q	P will result in Q;
not q	~q	but, result Q did not occur.
———	———	———
so, not p	∴ ~p	So, P must not have occurred.

1. If the Cubs won the Series, then Chicago had a great celebration for them.

2. Wait, Chicago did not have a great celebration for the Cubs.

So, the Cubs must not have won the Series.

Hypothetical Syllogism (Hyp Syll) (HS)

Our logical thoughts are linear; they are paths that go from point A to point B, and from point B to point C. But in addition, and this is crucial, we always keep track of the fact that the *last* point reached is a consequence of the *first* point with which we began. The rule of Hypothetical Syllogism is devoted to precisely this kind of book-keeping.

if p then q	p ⊃ q	P will result in Q, and
if q then r	q ⊃ r	Q in turn will result in R.
———	———	———
so, if p then r	∴ p ⊃ r	So, P must result in R.

1. If the Cubs win all their games, then the Cubs win the World Series.

2. If the Cubs win the World Series, then all of Chicago will celebrate.

So, if the Cubs win all their games, then all of Chicago will celebrate.

Complex Dilemma (Dilem)

The Dilemma rule tells you how to reason with given *choices*. You must look at the *results* of those choices, so that you may infer the choice of those results, which is new information that could be useful to the argument.

either p or q	p ∨ q	Either P or Q will occur;
if p then r	p ⊃ r	but, P will result in R,
if q then s	q ⊃ s	and, Q will result in S.
————	———	———
so, either r or s	∴ r ∨ s	So, one of those results must occur

1. Either the Chicago Cubs or the Pittsburgh Pirates are going to win.
2. If the Cubs win, then Chicago will have a celebration.
3. If the Pirates win, then Pittsburgh will have a celebration.

So, either Chicago or Pittsburgh is going to have a celebration.

Simple Dilemma (Dilem)

The Simple Dilemma is a special case of the Complex Dilemma, where the two choice results are one and the same.

either p or q	p ∨ q	Either P or Q will occur;
if p then r	p ⊃ r	but, P will result in R,
if q then r	q ⊃ r	and, Q will also result in R.
————	———	———
so, r	∴ r	So, the one result R must occur.

1. Either the Chicago Cubs or the Pittsburgh Pirates are going to win.
2. If the Cubs win, then some city will have a celebration.
3. If the Pirates win, then, again, some city will have a celebration.

So, definitely, some city is going to have a celebration.

Simplification (Simp)

This rule (and the next) define the idea of conjunction. An asserted conjunction may always be broken up into its two parts. That's what conjunctions are all about, and strategically, such reduction is always recommended.

p and q	p & q	Both P and Q are occurring.
———	———	———
so, p	∴ p	So, P is occurring.
so, q	∴ q	So, Q is occurring.

1. Both the Cubs and the Pirates are going to win a game this year.

So, there you have it, the Cubs are going to win a game this year.

Conjunction (Conj)

As noted with the rule Simp, this rule is part of the very idea of conjunction. Two separate assertions may be combined into a conjunction, with no change of meaning.

p	p	P is occurring.
q	q	Also, Q is occurring.
———	———	———
so, p and q	∴ p & q	So, both P and Q are occurring.

1. The Cubs won a game this year.
2. And the Pirates won a game this year.

So, both the Cubs and the Pirates won a game this year.

Disjunctive Syllogism (Disj Syll) (DS)

The rule of Disjunctive Syllogism provides a very simple way of dealing with choices. Given two choices, when we *eliminate* one choice, the other choice *remains*.

p or q	p ∨ q	Either P or Q will occur;
not p	~p	but, P is not occurring.
———	———	———
so, q	∴ q	So, Q must be the one to occur.

1. Either the Cubs or the Pirates are going to win.
2. Aww gee, the Cubs didn't win.

So, the Pirates won.

Disjunctive Addition (Disj Add) (Add)

This rule is designed to mirror the inclusive nature of disjunction. "Is either of these cases true?" The answer is "Yes," if the one case is true, and the answer is "Yes," if the other case is true. Sometimes people are interested in the general case where either is true, without really being interested in which case it is.

p	p	P definitely occurs.
_____	_____	_____
so, p or q	∴ p ∨ q	So, at least one of P or (any) Q occurs.

The Cubs are definitely going to win some game this year.

So, either the Cubs or Queen Elizabeth will win some game this year.

Reductio ad Absurdum (RAA)

Sometimes a hypothesis p produces a contradictory result q and ~q. Since contradictions are impossible, this result is false, and the law of Modus Tollens forces us to conclude that the hypothesis p is false as well. This kind of reasoning take the following form:

if p, then q	p ⊃ q	Hypothesis P will result in Q;
if p, then not q	p ⊃ ~q	and, P will also result in not-Q.
_____	_____	_____
so, not p	∴ ~p	So, this hypothesis P is impossible.

1. If a number N is the largest number, then no number is larger than N

2. If a number N is the largest number, then some number (N+1) is larger than N.

So, there can be no number N that is the largest number.

Double Thens (Dbl Thens) ↻

This rule is not as fundamental as some of the other rules, but it is nevertheless an important and *constantly used* principle in our reasoning. When a certain *condition* has a *double result*, we are allowed to state those results together or separately.

if p then (q and r)	p ⊃ (q & r)	P will result in both Q and R.
_____	_____	_____
so, if p then q	∴ p ⊃ q	So, P will result in Q.
so, if p then r	∴ p ⊃ r	Also, P will result in R.

Comment: This rule also works in the reverse.

If the Cubs win, then Chicago is happy and Pittsburgh is sad.

So, if the Cubs win, then Pittsburgh is sad.

Bicondition (Bicond) ↻

The biconditional connective represents an important conceptual relationship. This connective is not a basic connective, but is rather a combination of other connectives acting as a unit. This present rule reflects the *definition* of this relationship.

p if and only if q	$p \equiv q$	P and Q each result in the other.
so, if p then q	$\therefore p \supset q$	So, if one occurs, the other occurs.
so, if q then p	$\therefore q \supset p$	

Comment: This rule also works in the reverse.

Chicago is truly happy, when, and only when, the Cubs are winning.

So, if the Cubs are winning, then Chicago is truly happy.

Also, if Chicago is truly happy, then the Cubs are winning.

Law of Double Negation (Dbl Neg) (DN) ↻

When someone *denies* a *negated* assertion, then that is the same as *affirming* the assertion. *Double negatives* cancel when they have this unique arrangement.

not (not p)	$\sim(\sim p)$	The denial of a denial of a sentence
so, p	$\therefore p$	= an affirmation of the sentence.

Comment: This rule also works in the reverse.

It is false that the Cubs will not win

So, the Cubs will win.

De Morgan's Laws (DeMorg) ↻

There are two similar kinds of problems. Problem #1. You ask whether *both* P and Q will happen, and someone says, *no*. What does that mean? Problem #2. You ask whether *either* P or Q will happen, and someone says, *no*. What does that mean?

not (both p and q)	$\sim(p \mathbin{\&} q)$	A double assertion is false
so, (not p) or (not q)	$\therefore \sim p \lor \sim q$	= some part is false.

not (either p or q)	~(p ∨ q)	A statement of choices is false
———	———	= both parts are false.
so, (not p) and (not q)	∴ ~p & ~q	

Comment: These rules also work in the reverse.

Not both the Cubs and the Pirates will win.
So, either the Cubs won't win, or the Pirates won't.

Not either the Cubs or the Pirates will win.
So, both the Cubs won't win, and also the Pirates won't win.

Law of Contraposition (Contrap) ↻

For any *conditional* assertion, there is a *negative* form of it that means the same thing. This is similar to the law of Modus Tollens.

if p then q	p ⊃ q	P will result in Q
———	———	= if Q is not occuring,
so, if (not q) then (not p)	∴ ~q ⊃ ~p	then P is not occurring.

Comment: This rule also works in the reverse.

If the Cubs win, then the Pirates will lose.
So, if the Pirates don't lose, then the Cubs will not win.

Law of Conditional Relation (Cond) ↻

There is a special relationship between "if then" sentences and "either or" sentences. Each can be re-expressed into the other, without change of meaning, but with appropriate compensations. An important consequence of this is that two people can be discussing some matter, the one by using conditional relationships and another person by using disjunctive relationships, and they can be in perfect agreement, just different means to the same end.

if p then q	p ⊃ q	A conditional sentence can be re-expressed as
———	———	two choices: *either* the indicated *condition* is
so, either (not p) or q	∴ ~p ∨ q	*not* met, *or* (it is, and then) the indicated *result*
		happens.

Comment: This rule also works in the reverse.

If the Cubs lose, then Chicago will be a depressing place.

So, either the Cubs win, or Chicago will be a depressing place.

Law of Double Ifs (Dbl Ifs) (Exportation) (Exp) ↻

Many of our conditional sentences have a *double* condition, e.g., there is a double condition for it to start snowing: (a) it must cold enough; (b) there has to be moisture in the air. Neither of these conditions by itself is sufficient; you need both. There are two different ways of saying that something has a double condition.

if (p and q) then r	$(p \,\&\, q) \supset r$	A *double* condition can be expressed in two ways: (1) as a single conjunctive condition, or (2) as a sequence of two separate conditions.
so, if p then (if q then r)	$\therefore p \supset (q \supset r)$	

Comment: This rule also works in the reverse.

If the Cubs and the White Sox win, then Chicago will go wild.

So, if the Cubs win, then, if the White Sox also win, then Chicago will go wild.

The four rules that follow are of a more technical nature. They are not likely to enter into the thinking of ordinary arguments, but they might occur in technical proofs, for example, about which rules can be derived from other rules. A system of rules must be general enough to cover all possible uses, and so they are also presented here.

Law of Duplication (Dupl) ↻

Duplicated *ands* reduce to one. Also, duplicated *ors* reduce to one.

both p and p = p $p \,\&\, p = p$

either p or p = p $p \lor p = p$

There are only two choices: either the Cubs will win, or the Cubs will win.
So, the Cubs will win.

Note: A number of logic books inadvisably use the label "Tautology" to refer to this law. Doing so ignores the fact that in logic this label has always been *reserved* for a different purpose.

Law of Commutation (Comm) ⟳

There is no preferred *order* to multiple conjunctions. Also, there is no preferred order to multiple disjunctions.

p and q = q and p $\qquad\qquad$ p & q = q & p

p or q = q or p $\qquad\qquad$ p ∨ p = q ∨ p

The Cubs and the White Sox will win next week.

So, the White Sox and the Cubs will win next week.

Law of Association (Assoc) ⟳

There is no preferred *ranking* in triple conjunctions. Also, there is no preferred ranking in triple disjunctions.

p and (both q and r) = (both p and q) and r $\qquad$ p & (q & r) = (p & q) & r

p or (either q or r) = (either p or q) or r $\qquad$ p ∨ (q ∨ r) = (p ∨ q) ∨ r

The Cubs will win, and so will the White Sox and the Pirates.

So, the Cubs and the White Sox will win, and so will the Pirates.

Law of Distribution (Dist) ⟳

One disjunct can be *distributed over* a conjunction. Also, one conjunct can be distributed over a disjunction.

p or (q and r) = (p or q) and (p or r) $\qquad$ p ∨ (q & r) = (p ∨ q) & (p ∨ r)

p and (q or r) = (p and q) or (p and r) $\qquad$ p & (q ∨ r) = (p & q) ∨ (p & r)

The Cubs will win, or the White Sox and the Pirates will win.

So, the Cubs or the White Sox will win, and, the Cubs or the Pirates will win.

The Cubs will win, and the White Sox or the Pirates will win.

So, the Cubs and the White Sox will win, or, the Cubs and the Pirates will win.

The Rule of Logical Truth (Taut)

Logical truths are sentences that are necessarily true in virtue of their logical form; that is, the logical form that these sentences have forces them to be true in every possible world. Because of this feature, logical truths are *laws of logic* in their own right, and they may consequently be used at any point in any form of argumentation. In logic these logical truths are also called *tautologies*; so, it is natural to use the label "Taut" to refer to these laws. As a *practical* measure, we list only seven logical truths that have a potential to be *useful* in the making of deductions.

- $p \lor {\sim}p$ Law of Excluded Middle
- ${\sim}(p \mathrel{\&} {\sim}p)$ Law of Non-contradiction
- $p \supset p$ Law of Implication
- $(p \mathrel{\&} q) \supset p$ Law of Implication
- $(p \mathrel{\&} q) \supset q$ Law of Implication
- $p \supset (p \lor q)$ Law of Implication
- $p \supset (q \lor p)$ Law of Implication

An Important Note on Using the Rules

Now that we have presented the rules of Propositional Logic, we must also explain how they are to be used. We will have much to say about this in the coming sections, but even now we can emphasize something that is implicit in the very idea of a rule. Rules are *general* instructions for doing something. This means that the rules of logic apply to *all* sentences, whether they are simple or compound, no matter what their complexity, and while this seems obvious enough, this matter can sometimes be a little confusing. Notice that all the rules were stated using the lower case letters: p, q, r, s. These letters are *variables* that represent *all* possible sentences. This means that they not only represent single capital letters, A, B, C, etc., for simple sentences, they also represent negative sentences, ~A, ~B, ~C, etc., as well as conjunctive sentences, (A & M), (C & S), etc., as well as all the other types of compounds, as well as any *combination* of any of these. And that means, then, that the following three arguments are all correct instances of the rule of Modus Ponens:

Modus Ponens	$M \supset U$	${\sim}G \supset {\sim}H$	$(R \lor Q) \supset {\sim}(W \mathrel{\&} A)$
	M	${\sim}G$	$R \lor Q$
$p \supset q$	——	——	——
p	$\therefore U$	$\therefore {\sim}H$	$\therefore {\sim}(W \mathrel{\&} A)$
——			
$\therefore q$	$p = M$	$p = {\sim}G$	$p = (R \lor Q)$
	$q = U$	$q = {\sim}H$	$q = {\sim}(W \mathrel{\&} A)$

This, then, completes the presentation of the rules that we will be using when we prove that arguments are valid. We turn now to the second method for demonstrating the validity of arguments, a method that is devoted entirely to the use of these laws. This method is known as the *Method of Deduction*.

Reference Sheet for the Propositional Rules of Deduction

I. BASIC ARGUMENT FORMS

MP	MT	Hyp Syll	Dilem	
p ⊃ q	p ⊃ q	p ⊃ q	p ∨ q	p ∨ q
p	~q	q ⊃ r	p ⊃ r	p ⊃ r
			q ⊃ r	q ⊃ s
————	————	————	————	————
∴ q	∴ ~p	∴ p ⊃ r	∴ r	∴ r ∨ s

Simp	Conj	Disj Syll		Disj Add
p & q	p	p ∨ q	p ∨ q	p
————	q	~p	~q	————
∴ p		————	————	∴ p ∨ q
∴ q	————	∴ q	∴ p	∴ q ∨ p
	∴ p & q			

Dbl Thens		Bicond		RAA
p ⊃ (q & r)	p ⊃ q	p ≡ q	p ⊃ q	p ⊃ q
————	p ⊃ r	————	q ⊃ p	p ⊃ ~q
∴ p ⊃ q	————	∴ p ⊃ q	————	————
∴ p ⊃ r	∴ p ⊃ (q & r)	∴ q ⊃ p	∴ p ≡ q	∴ ~p

II. BASIC EQUIVALENCE FORMS

Dbl Neg	$p = \sim(\sim p)$
DeMorg	$\sim(p \& q) = \sim p \lor \sim q$
DeMorg	$\sim(p \lor q) = \sim p \& \sim q$
Contrap	$p \supset q = \sim q \supset \sim p$
Cond	$p \supset q = \sim p \lor q$
Bicond	$p \equiv q = (p \supset q) \& (q \supset p)$
Dbl Ifs	$(p \& q) \supset r = p \supset (q \supset r)$
Dupl	$p \& p = p$
Dupl	$p \lor p = p$
Comm	$p \& q = q \& p$
Comm	$p \lor q = q \lor p$
Assoc	$(p \& q) \& r = p \& (q \& r)$
Assoc	$(p \lor q) \lor r = p \lor (q \lor r)$
Dist	$p \& (q \lor r) = (p \& q) \lor (p \& r)$
Dist	$p \lor (q \& r) = (p \lor q) \& (p \lor r)$

III. LOGICAL TRUTHS

(Taut)
- $p \lor \sim p$
- $\sim(p \& \sim p)$
- $p \supset p$
- $(p \& q) \supset p$
- $(p \& q) \supset q$
- $p \supset (p \lor q)$
- $p \supset (q \lor p)$

IV. ASSUMPTION RULES (§ 2.10)

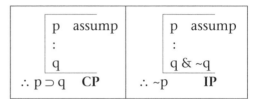

Exercise 2.7. A,B Practicing the Rules

Part A. For each of the following inferences, determine whether the conclusion follows from the premisses by the rule listed. Use the available **Exercise Work Sheet** to submit your work.

1. $\sim J \supset (A \lor S)$, $\sim J$	$/\therefore$ $(A \lor S)$	Is it MP?
2. $(A \lor S) \supset \sim J$, $\sim J$	$/\therefore$ $(A \lor S)$	Is it MP?
3. $(A \lor S) \supset J$, $\sim J$	$/\therefore$ $\sim(A \lor S)$	Is it MT?
4. $J \supset (A \lor S)$, $\sim J$	$/\therefore$ $\sim(A \lor S)$	Is it MT?
5. $A \supset \sim C$, $\sim B \& \sim C$	$/\therefore$ $\sim C$	Is it Simp?
6. $T \lor \sim E$, $\sim T$	$/\therefore$ $\sim E$	Is it Disj Syll?
7. $H \lor \sim I$, $H \supset \sim P$, $\sim A \supset \sim I$	$/\therefore$ $\sim P \lor \sim A$	Is it Dilem?
8. $\sim B \supset \sim C$, $\sim B \supset A$	$/\therefore$ $\sim C \supset A$	Is it Hyp Syll?
9. $(T \& B) \lor \sim E$, $\sim(\sim E)$	$/\therefore$ $T \& B$	Is it Disj Syll?
10. $\sim T \lor \sim E$, $\sim T$	$/\therefore$ $\sim E$	Is it Disj Syll?
11. $A \supset Q$, $\sim C \equiv B$	$/\therefore$ $\sim C \supset B$	Is it Bicond?
12. $\sim E$	$/\therefore$ $\sim E \lor (M \& S)$	Is it Disj Add?
13. $B \supset \sim C$, $\sim A \supset B$	$/\therefore$ $\sim A \supset \sim C$	Is it Hyp Syll?
14. $H \lor \sim I$, $H \supset \sim P$, $\sim I \supset \sim J$	$/\therefore$ $\sim P \lor \sim J$	Is it Dilem?
15. $L \supset (B \& E)$, $L \supset \sim(B \& E)$	$/\therefore$ $\sim L$	Is it RAA?

16. (B & E) ⊃ ~C , ~A ⊃ (B & E)   /∴ ~A ⊃ ~C   Is it Hyp Syll?
17. ~(A ∨ B) ⊃ C   /∴ (A ∨ B) ⊃ ~C   Is it Contrap?
18. ~(A ∨ B) ⊃ C   /∴ ~C ⊃ (A ∨ B)   Is it Contrap?
19. ~(A ∨ B)   /∴ ~A ∨ ~B   Is it DeMorg?
20. ~(S & E)   /∴ ~S ∨ ~E   Is it DeMorg?
21. ~A ∨ ~B   /∴ A ⊃ ~B   Is it Cond?
22. (Q & P)   /∴ (~Q & ~P) ∨ A   Is it Cond?
23. L ⊃ [(B & E) & A]   /∴ L ⊃ (B & E)   Is it Dbl Thens?
24. L ⊃ (B & E)   /∴ L ⊃ (~B ∨ L)   Is it Taut?

Part B. For each of the following inferences, the listed conclusion follows from the premises by one of the allowed rules. In each case, *name the rule* that was used. Use the available **Exercise Work Sheet** to submit your work.

1. ~(A ∨ ~B)   /∴ ~A & ~(~B)
2. (A ∨ S) ⊃ J , ~J   /∴ ~(A ∨ S)
3. ~(A ∨ B) ⊃ C   /∴ ~C ⊃ (A ∨ B)
4. (A ∨ S) ⊃ ~J , (A ∨ S)   /∴ ~J
5. H ∨ ~I , H ⊃ ~P , ~I ⊃ ~J   /∴ ~P ∨ ~J
6. J ⊃ (A ∨ S) , ~(A ∨ S)   /∴ ~J
7. ~S & ~E   /∴ ~(S ∨ E)
8. T ∨ ~E , ~T   /∴ ~E
9. ~H ⊃ Q , ~H ∨ I , I ⊃ M   /∴ Q ∨ M
10. (T & B) ∨ ~E , ~(~E)   /∴ T & B
11. ~T ∨ ~E , ~T   /∴ ~T & (~T ∨ ~E)
12. A ⊃ B , ~C ≡ B   /∴ ~C ⊃ B
13. L ⊃ (B & E)   /∴ (B & E) ⊃ B
14. ~E   /∴ ~E ∨ (M & S)
15. Q ⊃ [(B & E) & A]   /∴ Q ⊃ (B & E)
16. B ⊃ ~C , ~A ⊃ B   /∴ ~A ⊃ ~C
17. ~J ⊃ (A & S) , ~J   /∴ (A & S)
18. ~(Q & P) ∨ A   /∴ (Q & P) ⊃ A
19. A ⊃ ~C , ~B & ~C   /∴ ~C
20. (B & E) ⊃ ~C , ~A ⊃ (B & E)   /∴ ~A ⊃ ~C
21. (A ∨ B) ⊃ C   /∴ ~(A ∨ B) ∨ C
22. A ∨ ~B , D   /∴ D & (A ∨ ~B)
23. (B ⊃ ~C) & (~B ⊃ A)   /∴ ~B ⊃ A
24. L ⊃ (~B & ~E)   /∴ L ⊃ ~E

Section 2.8 Making Deductions for Arguments

There is another important method for showing that arguments are valid, and this method is actually superior to the truth-table method. The truth-table method is very precise, very simple, and completely comprehensive, but it is also extremely cumbersome and, well, rather unnatural. Many simple examples can illustrate this point. Consider the easy argument:

$(A \& B \& C) \supset (D \& E)$

$A \& B \& C$

_____

$\therefore E$

The truth-table method requires a truth-table with 32 rows (holy smokes!) to show that this easy argument is valid, since there are five simple components and 2×2×2×2×2=32. So, that method is indeed cumbersome, in view of the effort it takes. But more importantly, the truth-table method is literally unnatural, since that is *not* how we *actually* reason things out. Rather, the natural method is to *deduce* the conclusion from the premises in a series of steps using the *rules* of logic. For example, we already know that the rules Modus Ponens and Simplification are valid,

$p \supset q$
p
_____ MP

$\therefore q$

$p \& q$
_____ Simp

$\therefore q$

and we can apply these rules to the given premises to generate the desired conclusion. We start with lines 1 and 2:

1. $(A \& B \& C) \supset (D \& E)$ $= p \supset q$
2. $A \& B \& C$ $= p$

Here, line 1 matches the pattern $p \supset q$ of the first premise of Modus Ponens, and line 2 in the same way matches the pattern p of the second premise of Modus Ponens. This rule now guarantees that the sentence that matches the pattern q of the conclusion of Modus Ponens may be validly inferred; that is, we may infer line 3:

3. $D \& E$

But line 3 in turn matches the pattern p & q of the premiss of the rule of Simplification, so that we can now validly infer the sentence matching the pattern q of the conclusion of the Simplification rule, that is, we may infer the final conclusion:

4. E

We can put all this information into a compact arrangement that we call a *deduction* (or a *derivation*) for the original argument:

1. (A & B & C) ⊃ (D & E)   prem
2. A & B & C   prem   ∴ E
_____

3. D & E   1, 2, MP
4. E   3, Simp

Let's pause a moment to notice some of the features of this display. There is a left column consisting of the *lines* (steps) of the deduction, and there is a right column consisting of the *reasons* for each of the steps on the left. Notice that the two columns are perfectly *aligned*, for ease of visual inspection. And notice that the lines on the left are *numbered*, never lettered, since lettering would make the deduction very difficult to read. Notice also that the reasons are written in a *very compact* form, citing only the numbers of the lines used together with the official *abbreviation* of the name of the rule used. (This requires not only that every rule has an official name, but also that every name in turn has an official abbreviation.) With this understanding of how deductions are displayed, we now give the official definition of what a deduction is:

A *deduction* for an argument is a listed sequence of sentences such that

1.   All the premisses of the argument are listed *first* in the sequence.

2.   The conclusion of the argument is listed *last* in the sequence.

3.   All sentences in the sequence, except for the premisses, are derived from *earlier* sentences in the sequence by means of *the rules of inference*. (For a list of these rules, see section 2.7.)

4.   All the sentences in the sequence are properly *displayed*, as described above.

How are *deductions* related to *valid arguments?* First of all, recall that we already showed in sections 2.5 and 2.6 that all the rules of inference are valid argument and equivalences patterns in the truth-table sense. This means, then, that all of the individual steps in the deduction, after the premisses, are subconclusions produced by valid patterns. And that also means that the *overall* pattern starting with the premises and ending with the final conclusion must also be a valid pattern.

> **Method of Deduction:**
>
> If a deduction has been given for an argument, then the argument is valid.

This all means that we have a new method, one to replace the truth-table method, by which we can demonstrate the validity of arguments. Let's try another example.

A & B

A ⊃ (C ∨ D)

B ⊃ ~C

∴ (D & A) & B

To show that this argument is valid, we give a deduction for it. Keep in mind that the definition of a deduction does *not* require that the steps are to be done in any special order. The steps of a deduction are entirely your own creations. What *is* required is that you do not make any *mistakes* when you apply the rules to the given lines. As a result of this kind of freedom, there are always several deductions that one can construct to show that a given argument is valid.

1. A & B	prem	
2. A ⊃ (C ∨ D)	prem	
3. B ⊃ ~C	prem	∴ (D & A) & B
4. A	1, Simp	
5. B	1, Simp	
6. C ∨ D	2, 4, MP	
7. ~C	3, 5, MP	
8. D	6,7, Disj Syll	
9. D & A	8, 4, Conj	
10. (D & A) & B	9, 5, Conj	

Notes on the Method of Deduction

Note 1. The rules of inference constitute the very heart of logic. You must know *all* these rules *in their entirety*: You must know their *English form*; you must know their *symbolic form*; you must know their *conceptual content*; you must know their *names*; you must be able to give *easy examples*. MEMORIZE. MEMORIZE. MEMORIZE. Your ability to do deductions will be directly proportional to your knowledge of these rules.

Note 2. The rules of inference are so intended that the *written order* of the premisses of a rule is *not* significant. The fact that one premiss is written before or after another premiss does not in any way affect what the *consequences* of these two steps are. When we list a rule, we naturally have to write the steps in a certain chronological order, but that order is intended to be arbitrary. The Dilemma rule, for example, can be written in any of the following ways:

$p \lor q$	$p \supset r$	$p \supset r$	$p \supset q$
$p \supset r$	$q \supset s$	$p \lor q$	$r \supset s$
$q \supset s$	$p \lor q$	$q \supset s$	$p \lor r$
———	———	———	———
$\therefore r \lor s$	$\therefore r \lor s$	$\therefore r \lor s$	$\therefore q \lor s$

The last version has not only changed the order of the premisses, it has also changed which meta-variables were used to represent the parts of the rule.

Note 3. All of the rules of inference have an *infinitely large scope* of application. The rules are stated in terms of the meta-variables "p", "q", "r", and "s". Here we must remember that these labels represent *all* sentences of any kind: all the simple ones, all the negative ones, and all the conjunctive, disjunctive, conditional, and biconditional ones as well. It is this infinite variability that gives the rules the power to form deductions. Thus, the following five arguments are *all* examples of the rule of Modus Ponens:

	(1)	(2)	(3)	(4)	(5)
$p \supset q$ →	$M \supset A$	$R \supset {\sim}S$	$(B \,\&\, C) \supset (A \,\&\, D)$	${\sim}U \supset {\sim}H$	${\sim}(K \lor M) \supset {\sim}{\sim}H$
p →	M	R	$B \,\&\, C$	${\sim}U$	${\sim}(K \lor M)$
$\therefore q$ →	$\therefore A$	$\therefore {\sim}S$	$\therefore A \,\&\, D$	$\therefore {\sim}H$	$\therefore {\sim}{\sim}H$

Even though some of these inferences contain negative sentences, they are *not* examples of the rule of Modus Tollens (since the second premiss is not the opposite of the back part of the first premiss).

Note 4. A single sentence can use many different rules. The reason for this is that a single sentence, when it is compound, can be viewed as having several different *sentence patterns*, and all these different patterns enable the sentence to use different rules. We illustrate this matter with the sentence ${\sim}A \lor {\sim}B$. This sentence obviously has the pattern p , since it is just a sentence. It also has the pattern p $\lor$ q , since it is a disjunction, and it has other patterns as well, as we list below. With each pattern come certain rules of inference that can be applied:

sentence
~A ∨ ~B
_____

pattern		candidate rules
p	→	MP, Conj, Disj Add, DN, Dupl
p ∨ q	→	Disj Syll, Dilemma, Comm, (and the above)
~p ∨ q	→	Cond (and the above)
p ∨ ~q	→	Comm (and the above)
~p ∨ ~q	→	DeMorg (and the above)

Note 5. *Deductive elegance* is really nice, but it is *not* required. Deductions are free creations. There is nothing in the definition of a deduction that requires that the steps be written in a certain order, or that the steps are as compact as possible, or that all the steps are necessary ones. The definition does require, however, that all the steps are correct applications of the rules. You are not allowed to make even the smallest mistake. There is, of course, a *practical* value to working with deductions that are orderly and compact, but that value has no logical significance.

Wow, that's beautiful, and correct!

1. ~(~S)	Prem
2. S ⊃ W	Prem ∴ ~(~W)
_____	
3. S	1, DN
4. W	2, 3, MP
5. ~(~W)	4, DN

(An *even more beautiful* deduction can be given. Can you think of it?)

Man, that's ugly, and correct!

1. ~(~S)	Prem
2. S ⊃ W	Prem ∴ ~(~W)
_____	
3. ~W ⊃ ~S	2, Contrap
4. ~W ⊃ ~(~(~S))	3, DN
5. ~(~W) ∨ ~(~(~S))	4, Cond
6. W ∨ ~(~(~S))	5, DN
7. W ∨ ~S	6, DN
8. ~(~W)	1, 3, MT

Argument Forms, Equivalence Forms, and Logical Truths

The rules of inference fall into three different groups with respect to the manner in which they *behave*. These groups are:

> Group 1: basic argument forms
>
> Group 2: basic equivalence forms
>
> Group 3: logical truths

Group 1. *The basic argument forms* are rules that behave in the same way that arguments behave: you start with some given premises, and then you *infer a new conclusion*, a conclusion that is different in content and form from the premises. On the rule sheet, these are the rules that use "therefore," the *triple dot* inference indicator. This includes, then, the following eleven rules:

MP, MT, Hyp Syll, Dilemma

Simp, Conj, Disj Syll, Disj Add

Dbl Thens, Bicond, RAA

What is important about *these* rules is that they *apply only to whole lines* of a deduction, and *never to parts of lines*. Consider the rule Disj Syll:

12. K ∨ (S & ~B)	. . . .	← whole line is p ∨ q
13. ~K	. . . .	← whole line is ~p
14. S & ~B	12,13,Disj Syll	← whole line is q , CORRECT USE
12. R & (A ∨ L)	. . . .	← only *part* of line 12 is p ∨ q
13. ~A	. . . .	← whole line is ~p
14. L	12,13,Disj Syll ??	← WRONG: only *part* of 12 is p ∨ q
15. R & L	12,13,Disj Syll ??	← WRONG: only *part* of 12 is p ∨ q
		and WRONG: only *part* of 15 is q

Group 2. *The basic equivalences forms* behave like rules for making *substitutions* with items that *mean the same thing*. Unlike the previous group of rules, these rules do not generate a new conclusion, but rather, they *restate* existing information in an alternate form, without changing the content. On the rule sheet, the equivalence rules are the ones that use the *equal sign* between the equivalent sides. This includes then the following ten rules:

Dbl Neg, DeMorg, Contrap,

Cond, Bicond, Dbl Ifs,

Dupl, Comm, Assoc, Dist

Because these rules manipulate parts that are entirely equivalent in meaning, there is no restriction on the context in which these rules may be used. In particular, the equivalence rules may be applied *both* to *whole* lines of a deduction as well as to *parts* of lines. Consider the two equivalence rules known as De Morgan's Law and Double Negation:

18. ~(M ∨ ~B)	. . . .	← whole line is ~(p ∨ q)
19. ~M & ~(~B)	18, DeMorg	← whole line is ~p & ~q , CORRECT USE
19. ~M & ~(~B)	. . . .	← *part* of line is ~(~p)
20. ~M & B	19, DN	← same *part* of line is p , CORRECT USE

Group 3. The rule for *logical truths* is a rule that makes no inference whatsoever. It simply permits someone to write down a sentence that in itself is a *logical truth* at any point in the deduction. (This rule agrees well with the common practice of writing any mathematical theorem at any point in a mathematical deduction.) The rule sheet gives a small list of logical truths that may be inserted into any deduction at any point. As a practical matter, this list includes only those logical truths that are likely to be *useful* in a deduction. The rule of logical truths may be cited simply as "Logical Truth," or by the shorter abbreviation "Taut." Logic books commonly refer to logical truths as *tautologies*, hence the abbreviation "Taut."

10.	H ⊃ (A & ~E)	. . . .	← any line whatever
11.	(A & ~E) ⊃ ~E	Taut	← any logical truth, CORRECT
12.	H ⊃ ~E	10,11,Hyp.Syll	← How about that!
			Perfect for Hyp Syll

A Sample Deduction

We are done with our general comments, and we are now *eager* to actually start doing deductions. We'll walk through one and make some comments as we go. The premisses and the conclusion are as indicated:

1.	(~A ⊃ D) & (A ⊃ I)	Prem	
2.	(I ⊃ Q) & (~S ⊃ ~D)	Prem	/∴ Q ∨ S
	_____		
3.	?		

What do we do next? There is an important answer to this question, and it is called *strategy*. We will spend the entire next section on that idea, but for the moment, let's just do what comes to mind. (Sometimes that's the only strategy available.) What is immediately obvious is that the premisses are *conjunctions*, and that means there's only one thing to do: *break up* the conjunctions into their individual pieces.

3.	~A ⊃ D	1, Simp
4.	A ⊃ I	1, Simp
5.	I ⊃ Q	2, Simp
6.	~S ⊃ ~D	2, Simp

What comes to mind next is that lines 4 and 5 have an easy connection by the rule Hyp Syll, and so we should definitely try that, and also, looking at line 6, we can see that the negatives can be eliminated by the rule Contrap, and that kind of reduction is always a good idea.

7. A ⊃ Q	4,5, Hyp Syll
8. D ⊃ S	6, Contrap

And *now* another new connection has appeared between line 3 and line 8, through another Hyp Syll, and so, we won't hold back. We do it.

3. ~A ⊃ D	1, Simp
4. A ⊃ I	1, Simp
5. I ⊃ Q	2, Simp
6. ~S ⊃ ~D	2, Simp
7. A ⊃ Q	4,5, Hyp Syll
8. D ⊃ S	6, Contrap
9. ~A ⊃ S	3,8, Hyp Syll

Well, the immediate connections have stopped, and we pause to check the conclusion, Q ∨ S. Hmm, now what? We must *scan*. We must scan what we have. Line 7 has Q in it, and line 9 has S in it. Hmm. Those are two "if thens," and the conclusion is "or," so that sort of looks like a *Dilemma*. But that means we also need an "or" sentence to start the Dilemma, and that sentence would be A ∨ ~A. Hmm, how can we get *that* one. . .? BINGO! The missing "or" sentence is a *logical truth*, so we can just write *that* logical truth wherever and whenever we want. Done.

1. (~A ⊃ D) & (A ⊃ I)	Prem
2. (I ⊃ Q) & (~S ⊃ ~D)	Prem /∴ Q ∨ S
———	
3. ~A ⊃ D	1, Simp
4. A ⊃ I	1, Simp
5. I ⊃ Q	2, Simp
6. ~S ⊃ ~D	2, Simp
7. A ⊃ Q	4,5, Hyp Syll
8. D ⊃ S	6, Contrap
9. ~A ⊃ S	3,8, Hyp Syll
10. A ∨ ~A	Taut
11. Q ∨ S	10,7,9, Dilem

Advanced rules: Conditional Proof and Indirect Proof. A closing comment. There are two other rules that are important deduction tools. They are more advanced and more powerful logical techniques than the rules presented thus far. These are known as the rule of *Conditional Proof* and the rule of *Indirect Proof*. We present these rules in section 2.10 below.

Exercise 2.8. A,B Deductions, Supply Reasons

Part A Supply the missing reasons in the following deductions. Use the standard method of annotating deductions, as in Problem #1. Always cite the line numbers used (if any), and cite the abbreviated name of the rule used. In all these problems lines 1 and 2 are premises, and they are annotated as "Prem." Use the available **Exercise Work Sheet** to submit your work.

1) 1. A ⊃ B   Prem
    2. B ⊃ C   Prem
    3. A ⊃ C   1,2, Hyp Syll
    4. ~C ⊃ ~A   3, Contrap

2) 1. T ∨ (D & ~E)
    2. ~T
    3. D & ~E
    4. ~E

3) 1. (A ∨ B) ⊃ C
    2. (A ∨ B) & F
    3. A ∨ B
    4. C

4) 1. ~(Q ∨ S)
    2. B
    3. ~Q & ~S
    4. B & (~Q & ~S)

5) 1. ~B & A
    2. (K & ~E) ⊃ B
    3. ~B
    4. ~(K & ~E)
    5. ~K ∨ ~(~E)

6) 1. ~J ⊃ ~I
    2. (H ⊃ P) & (H ∨ ~J)
    3. H ⊃ P
    4. H ∨ ~J
    5. P ∨ ~I

7) 1. L ⊃ (B & E)
    2. E ⊃ S
    3. L ⊃ B
    4. L ⊃ E
    5. L ⊃ S

8) 1. L ⊃ (B & E)
    2. ~E
    3. (B & E) ⊃ E
    4. ~(B & E)
    5. ~L

9) 1. A ≡ ~B
    2. C ≡ ~B
    3. A ⊃ ~B
    4. ~B ⊃ C
    5. A ⊃ C
    6. ~C ⊃ ~A

10) 1. (~S ∨ Y) ∨ ~A
    2. ~Y
    3. (Y ∨ ~S) ∨ ~A
    4. Y ∨ (~S ∨ ~A)
    5. ~S ∨ ~A
    6. ~(S & A)

Part B. Supply the missing reasons in the following deductions. Use the standard method of annotating deductions, always citing both the line numbers used, and the abbreviated name of the rule used, in that order. In each deduction, the steps above the horizontal line are the premises, and they are annotated as "Prem." Use the available **Exercise Work Sheet** to submit your work.

1) 1. F ≡ G
    2. E ⊃ (F ∨ G)
    3. ~G & (A ∨ B)
    4. (B ⊃ E) & H
    ———————
    5. ~G
    6. A ∨ B
    7. B ⊃ E
    8. F ⊃ G
    9. ~F
    10. ~F & ~G
    11. ~(F ∨ G)
    12. ~E
    13. ~B
    14. A

2) 1. A ∨ (N ∨ W)
    2. W ⊃ ~(~B)
    3. K & ~S
    4. (N ⊃ L) & ~A
    5. (~S ∨ M) ⊃ Q
    ———————
    6. ~S
    7. ~S ∨ M
    8. Q
    9. ~A
    10. N ∨ W
    11. N ⊃ L
    12. W ⊃ B
    13. L ∨ B
    14. Q & (L ∨ B)

3) 1. M ⊃ (~P ∨ T)
    2. ~M ⊃ Q
    3. (P ∨ A) & (~Q & ~A)
    ———————
    4. P ∨ A
    5. (~Q & ~A)
    6. ~Q
    7. ~(~M)
    8. M
    9. ~P ∨ T
    10. ~A
    11. P
    12. ~(~P)
    13. T
    14. ~S ∨ T

4) 1. A ⊃ (B ⊃ C)
    2. D ⊃ (E & F)
    3. (B ⊃ C) ⊃ (A ⊃ D)
    4. (~A ∨ E) ⊃ (B ⊃ C)
    5. ~C
    ———————
    6. A ⊃ (A ⊃ D)
    7. (A & A) ⊃ D
    8. A ⊃ D
    9. A ⊃ (E & F)
    10. A ⊃ E
    11. ~A ∨ E
    12. B ⊃ C
    13. ~B
    14. ~B & ~C

Section 2.9 Strategy in Deductions

The Method of Deduction is not a mechanical method, in the sense that the Truth-table Method is a mechanical method. One constructs a complete truth-table for an argument, that's mechanical, and one applies the validity test, that's mechanical, and the outcome is automatic. By contrast, making a deduction for an argument is a *creative* process that requires ability and insight: the reasoner must *somehow* figure out how the laws of logic can be used to deduce the conclusion from the premises in a manageable number of steps. Maybe the reasoner will succeed; but maybe not, even if no mistakes are made. It is tempting to think that not being able to find a deduction (while making no mistakes) is actually a success of another kind: a demonstration that the argument is invalid. But that would not be true. Not being able to find a deduction *could* mean that the argument is invalid, and that a deduction is impossible. It could also mean that the argument is valid after all, and a deduction can be found, but *you* have not succeeded in finding one.

But there are positive aspects. (1) First of all, most arguments we are likely to meet are not so complex that we cannot demonstrate their validity, or invalidity. With some logic education, our creative abilities are well-suited to the task. And that is also the second point. (2) *Practice* will help us become better deduction makers. All skills are like that, and making deductions is a skill. So, PRACTICE, PRACTICE, PRACTICE. (3) Thirdly, our creative abilities are helped not only by practice, we can also use *strategy*. We should never proceed randomly in deductions, because random steps usually produce nothing of interest. The strategy at issue is very general, and it can be applied to solving most problems. Of course, strategy is not a mechanical method that guarantees a result. But, like most strategy, it is effective. There are two main parts.

Strategy #1: Simplify Complexity

Normally, we will not be able to construct a deduction unless we can see how the various sentences are related. But we can't see those relationships if they are hidden from us by the complex structures of the sentences. So, in order to do a deduction, we must eliminate the complex structures that hide the relationships. As much as possible, we have to *reduce complex sentences to simpler ones.*

We do have rules that will perform the needed reductions. In fact, many of our rules of deduction are also rules of reduction. The important ones are:

Simp	MP	MT	Disj Syll	DN	Contrap
5. p & q	5. p ⊃ q	5. p ⊃ q	5. p ∨ q	5. ~(~p)	5. ~q ⊃ ~p
	6. p	6. ~q	6. ~p		
6. p	7. q	7. ~p	7. q	6. p	6. p ⊃ q

Here the reduction results have been highlighted. What is important is that when sentences are simpler, we can better see the connections. And there is a matching *negative strategy* that goes along with this: *DO NOT make simpler sentences more complicated!* For example, the following is a strategic blunder:

5.	~A ⊃ B	. . . . . .	
6.	~B ⊃ ~(~A)	5, Contrap	
7.	~(~B) ∨ ~(~A)	6, Cond.	Strategy mistake: Should be: 6, Dbl Neg
8.	~(~B & ~A)	7, DeMorg	What a mess!
9.	B & A	8, Dbl Neg ???	ERROR. See what happens?

The above procedure is too complicated, and it's unnatural (real people don't do that), and such unnatural complexities will likely lead to error. Unless you happen to have a very good reason for introducing complexity (like when the desired conclusion itself is complex), *don't* do it; otherwise, the best you can hope for is confusion. Here is an example of a series of typical reductions:

1. O & ~K	Prem		
2. U & (R ∨ K)	Prem		
3. R ⊃ (S & W)	Prem	∴ S	
4. O	1, Simp	= reduce line 1	
5. ~K	1, Simp	= reduce line 1	
6. U	2, Simp	= reduce line 2	
7. R ∨ K	2, Simp	= reduce line 2	
8. R	5,7, Disj Syll	= reduce line 7	
9. S & W	3,8, MP	= reduce line 3	
10. S	9, Simp	= reduce line 9	

Strategy #2: Always Proceed in Accordance with Set Goals

The second strategy is perhaps more important than the first, because it controls the *direction* that the construction of the deduction takes. There are so many things that the rules *allow* us to do—what should we do *first*? The answer is: We should do those things that will accomplish the *goal* that we have set. Clearly, every problem sets the first goal for us, which is to find the solution, and in deductions that goal is to derive the *conclusion*. So, that is the *starting* point in our strategy (and the *ending* point in finishing the deduction). The first question we ask is, *Which one* of the premisses is relevant to getting the conclusion, and *exactly how* will this premiss do this? For example, suppose the argument is:

1. ~A ⊃ (A ∨ B)	Prem	
2. M ⊃ S	Prem	
3. M & (S ⊃ ~A)	Prem	∴ A ∨ B
. . . .	?	
x. A ∨ B	Conclusion	← That's the goal

The conclusion is A ∨ B. We look at the premisses, and we see that one of them is ~A ⊃ (A ∨ B). Bingo! That's the premiss we focus on. That premiss gives us a strategy for deriving the conclusion. We need to use the rule MP, and, therefore, we need the additional, independent line ~A to *match* the condition part:

1. ~A ⊃ (A ∨ B)	Prem	
2. M ⊃ S	Prem	
3. M & (S ⊃ ~A)	Prem	
——————		
. . . .	?	
x. ~A	?	← That's the new goal
x. A ∨ B	1, x, MP	← That's the first goal

This is real progress. We have set a new goal, to derive ~A , and when we have done that, we are all done. So, again, the question is, *which one* of the available lines is relevant to getting the new goal, and *exactly how* will this line produce it? The relevant line is Premiss 3. It is a conjunction, so we need to use the rule Simp to break it up. This produces the new line S ⊃ ~A , and this new line gives us a new strategy for getting what we want. What we need is the additional line S, and those two lines will produce ~A by means of the rule MP:

1. ~A ⊃ (A ∨ B)	Prem	
2. M ⊃ S	Prem	
3. M & (S ⊃ ~A)	Prem	
——————		
4. S ⊃ ~A	3, Simp	
. . . .	?	
x. S	?	← That's the new goal
x. ~A	4, x, MP	← That's the second goal
x. A ∨ B	1, x, MP	← That's the first goal

We are getting close to the end. Our goal is to derive S. We search for a relevant line, and we see that it is line 2. This gives us a new goal. We need to get M. We look and find M in line 3. Bingo! The rule Simp completes the strategy.

1. ~A ⊃ (A ∨ B)	Prem	
2. M ⊃ S	Prem	
3. M & (S ⊃ ~A)	Prem	
——————		
4. S ⊃ ~A	3, Simp	
5. M	3, Simp	← That's the last goal
6. S	2, 5, MP	← That's the third goal
7. ~A	4, 6, MP	← That's the second goal
8. A ∨ B	1, 7, MP	← That's the first goal

Of course, not all arguments fall so easily under the two main strategies. You may well have to supplement these strategies with some *cleverness* of your own. Also, there are some *special* strategies for some special conclusions, as described next.

Particular Strategies

In addition to the two main strategies there are also more particular strategies that must be used. In fact, we need these particular strategies to do what is asked by the second main strategy: to always proceed in accordance with set goals. If the sought-after line (the final conclusion or an intermediate conclusion) does not appear in the premisses, then one will have to *construct* this line *from pieces* that are available or that still have to be derived. At this point, a thorough *knowledge of the rules of inference* is required. Our discussion here refers to the conclusion, but the same strategy points apply to any intermediate conclusions along the way as well. Here are the specific cases.

1. The conclusion is a *conjunction* p & q :

   Here, you must derive two lines, one line p and the other line q, and then use the rule Conj.

2. The conclusion is a *disjunction* p $\lor$ q :

   Case 1. q is an *extra* component that does not occur anywhere else in the premisses. Here you must derive the line p and then use the rule Disj Add to get p $\lor$ q .

   Case 2. There are three other rules that *generate* p $\lor$ q: DeMorg, Cond, Dilem.

3. The conclusion is a *biconditional* p $\equiv$ q :

   Here, you must derive the two sentences p $\supset$ q and q $\supset$ p and then use the rule Bicond. Only the rule Bicond will generate a biconditional sentence.

4. The conclusion is a *conditional* p $\supset$ q :

   There are various rules that *generate* conditional sentences. The rule Hyp Syll is at the top of the list. Other candidates to consider are: Cond, Bicond, Contrap, Dbl Thens, Dbl Ifs. The advanced rule CP is also a good rule to use here.

5. The conclusion is a *negation* of a compound sentence:

   Case 1. ~(p & q). Use DeMorg to get it.

   Case 2. ~(p $\lor$ q). Use DeMorg to get it.

   Case 3. ~(p $\supset$ q). Ordinary English does *not* have cases like this, but in the symbolic language this could occur. Start with: p & ~q , and then do: ~(~p) & ~q , ~(~p $\lor$ q) , ~(p $\supset$ q) , by the rules Dbl Neg, DeMorg, Cond, respectively. This is a bit tedious, and the advanced rule IP is a better rule to use for this case.

   Case 4. ~(p $\equiv$ q). Ordinary English does *not* have cases like this, but in the symbolic language this could occur. One must start with: (p & ~q) $\lor$ (q & ~p), and then do:

(~~p & ~q) ∨ (~~q & ~p), ~(~p ∨ q)∨ ~(~q ∨ p), ~(p ⊃ q)∨ ~(q ⊃ p) , ~[(p ⊃ q) & (q ⊃ p)], ~(p ≡ q) , using the rules Dbl Neg, DeMorg, Cond, DeMorg, Bicond, respectively. This is very tedious, and the advanced rule IP is a better rule to use in this case.

6. For the remaining cases, a general strategy is to derive an *equivalent* form of the desired sentence. For example, to derive A ⊃ ~(C ∨ D) we should first get its DeMorg equivalent A ⊃ (~C & ~D) , and the latter can be derived by the rule Dbl Thens from A ⊃ ~C and A ⊃ ~D .

We illustrate a couple of these strategies in the next two examples. Notice that in each of these problems, an extended list of strategies was mapped out and recorded in the space on the right. You should momentarily *cover up* the deduction steps on the left and concentrate on the strategy steps on the right. The strategy steps start with the final conclusion and then grow more and more, as we try to push our goals deeper to where the original premises can be used to give us what we need. *After* the strategies are finished, we begin to write the deduction steps by using the strategy steps in the *reverse order*, beginning with the last strategy step.

1. (A & B) ∨ D	Prem	want: U & W , use Conj
2. (~D & ~E) ∨ S	Prem	need: U , get from 3
3. A ⊃ U	Prem	need: W , get from 4
4. W & ~S	Prem ∴ U & W	————————
————————		want: U , from 3
5. ~S	4, Simp	need: A , get from 1
6. ~D & ~E	2,5, Disj Syll	————————
7. ~D	6, Simp	want: A , from 1
8. A & B	1,7, Disj Syll	need: ~D , get from 2
9. A	8, Simp	————————
10. U	3,9, MP	want: ~D , from 2
11. W	4, Simp	need: ~S , get from 4
12. U & W	10,11, Conj	*reverse for deduction*

1. M ⊃ ~H	Prem	want: P ⊃ ~(S ∨ M)
2. P ⊃ H	Prem	= P ⊃ (~S & ~M)
3. P ⊃ ~S	Prem	get this by rule Dbl Thens
∴ P ⊃ ~(S ∨ M)		from P ⊃ ~S , P ⊃ ~M
————————		
4. H ⊃ ~M	1, Contrap	want: P ⊃ ~S , from 3
5. P ⊃ ~M	2,4, Hyp Syll	want: P ⊃ ~M , from 1,2
6. P ⊃ (~S & ~M)	3,5, Dbl Thens	
7. P ⊃ ~(S ∨ M)	6, DeMorg	*reverse for deduction*

What follows is twenty sample deductions. We give these so that you can go through them at your leisure. Most of these are not difficult, but until you have practiced doing some of these on your own, you will not feel comfortable doing any of the deductions. We have also reproduced these problems in the exercises for optional practice, so that you can compare your own answers to the ones provided here. And as you compare answers, remember that there is always more than one way to do any deduction. We also give another reminder that you should master the rules of inference ASAP. The better you know the rules, the easier the deductions become.

Twenty Sample Deductions

1.
1.	D ⊃ E	Prem
2.	E ⊃ F	Prem
3.	F ⊃ G	Prem ∴ D ⊃ G
4.	D ⊃ F	1,2 Hyp Syll
5.	D ⊃ G	4,3 Hyp Syll

2.
1.	E ∨ F	Prem
2.	E ⊃ G	Prem
3.	~F	Prem ∴ G
4.	E	1,3, Disj Syll
5.	G	2,4, MP

3.
1.	G ∨ ~F	Prem
2.	H ⊃ F	Prem
3.	~G	Prem ∴ ~H
4.	~F	1,3, Disj Syll
5.	~H	2,4, MT

4.
1.	(~E ∨ P) ∨ U	Prem
2.	(~E ∨ P) ⊃ A	Prem
3.	U ⊃ B	Prem
4.	~A	Prem ∴ B
5.	A ∨ B	1,2,3, Dilem
6.	B	5,4, Disj Syll

5.
1.	~R ⊃ (A ⊃ M)	Prem
2.	~R	Prem
3.	~M	Prem.∴ ~A&~M
4.	A ⊃ M	1,2, MP
5.	~A	3,4, MT
6.	~A & ~M	3,5, Conj

6.
1.	~M ∨ ~O	Prem
2.	O ∨ N	Prem
3.	M	Prem ∴ N
4.	~(~M)	3, DN
5.	~O	1,4, Disj Syll
6.	N	2,5, Disj Syll

7.
1.	A ⊃ (B & C)	Prem
2.	~B & E	Prem ∴ ~A
3.	A ⊃ B	1, D.Thens
4.	~B	2, Simp
5.	~A	2,4, MT

8.
1.	A ⊃ (B & C)	Prem
2.	~B	Prem ∴ ~A
3.	~B ∨ ~C	2, Disj Add
4.	~(B & C)	3, DeMorg
5.	~A	1,4, MT

9.
1.	(A & B) ⊃ C	Prem
2.	A & D	Prem
3.	B	Prem ∴ B & C
	———————	
4.	A	2, Simp
5.	A & B	4,3, Conj
6.	C	1,5, MP
7.	B & C	3,6, Conj

10.
1.	B ⊃ [C ∨ (D & E)]	Prem
2.	B & ~C	Prem ∴ E
	———————	
3.	B	2, Simp
4.	C ∨ (D & E)	1,3, MP
5.	~C	2, Simp
6.	D & E	4,5, Disj Syll
7.	E	6, Simp

11.
1.	~M ⊃ O	Prem
2.	U ⊃ ~M	Prem
3.	S & ~O	Prem ∴ ~U&~O
	———————	
4.	U ⊃ O	2,1, Hyp Syll
5.	~O	3, Simp
6.	~U	4,5, MT
7.	~U & ~O	6,5, Conj

12.
1.	(A ∨ B) ⊃ K	Prem
2.	C ⊃ (A ∨ B)	Prem
3.	D ≡ C	Prem.∴ ~K ⊃~D
	———————	
4.	C ⊃ K	2,1, Hyp Sll
5.	D ⊃ C	3, Bicond
6.	D ⊃ K	5,4, Hyp Syll
7.	~K ⊃ ~D	6, Contrap

13.
1.	~(A & ~H)	Prem
2.	~H ∨ ~E	Prem
3.	N & A	Prem ∴ SV~E
	———————	
4.	A	3, Simp
5.	~A ∨ ~(~H)	1, DeMorg
6.	~(~H)	4,5, Disj Syll
7.	~E	2,6, Disj Syll
8.	S ∨ ~E	7, Disj Add

14.
1.	U ⊃ C	Prem
2.	L ∨ U	Prem
3.	(M & H) ⊃ ~L	Prem.∴ (M&H)⊃C
	———————	
4.	~(~L) ∨ U	2, DN
5.	~L ⊃ U	4, Cond
6.	~L ⊃ C	5,1, Hyp Syll
7.	(M & H) ⊃ C	3,6, Hyp Syll

15.
1.	~B & ~U	Prem
2.	~U ⊃ (W ∨ S)	Prem
3.	(W ⊃ Q)&(S ⊃ A)	Prem ∴ Q ∨ A
	———————	
4.	~U	1, Simp
5.	W ∨ S	2,4, MP
6.	W ⊃ Q	3, Simp
7.	S ⊃ A	3, Simp
8.	Q ∨ A	5,6,7, Dilem

16.
1.	(A ∨ B) ⊃ K	Prem
2.	C ⊃ (A ∨ B)	Prem
3.	~C ⊃ ~D	Prem ∴ D ⊃ K
	———————	
4.	C ∨ ~C	Taut
5.	(A ∨ B) ∨ ~D	4,2,3, Dilem
6.	~D ∨ (A ∨ B)	5, Comm
7.	D ⊃ (A ∨ B)	6, Cond
8.	D ⊃ K	7,1, Hyp Syll

17. 1. A ≡ (B & C)   Prem
     2. ~(A ∨ ~C)   Prem ∴ ~B
     _____
     3. (B & C) ⊃ A   1, Bicond
     4. ~A & ~(~C)   2, DeMorg
     5. ~A   4, Simp
     6. ~(B & C)   3,5, MT
     7. ~B ∨ ~C   6, DeMorg
     8. ~(~C)   4, Simp
     9. ~B   7,8, Disj Syll

18. 1. (M ∨ S) ⊃ (N&O)   Prem
     2. ~S   Prem
     3. O ⊃ S   Prem ∴ ~M
     _____
     4. (M ∨ S) ⊃ O   1, Dbl Thens
     5. ~O   2,3, MT
     6. ~(M ∨ S)   4,5, MT
     7. ~M & ~S   6, DeMorg
     8. ~M   7,Simp

19. 1. (~A ⊃ D)&(A ⊃ I)   Prem
     2. (D ⊃ S) & (I ⊃ Q) Prem ∴ Q ∨ S
     _____
     3. ~A ⊃ D   1, Simp
     4. A ⊃ I   1, Simp
     5. D ⊃ S   2, Simp
     6. I ⊃ Q   2, Simp
     7. ~A ⊃ S   3,5, Hyp Syll
     8. A ⊃ Q   4,6, Hyp Syll
     9. A ∨ ~A   Taut
     10. Q ∨ S   9,8,7, Dilem

20. 1. E ⊃ (U ⊃ D)   Prem
     2. E ⊃ U   Prem
     3. ~D   Prem ∴ ~(EVD)
     _____
     4. (E & U) ⊃ D   1, double ifs
     5. ~(E & U)   3,4, MT
     6. ~E ∨ ~U   5, DeMorg
     7. E ⊃ ~U   6, Cond
     8. ~E   2,7, RAA
     9. ~E & ~D   8,3, Conj
     10. ~(E ∨ D)   9, DeMorg

Practice the Twenty Previous Sample Deductions

Practice these problems yourself, and compare your answers to the solutions given above. There is an available **Exercise Work Sheet** for these problems.

1. D ⊃ E , E ⊃ F , F ⊃ G /∴ D ⊃ G

2. E ∨ F , E ⊃ G , ~F /∴ G

3. G ∨ ~F , H ⊃ F , ~G /∴ ~H

4. (~E ∨ P) ∨ U , (~E ∨ P) ⊃ A , U ⊃ B , ~A /∴ B

5. ~R ⊃ (A ⊃ M) , ~R , ~M /∴ ~A & ~M

6. ~M ∨ ~O , O ∨ N , M /∴ N

7. A ⊃ (B & C) , ~B & E /∴ ~A

8. A ⊃ (B & C) , ~B /∴ ~A

9. (A & B) ⊃ C , A & D , B /∴ B & C

10. B ⊃ [C ∨ (D & E)] , B & ~C /∴ E

11. ~M ⊃ O , U ⊃ ~M , S & ~O /∴ ~U & ~O

12. $(A \lor B) \supset K , C \supset (A \lor B) , D \equiv C \ / \therefore \ \sim K \supset \sim D$

13. $\sim (A \ \& \ \sim H) , \sim H \lor \sim E , N \ \& \ A \ / \therefore \ S \lor \sim E$

14. $U \supset C , L \lor U , (M \ \& \ H) \supset \sim L \ / \therefore \ (M \ \& \ H) \supset C$

15. $\sim B \ \& \ \sim U , \sim U \supset (W \lor S) , (W \supset Q) \ \& \ (S \supset A) \ / \therefore \ Q \lor A$

16. $(A \lor B) \supset K , C \supset (A \lor B) , \sim C \supset \sim D \ / \therefore \ D \supset K$

17. $A \equiv (B \ \& \ C) , \sim (A \lor \sim C) \ / \therefore \ \sim B$

18. $(M \lor S) \supset (N \ \& \ O) , \sim S , O \supset S \ / \therefore \ \sim M$

19. $(\sim A \supset D) \ \& \ (A \supset I) , (D \supset S) \ \& \ (I \supset Q) \ / \therefore \ Q \lor S$

20. $E \supset (U \supset D) , E \supset U , \sim D \ / \therefore \ \sim (E \lor D)$

Exercise 2.9. A,B,C,D Deductions, Full Blast

Part A. Give deductions for the following arguments. These are easy. Use the available **Exercise Work Sheet** to submit your work.

1. $\sim A , \sim B , B \lor C , A \lor D \ / \therefore \ C \ \& \ D$

2. $\sim A \ \& \ \sim B , B \lor C \ / \therefore \ C \ \& \ \sim A$

3. $A \supset B , \sim P \supset \sim T , B \supset \sim P \ / \therefore \ A \supset \sim T$

4. $G \lor \sim H , \sim G , I \supset H \ / \therefore \ \sim I$

5. $(A \ \& \ B) \lor (Q \ \& \ R) , \sim Q \lor \sim R \ / \therefore \ B$

6. $C \supset (A \ \& \ S) \ / \therefore \ \sim S \supset \sim C$

7. $M \equiv \sim O \ / \therefore \ \sim M \supset O$

8. $F \supset (G \lor A) , \sim G , \sim A \ / \therefore \ \sim F$

Part B. Give deductions for the following arguments. These are just a bit harder. Use the available **Exercise Work Sheet** to submit your work.

1. $\sim (A \ \& \ B) , A , \sim B \supset D \ / \therefore \ D$

2. $\sim (G \ \& \ \sim (\sim H)) , \sim H \supset D \ / \therefore \ G \supset D$

3. $\sim L , \sim N \ / \therefore \ \sim (L \lor N) \lor Q$

4. $K \lor M , \sim M \ / \therefore \ \sim (\sim K \lor M)$

5. $\sim R \lor \sim S , \sim R \lor S \ / \therefore \ \sim R$

6. $F \supset (G \ \& \ A) , (\sim G) \ \& \ M \ / \therefore \ \sim F$

7. $F \supset A , G \ \& \ \sim A \ / \therefore \ \sim F \lor X$

8. $S \supset \sim M , M \lor T , S \supset \sim T \ / \therefore \ \sim S$

Part C. Give deductions for the following arguments. These are a bit harder yet. Use the available **Exercise Work Sheet** to submit your work.

1. A ∨ W , ~A ∨ ~W /∴ ~W ≡ A
2. S ≡ ~K , K , ~B ⊃ S /∴ B & K
3. (S ∨ ~S) ⊃ ~B , (A & P) ⊃ B /∴ ~A ∨ ~P
4. (A & B) & ~(~C) , (D ∨ D) & M /∴ (C & B) & D
5. U ⊃ R , ~N ⊃ ~F , N ⊃ J , ~U ⊃ ~J /∴ F ⊃ R
6. P ⊃ T , ~T ⊃ ~Q , ~(~P & ~Q) /∴ T
7. ~Q ⊃ E , ~A ⊃ E , ~E /∴ (A & Q) ∨ (A & E)
8. A ∨ (B & C) , A ⊃ M , M ⊃ D /∴ D ∨ B

Part D. Give deductions for the following arguments. These are difficult. The rule of Tautology may be useful here. You may want to practice these first on a separate sheet. Use the available **Exercise Work Sheet** to submit your work.

1. A ⊃ (B ∨ C) , C ≡ B /∴ A ⊃ B
2. ~(A & B) , (A ∨ B) & (A ∨ ~B) /∴ A & ~B
3. A ⊃ B , C ⊃ D /∴ (A ∨ C) ⊃ (B ∨ D)
4. P ⊃ (Q & R) , (Q ∨ R) ⊃ S , P ∨ S /∴ S
5. (A ∨ B) ⊃ (A ⊃ ~B) , (B & ~C) ⊃ (A & B) , ~A ⊃ B /∴ A ∨ C
6. ~(T & R) , (P ⊃ Q) & (R ⊃ S) , T & (P ∨ R) , ~Q ≡ S /∴ ~R & ~S
7. G ⊃ F , (D ⊃ A) & (E ⊃ B) , G ∨ (D ∨ E) , ~(F ∨ C) , B ⊃ C /∴ A
8. (E ∨ R) ≡ D , (K ⊃ L) & (G ⊃ H) , (~E ∨ L) ⊃ (D ∨ G) , ~(D ∨ L) /∴ E ∨ H
9. (N & E) ∨ (N & H) , (B ∨ P) ≡ ~(B & K) , (E ∨ P) ⊃ ~N , H ⊃ B /∴ ~K
10. (K & L) ⊃ ~M , S ⊃ (M & P) , T ⊃ (Q & R) , L & (S ∨ T) , K ≡ L /∴ Q ∨ ~L

MORE ADVANCED TOPICS IN PROPOSITIONAL LOGIC

Section 2.10 The Rules of Conditional Proof and Indirect Proof

Sometimes when people reason they make use of *temporary hypotheses* to investigate possible outcomes of some situation. This is the well-known type of "what if . . ." thinking. Suppose you have just taken the LSAT and are waiting for the results:

Your friend asks, "What if you got a perfect LSAT score?" [P]

And you respond, "Well, then my future is guaranteed." [F]

Your friend asks you what you mean by that, and you answer, "Because, then I would be admitted to Harvard Law School [A], and then I would get a Harvard Law degree [D], and then I would have a great job [J] with a great future [F]." Let's have a closer look at this reasoning. The progression has the following *format*:

1.	P ⊃ A	Premiss, assertion of fact
2.	A ⊃ D	Premiss, assertion of fact
3.	D ⊃ (J & F)	Premiss, assertion of fact

4.	P	Temporary "what if" assumption
5.	A	1,4, MP
6.	D	2,5, MP
7.	J & F	3,6, MP
8.	F	7, Simp

9.	P ⊃ F	"what if" summary

This is good reasoning, and this is something all of us do very often. One begins with a temporary assumption and, in the presence of other known facts, deduces a corresponding temporary conclusion. This procedure then allows one to make an overall *summary* of the deductive relationship: "So, if this, then that." This logical technique is known as the rule of *Conditional Proof*, and it takes the following form:

The Rule of Conditional Proof (CP)

1.	. . .	
2.	. . .	
	. . .	
k.	p	Assumption
	. . .	. . .
	. . .	. . .
n.	q	. . .
n+1.	p ⊃ q	k—n, CP

The purpose of this new rule is to *create* conditional sentences. The rule allows you to start a *Conditional Proof Box* at *any* point in a deduction. The first line in this box is *any* sentence that you select, and it receives the label *assumption*. Using this assumption and the previous lines of the deduction, you may derive additional lines inside the CP-box. You may terminate the CP-box whenever you wish. When you terminate it, you simply make sure that the bottom border is drawn, and outside the box as the next line, you write a "summary" of what happened in the box. This summary is a conditional sentence p ⊃ q, where p is the same sentence as was the assumption of the box, and where q is the same sentence as was the last line of the box. This new line is justified by citing the sequence of line numbers in the box, as well as the rule CP.

One important restriction in using the rule CP is that when the CP-box is terminated and the conditional sentence has been derived, all the lines inside the box become *de-activated*. From that point on, all the lines inside the box *cease to exist*. (This gives that other meaning to the word "terminate": you don't just stop it, you also *kill* it.) That means, of course, that you cannot derive later lines outside the box by using lines from inside the box—because those inner lines no longer exist.

Another point is that since CP-boxes may be introduced at any point, they may also be put one *inside* the other, *nested* CP-boxes, as they are called. We illustrate the method with the next two examples.

Example #1.

1. A ⊃ ~B   Prem
2. A ⊃ (B ∨ C)   Prem ∴ A ⊃ C

3. A	Assumption
4. ~B	1,3, MP
5. B ∨ C	2,3, MP
6. C	4,5, Disj Syll

7. A ⊃ C   3–6, CP

Example #2.

1. A ⊃ ~B   Prem
2. A ⊃ (B ∨ C)   Prem ∴ A ⊃ [(C ⊃ K) ⊃ K]

3. A	Assumption
4. ~B	1,3, MP
5. B ∨ C	2,3, MP
6. C	4,5, Disj Syll
7. C ⊃ K	Assumption
8. K	6,7, MP

9. (C ⊃ K) ⊃ K   7—8, CP

10. A ⊃ [(C ⊃ K) ⊃ K]   3—9, CP

The rule CP is a very *powerful* deductive technique. Admittedly, the rule CP is not a necessary addition to the system, because the previous rules are themselves adequate to achieve the same final results. But what is important here is that when you use the rule CP, results can often be derived in a very *simple* and *natural* manner, but if you do *not* use this rule, the derivation is very technical and complex. Look, for example, at the deduction for the argument of *Example #1* when it is done using Direct Proof. This deduction is entirely correct, and it is as short as possible using just the previous rules; but, no human being has ever reasoned in *this* way.

1. A ⊃ ~B   Prem
2. A ⊃ (B ∨ C)   Prem
_____
3. A ⊃ (~B ⊃ C)   2, Cond
4. (A & ~B) ⊃ C   3, Dbl Ifs
5. (~B & A) ⊃ C   4, Comm
6. ~B ⊃ (A ⊃ C)   5, Dbl Ifs
7. A ⊃ (A ⊃ C)   6,1, Hyp Syll
8. (A & A) ⊃ C   7, Dbl Ifs
9. A ⊃ C   8, Dupl

The Rule of Indirect Proof (IP)

Here is the second type of reasoning that uses temporary hypotheses. This type is known as the method (the rule) of *Indirect Proof*. This rule is a more powerful version of the rule RAA that we introduced earlier. Recall that RAA is the rule:

p ⊃ q , p ⊃ ~q ∴ ~p . And also, ~p ⊃ q , ~p ⊃ ~q ∴ p

When a *hypothesis* produces a contradiction, q and ~q , then we know that the hypothesis is WRONG, and we must conclude the *opposite* of the hypothesis. One practical problem with RAA is that it is sometimes difficult to derive the two conditional sentences containing the contradictory results. This is where the rule IP can help. If an assumption has the *potential* to produce contradictory results, then the method of IP is the *easiest* way to bring the contradiction out in the open.

The Rule of Indirect Proof (IP)

```
1. . . .
2. . . .
    . . .
            ┌─────────────────────────────────────┐
            │   k. ~p           Assumption         │
            │      . . .            . . .          │
            │      . . .            . . .          │
            │   n. q & ~q           . . .          │
            └─────────────────────────────────────┘
    n+1. p              k—n, IP
```

Again, as before, this rule allows you to start an *Indirect Proof Box* at *any* point in a deduction. The first line in this box is *any* sentence you select, and it receives the label *assumption*. Using this assumption and the previous lines of the deduction, you may derive additional lines inside the IP-box. Now, here is where the rule IP begins to differ from the rule CP. Once you have derived any contradiction of the form q & ~q inside the IP-box, at *that* point you may terminate the IP-box. When you terminate the IP-box, you must make sure the bottom border of the box is drawn, and outside the box as the next line, you must write the opposite of the assumption that is at the head of the box. This new line is justified by citing the sequence of line numbers in the box, as well as the rule IP. Again, keep in mind that once a box has been terminated, all the lines inside the box are *de-activated* and cease to exist. Those lines cannot be used later by lines that lie outside the box. And again, CP-boxes and IP-boxes can be nested inside other CP-boxes and IP-boxes.

Let's look at some examples of deductions using Indirect Proof. Today, perhaps, you have a brain cloud, and you cannot find *direct proofs* for these arguments:

- S ∨ M , ~M ∨ S ∴ S
- S ⊃ (A ∨ B) , B ⊃ (S ⊃ A) ∴ S ⊃ A

Not to worry. We will use the rule IP for the first problem, and the rules CP and IP for the second problem.

```
1. S ∨ M               Prem
2. ~M ∨ S              Prem  ∴ S = original goal
   ┌──────────────────────────────────────────────────┐
   │ 3. ~S             Assumption (IP) ∴ q & ~q = new goal │
   │ 4. M              1,3, Disj Syll                    │
   │ 5. ~M             2,3, Disj Syll                    │
   │ 6. M & ~M         4,5, Conj                         │
   └──────────────────────────────────────────────────┘
7. S                   3—6, IP
```

| 1. S ⊃ (A ∨ B) | Prem |
| 2. B ⊃ (S ⊃ A) | Prem ∴ S ⊃ A |

| 3. | S | Assumption (CP) ∴ A |
| 4. | A ∨ B | 1,3, MP |

5.	~A	Assumption (IP) ∴ q & ~q
6.	B	4,5, Disj Syll
7.	S ⊃ A	2,6, MP
8.	~S	7,5, MT
9.	S & ~S	3,8, Conj

| 10. | A | 5–9, IP |

| 11. S ⊃ A | 3–10, CP |

Exercise 2.10. A,B Conditional Proof and Indirect Proof

Part A. Give deductions for the following arguments, using the rules CP and IP. Use the available **Exercise Work Sheet** to submit your work.

1. (A ∨ B) ⊃ (C & D) /∴ A ⊃ D

2. (A ∨ B) ⊃ (A & B) /∴ A ≡ B

3. A ∨ (B & C) , A ⊃ D , D ⊃ E /∴ ~E ⊃ B

4. C ⊃ [A ∨ (B & C)] , ~B /∴ C ⊃ (A ∨ D)

5. A ⊃ (B & C) , (D & C) ⊃ (E & F) /∴ (A & D) ⊃ E

6. (A & ~B) ⊃ C , B ⊃ C , ~(~A & ~B) /∴ C

7. A ⊃ ~B , C ⊃ (D ⊃ B) /∴ D ⊃ (~A ∨ ~C)

8. E ⊃ (A ⊃ B) /∴ E ⊃ [(A ∨ B) ⊃ B]

9. (A & B) ⊃ C , (A & ~B) ⊃ E /∴ A ⊃ (C ∨ E)

10. (A ⊃ B) ∨ (A ⊃ C) , B ⊃ D , C ⊃ D ∴ A ⊃ D

Part B. Give deductions for the following arguments, using the rules CP and IP. These are more difficult. Use the available **Exercise Work Sheet** for your work.

1. (P ∨ Q) ⊃ ~R , S ⊃ (~U & ~W) , M ⊃ (R & U) /∴ (P ∨ S) ⊃ ~M

2. ~[A & (B ∨ C)] , D ⊃ B , E ⊃ C /∴ ~[A & (D ∨ E)]

3. (P ∨ Q) ⊃ (R & S) , (T ∨ U) ⊃ (U & W) /∴ (P ∨ T) ⊃ (R ∨ W)

4. A ∨ B , ~A ∨ ~B /∴ ~(A ≡ B)

5. (A & B) ⊃ C , A ⊃ B , (A ∨ C) ∨ ~D /∴ D ⊃ C

6.   (A & B) ⊃ (C ∨ D) , (~A ∨ C) ⊃ D /∴ B ⊃ D

7.   (B ∨ C) ⊃ ~A , (D & ~E) ⊃ B , A ⊃ ~E /∴ A ⊃ ~D

8.   A ⊃ [B ⊃ (C ∨ D)] , (Q & ~C) ⊃ B /∴ ~C ⊃ [A ⊃ (Q ⊃ D)]

Section 2.11 Further Uses of Deductions

The Method of Deduction is very versatile. The *main* use of deductions is to produce the conclusions of valid arguments. Indeed, there is no better method available to demonstrate that a conclusion follows from its premises, than to present a step-by-step deduction. We have finished our introduction to this method, and we now turn to other applications that this method has. We continue here the ideas that we first introduced in Section 2.6, where we noted that in addition to (1) validity, logic also has the following important concerns: (2) the *equivalence* of two sentences; (3) the *logical status* of an individual sentence, with respect to it being a *logical truth*, or a *contradiction*; and (4) the *consistency* of a *group* of sentences. We will look at these further concerns as they relate to the method of deduction.

Earlier, we defined the notion of equivalence, in the following way: Two sentences p and q are *equivalent* if and only if, in every possible situation, p and q have the same truth-value. If we compare this with the definition of validity, we see that equivalence means the following:

Two sentences p and q are equivalent if and only if

the argument p ∴ q is valid, and the argument q ∴ p is valid

Since we use deductions to demonstrate validity, we can now also demonstrate equivalence by the method of deduction:

Two sentences p and q are *equivalent* if there are *two* deductions: one deduction that starts with p and ends with q, and another deduction that starts with q and ends with p.

To demonstrate: P & (P ⊃ Q) is equivalent to P & Q

Deduction #1			*Deduction #2*	
1. P & (P ⊃ Q)	Prem		1. P & Q	Prem
2. P	1, Simp		2. P	1, Simp
3. P ⊃ Q	1, Simp		3. Q	1, Simp
4. Q	2,3, MP		4. ~P ∨ Q	3, Disj Add
5. P & Q	2,4, Conj		5. P ⊃ Q	4, Cond
			6. P & (P ⊃ Q)	2,5, Conj

To demonstrate: P is equivalent to (P & Q) ∨ (P & ~Q)

Deduction #1	*Deduction #2*
[We leave this as an exercise.	[We leave this as an exercise.
Hint: use the Dist Law.]	Hint: use the Dist Law.]

The next logical concern is the logical status of a single sentence, according to which a sentence is either a *truth of logic*, or a *contradiction*, or (whatever is left over) *neither* of these two. Let's start with the logical truths.

We already have the Rule of Logical Truth that identifies seven individual sentence patterns as being truths of logic, for example, (p & q) ⊃ p, and others. Such sentences may be introduced in a deduction at any point. They require no previous premisses from which they are derived, and no rule is cited as their justification, except that they are *themselves* laws of logic, and they can therefore cite themselves as their own justification, so that we may write as their reason, "logical truth." What about *other* sentences that are different from the given seven patterns? How do we show that they are truths of logic? We may extend the situation in the following way:

> If a sentence can be *derived* in a deduction *from nothing*, then that sentence is a *Truth of Logic*.

This means that (1) the deduction contains *no* premisses, and (2) the sentence does not occur as an item *inside* a Conditional Proof box or an Indirect Proof box, because then the sentence would depend on the Assumption step that begins such a box.

1. zero premisses	←	No premisses are allowed.
2. derived sentence	←	Because all these derived
3.		sentences do not depend on
4.		any premisses, nor on any
5. derived sentence	←	Assumption steps, all these
6. derived sentence	←	derived sentences have the
7. derived sentence	←	status of being a Truth of Logic.

If a deduction starts with *no* premisses, then how can there even be a deduction? Without any premisses, what can be the *next* step? A good question, and it points out how *special* these kinds of deductions are. There are two ways to get the next step.

Way #1. Just write one of the seven tautologies allowed by the Rule of Logical Truth.

1. zero premisses	start with nothing	
2. (A ⊃ B) ∨ ~(A ⊃ B)	Tautology	
3. (~A ∨ B) ∨ ~(A ⊃ B)	2, Cond	Each of these lines by
4. ~A ∨ [B ∨ ~(A ⊃ B)]	3, Assoc	itself has the status
5. ~A ∨ [~(A ⊃ B) ∨ B]	4, Comm	of a Truth of Logic.
6. [~A ∨ ~(A ⊃ B)] ∨ B	5, Assoc	
7. ~[A & (A ⊃ B)] ∨ B	6, DeMorg	
8. [A & (A ⊃ B)] ⊃ B	7, Cond	← Hey, that's a good one!

Most of the logical truths generated in this deduction are boring, and they are entered only to get to the next step. But the last one is actually interesting. It looks just like the rule Modus Ponens, except that it is a *single* "if then" sentence.

Way #2. Start with an Assumption step in a CP-box or an IP-box. When the box is closed, the sentence that is then introduced by the closure of the box is a sentence that depends on nothing, so that it has the status of a Truth of Logic.

1. zero premisses	start with nothing	
2. (K & R) & (K ⊃ S)	Assumption	
3. K	2, Simp	Lines 2–7 are
4. R	2, Simp	inside the box,
5. K ⊃ S	2, Simp	and so, are *not*
6. S	3,5, MP	Truths of Logic
7. R & S	4,6, Conj	
8. [(K & R) & (K ⊃ S)] ⊃ (R & S) 2—7, CP	← a Truth of Logic	

Notice that each of lines 2 through 7 is not a Truth of Logic because *none* of those lines have been derived from nothing. Line 2 is an assumption, and the other steps are all derived from that assumption. When the CP-box is closed, that box in effect disappears and is replaced by a conditional sentence. What *remains* of the deduction is a deduction whose only line is a Truth of Logic, one that depends on nothing.

The next logical concern is how one shows that a single sentence has the status of being a *contradiction*. Such a sentence is also said to be a *self-contradictory* sentence. The most *explicit* form of a contradiction is the form p & ~p. But other contradictions are *implicit* ones, in the sense that even though they do not have that explicit form, they are nevertheless self-contradictory, because an explicit contradiction p & ~p can be *derived* from them. So, *that* will be the criterion:

> Any sentence from which one can *derive* an explicit contradiction, p & ~p, has the status of being a *contradiction*. So, one must *start* with that sentence as the only premiss and then derive an explicit contradition as a *conclusion*.

To demonstrate: B & (B ⊃ G) & ~G is a contradiction.

1. B & (B ⊃ G) & ~G	Prem	←	Start with the sentence

2. B	1, Simp	
3. B ⊃ G	1, Simp	
4. ~G	1, Simp	
5. ~B	3,4, MT	
6. B & ~B	2,5, Conj	← End with a contradiction

The last logical concern is how one can show that a *group* of sentences is *inconsistent*. Inconsistency is simply a form of contradiction, but the contradiction does not characterize any individual sentence, but rather, it characterizes the group taken as a whole, when they are all asserted together. So, the criterion is as follows:

> A *group* of sentences is *inconsistent* if one can *derive* an explicit contradiction from the sentences in the group. So, one must *start* with all of the sentences in the group as the premisses and then derive an explicit contradiction as the *conclusion*.

To demonstrate: The four sentences A, B ∨ C, ~(A & B), ~(A & C) together form an inconsistent set.

1. A	Prem	←	Start with all of
2. B ∨ C	Prem	←	the sentences of
3. ~(A & B)	Prem	←	the set as they are
4. ~(A & C)	Prem	←	originally given

5. A & (B ∨ C)	1,2 Conj	
6. (A & B) ∨ (A & C)	5, Dist	
7. A & C	3,6, Disj Syll	
8. (A & C) & ~(A & C)	7,4, Conj	← End with a contradiction

It is, of course, the implicit nature of such contradictions that causes the concern. Explicit inconsistencies are so obvious that no one is likely to embrace them. But implicit inconsistencies are hidden, and they can more easily find a home in our thoughts, unless we are vigilant.

A Terminological Distinction

In this chapter we are studying Propositional Logic, which is a study of logic with respect to the *connective structure* of sentences. In chapters 3 and 4 we will study more detailed structures, including both connective structures and *subject–predicate structures*. If we consider *only* the connective structure of sentences (as in Chapter 2), then the various logical characteristics we have been studying, including validity, equivalence, logical truth, logical falsehood, consistency, and inconsistency, are called *truth-functional* validity, *truth-functional* equivalence, etc. (because the connectives involved have a truth-functional character). When *all types* of logical structures are considered, as in chapters 3 and 4, these logical characteristics are said to be characteristics *in the general sense*, and we speak of validity *in the general sense*, and consistency *in the general sense*, etc. There are, therefore, various distinctions and relationships between and among the various characteristics, truth-functional and general. For example (here we abbreviate "truth-functional" as "t-f"):

(a) t-f valid arguments form one subgroup of generally valid arguments

(b) generally invalid arguments form one subgroup of t-f invalid arguments

(c) t-f inconsistent sets form one subgroup of generally inconsistent sets

(d) generally consistent sets form one subgroup of t-f consistent sets

We illustrate (c) and (d) in the following diagram:

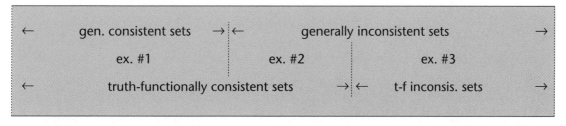

Example set #1: { some X are Y , some X are non-Y , some non-X are Y }

Example set #2: { all X are Y , all Y are Z , some X are non-Z }

Example set #3: { A , A ⊃ B , A ⊃ ~B }

Exercise 2.11. A,B,C,D Further Uses of Deductions

In the deductions below, you will find the following rules to be especially helpful: **Taut, CP, IP, Dist.**

Part A. Give deductions to show that the following listed pairs are equivalent. Use the available **Exercise Work Sheet** to submit your work.

1.   ~(D & H) , D ⊃ ~H
2.   S , (A ∨ ~A) ⊃ S
3.   M , [(M ∨ ~~M) & M] ∨ M
4.   ~Q & E , ~Q & (Q ∨ E)
5.   A ∨ (B & C) , (~B ⊃ A) & (~C ⊃ A)
6.   F ⊃ ~(G ∨ H) , (F ⊃ ~G) & (F ⊃ ~H)
7.   (P ∨ Q) ⊃ S , (P ⊃ S) & (Q ⊃ S)
8.   ~(W ∨ K) , ~K & [W ⊃ (H & ~H)]

Part B. Give deductions to show that the following sentences are truths of Logic, i.e., tautologies. Use the available **Exercise Work Sheet** to submit your work.

1.   (B ∨ S) ⊃ (~B ⊃ S)
2.   P ∨ (P ⊃ Q)
3.   (A & (B & C)) ∨ [A ⊃ (~B ∨ ~C)]
4.   (S & ~M) ⊃ (S ∨ M)
5.   (A & B & C) ⊃ (B ∨ Q)
6.   [(Q ⊃ U) & ~U] ⊃ ~Q
7.   [(P ∨ Q) & (P ⊃ R)] ⊃ (R ∨ Q)
8.   (A & B) ∨ (A & ~B) ∨ (~A & B) ∨ (~A & ~B)

Part C. Give deductions to show that the following sentences are contradictions. Use the available **Exercise Work Sheet** to submit your work.

1.   (B ∨ S) & (~B & ~S)
2.   (F ⊃ G) & (F & ~G)
3.   (S & ~M) & ~(S ∨ M)
4.   ~[P ∨ (P ⊃ Q)]
5.   ~[(A ∨ B) ∨ (~A ∨ C)]

6. A ≡ ~A

7. O & (O ⊃ P) & (P ⊃ R) & ~R

8. (A ∨ B) & (~A ∨ C) & (~B & ~C)

Part D. Give deductions to show that the following sets are inconsistent. Use the available **Exercise Work Sheet** to submit your work.

1. M ⊃ D , (D ∨ ~M) ⊃ S , ~S

2. A ∨ B , ~A ∨ C , ~B & ~C

3. W ≡ P , ~P , (A ∨ ~A) ⊃ W

4. ~(R & S) , ~(S & T) , S & (R ∨ T)

5. (A & B) , [(A & ~B) ∨ (B & ~A)]

6. (A ∨ B) ∨ C , A ⊃ C , C ⊃ ~C , B ≡ C

7. M ≡ ~N , N ≡ ~O , ~M ≡ O

8. (A ⊃ B) ⊃ A , (B ⊃ A) ⊃ ~A

CHAPTER 3

TRADITIONAL LOGIC

Section 3.1 Introduction: New Perspectives

In Chapter 2 we studied the patterns of *compound sentences* and their arrangements in arguments. These patterns focus on the overall *connective structure* that sentences and arguments have, structures consisting of the connectives ~, &, ∨, ⊃, ≡ , together with the symbols that represent simple sentences. Connective structure is a *high level* logical structure, because two sentences can have the same connective structure, for example, p ∨ q, even though they have significantly different logical structures at the *low level*. Chapter 3 will investigate the *low level* logical structure that all sentences have. Consider the argument:

1. Either all persons are moral agents, or no persons are moral agents.
2. Some persons are not moral agents.

So, all persons are not moral agents.

This argument is valid. (Even now, without yet having studied this kind of pattern, most of us are able, with some effort, to figure out how this argument is valid.) But one can easily see that the *connective* structure of this argument is *not* what makes it valid. Let's symbolize the argument with respect to its connective structure:

1. A ∨ B	where, A = "all persons are moral agents"
2. C	B = "no persons are moral agents"
∴ D	C = "some persons are not moral agents"
	D = "all persons are not moral agents"

This pattern fails to capture the logical relationships that are at play in the argument, because these relationships lie at a deeper level: these relationships also involve the arrangements of the parts that are *inside* the simple sentences A, B, C, D. As a preview of what we will study in this chapter, consider the more revealing pattern:

1. (all P are M) $\vee$ (no P are M)   where,
2. some P are not M   P = "person,"
∴ all P are not M   M = "moral agent"

We will have to wait to see how we can demonstrate that this argument is valid, but the new symbolization already gives some good hints how this is to be done.

The Greek philosopher Aristotle was the first formal logician. In the fourth century B.C.E. he introduced a system of formal logic that is still used to this day. This system now goes by different names: *Aristotelian Logic, Traditional Logic, Syllogistic Logic*. We will study this system next. In modern times, Traditional Logic came under criticism, mainly because it is inherently *limited* with regard to what sentences can be represented in it. By about 1950 another system of logic known as *Quantificational Logic* (also known as *Predicate Logic*) had become popular in university curriculums, right alongside Traditional Logic, and as a corrective to it. But Quantificational Logic, to this day, remains a rather technical and even impractical system, and as a result, Traditional Logic, in spite of its *limitations*, is still a favorite introduction to logic.

We need to make an important clarification. Traditional Logic, for all its merits, has always been presented in a peculiar manner, which, from a more contemporary perspective, makes the system less desirable. There is a problem with the *customary* way in which Traditional Logic is done. This customary approach consists of making many *technical distinctions* regarding the various ways that permissible arguments, called *categorical syllogisms*, can be composed. It is true that within this customary approach all these special, technical distinctions are necessary to get the job done. But, in the *new* deductive approach that we take, all these complicated distinctions are completely *unnecessary*, and in fact, they have no role to play at all. We mention these things now, to warn the readers that they should not expect to deal with these technical distinctions (see the note below), even though other logic books require them to do so.

Our treatment of Traditional Logic will *not* include these just-mentioned technical distinctions, for two important reasons. First of all, none of these distinctions are distinctions of *common sense*, and their employment, therefore, would promise to be an uphill battle. Secondly, all of these distinctions are completely *unnecessary* for the purpose of developing an easy and efficient system of syllogistic reasoning. Our purpose will be to present Traditional Logic as a *commonsense* system of deduction, a system that is complete and formal in the *style* of the deductive system for Propositional Logic. This system will apply not only to all simple categorical syllogisms (with just two premises and just three terms), but it will also apply to all syllogistic arguments with any number of premises, and thus involving any number of terms. Such a simplified deductive system, and one presented in simple, everyday terms, is absent from present-day treatments of Traditional Logic, and in this regard, then, our treatment is both unique and important.

[Note. Here is an outline of the details. They are stated here for possible future reference and comparison purposes only. The customary approach for Traditional Logic makes many special distinctions regarding the *composition* of categorical syllogisms, such as:

(1) identifying the *major, minor,* and *middle* terms of a syllogism,
(2) fixing the *major/minor* premiss order of a syllogism,
(3) finding the *distribution* of the terms of each sentence of a syllogism,
(4) dividing all categorical sentences into strict *types,*
(5) finding the *mood* of a syllogism, determined by its sentence types,
(6) finding the *figure* of a syllogism, determined by the premisses' term order,
(7) obeying five special *design rules* for syllogisms, involving these distinctions.

Remarkably, none of these five design rules are themselves laws of logic. The study of Traditional Logic has focused on these technical distinctions throughout its history, including the present time, with a great loss of opportunity to present a simple, elegant, and efficient system of deductive logic.]

Section 3.2 Categorical Sentences in Traditional Logic

When we introduced the language of Propositional Logic, we made a distinction between simple and compound sentences. Sentences are *compound* when they are grammatically constructed out of other sentences using special *sentence operators*. They are *simple* when they are not constructed out of other sentences using the special sentence operators. This led us to distinguish the following six types of sentences: simple sentences, ~p, p & q, p ∨ q, p ⊃ q, p ≡ q. In all of this, simple sentences themselves were left unanalyzed, and they were simply represented by individual capital letters. No longer. We now have a new purpose: to analyze the various complex structures that simple sentences themselves possess.

The Language of Traditional Logic

In Traditional Logic, simple sentences are usually called *categorical sentences*, and categorical sentences must have the following general form:

quantifier + term + copula + term

The *quantifier* together with the first *term* constitute the *subject side* of the sentence, and the *copula* together with the second *term* constitute the *predicate side* of the sentence, similar to the distinction made in regular English. In addition, these parts are defined very specifically as follows:

> *quantifiers*: all, some, no
>
> *copula*: are
>
> *terms*: expressions that represent a group of items, symbolized as:
>
> *affirmative terms*: A, B, C, D, E, . . .
>
> *negative terms*: non-A, non-B, non-C, non-D, non-E, . . .
>
> (not A), (not B), (not C), (not D), (not E), . . .

Some examples of categorical sentences are:

All animals are living things	= all A are L
Some red boxes are flexible containers	= some R are F
No bananas are made of gold	= no B are G
Some people under 20 are not things that can dance	= some P are non-D

The notion of a term is one that we have not used before. A *term* is a word or phrase that *describes* a group of things. Such a group may consist of physical things, like the group of all the cats that live in Paris, or it may consist of non-physical things, like numbers, ideas, and feelings. English expressions that count as terms are nouns, adjectives, noun phrases, and adjective phrases. Examples are:

	Symbolization
• elephant	E
• poisonous	P
• book with hard covers	H
• even number greater than 10	N
• red car	R
• red car owned by someone in Chicago	O
• red car in Chicago owned by Madonna	M
• billionaire that lives on the Moon	B
• non-elephant	non-E
• thing that does not swim or fly	non-S

One can see right away that term expressions *in English* have a considerable amount of structure, but in Traditional Logic there is *not* a corresponding *logical* structure for terms. For example, the expression "red and square box" is constructed out of three words that are themselves terms—"red," "square," "box"—and one *might* have expected it to be symbolized something like "(R & S) & B." But that is *not* how it is done in Traditional Logic.

Traditional Logic *is not capable* of analyzing the structure of complex terms, with the one exception of *negative terms*. This is important. *All* terms, regardless of their complexity, are symbolized by a single capital letter, *except* for negative terms; they are symbolized by applying the term operator "non-" or "not" to a capital letter, and in the second case, enclosing it all in parentheses.

It is important that we represent *negative terms* in an explicit manner. Negations may never be hidden. When an expression has the meaning of being the negation of some affirmative term, say T, then it must be construed as the negative term, non-T. Sometimes these terms will sound artificial, but negative terms are quite common in English, though they often use variations on the "non-" operator, as in: *ir*responsible, *im*mortal, *un*usual, *in*active, *il*legal, *a*symmetric, and so on.

Some plants are inorganic	some P are non-O
Some items are non-electronic	some I are non-E
Some organizations are not-for-profit	some O are non-P
Some customs are unusual	some C are non-U
Some foods are nonfattening	some F are non-F
Some books are not available	some B are (not A)

Types of Categorical Sentences

The various simple sentences that can be constructed in this new logical grammar are called *categorical sentences*. There are actually twelve different types of these, since there are three quantifiers, two types of subject terms, and two types of predicate terms. That gives a total of $3 \times 2 \times 2 = 12$ types of sentences:

$$\left.\begin{array}{c}\text{all}\\\text{some}\\\text{no}\end{array}\right\} \;+\; \left\{\begin{array}{l}\text{affir. term}\\\text{neg. term}\end{array}\right\} \;+\; \text{are} \;+\; \left\{\begin{array}{l}\text{affir. term}\\\text{neg. term}\end{array}\right.$$

Here are examples of these types using the terms "A" = "apples" and "B" = "blue":

all A are B	some A are B	no A are B
all non-A are B	some non-A are B	no non-A are B
all A are non-B	some A are non-B	no A are non-B
all non-A are non-B	some non-A are non-B	no non-A are non-B

So, these twelve sentences are the kinds of things that one can say in Traditional Logic. Just these twelve. This is a very manageable number of patterns. And it gets better: the *logic* of Traditional Logic is even simpler than these twelve patterns. All the rules of Traditional

Logic are formulated with just *four general sentence patterns*. (Actually, there are *five* patterns here, but two are equivalent and are treated as the same). These general categorical patterns are:

> all **S** are **P**
>
> all **S** are non-**P** = no **S** are **P**
>
> some **S** are **P**
>
> some **S** are non-**P**

These patterns have a very wide range, because here the letters "**S**" and "**P**" are used as *variables* and represent all terms whatsoever—both affirmative terms and negative terms. You can see that by using these variables we are able to represent all twelve patterns listed above. These general categorical patterns are often displayed in the form of a square, also known as *the Square of Opposition*:

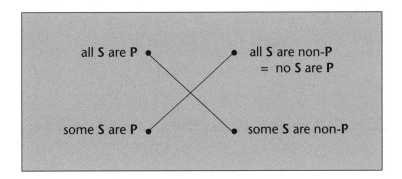

[A historical note. Contrary to our own approach, the customary approach for Traditional Logic actually recognizes *two* copulas instead of one. It counts both "are" and "are not" as copulas, generating thereby extra forms of categorical sentences. Strangely however, the customary approach also considers *some* of these extra forms to be *inferior* and not permitted. In particular, the negative copula is not permitted with the quantifiers "all" and "no," but it is permitted with the quantifier "some." So, the customary approach adds to the list of categorical sentences, all sentences of the form, "some **S** (are not) **P**," with the following distinction: a sentence "some **S** (are not) **P**" is different in form, but identical in meaning to "some **S** are non-**P**."

Well, as it turns out, adding the extra copula "are not" adds an unacceptable degree of complication to the entire exposition of Traditional Logic, and it does so *without* any real benefit. For this reason our own approach will *not* permit the addition of the negative copula. You may have noticed, of course, that our second way of writing negative terms, ". . . are (not **P**)," is a *compromise* of sorts, on this very point.]

Translating English Sentences into Categorical Form

To help us better manage these new logical patterns, we will initially use a practical technique for analyzing and symbolizing English sentences with respect to their categorical form.

Step 1. We first make sure that the sentence in question is worded in such a way that it is in categorical form: a quantifier, followed by a term, followed by a copula, followed by a term. If the original sentence is not in categorical form, then it is our task to reword the sentence in such a way that it is in categorical form.

Step 2. Superimpose brackets [ ] around the subject term expression and around the predicate term expression. The result will be: quantifer [term] copula [term].

Step 3. Replace the terms *and* brackets by an appropriate capital letter.

Here are some examples:

- original sent.:   Every person in the room was yelling and screaming loudly.
- analysis: All [persons in the room] are [loud yellers and screamers]
- symbolization: All R are L

- original sent.:   Some cat that was sitting on the sofa meowed.
- analysis: Some [cats that are sitting on the sofa] are [meowers]
- symbolization: Some C are M

- original sent.:   All non-emplyees of SilCo are not insured by AllSafe.
- analysis: All [non-employes of SilCo] are [not insured by AllSafe]
- symbolization: All non-E are non-I , or
                      All non-E are (not I)

We will spend a lot of time in the next section learning how to turn ordinary English sentences, of a wide variety, into sentences that are in categorical form. But already here we must stress that the requirements of categorical form are *unforgiving*, in that no deviations are permitted. Ironically, the great benefit of having commonsense symbolism ("all," "some," "no," "are") fights against itself to some extent, because it invites people to blur the distinction between precise logical symbolism and everyday speech. In the next exercise, for example, you must make sure that the copula "are" is the *only* "verb" in the reconstructed sentence. In particular, sentences about the past, or future, must be recast by using the *logical* copula "are," and English copulas like "were" or "will be" are just plain *illegal*. And the quantifiers are equally strict.

Exercise 3.2. A,B Categorical Form

Part A: For each of the following sentences, (1) rewrite the sentence so that it is in categorical form; (2) put brackets "[ ]" around the subject term and the predicate term; and (3) symbolize the sentence, using the indicated capital letters for the bracketed terms. Remember to use the operator "non-" or "(not . . .)" for English negative terms. Use the available **Exercise Work Sheet** to submit your work.

0.   Each person is an artist. (P, A):   all [persons] are [artists] ,   all P are A
1.   All bananas are unsalted. (B, S)
2.   Some brightly colored snakes are poisonous. (B, P)
3.   Some contestants will be happy winners. (C, H)
4.   All ancient Greek philosophers were materialists. (A, M)
5.   No animals were injured in the making of the film. (A, I)
6.   Every automobile has an engine. (A, E)
7.   Some students are ineligible for a loan. (S, E)
8.   Some non-students are eligible for a loan. (S, E)
9.   No non-students are ineligible for a loan. (S, E)
10.   All trees are not inorganic. (T, O)
11.   There are people that climb mountains. (P, C)
12.   There are no people that can fly. (P, F)

Part B. With respect to the requirements for categorical form, find the errors in each of the sentences below. Use the error codes "Q," "S," "C," "P" to indicate if an error is made in the quantifier (Q), in the subject term (S), in the copula (C), or in the predicate term (P). Most, but not all of the sentences make one or more errors. Use the available **Exercise Work Sheet** to submit your work.

0.   Many [cities] have [large skyscrapers]   <u>Q, C, P</u>
1.   Each [persons who take logic] are [careful thinkers]
2.   Some [old books] in the library are [dusty books] that no one reads
3.   Some [students at Loyola] will get [their Ph.D. from Oxford]
4.   No [visitors to Chicago] are [not people impressed by the view of the lake]
5.   Some of the [cars at the exhibition] were [made out of plastic]
6.   Any [persons that can sing well] are [not persons likely to get rich]
7.   No [animals in the Lincoln Park Zoo] are unable [to be set free]
8.   None [who are naturalized citizens] can be [presidents of the U.S.]

9.   All [fish that are fish that are able to fish] are [fish that are fishing fish]

10.   [Students who take logic] are [students likely to get into law school]

11.   No [books that] are [Inexpensive do not cost a lot of money]

12.   Somethings [sitting in the attic] are [scary old skeletons]

Section 3.3 English Variations on Categorical Forms

The aim of logic is to provide a set of formal principles for correct reasoning. Such principles can then be used to guide and evaluate the inferences we make in our everyday discussions and writings. Traditional Logic is a system that focuses on certain kinds of patterns that are called *categorical forms*, and we have already dealt with sentences that are in categorical form. One problem. Most of the sentences that we commonly use are not in categorical form, and they cannot therefore be used in Traditional Logic—at least, as long as they remain in such non-categorical form. But we can manage this obstacle. Many of the sentences we use can be *reworded* so as to turn them into categorical form. There is no precise translation list, but there are a number of very useful *translation rules*, and even beyond such rules, we can rely to some extent on our commonsense understanding of our language to make the necessary adjustments. (It must be admitted that there are some inherent limitations to Traditional Logic with respect to its ability to capture certain complex types of reasoning, and for those types of inferences we will need to go to another part of logic, presented in Chapter 4. But it remains a fact that Traditional Logic is just the right system for the *bulk* of ordinary reasoning.) Our first task, then, is to learn how to re-write regular English sentences so that they will be in the required categorical form.

1. Some Simple Variations

The following lists are easy variations on the three standard quantifiers "all," "some," and "no." These variations are more easily recognized and learned when they are presented in *schematic* English form.

all snakes are pink	*some snakes are pink*	*no snakes are pink*
all S are P	*some S are P*	*no S are P*
every S is P	at least one S is P	all S are not P
each S is P	there are P S	not any S are P
any S is P	there are S that are P	there are no S that are P
whatever is a S is P	P S exist	S that are P don't exist
if anything is a S, it is P	S that are P exist	nothing is a S and P
if something is S, it is P	something is a S and P	none [of them] are P
if you're a S, you're P	A few S are P	(where S refers to "them")

2. Plural vs. Singular has no Logical Significance

One can easily observe that sentences that use the plural construction can be written in the singular construction without loss of meaning, and the reverse is equally true. There is therefore no logical distinction between the singular and plural constructions. In Traditional Logic the plural construction has been selected (arbitrarily) to be the *standard* form for representing sentences.

some person is smart	= some persons are smart	= some P are S
every house is expensive	= all houses are expensive	= all H are E
no problem is difficult	= no problems are difficult	= no P are D

3. Past and Future Become Present Tense

Most ordinary sentences are stated in the present tense, the past tense, or the future tense; that is, the verb indicates an action in the present, in the past, or in the future. But what is very useful in the analysis of arguments is that one can just *ignore* the tenses of sentences. For the most part, one can correctly display the logical form of an argument *without* representing the tenses of the sentences that make up the argument. In logic, sentences are considered to be stated in what is sometimes called "the eternal present." Consider the following examples:

All things that are born are mortal.

All my cat's kittens *were* born.

So, all my cat's kittens are mortal.

B = born, things that are born; M = mortal; C = kittens of my cat.

all [things that are born] are [mortal]	= all B are M
all [kittens of my cat] are [born]	= all C are B
So, all [kittens of my cat] are [mortal]	= so, all C are M

Some Romans (such as Julius Caesar) *were* shapers of history.

All shapers of history are responsible for what happens in history.

So, some Romans *were* responsible for what happens in history.

R = Romans; S = shapers of history; H = responsible for what happens in history.

some [Romans] are [shapers of history]	= some R are S
all [shapers of history] are [resp. for what happens in history]	= all S are H
So, some [Romans] are [resp. for what happens in history]	= so, some R are H

4. Verbs become Copulas with some Adjustment

One of the most obvious differences between ordinary English sentences and sentences that are in categorical form is that ordinary sentences have verbs other than the copula "are." But there is an easy translation, even if it is grammatically frightening: simply put a hyphen between all the words of the *entire* predicate side of the sentence, and turn that monstrosity into a noun by appending the transformer "-*ers*." This actually works! So, "sing" becomes "are sing*ers*," and "jumped over the fence" becomes "are jumped-over-the-fence-*ers*," or a little better, "are jump*ers*-over-the-fence."

All cats like to sleep	= all cats are likers-of-sleep	= some P are L
No snails move fast	= no snails are fast-movers	= no S are C
All cars have wheels	= all cars are wheeled	= all C are W
No books have no pages	= no books are non-paged	= no B are non-P

One can also use a *second* translation rule:

> Put the phrase *"things that"* in front of the English predicate expression

So, there are two ways to handle English verb phrases:

> Some people like to spend money
>
> = Some people are [lik*ers* of spending money]
>
> = Some people are [*things that* like to spend money]

Regardless of which of these two rules one uses, one must always treat *negative expressions* in the required way, by using the negative term operator "non-" or "(not . . .)." One may never "bury" a negation when it is available. For example,

> Some people do not like to spend money

• Some people are [things that do not like to spend money]	???
Some P are M	WRONG
• Some people are [do-not-like-to-spend-money-ers]	???
Some P are M	WRONG
• Some people are [not things that like to spend money]	YES!
Some P are (not L)	GOOD
• Some people are [non-things-that-like-to-spend-money]	YES!
Some P are non-L	GOOD
• Some people are [non-likers-of-money-spending]	YES!
Some P are non-L	GOOD

5. Adjectives become Terms

There are two methods that one may use to translate adjectives into term expressions. These methods produce results that have exactly the same meaning, and both methods are equally acceptable.

> *Method 1*. Add the noun "things" to the adjective.
>
> *Method 2*. Adjectives are treated as terms, and they are left unchanged.

Method 1	*Method 2*
All snakes are poisonous	All snakes are poisonous
All [snakes] are [poisonous *things*]	All [snakes] are [poisonous]
All S are P	All S are P

Note that the *same* capital letter is used to symbolize *both* the phrase "poisonous thing" and the adjective "poisonous." We are allowed to do this because these two expressions have exactly the *same* meaning. Adding the word "things" keeps the meaning the same.

But, by the same reasoning, we can see that it is a *mistake* to add a noun that is *different* from the noun "things," because a different noun will give the reworded phrase a more restricted meaning than the original meaning:

> *Wrong method*. Add the noun from the subject term to the adjective.
>
> All snakes are poisonous
> All [snakes] are [poisonous *snakes*]
> All S are P

Here the original adjective "poisonous" describes a very large group of things, but the reworded phrase "poisonous snakes" describes a much smaller group of things. This change in meaning shows that there was a translation mistake. And this mistake will correspondingly assign an invalid form to many valid arguments:

Method 2 (no changes)	*Arg form is valid*
Some [snakes] are [poisonous]	Some S are P
No [good pets] are [poisonous]	No G are P
So, Some [snakes] are [not good pets]	So, some S are (not G)

Wrong method (repeat the subject)	*Arg form has become invalid*
Some [snakes] are [poisonous snakes]	Some S are Q
No [good pets] are [poisonous pets]	No G are R [can't use Q again!]
So, Some [snakes] are [not good pets]	So, some S are (not G)

6. The Missing Quantifier

It is very normal for a sentence not to have a quantifier. But we must consider this absence to be a feature of the customary, "surface" grammar, not of the deeper logical grammar. Missing quantifiers are a convenient shortcut: Why say "all" or "some," when the rest of the sentence *also* gives that information? Still, logic must be exact, and logic must have its quantifers.

Birds sing	= all birds are singers	= all B are S
Cars have wheels	= all cars are wheeled	= all C are W
Elephants have a trunk	= all elephants are trunked	= all E are T
Airplanes float on air	= all airplanes are air-floaters	= all A are F
Pigs cannot fly	= all pigs are non-flyers	= all P are non-F
Birds sat on the fence	= some birds are fence-sitters	= some B are S
Cars hit the wall	= some cars are the-wall-hitters	= some C are W
Elephants trumpeted	= some elephants are trumpeters	= some E are T
Planes flew overhead	= some planes are fliers-over-us	= some A are F

An amazing difference! Did you figure it out? It's all about the predicate. Here's the rule (and you won't find this in other books):

Rule of translation for the missing quantifier:

If the action of the *verb* of the English sentence has a *restriction* in either space or time, then the missing quantifier is replaced by the quantifier "some."

If the action of the *verb* of the English sentence has *no restriction* in space, nor in time, then the missing quantifier is replaced by the quantifier "all."

7. The "A" Quantifier

There is a similar situation with the "a" quantifier. The regular quantifier is missing, and in its place is the quantifier "a."

A bird sings	= all birds are singers	= all B are S
A car has wheels	= all cars are wheeled	= all C are W
An elephant has a trunk	= all elephants are trunked	= all E are T
An airplane floats on air	= all airplanes are air-floaters	= all A are F
A bird sat on the fence	= some birds are fence-sitters	= some B are S
A car hit the wall	= some cars are the-wall-hitters	= some C are W
An elephant trumpeted	= some elephants are trumpeters	= some E are T
A plane flew overhead	= some planes are fliers-over-us	= some A are F
A bird is singing (now)	= some birds are singing now	= some B are S

Interestingly enough, the rule that governs these cases is the same rule as before. Amazing! It is quite unexpected that a natural grammar should behave in this way.

Rule of translation for the "a" quantifier:

If the action of the verb of the English sentence has a restriction in either space or time, then the "a" quantifier is replaced by the quantifier "some."

If the action of the verb of the English sentence has no restriction in space, nor in time, then the "a" quantifier is replaced by the quantifier "all."

A word of caution. Logic books often recommend that we take an *intuitive* approach in reconstructing a missing quantifier or the "a" quantifier, with the following possible outcomes:

(1) if the sentence *feels* like a *generic* description, then the quantifier is "all;"

(2) if the sentence *feels* like a *limited* description, then the quantifier is "some;"

(3) if the sentence *feels ambiguous*, then one must supply *both* possible versions.

In part this is good advice, although we have improved on (1) and (2), but part (3) is making a *mistake*. We already addressed this issue at the end of Section 2.3, where we noted that a written sentence has a *default* meaning. The mere fact that a *spoken* sentence *can* have a special meaning, by the special way it is spoken, does not in any way change the fact that a written sentence, one that is *not* spoken with a special meaning, has its default meaning. The sentence, "A bird sings," when *spoken*, may be spoken in the following ways:

(a) "Well, of course! A bird sings, as we have all experienced." Here, the special way that the sentence is spoken creates a special meaning for that spoken sentence, namely: all birds sing.

(b) "Oh, listen, can you hear it? A bird sings. What joy!" Here, the special way that the sentences is spoken creates a special meaning for that spoken sentence, namely: some bird is singing *here* and *now*.

But, the written sentence, "A bird sings," has its (one-and-only) default meaning: all birds sing.

8. The "Any" Quantifier

The quantifier "any" is a (super-duper) universal quantifier, but care must be taken when the quantifier is modfied by a negation operator. When a negation is present, do *not* just replace the word "any" by "all." Use the following rule:

Rule of translation for the "any" quantifier:

If a sentence contains the word "any," rewrite the sentence so that the *first* word is "all," and then finish the sentence, while preserving the meaning.

Any car has wheels	=	all cars . . .	YES
		all cars are wheeled	YES
Any novice can do this	=	all novices . . .	YES
		all novices are able to do this	YES
Not any car is cheap	= ?	not all cars . . .	NO! NO! NO!
		not all cars are cheap	WRONG
Not any car is cheap	=	all cars . . .	YES
		all cars are (not cheap)	YES

Of course, as we pointed out in Rule 1 above, an alternative way to translate the phrase "not any" is to use the "no" quantifier:

Not any car is cheap   =   no cars are cheap

This second way way of translating "not any" makes it very clear that "not all" is the *wrong* translation, because:

Not all cars are cheap   =   *some* cars are not cheap

So, for "not any" there are *two correct* translations you can choose from. Take your pick. There is also *one wrong* translation. Don't take that one.

9. The "Only" Quantifier

The "only" quantifier is more complicated. Let's compare the following two sentences to see whether they mean the same thing:

* Only elephants have trunks   [Start here.]
* All elephants have trunks   [Is this the same ? NO! Not even close!]

Clearly, these sentences are *not* the same in meaning. The first sentence *actually* says that dogs, and cats, people, ants, etc. do *not* have trunks. That was the whole point: *only* elephants have 'em. But the second sentence says nothing about dogs and cats: "Yeah, all elephants have 'em. I wonder what else does." See the difference? This tells us what the translation rule should be. There are *two* good versions.

Version 1: Only elephants have trunks = all *non*-elephants are *non*-trunked

Version 2: Only elephants have trunks = all trunked things are elephants

The second version follows from the first one by the Contraposition equivalence for universal-affirmative sentences, which we will study shortly. But even now, we can see that the second version works. "Look at that! That thing has a trunk! So, it must be an elephant, because *only* elephants have trunks." The translation rule is therefore as follows:

Version 1: Only F are G = all non-F are non-G

Version 2: Only F are G = all G are F   [the "flip" version]

WRONG: Only F are G ≠ all F are G

10. "One" and "Body" Subjects

English has dedicated words such as "everyone," "someone," "no one," "anyone," as well as "everybody," "somebody," "nobody," "anybody," all of which are used to refer to *persons*. You must be careful *not* to introduce a subject term "one," abbreviated by "O," or a subject term "body," abbreviated by "B," because such an analysis would be conceptually confused. What groups could these terms possibly represent? The group of Ones? The group of Bodies? In addition, these awkward terms will also break any *connection* the sentence has with *other* sentences containing the term "person." So, in all these cases, you must use "P" for the group of *persons*. Consider the argument:

original argument	*incorrect analysis*	*valid pattern*
Everybody is born with a soul	all B are S	all P are S
Things with souls are immortal	all S are non-M	all S are non-M
So, everyone is immortal	So, all O are non-M	So, all P are non-M

The initial analysis was incorrect, because the deeper connection between the sentences was lost. Clearly, the term letter "P" should replace the letters "B" and "O," so that throughout we are referring to *persons*. When this is done, the argument is easily seen to be valid.

11. Combined Subjects

Some sentences have a *combined subject*, which is a grammatical subject that is a *combination* of two subjects. Consider,

All dogs and cats have tails

= all D and C are T   ??   [NO! No way!]

The proposed analysis "All D and C are T" is *not allowed*. The symbolized sequence is not a categorical sentence. It is not a permitted sequence of symbols (in Traditional Logic), because the expression "D and C" is not permitted as a term. Terms are *single* capital letters. All this would suggest the following analysis:

$\quad$ = All Q are T   ??

This representation is properly formed, but it is nevertheless *inadequate* for two reasons. (1) What meaning can the term "Q" have here? What group of things can this term represent? Could it be the group of all things that are *both* dogs *and* cats? Wait a minute! The group of all things that are *simultaneously* dogs *and* cats? Holy smoking tobacco! Now, whether or not there are such strangely combined creatures in nature, it was surely *not* the intention of the original sentence to talk about *them*. (2) The original sentence clearly *says* that all dogs have tails, and it also clearly *says* that all cats have tails. But neither of these clear assertions is represented by the proposed analysis "all Q are T." Actually, this last point suggests how the sentence should be analyzed.

Combinations are superficial approximations of a deeper level of complexity. Good style and convenience have led us to combine longer, separated thoughts into shorter abbreviations. It is the job of the analyzer to retrieve and to display the original logical form of our thoughts. In the example at hand, that original form is:

$\quad$ All dogs have tails, *and* all cats have tails $\quad$ = (all D are T) & (all C are T)

Other examples now easily fall into place:

$\quad$ Students and teachers learn all the time $\quad$ = (all S are L) & (all T are L)

$\quad$ Broccoli and spinach are rich in vitamins $\quad$ = (all B are V) & (all S are V)

$\quad$ Books and papers covered the desk $\quad$ = (some B are C) & (some P are C)

12. Quantification in the Predicate

Many English sentences have patterns that are more complicated than the patterns of categorical form. But in some cases we can handle this complexity by means of a certain trick. This trick cannot be described by the ideas that define categorical form, and so we must appeal here to our *intuitive* understanding of these patterns. The trick involves switching back and forth between, what is known as, the *active* and *passive* voice of a sentence. When the switch is made, a quantified expression that occurs in the predicate becomes the quantified subject, and such results can then be reworded in categorical form. Here are some examples.

I ate some donuts	= some donuts are eaten-by-me	= some D are E
Sue hates all cats	= all cats are hated-by-Sue	= all C are H
Chicago has trees	= some trees are in-Chicago	= some T are C

13. Dealing with the Absolute Term "Thing"

Some sentences have as their *entire* subject term the word "thing," or "things." We call such sentences, *absolute* sentences. Absolute sentences have a special logical status, and to display this status we will *not* symbolize the subject "thing" by a capital letter, but we will leave the word in English and underline it. In (modern) English the quantifier can also be combined with the word "thing" to form a single compound quantifier-subject word, as is the case with "everything," "something," "nothing." Categorical form requires, of course, that we separate the quantifier from the subject term. We display this separation in Case 1 below.

Problems arise with English *complex terms*. All term expressions must be symbolized by a *single* term letter, with the result that logical connections that exist at the level of regular English are lost at this simplified symbolic level. (The exception to this is that negative terms are also symbolized by using the negative term operator.) We can remedy the situation to some extent by *restating* the original English sentence as another English sentence that has the same meaning and that is in categorical form. Four such sentences have an easy translation rule, as given in Case 2 below.

Case 1. Separate the quantifier from the word "thing."

Everything is A	→	all *things* are A
Nothing is A	→	no *things* are A
Something is A	→	some *things* are A
Something is not A	→	some *things* are (not A)

Case 2. When the English predicate is as indicated, reword as follows:

Something is B A	→	some A are B = some B are A
Nothing is B A	→	no A are B = no B are A
Everything is B, if it is A	→	all A are B
Nothing is B, if it is A	→	no A are B

Consider now the following argument.

Something is an indestructible force.
Whatever is indestructible is eternal.
So, something is an eternal force.

Inadequate analysis	*symbolization*
Some *things* are [indestructible-forces]	= some *things* are Q
All non-[destructible things] are [eternal]	= all non-D are E
So, some *things* are [eternal-forces]	= So, some *things* are W

It is pretty obvious that this analysis, while it makes no mistakes, completely misses the logical connections at work in the argument. Since the terms are all different, all different capital letters had to be used, and the resulting symbolic pattern is invalid. But if we judiciously reword the argument using the above rules, then we can display the argument in a form that is very clearly valid.

Good analysis	*symbolization*
Some [forces] are non-[destructible things]	= some F are non-D
All non-[destructible things] are [eternal]	= all non-D are E
So, some [forces] are [eternal]	= So, some F are E

14. Combined Quantifiers

On previous occasions we have considered combined English expressions. These combinations make their appearance at a surface level of grammar, but they correspond to *uncombined* items at the deeper level of logical grammar. Another such case is combinations of *quantifiers*. These combinations are "all and only" and "some but not all," as well as some variations on the latter. For all combinations, our method of analysis is always to restate the combined expression in its original uncombined doubled form.

1. **"all and only"**
   All and only elephants have trunks
   (all elephants have trunks) & (only elephants have trunks)
   (all E are T) & (all T are E)

2. **"some but not all"**
   Some, but not all, students will graduate
   (some students will graduate) & not (all students will graduate)
   (some S are G) & not (all S are G)
   = (some S are G) & (some S are (not G))

3. **Variations on "some but not all"**

some, but not all	Some, but not all, people dance
= some are, some aren't	= Some people dance; some don't
= a few are	= A few people dance
= only some are	= Only some people dance
= *some* are	= *Some* people dance [special emphasis required]
= not *all* are	= Not *all* people dance [special emphasis required]

15. Quantification over Times and Places

There are certain English words that are *time quantifiers*, and ones that are *place quantifiers*: "always," "never," "sometimes," "whenever," "everywhere," "nowhere," "somewhere," "wherever," and some others. One complication: time quantifier words are sometimes used as thing quantifiers rather than as time quantifiers, as in, for example, "Cats are never retrievers," which simply means "No cats are retrievers." But apart from that deviation, these words have the function of referring to times and places, and these words become *both* the *quantifier* and the *subject term* of a categorical sentence. We illustrate these quantifications in the following examples.

1. **Over Times**

Whenever it rains, it is dark	= all [times when it rains] are [dark times]
When it rained, it was dark	= some [times when it rained] are [dark times]
The Sun always shines	= all [times] are [times when the Sun shines]
Joe never says hello	= no [times] are [times when Joe says hello]
Sometimes Sue studies	= some [times] are [times when Sue studies]

2. **Over Places**

Where cows are, flies are	= all [places with cows] are [places with flies]
Where ants were, we sat	= some [places with ants] are [places we sat in]
You find bugs everywhere	= all [places you look] are [places with bugs]
Nowhere are there elves	= no [places] are [places with elves]
Somewhere stars explode	= some [places] are [places where stars explode]
Some places have junk	= some [places] are [places with junk]

When we analyze sentences with time quantifiers in this way, we can easily demonstrate the validity of a whole class of arguments made up of such sentences.

T = times;   S = times when Alex studies hard;
H = times when Alex gets a headache

Sometimes Alex studies hard.	= some T are S
Whenever he studies hard he gets a headache	= all S are H
So, sometimes Alex gets a headache.	= so, some T are H

16. Complexity Beyond Categorical Sentences

We should not forget that there are patterns of inference that involve *sentence connectives*, the ones we studied back in Chapter 2. These patterns are of a different kind than the categorical patterns we are studying now. But these extra patterns present no problem at all. The entire language of Propositional Logic is available for our use, because that language is a *foundational* part of all the levels of logic. Sentences such as the following are easily symbolized, as we have done:

> If some animals talk, then some animals have a mind
>
> = (some A are T) ⊃ (some A are M)

> Either every person has a mind, or no person has a mind
>
> = (all P are M) ∨ (no P are M)

And of course, these sentences can be manipulated by such propositional rules as Modus Ponens: p ⊃ q, p ∴ q , or the Disjunctive Syllogism: p ∨ q, ~p ∴ q .

There are still *other* kinds of patterns that go beyond the patterns of Traditional Logic and Propositional Logic. These patterns involve a complex structure *inside* the subject term and *inside* the predicate term (like atoms inside molecules). To deal fully with these other patterns we have to go to a new part of logic, and we do that in Chapter 4. Yet even here, we already have a special resource available—logical truths.

Consider the following argument. The predicate term of the premiss has a complex structure that relates to the predicate of the conclusion, but we are not able to symbolize that relationship.

> Some person knows all future events.
> So, some person knows what will happen tomorrow.

> Some [persons] are [knowers-of-all-future-events]   = some P are F
> So, some [persons] are [knowers-of-tomorrow's-events] = some P are T

Even though we are not able to symbolize the internal structure of the two predicate terms, we are allowed to enlist the aid of *logical truths* to display the implicit logical relationship. Admittedly, at this point, within the system of Traditional Logic, we have no formal way of demonstrating that the sentences we are introducing are in fact logical truths. We are relying here only on an intuitive understanding of the meaning of the sentences at issue. So, the following sentence is a logical truth, and because it is, we are allowed to add it along with the premisses:

all [knowers-of-all-future-events] are [knowers-of-tomorrow's-events]
= all F are T   [a logical truth]

Now, when we symbolize the original argument and add this logical truth, we can see a pattern that is obviously valid:

some P are F   original premiss
all F are T   added premiss (logical truth)

_____

So, some P are T   conclusion

Exercise 3.3. A,B More Categorical Translations

Part A. For each of the following sentences, (1) rewrite the sentence so that it is in categorical form; (2) put brackets "[ ]" around the subject term and the predicate term; and (3) symbolize the sentence, using the indicated capital letters for the bracketed terms. (These are a bit more difficult.) Use the available **Exercise Work Sheet** to submit your work.

1.   Ghosts roam these halls. (G, R)
2.   A very old map is quite valuable. (M, V)
3.   Some artistic works have no value. (A, V)
4.   Guys like to explore rugged places. (G, E)
5.   Some things that have wings cannot fly. (W, F)
6.   Some animals that have wings are birds that cannot fly. (A,B)
7.   Non-college students visited the campus yesterday. (C,V)
8.   A person who is angry is not rational. (P, R)
9.   Non-philosophers always have a good time. (P, G)
10. Nothing round is square. (R, S)
11. Only tigers have stripes. (T, S)
12. Not any person knows the secret password. (P, K)

Part B. For each of the following sentences, (1) rewrite the sentence so that it is in categorical form; (2) put brackets "[ ]" around the subject term and the predicate term; and (3) symbolize the sentence, using the indicated capital letters for the bracketed terms. (These are also more difficult.) Use the available **Exercise Work Sheet** to submit your work.

1. Whosoever loves gold, loves death. (G, D)
*2. Whatever you do, you cannot stop time. (A, S)

3. Insects exist everywhere. (P, I)

4. There are people who think they are divine. (P, T)

*5. Bureaucrats never work. (B, W)

6. Sometimes people are nasty. (P, N)

*7. People are sometimes nasty. (P, N)

8. Forgeries were found in the Art Institute. (F, A)

9. Not anyone showed up. (P, S)

10. A picture is worth a thousand words. (P, W)

11. Forgeries are fake works intended for deception. (F,W)

12. A statue of a sitting mermaid stands by the harbor. (M,S)

13. A statue of a sitting mermaid is delightful. (M, D)

*14. There are things that do not breathe that need oxygen. (B,O)

15. A group of people barged into the office. (P, B)

16. No rare books are without value. (R, V)

*17. Only senior executives have executive pension plans. (S,P)

18. Only professionals are ineligible. (P, E)

19. Only non-professionals are eligible. (P, E)

*20. Whenever the lights go out, things get real quiet. (T,Q)

*21. Well of course, *all* snakes are not poisonous. (S, P)

22. There are no good deeds that go unpunished. (G,P)

23. Cars that do not use gasoline exist. (C, U)

*24. Undetectable physical things do not exist. (P, D)

Answers to the starred problems of **Part B**.

2.	All [actions] are [not able to stop time].	All A are (not S)
5.	No [bureaucrats] are [workers].	No B are W
7.	All [persons] are [sometimes nasty].	All P are N
14.	Some [things that do *not* breathe] are [oxygen needers].	Some non-B are O
17.	All [havers of executive pension plans] are [senior executives].	All P are S
20.	All [times when the lights go out] are [times things get quiet].	All T are Q
21.	Not all [snakes] are [poisonous].	~(all S are P)
24.	No [physical things] are [*un*-detectable].	No P are non-D

Section 3.4 Venn Diagrams for Categorical Sentences

The formal structure of categorical sentences can be represented by certain diagrams known as *Venn diagrams*. A Venn diagram for a categorical sentence consists of two overlapping circles, one for the subject term of the sentence and one for the predicate term. Each circle is a graphic picture of the group of things that the term in question stands for. We require that the circles will *always* represent *affirmative terms*. These overlapping circles are then *marked up* to represent the content and the logical relationship of the two terms, as asserted by the categorical sentence. There are four ways to mark up a diagram:

(1) By *shading* some area of the diagram, as in the figure on the left. When some area is shaded, it means that that part of the group is *empty*; there is nothing in that part of the group. If the group has any members at all, they are located in its unshaded part. Here area #6 is entirely empty.

(2) By placing a *star* in some area of the diagram, as in the figure on the left. The star represents some unspecified thing, and when a star is inside an area, that means that the area is not empty, but that the area is *occupied* by something. In this case area #2 is occupied. (The star may be labeled by some name, like "Bill.")

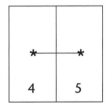

(3) By placing a *star* in a choice of two areas of the diagram, as in the figure on the left. The star represents some unspecified thing, and this thing is located **either** in area #4 **or** in area #5. There is a *connecting bar* for the *one* thing. So, either area #4 is occupied or area #5 is occupied.

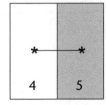

(4) By placing a *star* in a choice of two areas of the diagram (for one premiss), and by *shading out* one of the two choices (for another premiss), as in the figure on the left. After the shading, the star remains located in one area only. Either area #4 or #5 was occupied, but area #5 is now empty. So, area #4 is occupied.

(5) When an area contains *no marks*, that is, when it is not shaded and also not starred, as in the figure on the left, that means that the sentence makes *no assertion* about whether the corresponding portion of the group is empty or occupied. So, nothing is known about area #6.

All categorical sentences will be diagrammed with this common template. Remember that all group circles represent *only affirmative* subject and predicate terms. This is important. Violation of this requirement will destroy the ability to properly display the logical relationship between categorical sentences.

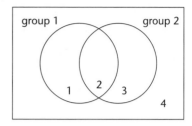

1. all S are P

Let us consider a specific sentence like "all cats are mellow." This is symbolized as "all C are M." The two groups C and M are related as follows:

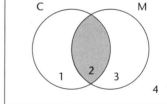

- All items in the C group are inside the M group.
- So, all items in C are limited to area #2.
- So, area #1 must be *empty*.

2. no S are P = all S are non-P

Let us consider a specific sentence like "no cats are mice." This is symbolized as "no C are M." The two groups C and M are related as follows:

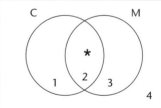

- No items in the C group are inside the M group.
- So, all items in C are limited to area #1.
- So, area #2 is *empty*.

3. some S are P

Let us consider a specific sentence like "some cats are mean." This is symbolized as "some C are M." The two groups C and M are related as follows:

- Some items in the C group are inside the M group.
- So, these items are in area #2.
- So, area #2 is *starred*.

4. some **S** are non-**P**

Let us consider a specific sentence like "some cats are not mean." This is symbolized as "some C are non-M." The two groups C and M are related as follows:

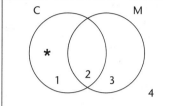

- Some items in the C group are inside the non-M group.
- So, these items in group C are outside group M.
- So, these items are in area #1.
- So, area #1 is *starred*.

Four Additional Venn Diagram Patterns

There are four additional Venn diagrams that make use of the two areas (#3 and #4), unlike the four special categorical sentences that use only areas #1 and #2. We mention these additional diagrams only for the purpose of comparison. It will be useful to keep in mind the expanse of the left-over areas for the negative terms:

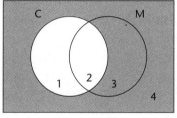
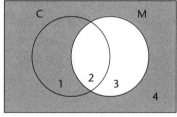
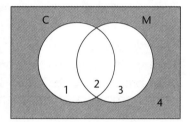

group non-C   group non-M   group non-C and non-M

Here the backgrounds have been colored only to indicate the boundaries of the areas for the negative terms. (This color here is not official "shading.") We can now illustrate the remaining possible diagrams with the following sentences.

- No non-cats are meowers.
- No non-C are M.

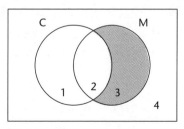

- No items in the non-C group are in the M group.
- So, area #3 is empty.

- Some non-cats are meowers.
- Some non-C are M.

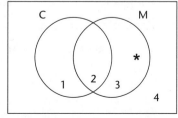

- Some items in the non-C group are in the M group.
- So, area #3 is starred.

- All non-cats are mean.
- All non-C are M.
- All items in the non-C group are in the M group.
- All items in non-C are limited to area #3.
- So, the outside area #4 is empty.

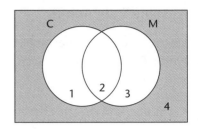

- Some non-cats are non-mean.
- Some non-C are non-M.
- Some items in non-C are also in non-M.
- So, some items not in C are also not in M.
- So, the outside area #4 is starred.

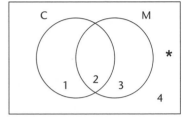

Non-Standard Venn Diagrams for Absolute Sentences

In Section 1.3 above we introduced a special group of sentences that we called *absolute* sentences. These are sentences whose entire subject term is the absolute term "things." We mentioned there that we would never symbolize the absolute term by a capital letter, but that we would symbolize it by the word "thing" underlined. There was a reason for that. The term *thing* cannot be represented by a group circle of things in the universe. The term *thing* can only be represented by the diagram for the *entire* universe. And here is where the "border" that we drew around the Venn diagrams comes into play. That border is the boundary of the entire universe, the set of all things that are real.

We can give Venn diagrams for absolute sentences in a similar way as we did for regular categorical sentences. For regular sentences, we have a subject circle overlapping the predicate circle, and the various areas are marked up with shading or starring. For absolute sentences, the subject "circle" is the entire universe box, and the predicate circle is a group circle that is completely inside the universe box, and the two areas inside the box can be marked up with shading or starring. Below is the general template for absolute sentences, followed by completed diagrams for the four types of absolute sentences.

- General template for absolute sentences.
- Subject term is "*things,*" represented by the universe.
- Predicate term is represented by the group X.
- The two areas X and non-X are shaded or starred.

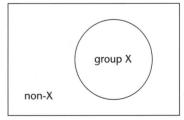

- Everything is made of matter.
- All *things* are M.

- All things in the universe are inside the M group.
- So, the area outside of M is *empty*.

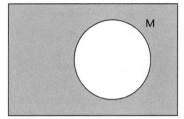

- Nothing is made of matter.
- No *things* are M.

- No things in the universe are inside the M group.
- So, the area M is *empty*.

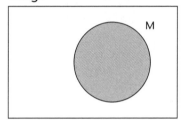

- Something is made of matter.
- Some *things* are M.

- Some things in the universe are inside the M group.
- So, the area M is *starred*.

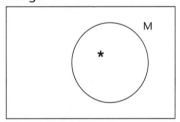

- Something is not made of matter.
- Some *things* are non-M.

- Some things in the universe are not in the M group.
- So, the area outside of M is *starred*.

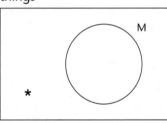

The Negation Correlation

Let's make some easy observations about the shading and starring that occurs in Venn diagrams for categorical sentences. Also, let's call the shading and starring, "area decorations."

1. A *star* in an area means: "the area is occupied by something."
2. *Shading* in an area means: "the area has been completely emptied out."

3. Categorical sentences are correctly represented by their Venn diagrams.

4. So, shading and starring are area decorations that are *logical opposites*.

5. So, sentences with opposite area decorations are *negation opposites*.

Observation #5 gives us the following *Negation correlation*:

If a categorical sentence **S** has a Venn diagram **D**, then its negation not (**S**) has the Venn Diagram that *swaps* the area decoration in **D** for its opposite.

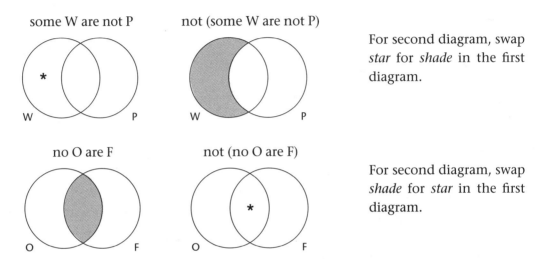

some W are not P	not (some W are not P)

For second diagram, swap *star* for *shade* in the first diagram.

no O are F	not (no O are F)

For second diagram, swap *shade* for *star* in the first diagram.

Exercise 3.4. A,B Venn Diagrams for Sentences

Part A. Symbolize the sentences. Also, draw the Venn diagram for each sentence. Remember that circles represent affirmative terms only. Use the available **Exercise Work Sheet** to submit your work.

1. All persons are artists. (P, A)
2. All bananas are unsalted. (B, S)
3. Some snakes are poisonous. (S, P)
4. Some contestants are not winners. (C, W)
5. No philosophers are materialists. (P, M)
6. All animals are not writers. (A, W)
7. Some non-cars are wheeled things. (C, W)
8. All trees are not inorganic. (T, O)
9. Some students are ineligible. (S, E)
10. Some non-students are eligible. (S, E)

11.   Some non-students are ineligible. (S, E)

12.   No non-students are ineligible. (S, E)

Part B. For each of the following sentence pairs, give a Venn diagram for the first sentence of the pair, and then use the *negation correlation method* to draw the Venn diagram for the second sentence. (Some of the left-side diagrams are difficult.) Use the available **Exercise Work Sheet** to submit your work.

1.   some G are H   , not (some G are H)

2.   all S are B   , not (all S are B)

3.   some U are non-R   , not (some U are non-R)

4.   all J are non-B   , not (all J are non-B)

5.   some non-A are W   , not (some non-A are W)

6.   no Q are K   , not (no Q are K)

7.   some non-W are non-P   , not (some non-W are non-P)

8.   all non-M are A   , not (all non-M are A)

9.   no E are non-D   , not (no E are non-D)

10.   all non-K are non-L   , not (all non-K are non-L)

11.   no non-T are S   , not (no non-T are S)

12.   no non-U are non-E   , not (no non-U are non-E)

Section 3.5 Venn Diagrams for Syllogisms and Equivalences

Argumentation in Traditional Logic is much the same as in any area of logic. Arguments have premises and a conclusion. Sometimes arguments are merely stated, sometimes they are established by a deductive demonstration, and sometimes they are shown to be invalid.

Certain arguments in Traditional Logic are known as *categorical syllogisms*. These arguments have two premises and a conclusion, all of which are categorical sentences. In addition, all these sentences are constructed out of (built up from) exactly three affirmative terms, each occurring twice. (This description allows that a syllogism can contain negative terms, since negative terms are themselves considered to be constructed out of the corresponding affirmative terms.) Here are some examples of categorical syllogisms (some of which are valid and some of which are not, as we will learn later on):

All K are M	Some B are A	All non-J are non-B	No L are M
All M are B	No A are H	No B are non-A	No S are M
So, all K are B	So, some B are non-H	So, all A are J	Some L are S

One can easily see the general character of categorical syllogisms (but we may focus on the first example). Each of these arguments has two premises and a conclusion, and each argument is built up from a total of three affirmative terms, each of which occurs twice. One of the three terms is special, and it is called the *middle term*. This term is always the one that occurs in *both* of the premises. In the first argument, for example, the middle term is the term M, and in the third argument the middle term is the term B. Now, because the middle term occurs in both premises, it *connects* the two premises, and because of this, it creates an *extra relationship* between the other two terms. The conclusion of the argument then states what that extra relationship is. If the conclusion gets that relationship right, the argument is valid, and if it gets that relationship wrong, the argument is invalid.

Venn Diagrams for Syllogisms

We begin with the well-known method of representing categorical sentences and syllogisms by means of *Venn diagrams*. In the preceding section we learned how to diagram all categorical sentences in this way. What is important in this method is that each sentence has a *picture* of its own logical form, and these pictures can be *added* to (superimposed on) other pictures, and one can *visually* compare the results. What is especially important is that when this diagram method is applied to arguments, one can literally *see* how the premises work together to create the conclusion when an argument is valid, and one can likewise see how the premises fail to create the conclusion when an argument is invalid. A picture is worth a thousand words, as they say.

The General Method

(1) The method begins with two Venn diagram *templates*, one for the two premises and one for the conclusion.

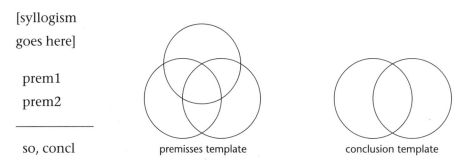

[syllogism
goes here]

prem1
prem2
_____
so, concl   premises template   conclusion template

(2) Next, the template for the premises is filled in with the diagrams for the two premises, and the template for the conclusion is filled in with the diagram for the conclusion.

(3) Finally, the resulting conclusion diagram is compared to the resulting premises diagram, and the *validity test* is applied. (We will not discuss the validity test until after we have discussed the details of constructing the diagrams.)

The Details

The Venn diagram for a syllogism directly incorporates the Venn diagrams for the sentences that make up the syllogism. Let us consider the following syllogism, with the already known diagrams for its component sentences:

Example 1

All K are M
All M are B
So, all K are B

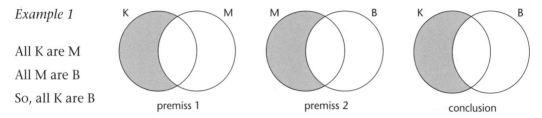

premiss 1   premiss 2   conclusion

It is pretty clear that *this* way of arranging the diagrams does *not* show anything about the logical arrangement of the argument. The information of the two premisses is isolated—it has not been allowed to interact. What is needed is a *single diagram* that contains *all* the information. This is achieved by using three properly overlapping circles, one for each of the three terms, with one at the top and two at the bottom, and these circles are labeled by the terms letters in the *natural* order that these terms occur in the premisses. (So, don't label these in alphabetical order, unless that is also the natural order.) So, we start with the premisses template diagram below, on the left, and next, we *superimpose* the two diagrams for premiss 1 and premiss 2 on to this template. This results in the finished premisses diagram on the right.

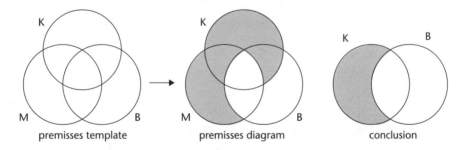

premisses template   premisses diagram   conclusion

A comparison of the premisses diagram and the conclusion diagram show that the two premisses interacted to produce the diagram of the conclusion. This means that the argument is *valid*. The validity procedure used here is explained below. Right now, we want to focus on how one constructs the diagrams in the first place. We will consider another example. The diagrams for its component sentences are as indicated.

Example 2

Some B are A
No A are H
So, some B are non-H

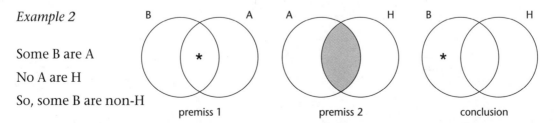

premiss 1   premiss 2   conclusion

Again let us consider how we will complete the premisses template below on the left. We first consider how the individual premisses appear when they are drawn in the premisses template.

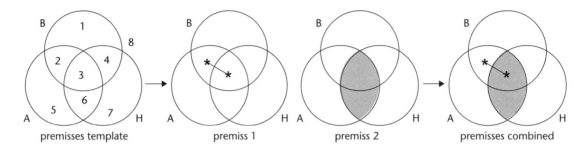

premisses template   premiss 1   premiss 2   premisses combined

Premiss 1 presents a *difficulty*. We know that the area common to B and A, consisting of sub-areas #2 and #3, must have a *star* in it, representing some unknown thing that is both B and A. But in which of the two sub-areas should the star be placed? If we put it in area #2, then we are saying that the unknown thing is in B and in A but also *outside* of H. That says too much. If we put the star in area #3, then we are saying that the unknown thing is in B and in A but also *inside* of H, and again that says too much. The solution is to say that the unknown thing is *either* in #2 *or* in #3.

We can just leave it as a *choice*. The way that we will draw the choice is to place the star in each sub-area connected with a *choice bar*.

Premiss 2 is drawn in the usual way. We know that the area common to A and H is empty. That means that the two sub-areas #3 and #6 are both empty. But now an interesting combination has occurred. Premiss 1 says that #2 or #3 has a star, and Premiss 2 says that #3 is empty, (shaded). Therefore, when both the premisses are drawn in the premisses template, the *result* is that #3 and #6 are shaded, and #2 has a star in it.

Of course, the Venn diagram for the argument does not include all the intermediate stages that we have been presenting. We only want the finished diagrams. So, the *official Venn diagram* for the argument is just the following:

Example 2

Some B are A

No A are H

So, some B are non-H

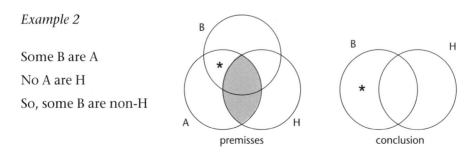

premisses   conclusion

A comparison of the premisses diagram and the conclusion diagram shows that the two premisses did indeed interact to actually produce the conclusion. This means that the argument is *valid*. The general procedure for such a validity check is what we will turn to next. Since there are some cases that are a little more complicated than others, we will present this procedure in a very detailed way, so that it can be easily understood.

A Special Procedure for Checking for Validity

The criterion for the validity of categorical syllogisms is the same as the criterion for the validity of any argument whatsoever. (In this regard, remember how we defined deductive validity in sections 1.6, 2.5, and 2.8.) With Venn diagrams, however, we can implement this criterion in a special pictorial way.

> *Criterion*: a categorical syllogism is *valid* if and only if
>
> the information in the premisses diagram *generates* the information in the conclusion diagram; in fact, the conclusion information is actually a part of the premiss information.

One can use a *special highlight procedure* to see whether this criterion is satisfied:

Step 1. Highlight the sub-area of the conclusion template where the conclusion info is located. Call this area the *claim-area*. (This area will be a "left moon," a "right moon," or a "lens.") The conclusion says *one of two* possible things about this claim-area:

(a)   this area is *shaded* [= it is empty], OR

(b)   this area is *starred* [= it is occupied]

Step 2. Next, highlight the *same* sub-area in the premisses template. It turns out that the premisses can say *one of three* possible things about the claim-area:

(a)   this area is *shaded*, OR

(b)   this area is *starred*, OR

(c)   *maybe* this area is starred

[The third case happens when a *choice-bar* is used, and *one half* of it is in the claim-area, and the other half has not been *eliminated*, so that the choice is still active. In this case the syllogism is *invalid*.]

Step 3. In a valid syllogism, what the conclusion says about the claim-area has to be guaranteed by what the premisses say about the claim-area. Watch out! If the premisses say, "Maybe the claim-area is starred," then that means the premisses do not guarantee that the claim-area *is* starred, and that uncertainty makes the argument invalid.

Here are some further examples of the Venn Diagram Method in action. First, we again present *Example 1*, this time using the highlight technique. We then continue with additional examples.

Example 1

All K are M

All M are B

So, all K are B

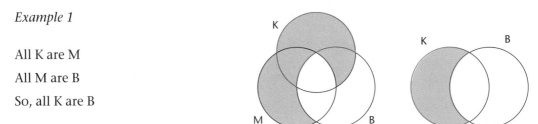

This syllogism is *valid*, because the premisses diagram agrees with the conclusion diagram that the claim-area "the entire K area outside of B" is shaded, empty.

Example 3

no S are B

All B are C

So, no S are C

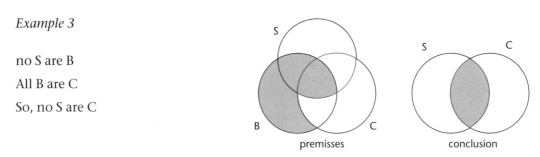

This syllogism is *invalid*, because the premisses diagram does not contain *all* the information that the conclusion is claiming, which is, that the *entire* claim-area is shaded. The conclusion asks for more than what the premisses can provide.

Example 4

some A are B

All B are C

So, some A are C

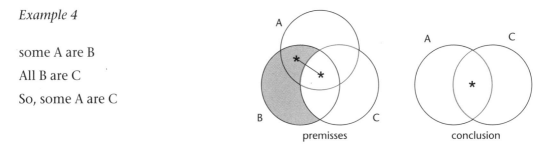

This syllogism is *valid*, because the "choice" that was first presented in the premisses was also later eliminated in the premisses, resulting in a specific starred area. The premisses diagram agrees with the conclusion diagram that the claim-area is starred.

Example 5

all K are M

some M are B

So, some K are B

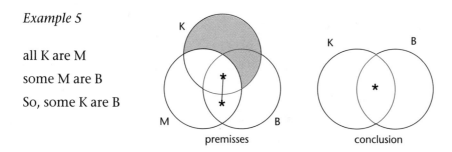

premisses   conclusion

This syllogism is *invalid*, because the "choice" presented in the premisses has been left unresolved. The premisses diagram only says that "maybe the claim-area is starred." But that is not good enough, because the conclusion diagram make the stronger claim that the claim-area is definitely starred.

Venn Diagrams for Equivalences

Testing the equivalence of two sentences by means of Venn diagrams is a straightforward matter. One simply diagrams each sentence, and then one compares the results. If the two diagrams are *the same*, then the sentences are *equivalent*, and if the diagrams are *different*, then the sentences are *not* equivalent.

Let us consider the two sentences "some B are non-H" and "some non-H are B." We must diagram these two sentences *separately*, but using the *same* template:

- Are the two sentences "Some B are non-H" and "some non-H are B" *equivalent*?

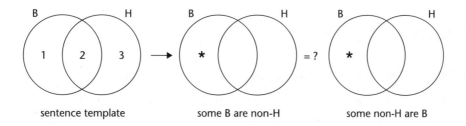

sentence template   some B are non-H   some non-H are B

The first sentence says that some item in B is also in non-H. So, a *star* must be placed in B, but *outside* of H, that is, the star must be in area #1.

The second sentence says that some item in non-H is also in B. So, a *star* must be placed *outside* of H but inside B. So, the star must be placed in area #1. The two diagrams are the *same*. The two sentences are *equivalent*. Here is another example:

- Are the two sentences "all K are M" and "all non-K are non-M" equivalent?

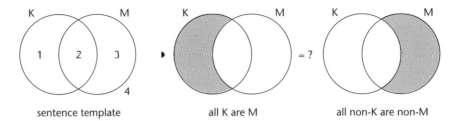

sentence template   all K are M   all non-K are non-M

We know that the first sentence is correctly diagrammed by the first diagram. The second sentence is more complicated. Let's see how that turns out:

All non-K are non-M.

All items not inside K are *not* inside M (area #3).

So, area #3 must be *empty* (otherwise, some star would be in #3, which would mean the star was in non-K and inside M).

So, the two sentences have *different diagrams*, and they are *not equivalent*.

Exercise 3.5. A,B Venn Diagrams for Syllogisms and Equivalences

Part A: For each syllogism, *draw* the premises in the premises diagram and the conclusion in the conclusion diagram, and say whether these diagrams show the syllogism to be *valid*. Label the circles with obvious letters in the order of their occurrence in the syllogism: the first letter for the top circle, the second letter for the left circle, the third letter for the right circle. Use the available **Exercise Work Sheet** to submit your work.

1. All poets are artists. All artists are inspired. So, all poets are inspired.

2. Some doctors are lawyers. No vets are lawyers. So, some doctors are not vets.

3. No apples are bananas. No bananas are oranges. So, no apples are oranges.

4. No cars are planes. Some wagons are cars. So, some wagons are not planes.

5. Some paintings are costly items. Some costly items are famous. So, some paintings are famous.

6. All golfers are athletes. All babies are not athletes. So, all babies are not golfers.

7. Some thinkers are not kings. No kings are scholars. So, some thinkers are scholars.

8. Some writers are not artists. No non-artists are poets. So, some writers are not poets. [Hint #8: *First* figure out the two-circle diagram for the second premiss.]

Part B: Use Venn diagrams to determine whether the following sentence pairs are *equivalent*. Symbolize the sentences. Draw a separate diagram for each sentence. Label the circles with the obvious letters. Remember that each *circle* represents an *affirmative* term only. Some of these diagrams will make use of the "outer region," so be sure to draw the rectangular border. Use the available **Exercise Work Sheet** to submit your work.

1. No kangaroos are monkeys, no monkeys are kangaroos

2. Some giraffes are not dragons, some dragons are not giraffes.

3. All fish are swimmers, all swimmers are fish.

4. All wizards are non-roosters, all roosters are non-wizards.

5. Some non-bananas are peaches, some peaches are non-bananas.

6. All hats are gigantic, no hats are non-gigantic.

7. Some ants are monsters, some non-monsters are non-ants.

8. All non-spirits are bulky, no non-spirits are non-bulky.

9. All planets are spheres, all non-planets are non-spheres.

10. Some non-ants are non-bugs, some bugs are not non-ants.

Section 3.6 Equivalence Operations

We turn our attention now to the *deductive* relationships that exist among categorical sentences. In Propositional Logic we studied logical relationships that are *external* ones, external in the sense that such logical relationships are created by the external arrangement of the connectives that form complex sentences. The internal structure that simple sentences have is not relevant to this external structure. Consider, for example, the following argument, along with its complete symbolic analysis:

All persons are free agents, or no persons are.	=	(all P are F) $\lor$ (no P are F)
But it is false that all persons are free agents	=	~(all P are F)
So, no persons are free agents.	=	$\therefore$ (no P are F)

What is immediately clear is that the *internal* categorical structure of the argument plays *no* role at all in making it a valid argument. The argument is valid only because it has the *external* form of a disjunctive argument, and in this case the rule of Disjunctive Syllogism applies: p $\lor$ q , ~p , so, q . Consider, on the other hand, the following argument and symbolization:

All babies are persons.	1. all B are P	1. p
All persons are moral agents.	2. all P are M	2. q
So, all babies are moral agents.	∴ all B are M	∴ r

This argument is valid, but not because of external relationships involving sentence connectives (in fact, there are none, as the displayed propositional form indicates). Rather it is valid because of the *internal* structure that each of the simple sentences has. What we shall do now is introduce the laws that govern the connections that exist between simple (categorical) sentences in virtue of their internal structure.

1. Predicate Double Negation (Pred-DN)

The first rule is a very easy one. It concerns *double negatives*. We already dealt with double negatives back in Chapter 2, when we learned how to use the Law of Double Negation, $p = \sim(\sim p)$, with precision. The present case is similar to the previous one, but there is a technical difference. The Double Negation Law concerns the denial of a sentence that is itself the denial of another sentence. It is *sentences* that are denied. But the present case concerns *predicates*, not sentences. Doubly negated predicates typically arise in the course of some discussion when some negative predicate is used ("People are so ungrateful"), and in *response* to that, another predicate is introduced that negates the other negative predicate ("Well, some people are not ungrateful"). Here are other examples:

Some topics are not inconsequential	= Some T are (not non-C)
Each human being is not immortal	= All H are (not non-M)
Non-administrators are not ineligble	= All non-A are (not non-E)

The symbolizations of these sentences show that none of them can be considered to have the form $\sim(\sim p)$. These are *not* doubly negated sentences, and so the Law of Double Negation cannot be used. Of course, what *is* true is that these sentences have doubly negated *predicates*. A doubly negated predicate term is a term to which the negative term operator has been applied two times. Since we actually have *two* versions of the negative operator, the doubles can take the following forms:

non-non-X

(not non-X)

non-(not X)

(not (not X))

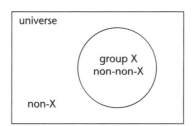

Of course, these double negatives *do* cancel each other, because if something is in the non-non-X group, then it is not in the non-X group, and then it must be in the X group, as the figure shows. This reasoning also works in the reverse.

Predicate Double Negation (Pred-DN)

> ... ... are **P** = ... are non-non-**P**
>
> Here the dotted notation represents any quantifier and subject term, both of which must be kept constant in the inference.
>
> This rule also hold for the other forms of doubly negated predicates.

We can see, then, that our previous examples reduce in the following way:

Some T are (not non-C)	= Some T are C
All H are (not non-M)	= All H are M
All non-A are (not non-E)	= All non-A are E

2. The Quantifier-Negation Laws (QN)

The most common logical inferences we make involve quantifiers and negations. We are told, "Not everyone here will have to pay the $1,000 fine," and we say "Oh, I hope that means me." Or, perhaps we hear "Relax. It won't happen that someone here will have to take the 7:30 am class," and *each* of us says "Thank you, Lord." Without reflection, and out of habit, we use the Quantifier-Negation Laws.

1. Not all [persons here] are [paying the fine]   Premiss
2. Some [persons here] are [**not** paying the fine]   1, QN Law

1. Not some [persons here] are [taking the class]   Premiss
2. All [persons here] are [**not** taking the class]   1, QN Law

Traditional Logic has always presented the QN Laws as a "Square of Opposition," whose corners are the four (five) main kinds of categorical sentences. These sentences are arranged so that the opposite corners are *negation* opposites. This is a very useful way to illustrate these fundamental logical relationships.

The Square of Opposition

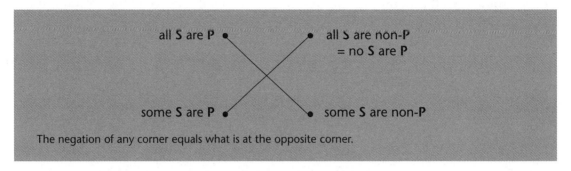

all S are P

all S are non-P
= no S are P

some S are P

some S are non-P

The negation of any corner equals what is at the opposite corner.

As a summary we can say that the QN Laws allow us to move back and forth between an *external negation* of a categorical sentence and an *internal negation* on the predicate side, compensating with a change of quantifier. Plus there are some rules for re-expressing "no." Here are the same relationships stated as equations.

Quantifier-Negation Laws (QN)

not (all S are P)	=	some S are non-P
not (some S are P)	=	all S are non-P
no S are P	=	all S are non-P
no S are P	=	not (some S are P)

One way to remember these relationships is to think of it as follows: for the "all" and "some" sentences, as a negative operator "moves through" the quantifier (either from front to back, or from back to front), the quantifier flips to the *other* one, from "all" to "some" and from "some" to "all," and the predicate either receives a negative or loses it. The quantifier "no" is a different idea: "no" just *means* "all are not," as well as, "not some are." There is one idea that holds for *all* of these relationships. The logical vocabulary has three negative words: "not," "no," "non-." When you use QN, the *total* number of negatives remains *constant*. The quantifier changes, the position of the negatives changes, but the number of negatives does not change.

1. all [people who live on the Moon] are [not Earthlings]   premiss
2. no [people who live on the Moon] are [Earthlings]   1, QN
3. not some [people who live on the Moon] are [Earthlings]   1, QN

1. not all [books that are not long] are [not interesting]   premiss
2. some [books that are not long] are [not (not interesting)]   1, QN

3. some [books that are not long] are [interesting]   2, Pred-DN
4. not no [books that are not long] are [interesting]   1, QN

1. some [buildings that don't have windows] are [not non-safe]   premiss
2. not all [buildings that don't have windows] are [non-safe]   1, QN
3. not no [buildings that don't have windows] are [safe]   2, QN

3. The Conversion Law (Conv)

Can the subject and the predicate of a sentence be reversed without changing the meaning of the sentence? Clearly, one cannot reverse the order of a sentence like "All dogs are animals." The reverse would mean an entirely different thing. On the other hand, sentences such as "Some persons are swimmers" *can* be reversed to say, "Some swimmers are persons," and it will mean the same as the original. (To see the identity, just try to *picture* what is said in each case.) The same is true of all sentences of the form "some **S** are **P**." In Traditional Logic, reversing the subject term and the predicate term of a sentence is called *conversion*, and so, the rule that we are considering is that sentences of the form "some **S** are **P**" may always be converted. Actually, it is easy to see why conversion works in this case. Intuitively, the sentence "Some **S** are **P**" means the same as "Some things are such that: they are **S** *and* they are **P**." Such particular sentences always have the *secret* meaning of a *conjunction*, p & q, and you will remember that conjunctions can always be reversed (by the Law of Commutation).

There is one extra form of Conversion. Universal negative sentences, "no **S** are **P**," can *also* be converted, as the following deduction shows. We may therefore also add this form to the Conversion Law (so that we never have to repeat this deduction).

1. no **S** are **P**   premiss
2. not some **S** are **P**   1, QN
3. not some **P** are **S**   2, Conv
4. no **P** are **S**   3, QN

Conversion (Conv)

some S are P	=	some P are S
no S are P	=	no P are S

We add a word of caution here about a possible misuse of the Conversion Law. We must make sure that the two terms being converted have been properly analyzed. There is no problem in this regard when we are dealing with sentences that have been symbolized, but error is very possible when sentences retain their *English* form. Here are some examples:

1. some cold-blooded animals are not lizards	premiss	
2. some lizards are not cold-blooded animals	1, Conv??	NO!!

~~1. some cold-blooded animals are not lizards~~	premiss,	BAD
1. some [cold-blooded animals] are [non-lizards]	premiss,	YES
1. some [non-lizards] are [cold-blooded animals]	1, Conv	YES

1. some [long hard problems] are [fascinating puzzles]	premiss	
2. some [fascinating puzzles] are [long hard problems]	1, Conv	

1. some [proper goals] are [non-achievable-ends]	premiss	
2. some [non-achievable-ends] are [proper goals]	1, Conv	YES
3. some [non-achievable-ends] are [not non-proper-goals]	2, Pred-DN	YES
4. not all [non-achievable ends] are [non-proper-goals]	3, QN	YES
5. not no [non-achievable ends] are [proper goals]	4, QN	YES

- "not no non-achievable ends . . ." Wow! Now *that* is impressive!

4. The Law of Contraposition (Contrap)

In earlier sections we had the opportunity to note that universal sentences such as "All cows are mooers" have a *secret* conditional structure, p ⊃ q, which is captured by the corresponding sentence, "**if** you are a cow **then** you are a mooer." We also know that conditional sentences obey the Law of Contraposition, so that this provides a further equivalence to "**if** you are a non-mooer, **then** you are a non-cow." But the latter, as just noted, is the secret conditional structure of the categorical sentence, "All non-mooers are non-cows." This example demonstrates that, according to the Law of Contraposition, all sentences of the form "all **S** are **P**" are equivalent to the corresponding form "all non-**P** are non-**S**;" and this relationship is true regardless of whether the terms involved are affirmative or negative.

To state this law efficiently, we introduce some *special notation*. We use the notation **opposite**[X] to represent the term that is the *negation opposite* of the term **X**, where **X** represents all terms, both affirmative and negative. (Of course, this notation is *not* a symbol in the symbolic language itself.) For example,

opposite["elephant"] = "non-elephant"

opposite["non-elephant"] = "elephant"

Contraposition (Contrap)

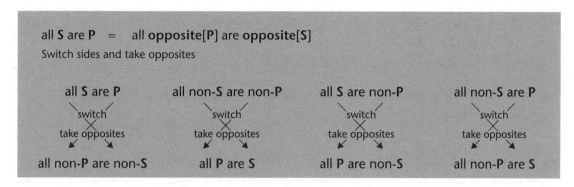

all S are P = all **opposite[P]** are **opposite[S]**
Switch sides and take opposites

But be careful. The law applies *only* to *universal* categorical sentences whose terms have been properly analyzed. This means that a sentence must have the universal quantifier "all" and the affirmative copula "are," and that any negative on the predicate side is properly *attached* to the predicate term. Consider some examples:

1.	all dogs are not cats	Premiss.
2.	all non-cats are not non-dogs	1, Contrap ?? ERROR

The correct method is to rewrite the premiss so that it is in categorical form:

1.	~~all dogs are not cats~~	premiss, BAD
1.	all dogs are non-cats	premiss, GOOD
2.	all cats are non-dogs	1, Contrap YES

1.	not some astronauts are medical-students	premiss
2.	all astronauts are non-medical-students	1, QN
3.	all medical-students are non-astronauts	2, Contrap

Here are some examples of deductions with all these laws when the sentences are all symbolized.

There is not a non-animal that is not made only of assembled pieces.

So, everything that is not made only of assembled pieces is an animal.

1.	not some non-A are (not M)	Premiss /∴ all (not M) are A
2.	all non-A are (not (not M))	1, QN
3.	all non-A are are M	2, Pred-DN
4.	all (not M) are A	3, Contrap

And here is yet another deduction for the same argument.

1.	not some non-A are (not M)	Premiss /∴ all (not M) are A
2.	not some (not M) are non-A	1, Conv
3.	all (not M) are A	2, QN

As you can see, in Traditional Logic (as in Propositional Logic) there is always more than one way to derive a conclusion from its premisses.

Exercise 3.6. Equivalences

Symbolize each of the following inferences, but keep them in the same form. If an inference is valid, give the *name* of the rule used; otherwise, say it is *invalid*. Use the available **Exercise Work Sheet** to submit your work.

0.	Some vegetables are tomatoes	/∴ Some tomatoes are vegetables
1.	All apples are fruits	/∴ All fruits are apples
2.	Some bananas are vegetables	/∴ Some non-bananas are non-vegetables.
3.	No peaches are blueberries	/∴ All peaches are non-blueberries
4.	All oranges are fruits	/∴ All non-fruits are non-oranges
5.	Not some bananas are green	/∴ All bananas are non-green
6.	All peaches are non-blue	/∴ Not some peaches are blue
7.	Not no watermelons are fruits	/∴ All watermelons are fruits
8.	No tomatoes are fruits	/∴ All non-tomatoes are fruits
9.	Some pears are not non-apples	/∴ Some pears are apples
10.	Some non-tomatoes are non-fruits	/∴ Some tomatoes are not non-fruits
11.	All apples are not tomatoes	/∴ All non-tomatoes are not non-apples
12.	Some oranges are non-vegetables	/∴ Some non-vegetables are oranges
13.	All strawberries are fruits	/∴ All non-strawberries are non-fruits
14.	All peaches are non-apples	/∴ All apples are non-peaches
15.	No mangos are non-fruits	/∴ All non-mangos are non-fruits
16.	Not all cherries are apples	/∴ Some cherries are non-apples
17.	Some apples are non-vegetables	/∴ Some vegetables are non-apples
18.	Some non-apples are vegetables	/∴ Some vegetables are non-apples
19.	No non-oranges are non-vegetab.	/∴ No vegetables are oranges
20.	All non-blueberries are non-fruits	/∴ All fruits are blueberries

Section 3.7 Deductions in Traditional Logic

Certain arguments may be shown to be valid by the Method of Venn Diagrams. But we should *not* consider this method to be good for general use, because the method is *limited*. The method is good for showing that certain basic patterns are valid, and that they can therefore be used as *rules* (and in this regard Venn Diagrams play a role similar to that of *truth-tables* in Propositional Logic), but the limitations become clear when one considers extended syllogisms (sometimes called *sorites* from the Greek) that are obviously valid, such as:

> All A are B
> All B are C
> All C are D
> All D are E
> So, all A are E

This argument uses five terms, and there are *no* practical Venn diagrams for using four, five, six, seven, eight, etc., terms. But the method *does* show that the following two simple syllogisms (called *Univ Syll* and *Part Syll*) are valid:

all **S** are **M**	some **S** are **M**
all **M** are **P**	all **M** are **P**
So, all **S** are **P**	So, some **S** are **P**

And, we can then use these two valid categorical syllogism patterns as official *rules* in our system of logic, that can be *repeatedly* used in a deduction:

1. all A are B	Prem
2. all B are C	Prem
3. all C are D	Prem
4. all D are E	Prem
5. all A are C	1,2, Univ Syll
6. all A are D	5,3, Univ Syll
7. all A are E	6,4, Univ Syll

Summary: The Venn Diagram methods can demonstrate that certain rules are valid. Thereafter, these rules can be used to do *deductions* in Traditional Logic, in exactly the same manner that we did deductions in Propositional Logic. This is an important approach in the study of logic, but, unfortunately, one that is *inexplicably* completely ignored in most other logic books and courses. (It makes you wonder.)

The System of Deduction

All the rules and methods of Propositional Logic continue to be available in the system of deduction for Traditional Logic. This includes, then, rules such as MP, MT, Disj Syll, DN, DeMorg, etc., and the methods of direct, indirect, and conditional proof. But we note here that, even though these rules are available, we will focus our attention on arguments that use only categorical (that is, simple) sentences. And without compound sentences, the rules of Propositional Logic have *no* role to play in these problems. (In the next section, however, we combine these two parts of logic.)

As was the case for Propositional Logic, the *new* deduction rules for Traditional Logic fall into two groups.

I. *Elementary argument forms*: two special syllogisms: the Universal Syllogism and the Particular Syllogism, whose operation we discuss below.

II. *Elementary equivalences*: the four equivalences we introduced above: Pred-DN, QN, Conv, Contrap.

We note once more that there is a difference between the way that the elementary argument forms and the equivalences are applied. The argument forms create *new* conclusions, and are therefore rules that apply only to entire lines of a deduction, never to parts of a line, while the equivalences merely *restate* in a different form what is already available, and are therefore rules that apply to all kinds and sizes of expressions, whether whole lines or parts of lines.

Elementary Equivalences

We have already discussed the elementary equivalences of Traditional Logic in the previous section. So, we can take that discussion for granted here. These rules are:

- The Predicate Double Negation Law   (Pred-DN)
- The Quantifier-Negation Laws   (QN)
- The Conversion Law   (Conv)
- The Law of Contraposition   (Contrap)

For example, the following seven sentences are all equivalent to each other:

11.	not some I are (not non-E)	. . . .	
12.	not some I are E	11, Pred-DN	
13.	not some E are I	12, Conv	
14.	all E are non-I	13, QN	
15.	all I are non-E	14, Contrap	[12, QN]
16.	no E are I	14, QN	[13, QN]
17.	no I are E	16, Conv	[12, QN] [15, QN]

The equivalences laws are important for two reasons. First of all, it is inherently important to be able to re-express complicated sentences in simpler form. Consider, "It is false that no one who doesn't like to dance isn't non-athletic." Few people are able to correctly restate this sentence in its simplest form. (But now, thanks to logic, *you* are one of those rare people, and it isn't that hard—go ahead, try it!) Secondly, the equivalences are important because they are absolutely necessary for restating sentences into the proper form required by the primary categorical syllogisms, which are the *primary* instruments available for making inferences, as we shall see.

Elementary Argument Forms

There are many valid categorical syllogisms that are *eligible* to be rules in our system, and we could pick, say, half a dozen of these. But that would be an inferior approach. Most syllogisms look alike, the good and the bad, the selected ones and the non-selected ones. It would be *too* confusing. But more importantly, there are *two* syllogisms that (i) are distinctly simple, (ii) are very intuitive, and (iii) are capable of doing the work of *all* the others. (This is a fact known throughout the history of logic.) We will select these two as our rules, and together we can call them the *primary* categorical syllogisms, to distinguish them from all other valid syllogisms. We will call the first one the *Universal Syllogism*, and the second one, the *Particular Syllogism*. (Historically, these are called by people names, *Barbara* and *Darii*, respectively.)

The Primary Categorical Syllogisms

Univ Syll	*Part Syll*
all **S** are **M**	some **S** are **M**
all **M** are **P**	all **M** are **P**
—————	—————
∴ all **S** are **P**	∴ some **S** are **P**

The connection provided by these basic syllogisms lies at the heart of all categorical reasoning. Consider, for example, the next argument:

> Only free agents are responsible for their actions. Only those who are responsible for their actions may be rewarded or punished for their actions. But, no animals are free agents. So, no animals may be rewarded or punished for their actions.

This argument may be symbolized and demonstrated as follows:

1. all non-F are non-R	Prem		
2. all non-R are non-M	Prem		
3. no A are F	Prem	∴ no A are M	
4. all A are non-F	3, QN		
5. all A are non-R	4,1, Univ Syll	Bingo!	
6. all A are non-M	5,2, Univ Syll	Bingo!	
7. no A are M	6, QN		

Correct Categorical Sequencing

The primary categorical syllogisms require that there be a *correct* sequence of linked terms, and this means three things.

(A) *Correct quantifiers*. The first requirement for a correct sequence is that the starting quantifier is either "all" or "some," and never the quantifier "no." So, an available sentence "no K are L" must be *changed* by the QN rule:

5. no K are L	. . .	[OK, but we can't use this form.]
6. all K are non-L	6, QN	[Yes. Ready for further action!]

(B) *Correct copula*. The second requirement is more about inferences made directly with English sentences than with symbolic sentences. One must make sure that the subject term and the predicate term have been properly analyzed, so that the copula of the sentence is "are," as required, and any negative operator on the predicate side has been incorporated into the predicate term.

8. ~~some people are not prepared~~	[Improper form for inference.]
8. some [people] are [non-prepared]	[Yes. Ready for action!]

(C) *Correct continuation*. The third requirement for a correct sequence is the presence of a *universal continuation*, in the following sense. One premiss *starts* the inference with a subject term **S** and a predicate term **M** that functions as a linking, middle term. Then, another premiss *continues* the inference by making a *universal* assertion about **M**, namely, all **M** are **P**. When an inference is continued, it must *always* be a universal-affirmative statement that does the continuation. For example,

6. all A are B   . . . .
7. some B are C   . . . .   [Stop. Need universal continuation!]
8. ~~some A are C~~ 6,7, Part Syll ?? [NO! DEAD WRONG]

Supersized Syllogisms

A related point. *How many* universal continuations may there be? Actually, *any number* of continuations. In other words, we could extend both of the syllogism rules into *super* syllogism rules. The super syllogism rules follow the three requirements just listed, with this added proviso: that *every* continuation must always be *universal*.

We *recommend*, but do not require, that you use the *supersized* versions of the two rules from this point on, whenever possible. For example, the first argument that started this section can be demonstrated in a single step—go back and check it out:

4. . . . .
5. all A are E   1,2,3,4, Super Univ Syll

Super Univ Syll	Super Part Syll
all S are M_1	some S are M_1
all M_1 are M_2	all M_1 are M_2
all M_2 are M_3	all M_2 are M_3
all M_3 are P	all M_3 are P
So, all S are P	So, some S are P

A New Deductive Strategy

We can make some useful points about deductive strategy. **The first point**. The two syllogism rules are the *only* deductive tool we have for deriving *new* conclusions from premisses. So, when we want a certain conclusion, we should think about how one of the syllogism rules would generate it. Of course, the available premisses or the desired conclusion might not be in a form required by the syllogism rules, and for that reason the *equivalences* are very important. We can use the equivalences to put sentences into the *right* form for the application of the syllogisms. Consider the following argument:

Some dogs are pets.

No dogs are meowers.

_____

So, not all pets are meowers

It is immediately clear that the second premiss does *not* fit the primary syllogisms, since the syllogisms do not allow the quantifier "no." So, we must change the second premiss. Also, the conclusion does not fit the primary syllogisms, since the syllogisms cannot end up with "not all." A little reflection tells us that the conclusion must be gotten from "some pets are non-meowers" by the rule QN. In addition, we need a universal *continuation* premiss, and that means that "dogs" has to be the *middle* term. This requires switching the sides of the first premiss. So, the deduction goes as follows:

1. some D are P	Prem	
2. no D are M	Prem ∴ not all P are M	
_____		
3. some P are D	1, Conv	
4. all D are non-M	2, QN	
5. some P are non-M	3,4, Part Syll	Bingo!
6. not all P are M	5, QN	

The second point concerns a special technique to use for deriving conclusions. When *several* premisses are involved, the equivalence rules provide *many* ways to modify the premisses, which, if all were performed, would produce a bewildering maze of related sentences. (You might find it interesting to try creating the maze-effect some time.) But there is an *excellent strategy* for navigating through the complex relations, and just to give this strategy some name, we call it **the chain technique**. The nice thing about a chain is that it can be of any *length*, and for the rest, a chain is a *sequence* of *linked* items, consisting of term letters, going from *left* to *right*. The chain technique is a way of producing the conclusion we are after, and we should think of chains as being just that, a *chain for the conclusion*. Let's suppose that the conclusion we want to produce is:

all A are non-W

Then, a chain for this conclusion could look something like this:

start   end

↓   ↓

A → M → non-C → non-B → E → Q → non-W

Let's have a closer look at how a chain is created. (1) Chains are instances of a *supersized* primary syllogism, in the sense that each *link* in the chain represents one of the lines used in the supersized syllogism rule, and the desired conclusion is then created by that supersized inference.

(2) The first term of the chain must be the subject term of the conclusion, and the last term of the chain must be the predicate term of the conclusion. That way, when the supersized rule is applied, the conclusion we are after will also be the conclusion generated by the supersized rule.

(3) Since the primary syllogisms are allowed to contain only "all" and "some" sentences, all of the links of the chain must be *such* sentences, and the conclusion generated will be *such* a sentence. This means that the following constructions may *not* be any part of the chain: "no," "not all," "not some." Such constructions must first be transformed into the proper form by using the Quantifier-Negation Laws.

(4) This is important: Except for the first link of the chain, *all* the other links in the chain must represent corresponding "all" sentences, because all *continuations* must always be "all": all/some. . . . all. . . . all. . . . all. . . . all. . . . all. . . . all. . . . all. . . . all. . . . all. . . . .

These four features give the chain the following configuration:

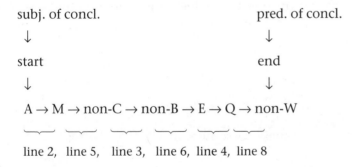

subj. of concl.   pred. of concl.
↓   ↓
start   end
↓   ↓
A → M → non-C → non-B → E → Q → non-W

line 2, line 5,   line 3,   line 6, line 4, line 8

So, inside the available lines of the deduction, we find the subject term that is also the subject term of the desired conclusion, and thereafter, we move through the terms in the available lines in a sequence until we arrive at the predicate term that is also the predicate term of the desired conclusion. Once that is done, we may infer the desired conclusion in *one fell swoop*:

  9. all A are non-W   2, 5, 3, 6, 4, 8, Super Univ Syll

Let's do an actual problem.

1. some K are B   prem
2. all A are M   prem   =   all non-M are non-A
3. no B are M   prem   =   all B are non-M
4. all non-A are P   prem
    _____

So, some K are P

Our goal is to map out the chain for the conclusion:

some K → B → . . . . → P

- *We start* with "some K"   – According to line 1, "B" is *next*.
- *Continue* with "B"   – Ln. 3 = "all B are non-M," by QN. So, "non-M" is *next*.
- *Continue* with "non-M"   – Ln. 2 = "all non-M are non-A," Contrap. So, "non-A" is *next.*
- *Continue* with "non-A"   – According to line 4, "P" is *next*.
- *Continue* with . . . Wait!   – Stop! We're done. "P" was the last term we needed.

So, the chain for the conclusion is:

some K → B → non-M → non-A → P

With this pre-mapped strategy, we can now do the deduction, without getting lost in a maze of our own making. Our task is to do *only* what is needed to produce the lines that are the links of the chain (they have been starred here):

1. some K are B *   prem
2. all A are M   prem
3. no B are M   prem
4. all non-A are P *   prem   so, some K are P
    _____

5. all B are non-M *   3, QN
6. all non-M are non-A *   2, Contrap
7. some K are P   1,5,6,4, Super Part Syll   HURRAY! HURRAY!

Expanding Traditional Logic to Include Names

One noticeable deficiency of Traditional Logic, but one that is easily remedied, is the lack of adequate and commonsense provisions for handling sentences and inferences about specific *individual things*. Traditional Logic is explicitly a logic of general terms, applied to groups, not individual things. By contrast, in everyday speech we readily discuss and make inferences about individual things, such as the Moon, the Sears Tower, Hillary Clinton, London, Europe, Donald Trump, and so on. These things are *not* groups, and therefore, the quantifiers "all," "some," and "no" do not apply to them. We need additional logical tools. When we focus on some specific arguments, we can readily see the pieces that are missing.

All planets orbit a sun	All [planets] are [sun-orbiters]
Earth is a planet	[Earth] is [a planet]
So, Earth orbits a sun	So, [Earth] is [a sun-orbiter]
Mars is a planet	[Mars] is [planet]
Mars is not inhabited	[Mars] is [non-inhabited]
So, some planets are not inhabited	some [planets] are [non-inhabited]

Intuitively, these are excellent inferences, and they indicate the way in which Traditional Logic must be augmented. First of all, we need a group of *name* expressions, that represent *individual things*. (These are also called *singular terms*, in contrast to the already available general terms.) Secondly we need one extra *copula* expression to accommodate name expressions. And thirdly, alongside the universal and particular categorical sentence forms, we need one extra *categorical* sentence form that incorporates these additional pieces into permissible sentences. All the elements that we are thus adding to the language of Traditional Logic are:

names: a, b, c, d, . . .

    [italicized lower case Roman letters, for English names:

      the Moon, the Sears Tower, Hillary Clinton, London, Europe, etc.]

singular copula: is
singular categorical sentences: name + singular copula + general term

The sample arguments we gave above can now be symbolized in the obvious way:

All planets orbit a sun	All P are O
Earth is a planet	*e* is P
So, Earth orbits a sun	∴ *e* is O
Mars is a planet	*m* is P
Mars is not inhabited	*m* is non-I
So, some planets are not inhabited	∴ some P are non-I

With this new addition to the language, it is also necessary to present additional rules of inference, to stipulate how these new sentences may be used in deductions. Again, the laws at issue are very simple and very intuitive, exactly what one would expect:

Singular Univ. Syllogism	*Singular Part. Syllogism*	*Name-Negation Law*
all S are P n is S ——————— ∴ n is P	n is S n is P ——————— ∴ some S are P	~(n is P) = n is non-P

There are some commonsense restrictions built into the very wording of the rules. One restriction is that, while these rules may use any names whatsoever, each such application may only use *one* name at a time. When a name is used, it must be used in a *consistent manner*. A second restriction is that only *name* expressions may be used in these rules, and one cannot substitute some quantified expression for these names. These are obvious points, but symbolic sentences can sometimes confuse us. Here are some examples that violate these restrictions, and in each case it is totally obvious that an error was made.

All [persons] are [thinkers] [Einstein] is [a person] So, [Chicago] is [a thinker]	all P are T *e* is P so, *c* is T	ERROR, the two names must be the same name
[Mars] is [a planet] [Einstein] is [smart] So, some [planets] are [smart]	*m* is P *e* is S so, some P are S	ERROR, the two names must be the same name
All [dinosaurs] are [humongous] [nothing] is [a dinosaur] So, [nothing] is [humongous]	all D are H [nothing] is P so, [nothing] is T	ERROR, "nothing" is not the name of an individual thing
[some cat] is [a fast animal] [Some cat] is [without legs] So, some [fast animals] are [without legs]	[some cat] is P [some cat] is S so, some P are S	ERROR, "some cat" is not the name of an individual thing

All these errors are just too obvious ever to be made by anyone, because we intuitively understand the error when ordinary language is used. But, in the symbolic language one can easily make mistakes by simply being careless.

Here are some examples of deductions within the augmented system.

(1) All non-human beings are without human feelings.
     Soxtrox has human feelings.
     All earthlings are things born on Earth.
     Soxtrox was not born on Earth.
     So, some human beings are not earthlings.

1. all non-H are non-F	PREM
2. *s* is F	PREM
3. all E are B	PREM
4. *s* is non-B	PREM /∴ some H are non-E
5. all F are H	1, Contrap
6. *s* is H	5,2, Sing Univ Syll
7. all non-B are non-E	3, Contrap
8. *s* is non-E	4,7, Sing Univ Syll
9. some H are non-E	6,8, Sing Part Syll

(2) All realtors manage large sums of money.
     No managers of large sums of money are soft-hearted.
     Donald Trump is a realtor, and he is a likable person.
     So, some likable persons are not soft-hearted.

1. All R are M	PREM
2. No M are S	PREM
3. *d* is R	PREM
4. *d* is L	PREM /∴ some L are non-S
5. *d* is M	1,3, Sing Univ Syll
6. all M are non-S	2, QN
7. *d* is non-S	6,5, Sing Univ Syll
8. some L are non-S	4,7, Sing Part Syll

When Traditional Logic is expanded to include names, it may be called *Augmented Traditional Logic*. A few logic books use the augmented system in part.

Other Traditional Rules, But Ones That Are Defective

If truth be told, there is something that we have *omitted* from Traditional Logic. Traditional Logic has traditionally included some rules that are now recognized to be incorrect rules. These purported rules all have one thing in common. They assume that universal categorical sentences, "all **S** are **P**," have an *existential commitment*, a commitment to the *existence* of things described by the subject term of the sentence. For example, the sentence, "All persons are free agents," is said to have this existential commitment, a commitment to the existence of persons. And, if such things do exist then the relationship asserted by the universal sentence must also apply to those things. Consequently, the existing persons are also free agents. So, the sentence, "Some persons are free agents," seems to follow. The now rejected *Rule of Subalternation* is precisely this inference:

- *All* persons are free agents.   So, *some* persons are free agents.
- *All* cars are wheeled.   So, *some* cars are wheeled.
- *No* dogs are purple.   So, *some* dogs are *not* purple.

But there is a problem here. The quantifier "all" does not work like that. The quantifier "all" has the functional meaning of "all, *if any*," and consequently, there are frequent exceptions to the conjectured correlation. In such cases, the "all" sentence is true, but the corresponding "some" sentence is false. Consider:

- All green horses are green. (**T**)   So, some green horses are green. (**F**)
- All round cubes are round. (**T**)   So, some round cubes are round. (**F**)
- No great-grandfathers *here* are   So, some great-grandfathers *here* are not
  without offspring. (**T**)   without offspring. (**F**)

And these are not the only counter-examples to the existential viewpoint. In fact, 50 percent of all universal sentences do not have existential commitment. (Try to figure out why it must be 50 percent.) As a result of this, Modern Logic *rejects* the existential viewpoint for universal sentences, and likewise, so do we. With this rejection, nothing of common sense is lost, much simplicity is gained, and truth is preserved. But one important consequence is that one must also reject those traditional rules that are based on the existential viewpoint. A word of *warning*: some logic books continue to include, even if apologetically, these invalid rules alongside the valid ones. Just be very careful if ever you use them.

Limitations of Traditional Logic

When Traditional Logic is presented in the simplified form that we have given it in the present chapter, the result is an easy and effective system of natural deduction, one that agrees well with our ordinary way of thinking and reasoning. But for all its goodness, Traditional Logic has significant practical and theoretical *limitations*. One of these limitations was the inability to adequately deal with named individual things, but, as we saw, that deficiency was easily remedied by means of a slight *expansion* of the system. The other limitations cannot be solved by such easy patches. The most significant of these limitations is the inability of Traditional Logic to deal with sentences that have *complex* subject terms and predicate terms. The kind of complexity at issue consists of the *combination* of several simple terms into a single larger complex term. The following argument illustrates the problem:

Some [hardworking persons] are [cow owners that live in Kalamazoo]

Therefore, some [persons] are [cow owners]

This argument contains four independent ideas, each of which creates relations to other sentences: H = hardworking, P = persons, C = cow owners, K = live in Kalamazoo. This argument *intuitively* suggests some sort of analysis like the following:

Some [H P] are [C K]

Therefore, some P are C

Intuitively this makes sense, but in Traditional Logic this is *complete nonsense*. In Traditional Logic only *single* capital letters are allowed to be used for the entire subject side and the entire predicate side, and such an analysis completely fails to capture whatever deeper logical relationships are at work in an argument, as in our example:

Q = hardworking persons   M = cow owners that live in Kalamazoo
P = persons   C = cow owners

some Q are M

Therefore, some P are C

So, we see that Traditional Logic does *not* have sufficient resources to deal with arguments that contain complex terms. There is a *general* solution for this *general* problem, but it is drastic—jump over to a *new logic*. But before we look at that general solution, there may be a *particular* solution for *particular* arguments, and one should always consider this possibility before taking the more drastic approach.

In fact, there is a particular solution for the argument just presented. (But there will be other arguments for which this kind of a solution will not work.) In the initial stages of analyzing the argument, we should consider whether the argument as given contains *intended* premisses that are *not* explicitly stated. In general, such arguments are also known as *enthymemes*, and when such intentions are clear, we are in fact required to *add* such additional premisses to the argument. At this early stage, then, a particular solution may be available to us: We may *add* to the stated premisses all relationships that are clearly intended, including intended *logical* relationships. This is something we do at the outset, as part of analyzing and symbolizing the argument. For our earlier example, the intended missing premisses are:

All [hardworking persons] are [persons]   = all Q are P
All [cow owners that live in Kalamazoo] are [cow owners]   = all M are C

When we add these extra premisses, we are able to represent and prove the original argument.

1. some Q are M	premiss	
2. all Q are P	intended missing premiss	
3. all M are C	intended missing premiss ∴ some P are C	
———		
4. some Q are C	1,3, Part Syll	
5. some C are Q	4, Conv	
6. some C are P	5,2, Part Syll	
7. some P are C	6, Conv	

Well, that one worked all right, and the approach is worth remembering. So, in as much as a very large part of our reasoning tends not to be extra complicated, Traditional Logic, with some such additions, is well suited to the task. Still, there must be a workable solution available for the complicated arguments as well, and that will force us to take the drastic approach. To deal with the complicated cases, we need to *abandon* Traditional Logic altogether, and we must start over with a new system of logic designed specifically to deal with the problem of complex terms, as well as a variety of other kinds of complications. This new system is the subject matter of the next chapter, and it is called *Modern Quantificational Logic*.

Reference Sheet for the Rules of Traditional Logic

S, **P**, **M** are variables that represent both *affirmative* terms and *negative* terms.

Elementary Equivalences For Traditional Logic

Predicate Double Negation (Pred-DN)

. . . . . are **P**   = ... are non-non-**P**

Here the dotted notation represents any quantifier and any subject term, both of which must be kept constant in the inference.

The Quantifier-Negation laws (QN)

not (all **S** are **P**)	=	some **S** are non-**P**
not (some **S** are **P**)	=	all **S** are non-**P**
no **S** are **P**	=	all **S** are non-**P**
no **S** are **P**	=	not (some **S** are **P**)

Conversion (Conv)

some **S** are **P**	=	some **P** are **S**
no **S** are **P**	=	no **P** are **S**

Contraposition (Contrap)

all **S** are **P**	=	all **opposite[P]** are **opposite[S]**

Elementary Argument Forms For Traditional Logic

Univ Syll	**Part Syll**	
all **S** are **M**	some **S** are **M**	One may also **supersize** these
all **M** are **P**	all **M** are **P**	rules by adding the appropriate
———————	———————	**continuation** premisses.
∴ all **S** are **P**	∴ some **S** are **P**	

Additional Rules for Traditional Logic

Sing Univ Syll	Sing Part Syll	Name-Negation Law
all S are P	n is S	~(n is P) = n is non-P
n is S	n is P	
∴ n is P	∴ some S are P	

Exercise 3.7. A,B,C Syllogistic Deductions

Part A. Here are some additional examples of deductions for syllogistic arguments. For some of these arguments, a solution has been provided so that you can compare your own answer to it. Do not be alarmed if your answer is different—there are several ways to do these problems. There is an available **Exercise Work Sheet** to practice on.

1.   There are very mellow persons. Everyone is endowed with free will. All who are endowed with free will are potentially very dangerous. So, some very mellow persons are potentially very dangerous.

1. some P are M	Prem	
2. all P are E	Prem	YOU TRY IT YOURSELF, TOO.
3. all E are D	Prem	
/∴ some M are D		
4. some M are P	1, Conv	
5. some M are E	4,2, Part Syll	
6. some M are D	5,3, Part Syll	

2.   No introverts are socialites. All who are not introverts are extroverts. So, all socialites are extroverts.

1. no I are S	Prem	
2. all non-I are E	Prem	YOU TRY IT YOURSELF, TOO.
/∴ all S are E		
3. all I are non-S	1, QN	
4. all S are non-I	3, Contrap	
5. all S are E	4,2, Univ Syll	

3. No one who is happy is depressed. All who are not depressed are not people whose candidate is losing. So, no one who has a candidate that is losing is a happy person.

1. no H are D	Prem	
2. all non-D are non-C	Prem	YOU TRY IT YOURSELF, TOO.
/∴ no C are H		
3. all H are non-D	1, QN	
4. all H are non-C	3,2, Univ Syll	
5. all C are non-H	4, contrap	
6. no C are H	5, QN	

4. Not everyone can dance. Whoever cannot dance didn't take lessons at the Arthur Murray School of Dance. Only those who take lessons at the Arthur Murray School of Dance pay money to that school. So, not everyone pays money to the Arthur Murray School of Dance.

1. not all P are D	Prem	
2. all non-D are non-T	Prem	YOU TRY IT YOURSELF, TOO.
3. all M are T	Prem	
/∴ not all P are M		
4. some P are non-D	1, QN	
5. some P are non-T	4,2, Part Syll	
6. all non-T are non-M	3, Contrap	
7. some P are non-M	5,6, Part Syll	
8. not all P are M	7, QN	

Now, give your own deductions for the following three arguments.

5.   some A are B , no B are non-C /∴ some A are C

6.   not all A are B , all A are C /∴ some non-B are C

7.   all K are non-S , all M are S , all non-B are K /∴ all M are B

Part B. Give deductions for the following arguments; use as many steps as you need. Use the available **Exercise Work Sheet** to submit your work.

1.   All babies are illogical. No one who can manage a crocodile is despised. Illogical persons are despised. So, babies cannot manage crocodiles.
   •   all B are I , no M are D , all I are D /∴ all B are non-M

2.   None of my books are interesting. Every one of your writings is interesting. Only your writings are criticized by you. So, you are critical about none of my books.
   •   no B are I , all W are I , all non-W are non-C /∴ no B are C

3.   No subscribers to the *New York Times* are not well-educated. No kangaroos can read. Whoever cannot read is not well-educated. So, kangaroos do not subscribe to the *New York Times*

   • no S are non-W , no K are R , all non-R are non-W /∴ all K are non-S

4.   No one who cannot stir the hearts of men is a true poet. No one who does not truly understand human nature can stir the hearts of men. Only exceptional people truly understand human nature. Exceptional people are capable of wielding great power. Those who are capable of wielding great power are potentially very dangerous. So, true poets are potentially very dangerous.

   • no non-S are T , no non-U are S , all non-E are non-U , all E are W , all W are P /∴ all T are P

5.   People who are sane can do logic. No lunatics are allowed to be on a jury. No one in your family can do logic. So, no one in your family is allowed to be on a jury.

   • all S are L , no non-S are A , no F are L /∴ no F are A

6.   All lions are cats. All cats are felines. No reptiles are felines. All snakes are reptiles. All boas are snakes. Some pets are boas. All pets are cared for animals. So, not all cared for animals are lions.

   • all L are C , all C are F , no R are F , all S are R , all B are S , some P are B , all P are A /∴ not all A are L

7.   Monkeys are bold. Nothing bold is scared of a baby. Some monkeys are unimaginative. Whatever is scared of a gigantic baby with a machine gun is scared of a baby. So, not everything that is not scared of a gigantic baby with a machine gun is imaginative.

   • all M are B , no B are S , some M are non-I , all G are S /∴ not all non-G are I

8.   To succeed in life, one must be able to achieve everything that is really important to one's life. No one can achieve everything that is really important to one's life if one does not know one's shortcomings. Knowing one's shortcomings means being able to admit that one makes mistakes. But, some people just can't admit that they make mistakes. So, some people will not succeed in life.

   • all S are A , no non-K are A , all K are M , some P are non-M /∴ some P are non-S

Part C. Give deductions for the following arguments; use as many steps as you need. Use the available **Exercise Work Sheet** to submit your work.

(#1)	(#2)	(#3)
1. no K are non-M	1. not all Q are B	1. b is non-M
2. some A are G	2. all W are K	2. all S are M
3. no non-S are G	3. all K are B	3. all R are E
4. all S are K	4. not some non-W are U	4. no E are non-S
————————	————————	————————
So, some A are M	So, some Q are non-U	So, not all non-M are R

(#4)
1. all D are non-Q
2. all D are S
3. c is D
4. all non-Q are M
5. no S are non-A
_____

So, not no A are M

(#5)
1. no A are B
2. all C are B
3. no U are M
4. all non-A are M
5. no non-U are K
_____

So, no C are K

(#6)
1. d is K
2. not some P are Q
3. all B are Q
4. no K are non-B
5. all non-M are P
_____

So, some K are M

Section 3.8 Combining Propositional Logic with Syllogistic Logic

We noted earlier that the system of Traditional Logic can be considered to also include the system of Propositional Logic. This means that we can demonstrate the validity of arguments that have *two* levels of complexity: (1) the lower level involving *quantifiers* and *terms*, and (2) the upper level involving *connectives*. So, when sentences have just the right connective structures, we can apply rules such as MP, MT, Hyp Syll, Disj Syll, DeMorg, Contrap, DN, and so forth, as in the following examples.

1. (all K are M) ∨ (some K are G)   . . . .
2. ~(all K are M)   . . . .
3. (some K are G)   1,2, Disj Syll

7. (some W are P) ⊃ (some H are A)   . . . .
8. (some W are P)   . . . .
9. (some H are A)   7,8, MP

As one might expect, many ordinary arguments *require* that we use *both* propositional rules and syllogistic rules to validly derive their conclusions, as the following three examples illustrate.

Argument #1. If some human beings are perfect, then some human beings are immortal. But, all human beings are mortal. So, no human beings are perfect.

1. (some H are P) ⊃ (some H are non-M)   Prem
2. all H are M   Prem   ∴ no H are P
_____

3. (all H are non-non-M)   2, Pred-DN
4. ~(some H are non-M)   3, QN
5. ~(some H are P)   1,4, MT
6. no H are P   5, QN

Argument #2. If some persons have free will, then some actions are good and some actions are evil. If no persons have free will, then no actions are good and no actions are evil. So, if some actions are good, then also, some actions are evil.

1.	(some P are F) ⊃ [(some A are G) & (some A are E)]	Prem
2.	(no P are F) ⊃ [(no A are G) & (no A are E)]	Prem
	∴ (some A are G) ⊃ (some A are E)	

3.	(some P are F) ⊃ (some A are E)	1, Dbl Thens
4.	(no P are F) ⊃ (no A are G)	2, Dbl Thens
5.	(some P are F) ∨ ~(some P are F)	Taut
6.	(some P are F) ∨ (no P are F)	5, QN
7.	(some A are E) ∨ (no A are G)	6,3,4,Dilemma
8.	(some A are E) ∨ ~(some A are G)	7, QN
9.	(some A are G) ⊃ (some A are E)	8, Comm, Cond

Argument #3. Either all people have a soul, or no person has a soul. If all people have a soul, then all people should be concerned about an afterlife. If all people should be concerned about an afterlife, then all people should be concerned about what good they do in their present life. Some people have willingly sacrificed their own lives to save others, and whoever willingly sacrifices his own life to save others must have a soul. So, everyone should be concerned about what good he does in his present life.

1.	(all P are S) ∨ (no P are S)	Prem
2.	(all P are S) ⊃ (all P are A)	Prem
3.	(all P are A) ⊃ (all P are G)	Prem
4.	(some P are W) & (all W are S)	Prem ∴ all P are G

5.	some P are W	4, Simp
6.	all W are S	4, Simp
7.	some P are S	5,6, Part Syll
8.	~(~(some P are S))	7, Dbl Neg
9.	~(no P are S)	8, QN
10.	all P are S	1,9, Disj Syll
11.	all P are A	2,10, MP
12.	all P are G	3,11, MP

By way of summary we present again all the rules that belong to the two systems of logic that we have studied thus far.

The Combined System of Rules

I.   **The Elementary Argument forms**

Propositional Logic: MP, MT, Hyp Syll, Dilem, Conj, Simp, Disj Syll, Disj Add, Dbl Thens, Bicond, RAA

Traditional Logic: Univ Syll, Part Syll, Sing Univ Syll, Sing Part Syll

II. **The Elementary Equivalences**

Propositional Logic: Dbl Neg, DeMorg, Contrap, Cond, Bicond, Dbl Ifs, Dupl, Comm, Assoc, Dist

Traditional Logic: Pred-DN, QN, Conv, Contrap, Name-Neg

III. **The Rule of Logical Truth**

Propositional Logic: Taut

IV. **The Rules of Hypothetical Reasoning**

Propositional Logic: Conditional Proof (CP)
Indirect Proof (IP)

Exercise 3.8. A,B Combined Logic—Symbolization and Deductions

Part A. Symbolize the following arguments, using the combined symbolic languages of Propositional Logic and Traditional Logic. Use the available **Exercise Work Sheet** to submit your work.

(1) 1. If everyone likes to sing or dance, then everyone likes to be active. 2. If everyone likes to be active, then it is false that someone is completely lethargic. So, if everyone likes to sing or dance, then no one is completely lethargic.

(2) 1. Some people invent important new theories. 2. All who invent important new theories are famous. 3. If some people are famous, then not all people are undistinguished. So, some people are distinguished.

(3) 1. If all even numbers are non-quintuple reals, then all multiples of four are non-quintuple reals. 2. Some multiples of four are also multiples of five (e.g., the number twenty). 3. But, no non-quintuple reals are multiples of five. So, some even numbers are not non-quintuple reals.

(4) 1. All actions performed out of physical necessity are not morally characterized actions. 2. Some things that people do are actions performed through brainwashing. 3. All actions performed through brainwashing are actions performed out of physical necessity. So, not all things that people do are morally characterized actions.

(5) 1. Either some physical things are atoms, or it is not the case that some physical things are atoms. 2. If some physical things are atoms, then all material things are made of atoms. 3. If it is not the case that some physical things are atoms, then no material things are made of atoms. So, all material things are made of atoms, or no material things are made of atoms, and consequently, if some material things are made of atoms, then all material things are made of atoms.

(6) 1. All beings that are perfect cannot be lacking in some feature that would make them greater if they had it than if they did not have it. 2. All beings that are not omnipotent are clearly lacking in some feature that would make them greater if they had it than if they did not have it, as are beings that are not omniscient, as are as beings that are not omnibenevolent, and as are beings that are not eternal. So, all perfect beings must be omnipotent; they must be omniscient; they must be omnibenevolent; and they must be eternal. [Hint: L = beings that lack some feature that would make them greater if they had it than if they did not have it.]

(7) 1. Either some persons have free will, or no persons have free will. 2. If some persons have free will, then some actions are good and some actions are evil. 3. If no persons have free will, then no actions are good and no actions are evil. So, either some actions are evil, or no actions are good.

(8) 1. Actions that are good are morally characterized actions, and they and only they deserve to be rewarded. 2. Also, actions that are evil are morally characterized actions, and they and only they deserve to be punished. So, actions that are not morally characterized actions do not deserve to be rewarded, nor do they deserve to be punished.

Part B. Give deductions for the following arguments. Use the available **Exercise Work Sheet** to submit your work.

1. (all P are L) ⊃ (all P are A) , (all P are A) ⊃ ~(some P are C) /∴ (all P are L) ⊃ (no P are C)

2. some P are I , all I are F , (some P are F) ⊃ ~(all P are non-D) /∴ some P are D

3. (all E are non-Q) ⊃ (all M are non-Q) , some M are F , no non-Q are F /∴ some E are non-non-Q

4. all N are non-M , some D are B , all B are N /∴ ~(all D are M)

5. (some P are A) ∨ ~(some P are A) , (some P are A) ⊃ (all E are M) ,

    ~(some P are A) ⊃ (no E are M)

    /∴ (all E are M) ∨ (no E are M) /∴ (some E are M) ⊃ (all E are M)

6.　all P are non-L , (all non-O are L) & (all non-S are L) & (all non-B are L) & (all non-E are L) /∴ (all P are O) & (all P are S) & (all P are B) & (all P are E)

7.　(some P are F) ∨ (no P are F) , (some P are F) ⊃ [(some A are G) & (some A are E)] , (no P are F) ⊃ [(no A are G) & (no A are E)]   /∴ (some A are E) ∨ (no A are G)

8.　(all G are M) & (all G are R) & (all R are G) , (all E are M) & (all E are P) & (all P are E) /∴ (all non-M are non-R) & (all non-M are non-P)

CHAPTER 4

MODERN QUANTIFICATIONAL LOGIC

Section 4.1 Introduction to Quantificational Logic

At the end of Chapter 3 we discussed several ways in which Traditional Logic was incomplete. The most important problems were the inability to deal with *singular terms*, the inability to deal with *complex terms*, and the inability to deal with *relational* terms. Modern Quantificational Logic was created to fix these problems in a final, comprehensive, and efficient manner.

Singular terms are words or phrases that represent *individual things*, such as "Joe," "Santa," "the Moon," "Chicago," "the Sears Tower," and so on. Singular terms are more commonly called the *names* of individual things. Singular terms, then, are different from the *general terms* that are provided in Traditional Logic: general terms represent *groups* of things, whereas singular terms represent *single* things, and not groups. Because of this difference, arguments about individual things cannot be properly represented in Traditional Logic.

The sentences of our everyday language usually contain *complex* descriptive phrases to represent groups of things. But Traditional Logic does not distinguish between *simple general terms* and *complex general terms*, with the one small exception that affirmative terms are distinguished from negative terms. The result of this deficiency is that a great many logical connections among sentences cannot be represented. For example, the following argument cannot be represented in Traditional Logic:

Original argument	*Traditional Logic*
Some (pink birds) are (long-legged)	Some Q are L
All (birds) are (winged)	All B are W
So, some (pink things) are (long-legged and winged)	So, some P are S

That is not even close. What is needed is a new kind of analysis with the following two features: (1) all the simple ideas that occur in an argument are individually represented, and

(2) all the simple ideas that occur in an argument can be combined or separated using familiar laws of logic.

Let's Start at the Very Beginning

We are going to replace the language of Traditional Logic with the significantly different language of Modern Quantificational Logic. But a word of warning. This language is somewhat strange, and it is intended only for *advanced* logical thinking.

The first thing we do is to officially introduce singular terms into the language of logic. These terms are words or phrases that *name* single things.

> *Singular terms (names)*:
> All singular terms are symbolized by unique lower case letters: a, b, c, d, . . . , w
> (but not including the letters: x, y, z).

Next, we will introduce terms to represent the *simple* ideas we have of the characteristics of things. One is able to think of these terms as representing groups of things, but that turns out not to be a useful way of thinking about them. Better just to think of these terms as representing the properties that things have.

> *Simple predicates*:
> All *simple* general terms are symbolized by unique capital letters: A, B, C, . . . , Z.
> (We will also call these *simple predicates*.)

Thirdly, the new language conceives of *sentences* in a new way. In Traditional Logic categorical sentences are thought of as expressing a relationship between two *groups* of things. The sentence "all cows moo" is reworded as "all cows are mooers," so that the relationship expressed is that the group of cows is included in the group of mooers.

But no longer in the new language. Groups are no longer important, and in their place are individuals with certain properties. Sentences function to express the *characteristics* that *individual things* have. The sentence "some person is happy" is not taken to be about the intersection of two groups; the sentence is about some individual thing: *it* has the characteristic of being a person, and *it* also has the characteristic of being happy. And so too with all other simple sentences. The fundamental ideas at play in the new logic are those of individuals and characteristics.

Name-Sentences (Singular Sentences)

Consider the sentence "Sue is a painter." This sentence is now thought of as saying that the characteristic "is-a-painter" is true of the individual thing "Sue." This sentence is analyzed as having two parts: "Sue" and "is-a-painter." The first part is a *name* and refers to some individual thing, and the second part is a *simple predicate* that identifies some characteristic. When we symbolize this sentence, the symbols for the two parts are written next to each other, but in a *special order*: the simple predicate symbol is written first, and the name symbol is written second. (The language is a little strange! Yes!)

Sue is a painter	→	Ps	"is-a-painter: Sue"
George is a president	→	Pg	"is-a-president: George"
Chicago is large	→	Lc	"is-large: Chicago"
Loyola is a university	→	Ul	"is-a-university: Loyola"
The Moon is round	→	Rm	"is-round: the Moon"

Compound Name-Sentences

A basic rule of analysis for the new language is that complex expressions must be broken up into *single, simple predications*, each of which is applied to the subject. *Each* idea gets *one* sentence. The proper combinations can then be formed by applying the appropriate connectives to the simple name-sentences involved.

The Moon is not square		
~ The Moon is square	→	~Sm
George is a sneaky president		
George is sneaky & George is president	→	Sg & Pg
Chicago is large and beautiful		
Chicago is large & Chicago is beautiful	→	Lc & Bc
Sue is a painter but not a writer		
Sue is a painter & ~ Sue is a writer	→	Ps & ~Ws
Loyola is inexpensive or it is challenging		
~ Loyola is expensive ∨ Loyola is challenging	→	~El ∨ Cl

Existentially Quantified Sentences

Sometimes we make assertions not about specific individuals, mentioned by name, but about some *unspecified* individuals, some individual things in general: "something scared me," or "there are things that have a great effect," or "spirits exist." Sentences such as these are analyzed in the new language as attributing some characteristic to some *unspecified* things. For this kind of sentence, the language requires a new kind of expression, called an *existential quantifier.* An existential quantifier introduces some unspecified thing(s) which will be referred to perhaps several times in the sentence. For this reason a special logical *pronoun* is introduced, akin to the English pronouns "he," "she," "it," "they," etc., by means of which the unspecified thing(s) are referred to later in the sentence. These special pronouns are usually called *variables*.

Variables (logical pronouns):

Variables are the symbols: x , y , z , with or without a subscript.

Variables occur in quantifiers to *begin* a reference to unspecified things, and they occur in the remainder of sentences to *continue* the reference to the things introduced by the quantifiers.

Existential quantifiers:

English expression	*symbolic form*
for some x , for some y , for some z	$(\exists x)$, $(\exists y)$, $(\exists z)$

Variables, existential quantifiers, and simple predicates combine to form simple existential sentences.

something is a spirit	→	for some x, x is a spirit	→	$(\exists x)Sx$
unicorns exist	→	for some x, x is a unicorn	→	$(\exists x)Ux$
there are red planets	→	for some x, x is a planet & x is red	→	$(\exists x)(Px \,\&\, Rx)$
there are non-red birds	→	for some x, x is a bird & ~ x is red	→	$(\exists x)(Bx \,\&\, {\sim}Rx)$

Universally Quantified Sentences

We can make yet another kind of assertion about unspecified individual things. We can say that *all* things have a certain kind of characteristic, for example, "all things are made of matter," or "everything is either physical or mental," or "nothing is uncaused," or "each person is able to sing." For these kinds of sentences the language has *universal quantifiers*, whose function it is to go through the entire list of things that exist and attribute to each of them some given characteristic. Again, these quantifiers introduce a variable that shifts its reference one at a time to each thing that exists, and this variable is later used in the sentence to make some predication.

Universal quantifiers:

English expression	symbolic form
for all x , for all y , for all z	$(\forall x) , (\forall y) , (\forall z)$

Variables, universal quantifiers, and simple predicates combine to form simple universal sentences.

all things are spiritual	$\rightarrow$	for all x, x is spiritual	$\rightarrow$	$(\forall x)Sx$
everything is not magical	$\rightarrow$	for all x, ~ x is magical	$\rightarrow$	$(\forall x)\text{\textasciitilde}Mx$
everything is a red star	$\rightarrow$	for all x, x is red & x is a star	$\rightarrow$	$(\forall x)(Rx \mathbin{\&} Sx)$
nothing is a talking bird	$\rightarrow$	for all x, ~(x is a bird & x talks)	$\rightarrow$	$(\forall x)\text{\textasciitilde}(Bx \mathbin{\&} Tx)$

The Need for Variables

The strangeness of the new language is most evident in its use of *variables* in both the quantifiers and in the remainder of sentences. Variables make the sentences look like mathematical formulas, rather than sentences of familiar English. But that is more a matter of appearances than how things actually are. In fact, variables are no stranger than the *pronouns* "he," "she," "it," "him," "her," "they," and "them," because in fact, the variables "x," "y," and "z" *are* these very pronouns. Consider,

For all x, x is made of matter.

This sentence may be considered to be an easy variation of the longer and more cumbersome sentence,

For everything in the universe [it is true that] it is made of matter.

The latter sentence is a *normal* English sentence, albeit a somewhat stuffy one. The strangeness of the new language is not that it uses variables; the strangeness comes from the fact that in place of regular, single word, quantifier expressions, the new language uses only the following quantifier expressions:

For everything in the universe [it is true that] . . .

For all x, . . .

For something in the universe [it is true that] . . .

For some x, . . .

These kinds of quantifier expressions are not only awkward in themselves but they also force the remainder of the sentence to be correspondingly awkward. Just compare the next two sentences:

> Some cats are very aloof.
> For something in the universe [it is true that] it is a cat and it is very aloof.

So that's the first point—the awkwardness. Secondly, there are variables. But why are *variables* necessary in all of this? The answer is that regular pronouns, like "he," "she," and "it," are *too imprecise* in their ability to refer to things. A typical English sentence makes several different references, and ordinary pronouns are unable to make these references in a simple and unambiguous manner. And, if variables are needed in *some* cases, then the formal method requires that they are needed in *all* cases. Consider this easy assertion:

> A man with a dog had a car, and he painted it blue.

The sentence is open to different interpretations, because of the ambiguous reference of the pronoun "it." What did the man paint? Did he paint the car, or did he paint the dog? Logic solves the problem of ambiguous reference by introducing *variables*, whereby pronouns can be "tagged," and in this way forcing a clear reference. For example, the intended meaning of the previous sentence could have been:

> A man$_x$ had a dog$_y$, and he$_x$ had a car$_z$, and he$_x$ painted it$_y$ blue.

(Why not? That could happen. People sometimes paint their dogs blue.) The new language goes one step further. Instead of using tagged English pronouns, the language just uses the *tags* themselves:

> A man$_x$ had a dog$_y$, and x had a car$_z$, and x painted y blue,

or, more precisely, using the new existential quantifiers:

> ($\exists$x) x is a man & ($\exists$y) y is a dog of x & ($\exists$z) z is a car of x & x painted y blue

Holy cow! That's complicated! Yes it is, but don't worry, we won't concern ourselves with *that* kind of complexity. (That's done in the advanced sections). For now, it is enough to know that precise meanings require the use of quantifiers and variables.

The Language of Quantificational Logic

Our discussion so far has introduced all the basic elements of the language of Quantificational Logic, including both the types of quasi-English expressions that it recognizes as well as the symbols for those expressions. Let's pull it all together. Here is the complete list of all the symbols of the new language:

name symbols:	a , b , c , d , . . . , w
variable symbols:	x , y , z
simple predicate symbols:	A , B , C , D , . . . , Z
quantifier symbols:	(∀x) , (∀y) , (∀z) , (∃x) , (∃y) , (∃z)
connective symbols:	~ , & , ∨ , ⊃ , ≡, ∴
parentheses:	(,) , [,] , { , }

Based on the examples that we have used in the previous section, we may observe that the following rules describe how one may combine these symbols into correct expressions of the language. We start with the idea of *sentential expressions*. These expressions are defined and then divided into two groups, namely, *complete* sentences, and *incomplete* sentential fragments:

1. *simple-name sentences*: Am , Da , Sd , Aa , Wb , . . .

These sentential expressions are *complete* sentences, and they consist of a simple predicate letter followed by a name letter.

2. *simple sentence fragments*: Ax , My , Gx , Wz , Mx , . . .

These sentential expressions consist of a simple predicate letter followed by a variable, and since this variable is *free* here, these expressions are *incomplete* sentential fragments. (A *free variable* is one not yet governed by a quantifier, and a *bound variable* is one that is being governed by a quantifier.)

3. *compound sentential expressions*: ~**S** , (**S** & **T**) , (**S** ∨ **T**) , (**S** ⊃ **T**) , (**S** ≡ **T**) ,

where **S** and **T** are sentential expressions. These compound expressions are *complete* sentences if both parts **S** and **T** are complete; otherwise, these compound expressions are *incomplete* sentential fragments.

4. *quantified sentential expressions*: (∀x)**S** , (∃x)**S** ,

where the part **S** by itself must have the variable x free, and also not already bound. If these quantified expressions (with the indicated quantifiers added) contain *no* free variables, then these quantified sentential expressions are *complete* sentences. If these quantified expressions *do* contain other free variables, these quantified expressions are still *incomplete* sentential fragments.

These formation rules divide all sentential expressions into two groups: complete sentences and incomplete sentential fragments. Expressions are complete if they contain *no* free variables, and they are incomplete if they *do* contain a free variable. An important consequence of this division is that complete sentences are fully meaningful, and they therefore have a truth-value: true, or false. Incomplete fragments, by contrast, are not meaningful, and they therefore are incapable of having a truth-value. We give some examples. Here, the name letter "s" means "the Sears Tower" (that information is needed to determine the real-world value of some of these sentences). Further explanations are given in the paragraph that follows.

sentential expressions	symbolization	grammatical status	truth-value*
(∃x) x is happy	(∃x)Hx	complete sentence	true
s is happy & (∃x) x is old	Hs & (∃x)Ox	complete sentence	false
s is happy ⊃ x is round	Hs ⊃ Rx	incomplete, "x" free	nonsense
(∃x) x is red & s is tall	(∃x)Rx & Ts	complete sentence	true
(∃x) x runs & y is old	(∃x)Rx & Oy	incomplete, "y" free	nonsense
x is happy & x is round	Hx & Rx	incomplete, "x" free	nonsense
(∃x) x is old & (∀y) y sings	(∃x)Ox & (∀y)Sy	complete sentence	false
~(∀x)(x is happy & x sings)	~(∀x)(Hx & Sx)	complete sentence	true

* If we give the preceding sentential expressions their full English wording, then we can more clearly see why the symbolic versions have the grammatical status and truth-value that we listed for them.

1. Something is happy.   = true
2. The Sears Tower is happy, and something is old.   = false
3. If the Sears Tower is happy, then x is round.   = Who is x ???
4. Something is happy, and the Sears Tower is tall.   = true
5. Something runs, and y is old.   = Who is y ???
6. x is happy, and x is round.   = Who is x ???
7. Something is old, and everything sings.   = false
8. Not everything both is happy and sings   = true

Exercise 4.1. A,B Symbolizing Quantificational Sentences

Part A. Symbolize the following sentences, using obvious letters for names and simple predicates. (Watch out for hidden negatives.) Use the available **Exercise Work Sheet** to submit your work.

1.   George is not happy.

2. Carlos is smart, but he is not rich.

3. Everything is mixed up.

4. Some things cannot be explained.

5. Not everything can be explained.

6. Nothing is greatest.

7. Not everything is immortal.

8. Expensive candy exists.

9. Inexpensive automobiles don't exist.

10. If there are unicorns, then some things are magical.

11. If there are no ghosts, then Carlos is not a ghost.

12. Everything is spiritual, or everything is not spiritual.

13. Everything is either spiritual or not spiritual.

14. Something is smart, and something is a computer.

15. There are ghosts if and only if there is no matter.

16. Everything is red and sweet or not red and not sweet.

Part B. Symbolize the following sentences, using obvious letters for names and simple predicates. These are harder. Use the available **Exercise Work Sheet** to submit your work.

1. George and Sue like to dance, but neither Liz nor George likes to sing.

2. None of George, Sue, Liz, and Bill know how to paint.

3. Simple, sober, silly Sally sits and Sophie sings.

4. Some things don't like to sing, including George, but some things do like to sing, although not George.

5. Some things are costly and trendy, and some things like that are useful as well.

6. George is such that he is definitely not a person who is generally very capable but specifically not able to sing.

7. Either something is good and something is bad, or nothing is good and nothing is bad.

8. If nothing is both alive and made of cement, then either something is not alive, or everything is not made of cement.

9. It is definitely false that nothing is both not alive and not made of gold. [Keep all the negatives.]

10. If everything has value, and everything is unique, then, if George is an atom, then unique atoms with value exist.

Section 4.2 Types of English Simple Sentences and Other Details

The previous sections introduced all the basic ideas of the language of Quantificational Logic, and these ideas are not difficult to grasp. Still, there is a general problem of how one goes about representing the sentences of English in this new language. The new language is, as we have noted, somewhat unnatural, and this raises the question of whether the new artificial language is adequate for all ordinary reasoning. This problem is more pressing in Quantificational Logic than in Traditional Logic, because Quantificational Logic *intends* to be a comprehensive treatment of all logical inference, and Traditional Logic never had such a goal.

Translation Rules

We have a good place to start. There are seven *translation rules* for seven very general types of *English* sentences. After we have finished with these seven types, we can enlarge our procedures to include a number of *variations* on these seven types. The net result turns out to be a rather comprehensive package. Because these types are so important, it will very useful to introduce some special *terminology*, to make these types more *recognizable*.

Type	Form	Symbolization
1. name-sentences	*name* is **P**	**Pn**
2. absolute, and existential	something is **P** for some x, x is **P**	(∃x) **Px**
3. absolute, and universal	everything is **P** for all x, x is **P**	(∀x) **Px**
4. absolute, and universal-negative	nothing is **P** everything is not **P** for all x, x is not **P**	(∀x) ~**Px**
5. categorical, and existential	some **S** are **P** for some x, x is **S** & x is **P**	(∃x)(**Sx** & **Px**)
6. categorical, and universal	all **S** are **P** for all x, x is **S** ⊃ x is **P**	(∀x)(**Sx** ⊃ **Px**)
7. categorical, and universal-negative	no **S** are **P** every **S** is not **P** for all x, x is **S** ⊃ x is not **P**	(∀x)(**Sx** ⊃ ~**Px**)

Type 1. Name-Sentences

Name sentences are the simplest of these seven types, and they can be propositionally simple or compound. Name sentences do not contain any quantifiers.

- William sneezes a lot → Sw
- Victoria is real smart, but she is not omniscient → Sv & ~Ov
- George and Ella are poor artists → (Pg & Ag) & (Pe & Ae)

Types 2–4. Absolute Sentences

Absolute sentences are sentences whose entire subject term is *exactly* the one word "thing(s)"—no additional words. The label *absolute* is appropriate because the group of things referred to by such a subject term is the *entire* universe, whatever there is. When absolute sentences are translated, the entire left side of the sentence (the subject side) becomes the quantifier "for all x," or "for some x." Their predicate side, on the other hand, may be very simple or very complex.

- Some*thing* made a noise. (What did? I don't know, just something.) → (∃x) Nx
- Every*thing* had a beginning. (What does? Everything, no exception.) → (∀x) Bx
- No*thing* is mental. (Nothing? Yep.) → all things are not mental → (∀x) ~Mx
- Some *things* are either inconsiderate and illegal or expensive and frustrating. → (∃x)[(~Cx & ~Lx) ∨ (Ex & Fx)]
- No*thing* is a green cow on the Moon → (∀x) ~ (Gx & Cx & Mx)

Types 5–7. Categorical Sentences

We call the three remaining types *categorical* sentences, partly because that's what we called them in Chapter 3, but also because their subject term is *not* just the word "thing," but is rather a word or phrase that describes a *category*, that is, a *limited group* of things. Examples of such subject terms are: "cat," or "large cat," or "mean, large cat," or "mean, large cat in Chicago," or "mean, large cat in Chicago that hates watermelons," or something like that. Categorical sentences have another important feature. They have a secret, underlying logical structure, which is captured by these translation rules. The indicated relationships are *mandatory* and have no exceptions. We can highlight these relationships in the following display:

| some . . . . are . . . . | → | (∃x)(. . . . & . . . .) | The "SOME–AND" rule |
| all . . . . are . . . . | → | (∀x)(. . . . ⊃ . . . .) | The "ALL–THEN" rule |

These two rules concern the *main connective* that connects the *subject* side to the *predicate* side of a categorical quantified sentence. When the quantifier is universal, the middle connective *must* be the connective "⊃," and when the quantifier is existential, the middle connective *must* be the connective "&," no exceptions.

Some people like to dance $\qquad\qquad\rightarrow$ (∃x) (Px & Lx)

Some people who like to dance are nevertheless shy and clumsy

$\qquad\qquad\qquad\qquad\qquad\rightarrow$ (∃x) [(Px & Lx) & (Sx & Cx)]

Every cat is deep-down-lazy $\qquad\rightarrow$ (∀x) (Cx ⊃ Lx)

All animals that can fly are either not humans or not fish

$\qquad\qquad\qquad\qquad\qquad\rightarrow$ (∀x) [(Ax & Fx) ⊃ (~Hx ∨ ~Ix)]

The rule for Type 7, categorical universal-negative sentences, emphasizes that the English quantifier "no" has no direct counterpart in the the symbolic language. Instead, this quantifier must be eliminated, by replacing replacing it with an "all . . . are not" construction. Here we follow the same manuever as in Chapter 3: the quantifier "no" changes to "all," the subject term stays exactly the same, and a negation "not" is added to the predicate.

No computers can think

$\quad\rightarrow$ all computers are not thinkers

$\quad\rightarrow$ (∀x)(Cx ⊃ ~ Tx)

No person on the Moon can talk or sing

$\quad\rightarrow$ all persons on the Moon are not talkers or singers

$\quad\rightarrow$ (∀x)[(Px & Mx) ⊃ ~ (Tx ∨ Sx)]

Variations on These Seven Types

By using the seven basic translation rules, one can reduce a large part of English to the new logical language, especially when one combines these rules with the built-in capability to translate complex subject terms and complex predicate terms into their various simple components. We can now go one big step further. In Chapter 3 we studied many English grammatical *variations* on the categorical forms, and what we can do now is simply apply those *same variation rules* to our present quantificational analysis. That means, of course, that you should *definitely* refresh your memory about how these variations work. (Now would be a good time.)

For example, a *missing quantifier*: **You must add it.**

People can't fly → all persons can not fly → $(\forall x)(Px \supset \sim Fx)$

Or how about, the *only quantifier*: **You must exchange it**.

Only cats meow → all meowers are cats → $(\forall x)(Mx \supset Cx)$

Again, the case of a *combined subject*: **You must divide it.**

Dogs and cats are pets → all dogs are pets, and all cats are pets

→ $(\forall x)(Dx \supset Px) \,\&\, (\forall x)(Cx \supset Px)$

Well, you get the idea. All the old ways of putting sentences into categorical form must now be used as *transitional stages* in Quantificational Logic.

Some Guidelines for Symbolization

As you try to translate English sentences to the symbolic forms of Quantificational Logic, remember the following guidelines.

1. Start by determining whether a sentence is propositionally *simple* or propositionally *compound*.

If the sentence is simple, then use the seven translation rules together with the rules for variations to symbolize the sentence. If, on the other hand, the sentence is compound, then symbolize all the simple parts in the way we just mentioned, and when that is done, connect them together with the appropriate connectives.

2. Regarding the *number* of quantifiers there are in a symbolic sentence, the rule is that the number of symbolic quantifiers must equal the number of English quantifiers.
3. Regarding the *position* of quantifiers, the rule is that you must keep the position of a quantifier *exactly* where it is in the English sentence, especially in relation to negation operators.

Count the quantifiers. You may *not distribute* them, and you may *not collect* them. No exceptions. But this rule about numbers holds only for sentences that are already in *standard form*. Be sure to write variations back in their original form before you count quantifiers. For example, "exists" is a quantifier, as is "there are;" and you must re-introduce any missing quantifiers. Again, you must replace sentences with one quantifier and combined subject, with two sentences, each with its own quantifier. Also a word of caution. Do not use the *laws of logic* in the place of practical symbolization rules. It is one thing to analyze *the given form* of an English sentence, and *that* is what symbolization is all about, and it is quite another thing to worry about what logical *inferences* can be made. Keep these two matters separate. We will get to deductions *later*.

4.   Regarding the *number* of negation operators, the rule is that the number of symbolic negation operators "~" must equal the number of English negative words.

Recall that English has the following kinds of negative words: the external sentence negation "not," the internal verb negation "not," the quantifier "no," and the negative term operator "non-." Everyone of these will require, in its proper way, a symbolic operator "~." Again, don't use the law of double negation here to reduce the complexity. That comes *later*.

5.   Regarding the *position* of negation operators, the rule is that you must keep the position of a negation operator *exactly* where it is in the English sentence, especially in relation to quantifiers.

Of course, you have to make sure the sentence is in standard form before you apply this rule; in particular, you must replace the quantifer "no" right at the outset, as well as the quantifier "only." Always remember the following: In quantified sentences, when the *position* of a negation operator is changed, the *meaning* of the sentence also changes.

6.   We just discussed this, but it is worth repeating: remember the "SOME–AND" rule and the "ALL–THEN" rule.

7.   With *categorical* sentences, you must be sure that you have correctly identified the extent of the *subject* expression of the sentence.

This is more difficult when the subject term is complex. Try breaking the sentence into two parts, and *slice it with a vertical bar*, at a point where each part, by itself, has a normal term meaning.

Some Examples to Illustrate These Guidelines

Example 1.

There are mental things that aren't physical, and there are physical things that aren't mental.

Analysis: This is a conjunction p & q. Each part has its own quantifier; so, there are two quantifiers. Also, there are two negation operators that have their own location.

$(\exists x)(Mx \ \& \ {\sim}Px) \ \& \ (\exists x)(Px \ \& \ {\sim}Mx)$

Example 2.

Not no elephants do not fly.

Analysis: We need standard form. Eliminate the word "no" in the required way, and keep the rest constant. The original sentence has *three* negative operators, so the symbolic sentence must have *three* negations as well.

Not all elephants not do not fly.

Further analysis: This is the external negation of "all . . . are . . . ." Also, we must use the "ALL–THEN" rule. And, we finish the predicate side with two negatives, without cancelling them.

~ (∀x) . . . .
~ (∀x) (Ex ⊃ . . .)
~ (∀x) (Ex ⊃ ~(~Fx))

Example 3.

All green fruits that are picked too early will not ripen properly.

Analysis: This is a categorical sentence with a complicated subject term. Determine what the subject term is. Break the sentence into two parts.

All green fruits | that are picked too early will not ripen properly.

No way! Stop! The second half is supposed to be an English predicate expression, but the expression "that are picked too early will not ripen properly" makes no sense at all. Also, the subject idea is incomplete. We must try again:

All green fruits that are picked too early | will not ripen properly.

Yes! Each part makes good sense. The subject expression is "green fruits that are picked too early," and this is a meaningful, complete idea. The predicate expression is "will not ripen properly," and that too is a meaningful, complete idea. Now use the "ALL–THEN" rule. Also, the words "who," "which," "that" are relative pronouns, and they always mean "*and* he," "*and* she," "*and* it," "*and* they, which symbolically become ". . . & x . . ." The overall result is:

(∀x)[x is a green fruit that is picked too early ⊃ x will not ripen well]

(∀x)[(x is green & x is a fruit & x is picked too early) ⊃ x will not ripen well]

(∀x)[(Gx & Fx & Px) ⊃ ~Rx]

We finish this section with a list of 100 (yes, 100) symbolized sentences, grouped into the important types that sentences have. We invite you to review these sentences and their types and to even practice some of these yourself.

Symbolizing 100 Quantificational Sentences

Practice your symbolization skills. Cover up the answers with another sheet of paper, and then compare your own answers with the ones given here.

Group A. Name Sentences

1. Elmo is a hippo.	1. He
2. Sam is not made of matter.	2. ~Ms
3. George is a purple camel.	3. Pg & Cg
4. George is a camel or a hippo.	4. Cg ∨ Hg
5. Mickey is not a green hippo.	5. ~(Gm & Hm)
6. Edgar is green, but not an elephant.	6. Ge & ~Ee
7. Edgar is green, but not a green elephant.	7. Ge & ~(Ge & Ee)
8. If Elmo is a green hippo, then Sam is a cow.	8. (Ge & He) ⊃ Cg

Group B. Absolute Existential Sentences

1. There are hippos.	1. (∃x)Hx
2. Something is a camel.	2. (∃x)Cx
3. Angels exist.	3. (∃x)Ax
4. Something is not a hippo.	4. (∃x)~Hx
5. Some things aren't purple.	5. (∃x)~Px
6. It's not true that something is divine.	6. ~(∃x)Dx
7. Unicorns do not exist.	7. ~(∃x)Ux
8. There are no unicorns.	8. ~(∃x)Ux
9. There aren't any unicorns.	9. ~(∃x)Ux
10. A green elephant exists.	10. (∃x)(Gx & Ex)
11. There are no green camels.	11. ~(∃x)(Gx & Cx)

Group C. Absolute Universal Sentences

1. All things are made of matter.
2. Everything is spatial and temporal.
3. Everything is not spiritual.
4. Not everything is made of matter.
5. Nothing is spiritual.
6. Not anything is miraculous.
7. Nothing is a green elephant.
8. Nothing is a large green elephant.
9. Not everything is a divine spirit.

1. (∀x)Mx
2. (∀x)(Sx & Tx)
3. (∀x)~Sx
4. ~(∀x)Mx
5. (∀x)~Sx
6. (∀x)~Mx
7. (∀x)~(Gx & Ex)
8. (∀x)~(Lx & Gx & Ex)
9. ~(∀x)(Dx & Sx)

Group D. Categorical Existential Sentences

1. Some goats are pushy.
2. Some things that are impolite are also funny.
3. Some unpleasantries are also important.
4. Some camels are not hairy.
5. Some singing camels are funny entertainers.
6. Some elephants that are green are sick.
7. Some goats that are not hairy are polite.
8. Some camels that are purple are not sick.
9. Something that was not a camel did not moo.
10. Some goats are neither hairy nor polite.
11. Some non-cows are not either purple or sick.

1. (∃x)(Gx & Px)
2. (∃x)(~Px & Fx)
3. (∃x)(~Px & Ix)
4. (∃x)(Cx & ~Hx)
5. (∃x)[(Sx & Cx) & (Fx & Ex)]
6. (∃x)[(Ex & Gx) & Sx]
7. (∃x)[(Gx & ~Hx) & Px]
8. (∃x)[(Gx & Px) & ~Sx]
9. (∃x)(~Cx & ~Mx)
10. (∃x)[Gx & (~Hx & ~Px)]
11. (∃x)[~Cx & ~(Px ∨ Sx)]

Group E. Categorical Universal Sentences

1. Every goat is a menace.
2. Every goat is a hairy menace.
3. Every warm camel is hairy.
4. All camels that are hairy are warm.
5. All hairy goats are not warm.
6. Every green elephant is a sick animal.
7. What is not a goat is not a hairy menace.

1. (∀x)(Gx ⊃ Mx)
2. (∀x)[Gx ⊃ (Hx & Mx)]
3. (∀x)[(Wx & Cx) ⊃ Hx]
4. (∀x)[(Cx & Hx) ⊃ Wx]
5. (∀x)[(Hx & Gx) ⊃ ~Wx]
6. (∀x)[(Gx & Ex) ⊃ (Sx & Ax)]
7. (∀x)[~Gx ⊃ ~(Hx & Mx)]

Group F. The "No" Quantifier

1. No goats are polite.
2. No polite goats are a menace.

1. (∀x)(Gx ⊃ ~Px)
2. (∀x)[(Px & Gx) ⊃ ~Mx]

3. Not all hairy goats are polite.
4. Not all camels that are green are sick.
5. No camels don't like to sing.
6. There are no camels that don't like to sing, or, not some camels don't like to sing.
7. No green elephants are sick.
8. Nothing is a polite hairy goat.
9. Not any camel is a graceful dancer.

3. ~(∀x)[(Hx & Gx) ⊃ Px]
4. ~(∀x)[(Cx & Gx) ⊃ Sx]
5. (∀x)(Cx ⊃ ~(~Lx))
6. (∀x)(Cx ⊃ ~(~Lx)), or ~(∃x)(Cx & ~Lx)
7. (∀x)[(Gx & Ex) ⊃ ~Sx]
8. (∀x)~(Px & Hx & Gx)
9. (∀x)[Cx ⊃ ~(Gx & Dx)]

Group G. Quantifiers and Choices

1. Something is sick or not sick.
2. Everything is sick or not sick.
3. Some cow is sick or not sick.
4. Something is sick, or it is not sick.
5. Some cow is sick, or it is not sick.
6. Something is sick, or something is not sick.
7. Some cow is sick, or some cow is not sick.
8. Every cow is sick, or no cow is sick.
9. Everything is a cow or not a cow.
10. Everything is a cow or everything isn't a cow.
11. Everything is sick, or nothing is sick.
12. Something is sick, or nothing is sick.
13. All things are cows, or not all things are cows.
14. All things are cows, or all things are not cows.
15. All things are cows, or no things are cows.
16. Each thing is a cow, or it is not a cow.
17. Some cow is sick, or not some cow is sick.
18. Some cows are not either sick or not sick.

1. (∃x)(Sx ∨ ~Sx)
2. (∀x)(Sx ∨ ~Sx)
3. (∃x)[Cx & (Sx ∨ ~Sx)]
4. (∃x)(Sx ∨ ~Sx)
5. (∃x)[Cx & (Sx ∨~Sx)]
6. (∃x)Sx ∨ (∃x)~Sx
7. (∃x)(Cx&Sx)∨(∃x)(Cx&~Sx)
8. (∀x)(Cx⊃Sx)∨(∀x)(Cx⊃~Sx)
9. (∀x)(Cx ∨ ~Cx)
10. (∀x)Cx ∨ (∀x)~Cx
11. (∀x)Sx ∨ (∀x)~Sx
12. (∃x)Sx ∨ (∀x)~Sx
13. (∀x)Cx ∨ ~(∀x)Cx
14. (∀x)Cx ∨ (∀x)~Cx
15. (∀x)Cx ∨ (∀x)~Cx
16. (∀x)(Cx ∨ ~Cx)
17. (∃x)(Cx&Sx)∨~(∃x)(Cx&Sx)
18. (∃x)[Cx & ~(Sx ∨ ~Sx)]

Group H. Compound Sentences

1. If every cow is purple, then George is purple.
2. If some hippo is polite, then Dumbo is weird.
3. If smart hippos exist, then smart cows exist.
4. If all things are cows, all things are smart.
5. If all things are red cows, all hippos are red.
6. If anything is a red cow, then it is funny.
7. If anything is a red cow, then Sam is funny, or, if red cows exist, then Sam is funny.

1. (∀x)(Cx ⊃ Px) ⊃ Pg
2. (∃x)(Hx & Px) ⊃ Wd
3. (∃x)(Sx&Hx) ⊃(∃x)(Sx&Cx)
4. (∀x)Cx ⊃ (∀x)Sx
5. (∀x)(Rx&Cx)⊃(∀x)(Hx ⊃Rx)
6. (∀x)[(Rx & Cx) ⊃ Fx]
7. (∀x)[(Rx & Cx) ⊃ Fs], or (∃x)(Rx & Cx) ⊃ Fs

Group I. The "Only" Quantifier

1. Only elephants are green,
   or, all green things are elephants.
2. Only sick camels are purple,
   or, all purple things are sick camels.
3. Only *sick* camels are purple,
   or, all camels that are purple are sick.
4. Only polite goats are non-hairy,
   or, all non-hairy things are polite goats.
5. Only *polite* goats are non-hairy,
   or, all goats that are non-hairy are polite.
6. Only things that are not red cows are polite,
   or, all polite things are not red cows.

1. (∀x)(~Ex ⊃ ~Gx),
   or (∀x)(Gx ⊃ Ex)
2. (∀x)[~(Sx & Cx) ⊃ ~Px],
   or (∀x)[Px ⊃ (Sx & Cx)]
3. (∀x)[(Cx & ~Sx) ⊃ ~Px],
   or (∀x)[(Cx & Px) ⊃ Sx]
4. (∀x)[~(Px&Gx) ⊃ ~(~Hx)],
   or (∀x)[~Hx ⊃ (Px & Gx)]
5. (∀x)[(Gx&~Px) ⊃ ~(~Hx)],
   or (∀x)[(Gx & ~Hx) ⊃ Px]
6. (∀x)[~(~(Rx&Cx)) ⊃ ~Px],
   or (∀x)[Px ⊃ ~(Rx & Cx)]

Group J. Missing Quantifiers

1. Hairy goats are a menace.
2. Camels are not hairy animals.
3. Camels will bite you.
4. Camels were making a lot of noise.
5. Goats pushed Clinton, and then bit him.
6. An elephant has a good-memory.
7. An elephant stepped on my toe.

1. (∀x)[(Hx & Gx) ⊃ Mx]
2. (∀x)[Cx ⊃ ~(Hx & Ax)]
3. (∀x)(Cx ⊃ Bx)
4. (∃x)(Cx & Mx)
5. (∃x)[Gx & (Px & Bx)]
6. (∀x)(Ex ⊃ Mx)
7. (∃x)(Ex & Sx)

Group K. Combinations

1. Camels and eggplants are purple.
2. Goats and hippos are not polite.
3. Cows and hippos are large and funny.
4. Cows and hippos were making noises.
5. Some, but not all, camels are hairy.
6. Some cows are smart; some aren't.
7. Only a few hippos are clumsy.

1. (∀x)(Cx ⊃Px)&(∀x)(Ex ⊃Px)
2. (∀x)(Gx ⊃ ~Px) & (∀x)(Hx ⊃ ~Px)
3. (∀x)[Cx ⊃(Lx&Fx)]&(∀x)(Hx⊃(Lx&Fx))
4. (∃x)(Cx & Mx) & (∃x)(Hx & Mx)
5. (∃x)(Cx & Hx) & ~(∀x)(Cx ⊃ Hx)
6. (∃x)(Cx & Sx) & (∃x)(Cx & ~Sx)
7. (∃x)(Hx & Cx) & (∃x)(Hx & ~Cx)

Exercise 4.2. A,B,C Symbolizing Complex Sentences

Part A. Symbolize the following sentences. Be sure to symbolize each individual idea used in these sentences with a predicate letter, and symbolize each negative word. Use the available **Exercise Work Sheet** to submit your work.

1. Some problems are difficult.
2. All students are logical.
3. Some problems cannot be solved.
4. No student is omniscient.
5. Some easy problems can be solved.
6. All difficult problems can be solved.
7. No problem is unsolvable.
8. Some answers are difficult mathematical proofs.
9. Some unsolvable problems are incomprehensible.
10. No short answers are adequate solutions.
11. Not every person is a professional logician.
12. No person is a professional logician.
13. If difficult problems exist then logicians exist.
14. If all problems are difficult, all solutions are long.
15. Either problems exist, or no logicians have jobs.
16. Ella is a logician, but all problems are unsolvable.

Part B. Symbolize the following sentences. These are harder, and you will want to consult the translation rules back in Chapter 3. Use the available **Exercise Work Sheet** to submit your work.

1. Only graduate students are enrolled in graduate programs.
2. A great many metaphysical problems are both complex and unsolvable.
3. Tired students can't study very well.
4. Every person is irrational, if he or she is very angry.
5. All and only students with high GPAs are eligble for the award.
6. Everything is tolerable, except the creepy insects, they are definitely not.
7. Broccoli and spinach are delicious and nutritious.
8. A hungry tiger will eat you, if it can. (E = will eat you, A = is able to eat you)
9. If someone is poisoned, then he/she must get an antidote. (G = gets an antidote)
10. If anyone here starts to sing, George will get upset and leave. So, everyone, please, don't. (S = starts to sing, A = is allowed to sing)

Part C. Translate the following symbolic sentences into *regular* English sentences, using the listed meanings of the predicate letters. Use the available **Exercise Work Sheet** to submit your work.

T = triangle,	F = figure,	C = circle,	E = three-sided,
S = square,	G = green,	U = four-sided,	B = blue,
M = matter,	O = solid,	t = Sears Tower,	c = Chicago

1. (∀x)(Tx ⊃ Fx)
2. ~(∀x)(Fx ⊃ Tx)
3. (∀x)(Cx ⊃ ~Ex)
4. (∃x)~(Sx & Gx)
5. (∃x)(~Sx & ~Gx)
6. (∃x)[(Gx & Sx) & Ux]
7. (∀x)(Gx & Sx & Ux)
8. (∀x)[Tx ⊃ (Ex & Fx)]

9. (∀x)[Tx ⊃ ~(Ux & Fx)]
10. (∀x)[Tx ⊃ (~Ux & Fx)]
11. ~(∃x)[(Ex & Fx) & Cx]
12. (∀x)Mx ∨ (∀x)~Mx
13. (∀x)(Ox & Fx) & (∃x)~Mx
14. Bt ⊃ (∃x)[(Ox & Fx) & Bx]
15. (∀x)(Gx & Sx) ⊃ Sc
16. (∃x)(Sx &~Fx) ⊃ (∀x)~Fx

Section 4.3 The Truth-Value of Quantificational Sentences

Good news. You already know how to do what we deal with in this section. In Chapter 2 we studied the technique for calculating the truth-value of sentences. We will use the same technique for Quantificational Logic.

Let us begin by looking at the *status* of symbolic sentences. We take the symbolic language to be a direct *abbreviation* of a special part of the regular English language. This part is a cumbersome, stuffy, awkward part of English—but English it is. For example, when the following temporary abbreviations are *stipulated*,

R = "red," C = "car," P = "parked on the Moon,"

the symbolic sentence

(∃x)[(Rx & Cx) & Px]

becomes an abbreviation of the actual, but awkward, English sentence,

Something is such that it is red, and it is a car, and it is parked on the Moon.

It is only through such stipulated abbreviations that symbolic sentences have a real-world truth-value, that is, are **true**, or are **false**, in the real world. In the present example, the sentence (∃x)[(Rx & Cx) & Px] has the value **false** in the real world.

In addition, there are other more graceful sentences that we consider to be *stylistic variations* of these awkward sentences, such as:

A red car is parked on the Moon

Some red car is parked on the Moon

There is a red car parked on the Moon

There is a red car that is parked on the Moon

A red car that is parked on the Moon exists

Something is a red car that is parked on the Moon

Something is red, and it is a car, and it is parked on the Moon.

Because these are all equivalent variations, the symbolic abbreviation of any one of them is also a symbolic abbreviation of all the others. In this way, then, symbolic sentences not only represent English sentences but also themselves have a truth-value in the real world.

So, what then is the technique for determining the truth-value of the sentences of Quantificational Logic? As in Chapter 2, the answer divides into two main cases.

Case 1. Simple Sentences

We now know that there are *seven subcases* to consider, because there are seven kinds of simple sentences: (1) name sentences, (2) absolute existential sentences, (3) absolute universal sentences, (4) absolute universal-negative sentences, (5) categorical existential sentences, (6) categorical universal sentences, and (7) categorical universal-negative sentences. In each case the method is as follows:

Step 1. Determine what English sentence the symbolic sentence represents.

Step 2. Reflect carefully on what the truth-value of the English sentence is. (Here we may appeal to what we know through education, our experience, expert testimony, mathematics, ogic, or known definitions.)

Step 3. Assign that truth-value to the symbolic sentence at issue.

Let's consider the next symbolic sentence, with the stipulated term meanings,

$(\forall x)[\, Bx \supset (\sim Mx \,\&\, Qx)\,]$,   B = "bachelor,"   M = "married,"   Q = "male"

This symbolic sentence represents the English sentence

Every bachelor is an unmarried male

and we know that one to be true by definition of the word "bachelor." So, we must assign the value **true** to this symbolic sentence.

Case 2. Compound Sentences

The case of compound sentences is familiar territory. Once the truth-values of some given simple sentences are known, the truth-value of *any* propositional compounds of those sentences can be calculated using the official rules for calculating values. These rules were presented in Chapter 2, Section 4. The only difference between what we did in Chapter 2 and what we are doing now is that we are *now* writing simple symbolic sentences in a new style, using quantifiers and the like.

Let's consider the following four simple sentences:

$$(\forall x)(Tx \supset Bx),\ Tc,\ (\forall x)(Mx \supset Sx),\ (\exists x)(Lx \ \& \ Wx)$$

Let's suppose that we know the meanings of all these symbols, so that we also know (a) what English sentences these symbolic sentences represent, and (b) what truth-values these sentences have. Let's suppose that these truth-values are the following:

$$(\forall x)(Tx \supset Bx) = \mathbf{T},\quad Tc = \mathbf{F},\quad (\forall x)(Mx \supset Sx) = \mathbf{F},\quad (\exists x)(Lx \ \& \ Wx) = \mathbf{T}$$

Given these starting truth-values, we can calculate the truth-value of the next two compound sentences. The "tree method" introduced in Chapter 2 is useful here:

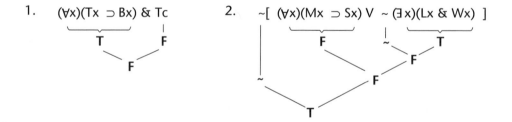

Back to Case 1. Working with Bits and Pieces

Let's have a closer look at step 2 of Case 1: "Reflect carefully on what the truth-value of the [corresponding] English sentence is." In some cases we need only *remember* what we learned earlier in life. For example, we learned earlier that the sentence, "All the planets in our solar system travel in elliptical paths," is indeed true. But sometimes we base these truth-values on some other facts that we know. We have learned many "bits and pieces" about the world around us, and we use that personal knowledge to *figure out* the truth-value of some simple quantifications. For example, suppose you see this big tree falling over in a storm on top of your car. You can hardly believe it. Later you tell the story and say, "Some big tree totalled my car." Hey, not so fast! You only saw a *particular* tree do this. Where did that *existential quantifier* come from? Clearly, there is some *method* at work here. This method is not a fixed, well-defined procedure, but it does employ some *logically valid* rules.

Given some personal observations about some particular things a and b, we may use the following *generalization* rules:

"a is F" = T, "a is G" = T → "Some F are G" = T, "No F are G" = F

"b is H" = T, "b is J" = F → "Some H are not J" = T, "All H are J" = F

Sometimes (but mostly not) our personal observations are able to exhaust *all* of the relevant instances for some matter, such as when we talk about *all the people in a room*. Since the entire range of relevant instances can be observed by us, those personal observations are sufficient for a generalization to "all":

the observed instances exhaust and agree → "All A are B" = T, "Some A are not B" = F
with the indicated correlation   "No C are D" = T, "Some C are D" = F

But do keep in mind that, in most cases, a few personal observations are *not* sufficient to determine correlations that require a knowledge of *all* the relevant cases.

Exercise 4.3. A,B,C Calculating Truth-Values

Part A. Translate each of the following sentences into a *regular* English sentence, using the listed meanings of the symbols; and then, state their truth-value, **T** or **F**. Use the available **Exercise Work Sheet** to submit your work.

T = triangle,	F = figure,	C = circle,	S = square,
U = four-sided,	G = green,	B = blue,	c = Chicago

1. $(\forall x)(Fx \supset Tx)$
2. $(\forall x)(Cx \supset {\sim}Sx)$
3. $(\exists x)(Sx \ \& \ Ux)$
4. $(\forall x)(Sx \ \& \ Gx)$
5. $(\exists x)({\sim}Sx \ \& \ {\sim}Cx)$
6. $(\forall x)(Bx \lor Gx)$
7. $(\forall x)({\sim}Bx \lor {\sim}Gx)$
8. Tc

Part B. Calculate the truth-values of the sentences below. Use the Tree Method and the *calculated truth-values* from Part A. Use the available **Exercise Work Sheet** to submit your work.

9. $Tc \supset (\exists x)(Sx \ \& \ Ux)$
10. $(\forall x)(Fx \supset Tx) \lor (\forall x)(Bx \lor Gx)$
11. $(\exists x)(Sx \ \& \ Ux) \equiv (\exists x)({\sim}Sx \ \& \ {\sim}Cx)$
12. ${\sim}[\, (\forall x)(Bx \lor Gx) \ \& \ Tc \,]$
13. ${\sim}Tc \lor {\sim}(\forall x)(Cx \supset {\sim}Sx)$
14. ${\sim}(\forall x)(Fx \supset Tx) \supset {\sim}(\exists x)(Sx \ \& \ Ux)$

Part C. Calculate the truth-values of the sentences below. Use the Tree Method and the *symbol meanings* from Part A. You must *first* determine the values of the simple component sentences. Use the available **Exercise Work Sheet** to submit your work.

15. $(\forall x)(Fx \supset Sx) \equiv [(\forall x)(Tx \supset Ux) \vee \sim(Bc \& Tc)]$

16. $(\exists x)(Fx \& Cx) \& (\exists x)(Fx \& \sim Cx) \& \sim(\exists x)[Fx \& (Cx \& \sim Cx)]$

17. $[(\forall x)(Tx \supset Bx) \vee (\forall x)(Tx \supset \sim Bx)] \& (\forall x)[Tx \supset (Bx \vee \sim Bx)]$

18. $(\forall x)[(Sx \& Bx) \supset (Fx \& Ux \& \sim Gx)] \supset [(\exists x)(Sx \& Tx) \vee (\exists x)(Bx \& Gx)]$

19. $[(\forall x)(Cx \supset Bx) \& (\forall x)(Bx \supset Cx)] \equiv (\forall x)(Cx \equiv Bx)$

20. $\{(\exists x)[Fx \& (Tx \& \sim Ux \& \sim Cx)] \vee (\exists x)[Fx \& (\sim Tx \& Ux \& \sim Cx)]\} \supset \sim(\forall x)Gx$

Section 4.4 Deductions in Quantificational Logic

Recall that one of the serious limitations of Traditional Logic was that there was no way to express the complexity of complex subjects and complex predicates. As we have seen in the preceding sections, we have certainly overcome this limitation through the powerful expressive features of the language of Quantificational Logic. What is needed next are appropriate rules of inference to enable us to reason in this language. While the language of Quantificational Logic is itself somewhat unnatural, the rules of inference for Quantificational Logic are surprisingly natural and simple.

Elementary Argument Forms

There are only five new rules. That is a welcome outcome. As in the previous divisions of logic, there is again the basic distinction between *elementary argument forms* and *elementary equivalences*. There are four elementary argument forms: Universal Instantiation (UI), Existential Instantiation (EI), Existential Generalization (EG), and Universal Generalization (UG); and one elementary equivalence: the Quantifier-Negation Laws (QN). We will discuss each of these rules in detail below.

Here is a revealing *preview* of the four argument forms.

U.I.	$\therefore (\forall x)\, Fx$	everything is flat.	This inference is VALID.
	$\overline{\quad\quad}$	$\overline{\quad\quad}$	
	Fa	$\therefore$ the Earth is flat.	
E.I.	$(\exists x)\, Fx$	something is flat.	This inference is INVALID.
	$\overline{\quad\quad}$	$\overline{\quad\quad}$	prem = T, concl = F
	$\therefore$ Fa	$\therefore$ the Earth is flat.	

E.G.	Fa	the Earth is round.	This inference is VALID.
	∴ (∃x) Fx	∴ something is round.	
UG	Fa	the Earth is round.	This inference is INVALID. prem = **T**, concl = **F**
	∴ (∀x) Fx	∴ everything is round.	

As this preview indicates, when four of these rules are stated in this *very* simple way, two of them are valid, and two are *invalid*. Luckily, when these rules are stated in a more *careful* way, all of them are valid.

Universal Instantiation (UI)

The first rule is very intuitive. It allows you to apply *universal* propositions to *particular* instances: "Whatever is true of *everything* is true of any particular thing."

Suppose you have *available* the assertion "Everything is deep-down mental." That is quite a sweeping result. Wow! Everything! No exception! Well then, you are entitled to now make this claim about any particular thing you wish to name.

1. Everything is deep-down mental	Prem
2. The Moon is deep-down mental	1, UI
3. Chicago is deep-down mental	1, UI
4. The number 5 is deep-down mental	1, UI
5. George Bush is deep-down mental	1, UI

Let's look at the symbolic version of the rule UI. In stating this rule let us represent all universal sentences in the general way as $(\forall x)(\ldots x \ldots)$, where the expression $(\ldots x \ldots)$ that follows the universal quantifier symbol is any symbolic sentential expression containing one or more occurrences of the variable **x**. The dots here indicate that the expression may be very simple or very complex.

Universal Instantiation UI

$(\forall x)(\ldots x \ldots)$
—————————   where **n** is any name, no restriction.
∴ $(\ldots n/x \ldots)$

Here the allowed conclusion is the sentence (. . . **n/x** . . .), which is just like the expression (. . . **x** . . .) except that *all* of the occurrences of the variable **x** have been replaced by the name **n** that was picked. Let's look at some examples.

18. (∀x)~Sx	. . . .
19. ~Sa	18, UI

45. (∀x)[Rx ⊃ (Mx & Gx)]	. . . .
46. Rg ⊃ (Mg & Gg)	45, UI

Since the rule UI is a basic argument form, and not an equivalence, one is allowed to apply this rule only to universal sentences that constitute an *entire line* of a deduction, and never to universal sentences that are a *part* of a line. Hence the following applications are all DEAD WRONG:

25. (∀x)Mx ⊃ (∀x)Px	. . . .
26. Mb ⊃ (∀x)Px	25, UI?? WRONG, can't UI on front part of 25

13. ~(∀y)(My & Uy)	. . . .
14. ~(Md & Ud)	13, UI?? WRONG, can't UI on the part after "~"

23. (∀x)Sx ∨ (∀x)Hx	. . . .
24. Sb ∨ Hb	23, UI?? WRONG, can't on front, can't on back

Existential Instantiation (EI)

This rule allows you to introduce a *momentary name* to refer to *something* that is completely unknown. This is actually something we do quite a bit in our conversations with others about the daily events in our lives. Everything that we can think of as a particular thing we can also *refer* to as such by some expression. That's how we talk about unknown things. Let's see this in action. Suppose you have just baked a yellow cake and have frosted it with chocolate frosting. Mmm-mmm good. You leave the cake on the table while you go to the store to buy some milk. When you come back, you find a big chunk missing from the cake. Right away you think, "Something ate the cake!" You also notice that whatever did this made a clean swipe, since there is no cake debris anywhere. You sound the alarm, people come running, and you explain the situation. During the discussion people start using the name "The muncher" to refer to the doer of this nasty deed. The investigation thus took the following form:

1. Something ate the cake	Premiss
2. Whatever ate the cake make a clean swipe	Premiss

3. Let's call the thing that did this "The muncher"	name selection
4. So, The muncher ate the cake	1, Existential Instantiation
5. So, The muncher made a clean swipe	. . . .
6. So, etc.	. . . .

By introducing a momentary name to refer to the unknown thing in question, we are able to start reasoning about that thing, and in this way we can come to some conclusion. This is always how one has to reason about "something."

We will make this introduction of the selected name an *official part* of this rule of inference. We will require that a separate, numbered line in the deduction be devoted to the introduction of this name, followed *immediately* by the line that makes the actual instantiation inference, in precisely the following manner:

15. select name: **n**	Selection
16. (. . . **n** . . .)	11, EI

where **n** is whatever name the writer has decided on, and where the line numbers involved will, of course, vary. The justification that one writes for the selection step will just be the one word "Selection." We note that our procedure here is not the *customary* one. Logic books never *write out* the selection step; they always leave it as a *mental* note. This is actually contrary to the custom in mathematics of explicitly writing out the selection steps in mathematical proofs: "Let n_0 be such a number . . ." Regardless, the practice of writing out the selection step will greatly prevent name-selection mistakes that are otherwise usually made at this juncture. In addition, this practice will *also* make the statement of the other rules easier.

Let's state the symbolic version of the rule of Existential Instantiation. In stating this rule let us represent all existential sentences as $(\exists x)(. . . x . . .)$. The expressions $(. . . x . . .)$ and $(. . . n/x . . .)$ are as described before.

Existential Instantiation EI

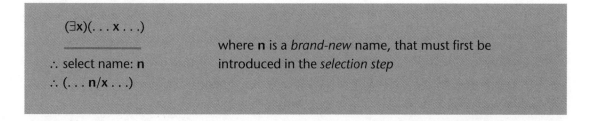

There is an important *restriction* that goes along with the special selection step. Every existential sentence claims the existence of something: something, *identity unknown*. Therefore, unlike with the rule UI, the name selected for EI is *not* permitted to be just any name. For this inference to be correct, one has to make sure that the name that is introduced has *no significance* whatsoever. It must be a name that has been *invented on the spot* to refer to the thing postulated by the existential sentence. We will officially call such names *brand-new* names. A brand-new name must satisfy the following two conditions:

(1) It is not the name of a *known* individual, such as, "Chicago," "Loyola University," "George Bush," "Plato," "The Moon," "The Sears Tower," etc.;

(2) It is a name that has *never been used* before (in the context of the argument and the deduction for the argument), since to pick a name that had been used before in some way would illicitly transfer the identity and significance of that previous thing to the new thing being referred to.

We can illustrate why these restrictions are necessary with the following bit of reasoning. We will use the information that *you* are a student who is always low on cash, and we will abbreviate your name as "*m*." We will also use the information that *some* people have tons of money, like those very rich people we hear about.

1. *m* is a student	Premiss	[this is you]
2. *m* is always low on cash	Premiss	[this is you]
3. (∃x) x has tons of money	Premiss	[maybe Bill Gates]
———————		
4. select name: *m*	3, selection ??	
5. *m* has tons of money	3, EI?? [this is you?]	
6. *m* is a student who has tons of money	1,5, Conj ["Oh, thank you!"]	

Thank me later, but doesn't it feel nice, now that **you have tons of money**? We proved it by logic, right? **No.** It is easy to see where things went wrong. One must always select a **brand new** name to replace any "**some**" quantifier, and we didn't do that here. From now on, we will pay extra attention to this. Here's another example:

1. (∃x)Mx & (∃x)(Rx & Gx)	Premiss	
———————		
2. (∃x)Mx	1, Simp	
3. (∃x)(Rx & Gx)	1, Simp	
4. select name: a	Selection	– Brand-new name? Yes.
5. Ma	2, EI	– Correct.

6. select name: a	Selection	– Brand-new name? NO. ERROR.
7. Ra & Ga	3, EI??	– NO, BLOCKED by line 6.
6. select name: b	Selection	– Brand-new name? Yes.
7. Rb & Gb	3, EI	– Correct.
8. Ma & (Rb & Gb)	3, 5, Conj	

A note about errors. As with the rule UI, the rule EI may never be applied to *parts* of a line. That is one possible source of errors. In addition, the rule E.I. has a strong *restriction* on the choice of names that may be selected: the name must always be brand-new. That is a second possible source of errors. We illustrated this in step 6 of this example. But there is also another kind of error one can make: a *strategic* error, as in the next example.

Everything is physical or mental.

Something is not physical (e.g. the number 2).

So, ...

1. $(\forall x)(Mx \lor Px)$	Prem	
2. $(\exists x)\sim Px$	Prem	$\therefore$ $(\exists x)Mx$
3. Pa $\lor$ Ma	1, UI	– Automatic OK.
4. select name: b	Selection	– Can't use name: a.
5. ~Pb	2, EI	– Correct.

We made no errors, but yet, things are not right here. We want the two premisses to *interact* to produce a conclusion. But that is not happening. If the name *a* could have been selected, that would have produced a nice Disj Syll interaction, but such a selection is illegal. So instead, the name *b* was correctly selected, but now there is no possibility of an *interaction*. Line 3 is about *Alex*, and line 5 is about *Barb*. These two lines have nothing to do with each other. We have come to a DEAD END.

The solution to this instantiation problem is to use a certain *strategy* in applying the quantificational rules. The strategy is this:

> Always EI before you UI

You can see that this solves the problem we just got into. When you UI first, you introduce a name, which can never be used later by EI. But, when you EI first, you can use that name again later by UI, because UI has no restriction on what names are used. So, the correct way to do the problem is:

1. (∀x)(Px ∨ Mx)	Prem	
2. (∃x)~Px	Prem	∴ (∃x)Mx

3. select name: a	Selection	– Brand-new name? Yes.
4. ~Pa	2, E.I.	– Correct. EI before UI.
5. Pa ∨ Ma	1, U.I.	– An automatic OK.
6. Ma	4,5, Disj Syll	– BINGO!

The desired conclusion, "Something is mental," is now staring us in the face; but we need yet another rule to finish up the deduction.

Existential Generalization (EG)

The third elementary argument form for Quantificational Logic is called *Existential Generalization* and it allows us to infer *existential conclusions* on the basis of concrete examples: "What is true of a particular individual, must be true of *something*." Here are some examples of this kind of inference:

Tantumalop lived on the Moon and was 200 years old.

So, *something* lived on the Moon and was 200 years old.

100 is a number greater than 10.

So, *something* is a number greater than 10.

Chicago is large and beautiful and lies on the edge of a great lake.

So, *something* is large and beautiful and lies on the edge of a great lake.

It is intuitively clear that these inferences are perfectly correct, and this maneuver works for *any* named individual, no exceptions. Let's state the symbolic version of the rule EG. As it turns out, this rule has a little more flexibility than the other rules, and there are two versions.

Existential Generalization EG

$$(\ldots n \ldots)$$
$$\overline{}$$
$$\therefore (\exists x)(\ldots x/n \ldots)$$

$$(\ldots n \ldots)$$
$$\overline{}$$
$$\therefore (\exists x)(\ldots x//n \ldots)$$

where **n** is any name

The first version is the more common of the two. Given some statement (. . . **n** . . .) about an individual **n**, one generalizes the statement by replacing *all* of the occurrences of the name

n by a variable **x** and adding a matching existential quantifier up front: (∃x)(. . . x/n . . .). For example,

> While Al owns a boat, Al owns a plane. So, something is   Ba & Pa
> such that while it owns a boat, it owns a plane.   ∴ (∃x)(Bx & Px)

The second version is the less common of the two, but it is nevertheless valid as well. Given some statement (. . . **n** . . .) about an individual **n**, one generalizes the statement by replacing *some* of the occurrences of the name **n** by a variable **x** and adding a matching existential quantifier up front: (∃x)(. . . x//n . . .). For example,

> While Al owns a boat, Al owns a plane. So, something is such   Ba & Pa
> that while Al owns a boat, it owns a plane.   ∴ (∃x)(Ba & Px)

Here are some other examples, based on the more common version.

18. ~Sa	. . . .
19. (∃x)~Sx	18, E.G.
13. Ma & Ua	. . . .
14. (∃y)(My & Uy)	13, E.G.
21. Rg ∨ (Mg & Gg)	. . . .
22. (∃x)[Rx ∨ (Mx & Gx)]	21, E.G.

Again, since the rule EG is a basic argument form, and not an equivalence, one is *not* allowed to apply this rule to a *part* of a line in a deduction. Hence the following inferences are all DEAD WRONG:

18. ~(Sa & Pa)	. . . .	
~~19. ~(∃x)(Sx & Px)~~	18, EG??	– WRONG, on a part
19. (∃x)~(Sx & Px)	18, EG	– Correct
13. Ma ∨ Ua	. . . .	
~~14. (∃x)Mx ∨ (∃x)Ux~~	13, EG??	– WRONG, on two parts
14. (∃x)(Mx ∨ Ux)	13, EG	– Correct
21. Ra	. . . .	
22. Gb	. . . .	
23. Ra & Gb	21, 22, Conj	
~~24.(∃x)(Rx & Gx)~~	23, EG??	– WRONG, different names
24. (∃x)Rx	21, EG	– Correct
25. (∃x)Gx	22, EG	– Correct
26. (∃x)Rx & (∃x)Gx	24, 25, Conj	

Universal Generalization (UG)

The fourth, and last, elementary argument form is also the most complicated of the four rules. This rule is known as Universal Generalization, and it allows the creation of universal conclusions, $(\forall x)(\ldots x \ldots)$. At the outset it must be noted that any simple statement of the rule, such as we had for Existential Generalization, would produce invalid inferences. Compare, for example, the following two simple inferences:

George is a student   George is a student
So, something is a student   So, everything is a student

The first argument is a valid argument and is justified by the rule EG. The second argument is clearly an invalid argument, and no rule will justify it. Yet, there are *special* circumstances under which inferences similar to this invalid one are in fact valid. Sometimes these inferences do work—it all depends on who George is, and what we are saying about him. Is George your next-door neighbor? Then the inference is invalid. Is George someone whom you have heard about on the news? Then the inference is invalid. Is George an absolutely arbitrary selected individual, and you were able to show, in general, that based on the universal claims of the premises, George would have to be a student? Well, that's entirely different. Then the inference is valid. And that's the trick. To derive a universal conclusion in this way, you have to be able to show that (1) the individual thing you are starting with is arbitrarily selected, and that (2) what you are asserting to be true of *this* individual is completely representative of *all* individual things in the universe—at least, according to the universal claims of the premises.

We will therefore always start with an explicit *selection step*, and such steps always require that the name selected be a *brand-new* name, a name that has never been used before. That will guarantee (1) that we are starting with an arbitrarily selected individual. Next, we will establish safeguards to insure that (2) only things that can be said about *everything* will be said about *this* selected thing. Finally, (3) whatever we are able to conclude about this selected thing, under these stringent conditions, we will also conclude about *everything*. We will employ a "box" technique, similar to the one we used for Conditional proof, to accomplish all these requirements.

Universal Generalization UG

```
        ⋮
    _____
    select name n
        ⋮                    1. The first line selects a brand-new name.
        ⋮
        ⋮                    2. The last line is not un-representative.
    (...n...)
    _____
∴   (∀x)(...x/n...)
```

Note that we have created a *special method* for employing the rule of Universal Generaliza-tion. We have done so because the danger of making invalid inferences with UG is extremely great. One is required to start a *UG-box*, and the very *first* step in the box must be a name *selection step*. Of course, the name selected must be a *brand-new* name. One then continues to infer other steps—necessarily, steps that include one or more uses of Universal Instantiation, which is the only way we can get information about the newly selected name—until one arrives at the kind of instance that one wants to universally generalize. At that point, the box is terminated and the UG inference is made.

The last line instance used for the UG inference is usually an automatic result that requires little attention. In such cases no special caution is required. But when sentences are very complicated (such as the relational sentences discussed in the advanced sections), things can go wrong, and caution is required. This is what the second condition is meant to control. The last line instance may not become *un-representative* of all things in the universe, which means that the line may not become *contaminated* with existential information that is not true of everything. We give an official definition of this idea, but again, we stress that this matter may be ignored when one is dealing with ordinary simple sentences.

A line *k* in a UG box is *un-representative* if and only if

some EI selection step occurs inside the UG box, and its name occurs in line *k*.

Here are some examples of arguments that use UG or that *attempt* to do so.

Example #1. George is happy and lucky. So, everything is happy.

1. Hg & Lg	Premiss ∴ (∀x)Hx	
~~2. select name: g~~	Selection for UG ??	– ERROR.
2. select name: a	Selection for UG	– Correct.
3. Hg	1, Simp	– Need: Ha
4. ???		– Dead end.
~~5. (∀x)Hx~~	BLOCKED	

Example #2. Something is happy. So, everything is happy.

1. (∃x)Hx	Premiss ∴ (∀x)Hx	
2. select name: a	Selection for EI	
3 Ha	1, EI	
~~4. select name: a~~	Selection for UG ??	– ERROR.
4. select name: b	Selection for UG	– Correct.
5. ???		– Need: Hb . Dead end.
~~6. (∀x)Hx~~	BLOCKED	

Example #3.

1. (∀x)Fx	Premiss
2. (∀x)Gx	Premiss ∴ (∀x)(Fx & Gx)
3. select name: a	Selection for UG
4. Fa	1, UI
5. Ga	2, UI
6. Fa & Ga	4,5, Conj
7. (∀x)(Fx & Gx)	6, UG Bingo!

Example #4.

1. (∀x)(Fx ∨ Gx)	Premiss
2. (∀x)~Fx	Premiss ∴ (∀x)Gx
3. select name: a	Selection for UG
4. Fa ∨ Ga	1, UI
5. ~Fa	2, UI
6. Ga	4,5, Disj Syll
7. (∀x)Gx	6, UG Bingo!

The previous examples were uncomplicated, because no *additional* selection steps were used inside the UG-box. But the next two examples *do* have additional selection steps inside the box, so *now* one has to check for *un-representativeness*. (You can take some comfort in the fact that the sentences in these examples are not ordinary English sentences, and you are not likely to run into them.)

Example #5.

1.	(∀x)Fx	Premiss
2.	(∃y)Gy	Premiss ∴ (∃y)(∀x)(Fx & Gy)

3. select name: a	Selection for UG
4. Fa	1, UI
5. select name: b	Selection for EI
6. Gb	2, EI
7. Fa & Gb	4,6, Conj

8. ~~(∀x)(Fx & Gb)~~	7, UG ?? ERROR. line 7 is un-representative.
9. ~~(∃y)(∀x)(Fx & Gy)~~	BLOCKED

Example #6.

1.	(∀x)(∃y)(Fx & Gy)	Premiss ∴ (∀x)Fx

2. select name: a	Selection for UG
3. (∃y)(Fa & Gy)	1, UI
4. select name: b	Selection for EI
5. Fa & Gb	3, EI
6. Fa	5, Simp

7. (∀x)Fx	6, UG. Yes. Line 6 is not un-representative.

Elementary Equivalences

We consider only one equivalence rule for Quantificational Logic. It is actually the earlier Quantifier-Negation rule that we studied in Traditional Logic. We can rely here on our earlier knowledge of that rule. Because there is a distinction between absolute and categorical quantified sentences, this rule must be stated in two forms:

QN for absolute sentences

not everything is **F** = something is not **F**   ~(∀x) Fx = (∃x) ~Fx
not something is **F** = everything is not **F**   ~(∃x) Fx = (∀x) ~Fx

QN for categorical sentences

not every F is G = some F is not G	~(∀x)(Fx ⊃ Gx) = (∃x)(Fx & ~Gx)
not some F is G = every F is not G	~(∃x)(Fx & Gx) = (∀x)(Fx ⊃ ~Gx)

A note about the mechanics of these rules. The QN laws for absolute sentences can be easily remembered if one remembers that

> as one *moves* a negation sign (left or right) through a quantifier, the quantifier mode switches to the *other* quantifier mode.

Also, with regard to these rules for categorical sentences, the *symbolic* inferences are perhaps the most easily performed if one (1) understands what *English* form is being used, then (2) performs the inference for the *English* form, and then (3) converts that result into the symbolic form. For example,

> 4. ~(∀x)(Wx ⊃ Kx)   Premiss

> [step 4 = not all W are K = some W are not K = step 5.]

> 5. (∃x)(Wx & ~Kx)   4, QN

When Do We Use the QN Laws?

Sentences like ~(∀x)(. . . x . . .) and ~(∃x)(. . . x . . .) have the form of *negation* sentences, and for that reason, only laws for *negation* sentences may be applied, when we infer *from* them or *to* them. That means, in particular, that the new rules UI, EI, EG, and UG may *not* be applied to them, since no argument-form rules may be applied to *parts* of sentences, which in this case would be the *un-negated* part: e.g.,

> 7. ~(∀x)(. . . x . . .) ln. 7 is not universal, only the "back" part of 7 is universal.
> 9. ~(∃x)(. . . x . . .) ln. 9 is not existential, only the "back" part of 9 is existential.

How, then, should we work with these negation sentences? *Answer*: We must use the Q.N. laws to change their form. Here are some examples.

14. ~(∀x)(Mx ∨ ~Bx)	. . . .	
~~15. ~(Ma ∨ ~Ba)~~	14, U.I. ??	ERROR, line 14 is not universal
15. (∃x)~(Mx ∨ ~Bx)	14, Q.N.	Yes, that's it
16. select name: a	Selection	Correct (the name is new)
17. ~(Ma ∨ ~Ba)	15, E.I.	Correct

6. ~(Gb & Ub)   . . . .
7. ~~(∃x)(Gx & Ux)~~   6, E.G. ??   ERROR, line 7 is not existential
7. (∃x)~(Gx & Ux)   6, E.G.   Yes, that's it
8. ~(∀x)(Gx & Ux)   7, Q.N.   Correct, if this extra step is wanted

Here is a problem that incorporates all these ideas.

"All monkeys are agile. Not everything is agile. So, not everything is a monkey."

1. (∀x)(Mx ⊃ Ax)	Prem	
2. ~(∀x)Ax	Prem	∴ ~(∀x)Mx
3. (∃x)~Ax	2, QN	The only way to deal with line 2.
4. select name: a	Selection.	Correct.
5. ~Aa	3, EI	Correct.
6. Ma ⊃ Aa	1, UI	Perfect, EI was before UI
7. ~Ma	5,6, MT	
8. (∃x)~Mx	7, EG	We *must* do this to produce line 9.
9. ~(∀x)Mx	8, QN	

This last example illustrates what is actually a general fact about ordinary reasoning: cases of ordinary reasoning readily make use of *all* the rules for quantiers: UI, EI, EG, UG, and QN. Here are some more examples of quantificational deductions.

More Examples of Quantificational Deductions

(1)
All things are mental. All things are squares. Not something is green. So, George is a non-green mental square.

1. (∀x)Mx	Prem	
2. (∀x)Sx	Prem	
3. ~(∃x)Gx	Prem ∴ ~Gg & Mg & Sg	
4. (∀x)~Gx	3, QN	
5. Mg	1, UI	
6. Sg	2, UI	
7. ~Gg	4, UI	
8. ~Gg & Mg & Sg	7, 5, 6, Conj	

(2)
Everything is a mental force. Everything mental is eternal. Nothing eternal is created. So, the Statue of Liberty is a force that was not created.

1. (∀x)(Mx & Fx)	Prem	
2. (∀x)(Mx ⊃ Ex)	Prem	
3. (∀x)(Ex ⊃ ~Cx)	Prem ∴ Fs & ~Cs	
4. Ms & Fs	1, UI	
5. Fs	4, simp	

	6. Ms	4, simp
	7. Ms ⊃ Es	2, UI
	8. Es ⊃ ~Cs	3, UI
	9. Ms ⊃ ~Cs	7,8, Hyp Syll
	10. ~Cs	6,9, MP
	11. Fs & ~Cs	5,10, Conj

(3)

If unbathed cows exist then flies exist. Bill is a cow. Cows never bathe. So, flies exist.

1. (∃x)(~Bx & Cx)	Prem
⊃(∃x)Fx	Prem
2. Cb	Prem ∴ (∃x)Fx
3. (∀x)(Cx ⊃ ~Bx)	
———	3, UI
4. Cb ⊃ ~Bb	2,4, MP
5. ~Bb	5,2, Conj
6. ~Bb & Cb	6, EG
7. (∃x)(~Bx & Cx)	1,7, MP
8. (∃x)Fx	

(4)

All things are green fruits. Something is round and noisy. So, something is a noisy fruit.

1. (∀x)(Gx & Fx)	Prem
2. (∃x)(Rx & Nx)	Prem ∴ (∃x)(Nx & Fx)
———	
3. select name: b	Selection for EI. Yes.
4. Rb & Nb	2, EI
5. Gb & Fb	1, UI
6. Nb	4, simp
7. Fb	5, simp
8. Nb & Fb	6,7, Conj
9. (∃x)(Nx & Fx)	8, EG

(5)

All monkeys are agile. Everything agile is fast. Everything fast is sneaky. So, all monkey are sneaky.

1. (∀x)(Mx ⊃ Ax)	Prem
2. (∀x)(Ax ⊃ Fx)	Prem
3. (∀x)(Fx ⊃ Sx)	Prem ∴ (∀x)(Mx ⊃ Sx)

———	
4. select name: g	Selection. Correct.
5. Mg ⊃ Ag	1, UI
6. Ag ⊃ Fg	2, UI
7. Fg ⊃ Sg	3, UI
8. Mg ⊃ Sg	5,6,7,Sup Hyp Syll

9. (∀x)(Mx ⊃ Sx)	4-8, UG

Reference Sheet for the Rules of Quantificational Logic

In what follows, α/β indicates putting α for *all* occurrences of β, and $\alpha//\beta$ indicates putting α for *some* occurrences of β.

The Quantifier-Negation Laws

QN $\sim(\forall x)\, Fx \;=\; (\exists x)\sim Fx$

QN $\sim(\exists x)\, Fx \;=\; (\forall x)\sim Fx$

Cat.QN $\sim(\forall x)(Fx \supset Gx) \;=\; (\exists x)(Fx \;\&\; \sim Gx)$

Cat.QN $\sim(\exists x)(Fx \;\&\; Gx) \;=\; (\forall x)(Fx \supset \sim Gx)$

Universal Instantiation UI

$$\frac{(\forall x)(\ldots x \ldots)}{\therefore\ (\ldots n/x \ldots)}$$

No restrictions on the name **n**.

Existential Instantiation EI

$$\frac{(\exists x)(\ldots x \ldots)}{\begin{array}{l}\therefore\ \text{select name } \mathbf{n}\\ \therefore\ (\ldots n/x \ldots)\end{array}}$$

1. **n** is a name that has *never* been used before

2. **n** must first be introduced in a *selection step*

Existential Generalization EG

$$\frac{(\ldots n \ldots)}{\therefore\ (\exists x)(\ldots x/n \ldots)} \qquad \frac{(\ldots n \ldots)}{\therefore\ (\exists x)(\ldots x//n \ldots)}$$

No restrictions on the name **n**.

Universal Generalization UG

$$
\begin{array}{|l}
\vdots \\
\hline
\text{select name } \mathbf{n} \\
\vdots \\
(\ldots \mathbf{n} \ldots) \\
\hline
\end{array}
$$

$\therefore (\forall x)(\ldots x/\mathbf{n} \ldots)$

1. The first line selects a name **n** never used before.

2. The last line is not un-representative.

Exercise 4.4. A,B,C,D Quantificational Deductions

Part A. For each of the following inferences, determine whether the conclusion follows by the rule listed. Answer YES or NO. (Premiss "Ma" is listed only to make the name "a" already present in the deduction.) Use the available **Exercise Work Sheet** to submit your work.

1. Ma , $(\forall x)(Fx \lor Gx)$	$\therefore Fb \lor Gb$	Is it UI?
2. Ma , $(\forall x)(Fx \lor Gx)$	$\therefore Fa \lor Ga$	Is it UI?
3. Ma , $(\forall x)(Fx \lor Gx)$	$\therefore Fa \lor Gb$	Is it UI?
4. Ma , $(\forall x)Fx \lor (\forall x)Gx$	$\therefore Fa \lor (\forall x)Gx$	Is it UI?
5. Ma , $Fb \& Gb$	$\therefore (\exists x)(Fx \& Gx)$	Is it EG?
6. Ma , $Fa \& Ga$	$\therefore (\exists x)(Fx \& Gx)$	Is it EG?
7. Ma , $Fa \& Gb$	$\therefore (\exists x)(Fx \& Gx)$	Is it EG?
8. Ma , $\sim Fb$	$\therefore \sim(\exists x)Fx$	Is it EG?
9. Ma , $(\exists x)Fx$	$\therefore Fb$	Is it EI?
10. Ma , $(\exists x)Fx$	$\therefore$ select name a $/\therefore$ Fa	Is it EI?
11. Ma , $(\exists x)Fx$	$\therefore$ select name b $/\therefore$ Fb	Is it EI?
12. Ma , $(\exists x)Fx$	$\therefore$ select name b $/\therefore$ Fc	Is it EI?
13. Ma , $\sim(\exists x)Fx$	$\therefore (\forall x)\sim Fx$	Is it QN?
14. Ma , $\sim(\forall x)Fx$	$\therefore (\forall x)\sim Fx$	Is it QN?
15. Ma , $(\exists x)\sim Fx$	$\therefore \sim(\forall x)Fx$	Is it QN?
16. Ma , $\sim(\exists x)\sim Fx$	$\therefore (\forall x)\sim\sim Fx$	Is it QN?
17. Ma , Fa	$\therefore (\forall x)Fx$	Is it UG?
18. Fa & Ga , $\boxed{\text{select name a, Fa Simp}}$	$\therefore (\forall x)Fx$	Is it UG?
19. Fa & Ga , $\boxed{\text{select name b, Fa Simp}}$	$\therefore (\forall x)Fx$	Is it UG?
20. $(\forall x)(Fx \& Gx)$, $\boxed{\text{select name b, Fb \& Gb U.I., Fb Simp}}$	$\therefore (\forall x)Fx$	Is it UG?

Part B, 1–5. Symbolize the following arguments, and give deductions for them. Check the symbolization answers given below. Use the available **Exercise Work Sheet** to submit your work.

1. Everything is either green or red. Chicago is not green, but it is square. So, Chicago is red and square.

2. All things are human or matter. All matter is expendable. Data is a non-human machine. So, Data is expendable.

3. All pink horses are rare. All rare horses are expensive. Allegro is a pink horse. So, Allegro is an expensive horse.

4. Queen Elizabeth is an orator, and she is funny too. All orators have had voice lessons. So, something funny had voice lessons.

5. Some people are smart and funny. All things are made of matter. So, some material things are smart funny persons.

Part C, 6–10. Symbolize the following arguments, and give deductions for them. Check the symbolization answers given below. Use the available **Exercise Work Sheet** to submit your work.

6. Some pink horses are rare and expensive. So, expensive horses exist.

7. All pink horses are rare. Some wild horses are pink. So, some horses are rare.

8. Every person in Chicago views the Lake and worries a lot. All Lake viewers enjoy nature. Beth is a person in Chicago. So, some worriers enjoy nature.

9. $(\forall x)(Fx \ \& \ Gx)$, $(\forall x)(Ox \ \& \ Px)$ ∴ $(\forall x)(Gx \ \& \ Px)$ [Use the rule UG]

10. $(\forall x)(Dx \ \& \ Sx)$, $[(\forall x)Sx] \supset (Ra \ \& \ Qb)$ ∴ $(\exists x)Rx$ [Use the rule UG]

Part D, 11–15. Symbolize the following arguments, and give deductions for them. Check the symbolization answers given below. These problems are *more difficult*. Use the available **Exercise Work Sheet** to submit your work.

11. Dogs are large animals suitable as pets. All large animals are potentially dangerous. So, dogs are potentially dangerous yet suitable as pets. (D, L, A, S, P)

12. If all dogs are potentially dangerous, then they all require insurance. Fido requires no insurance; but Fido does bark; and only dogs bark. So, some dogs are not potentially dangerous. (D, P, R, f, B)

13. Some dogs are wimpy; and some cats are ferocious. Wimpy things don't put up a fight, and ferocious things don't back down. So, some dogs don't put up a fight, and some cats don't back down. (D, W, C, F, P, B)

14. Betsy can't sing. But some can sing and climb mountains too. Others can't climb mountains, but they can dance. Now, if both singers and dancers exist, then no non-dancing non-singers exist. So, Betsy can't sing, but she can certainly dance. (b, S, M, D)

15. All kittens are felines. All felines are whiskered animals. If all kittens are whiskered, then all felines are carnivores. All carnivorous animals are predators. So, all kittens are predators. (K, F, W, A, C, P)

Symbolizations answers. (You have to give the deductions too).

For Part B:

1. (∀x)(Gx ∨ Rx) , ~Gc & Sc ∴ Rc & Sc

2. (∀x)(Hx ∨ Mx) , (∀x)(Mx ⊃ Ex) , ~Hd & Ad ∴ Ed

3. (∀x)[(Px & Hx) ⊃ Rx] , (∀x)[(Rx & Hx) ⊃ Ex] , Pa & Ha ∴ Ea

4. Oe & Fe , (∀x)(Ox ⊃ Vx) ∴ (∃x)(Fx & Vx)

5. (∃x)[Px & (Sx & Fx)] , (∀x)Mx ∴ (∃x)[Mx & (Sx & Fx & Px)]

For Part C:

6. (∃x)[(Px & Hx) & (Rx & Ex)] ∴ (∃x)(Ex & Hx)

7. (∀x)[(Px & Hx) ⊃ Rx] , (∃x)[(Wx & Hx) & Px] ∴ (∃x)(Hx & Rx)

8. (∀x)[(Px & Cx) ⊃ (Lx & Wx)] , (∀x)(Lx ⊃ Ex) , Pb & Cb ∴ (∃x)(Wx & Ex)

9. (∀x)(Fx & Gx) , (∀x)(Ox & Px) ∴ (∀x)(Gx & Px)

10. (∀x)(Dx & Sx) , [(∀x)Sx] ⊃ (Ra & Qb) ∴ (∃x)Rx

For Part D:

11. (∀x)[Dx ⊃ ((Lx & Ax) & Sx)] , (∀x)[(Lx & Ax) ⊃ Px] ∴ (∀x)[Dx ⊃ (Px & Sx)]

12. (∀x)(Dx ⊃ Px) ⊃ (∀x)(Dx ⊃ Rx) , ~Rf , Bf , (∀x)(Bx ⊃ Dx)) ∴ (∃x)(Dx & ~Px)

13. (∃x)(Dx & Wx) , (∃x)(Cx & Fx) , (∀x)(Wx ⊃ ~Px) , (∀x)(Fx ⊃ ~Bx)
    ∴ (∃x)(Dx & ~Px) & (∃x)(Cx & ~Bx)

14. ~Sb , (∃x)(Sx & Mx) , (∃x)(~Mx & Dx) , [(∃x)Sx & (∃x)Dx] ⊃ ~(∃x)(~Dx & ~Sx)
    ∴ ~Sb & Db

15. (∀x)(Kx ⊃ Fx) , (∀x)[Fx ⊃ (Wx & Ax)] , (∀x)(Kx ⊃ Wx) ⊃ (∀x)(Fx ⊃ Cx) ,
    (∀x)[(Cx & Ax) ⊃ Px] ∴ (∀x)(Kx ⊃ Px)

MORE ADVANCED TOPICS IN QUANTIFICATIONAL LOGIC

Section 4.5 Deductions with Conditional Proof and Indirect Proof

There are two main ways in which the rule of Conditional Proof is used in Quantificational Logic. The *first way* is the general method for deriving conclusions that are *conditional* sentences whose two sides involve quantifiers, such as, for example:

$(\forall x)(\ldots x \ldots) \supset (\exists x)(\ldots x \ldots)$, such as, in particular,

$(\forall x)(Ax \lor Bx) \supset (\exists x)(Cx \ \& \ Mx)$

We discussed this method back in Chapter 2, when we introduced the rule C.P. The method is always as follows:

1. Start a CP-box.

2. Write the condition part as the assumption, in this example, $(\forall x)(\ldots x \ldots)$.

3. Then, derive the result part, in this example, $(\exists x)(\ldots x \ldots)$.

4. Trade in the CP-box for the entire conditional sentence, by the rule CP.

Both Propositional Logic and Quantificational Logic contribute to the solutions in these cases. The overall method of CP belongs to Propositional Logic, but the detailed intermediate steps are performed by the special quantificational rules. For example:

All unicorns are magical.   ∴ $(\forall x)(Ux \supset Mx)$
So, if unicorns exist, then magical things exist.   ∴ $(\exists x)Ux \supset (\exists x)Mx$

Since the conclusion is a conditional sentence, we will use the rule CP to derive it.

1. $(\forall x)(Ux \supset Mx)$ Prem ∴ $(\exists x)Ux \supset (\exists x)Mx$

2. $(\exists x)Ux$	Assumption for CP
3. select name: e	selection
4. Ue	2, EI
5. Ue $\supset$ Me	1, UI
6. Me	4,5, MP
7. $(\exists x)Mx$	6, EG

8. $(\exists x)Ux \supset (\exists x)Mx$ 2-7, CP

The *second way* in which the rule CP is used in Quantificational Logic is to derive conclusions that are *universal categorical* sentences, that always take the form,

$(\forall x)[\,(\ldots x \ldots) \supset (\ldots x \ldots)\,]$, such as, in particular,

$(\forall x)[\,(Px \,\&\, Qx) \supset (Rx \,\&\, {\sim}Sx)\,]$

and the method for deriving such sentences always uses *both* the rule UG and, inside that one, the rule CP in the following nested manner:

1. Start a UG-box.
2. Write the selection step for a name **n**.
3. Now, write a CP box inside the UG box,
   and use CP to derive $(\ldots \textbf{n} \ldots) \supset (\ldots \textbf{n} \ldots)$.
4. This conditional sentence is now the last line in the UG box.
5. Trade in this UG-box for the whole universal sentence, by the rule UG.

Let's try this very method in the following example.

All computers are machines.	$(\forall x)(Cx \supset Mx)$
All clever things have a soul.	$(\forall x)(Kx \supset Sx)$
So, all clever computers are machines that have a soul.	$\therefore\ (\forall x)[(Kx \,\&\, Cx) \supset (Mx \,\&\, Sx)]$

1. $(\forall x)(Cx \supset Mx)$	Prem	
2. $(\forall x)(Kx \supset Sx)$	Prem $\quad \therefore\ (\forall x)[(Kx \,\&\, Cx) \supset (Mx \,\&\, Sx)]$	
3. select name: a	selection (UG)	$\therefore\ (Ka \,\&\, Ca) \supset (Ma \,\&\, Sa)$
4. Ka & Ca	Assumption (CP)	$\therefore\ Ma \,\&\, Sa$
5. Ca $\supset$ Ma	1, UI	
6. Ka $\supset$ Sa	2, UI	
7. Ma	4, Simp, 5, MP	
8. Sa	4, Simp, 6, MP	
9. Ma & Sa	7,8, Conj	
10. (Ka & Ca) $\supset$ (Ma & Sa)	4—9, C.P.	
11. $(\forall x)[(Kx \,\&\, Cx) \supset (Mx \,\&\, Sx)]$	3—10, UG	

The rule of Indirect Proof, IP, can also be used in Quantificational Logic. Like the rule CP, this rule is an overall method of Propositional Logic, but when quantificational sentences are present, the intermediate steps make use of the special quantificational rules. Suppose we are trying to derive a quantified line, say, (∃x)(. . . x . . .). The example could be a universal sentence instead, but the method is *routine*:

1. Start an IP-box.

2. Write the *negation* of the desired line as the assumption, and in this example, one would write: ~(∃x)(. . . x . . .) .

3. Use the rule QN to drive the negation inside, with a quantifier change.

4. Then, proceed to derive a contradiction p & ~p as the last line.

5. Trade in the IP-box for the orginal desired sentence, by the rule IP.

Of course, whether or not one actually succeeds in step 4, that is, whether or not one can derive that contradiction, depends on the content of the quantified sentence and the premisses that are available. This method will work only for sentences that are appropriately related to the original premisses. Here is an example.

Consider the following philosophical thesis. It is not always so easy to tell what the consequences are of some given proposals. In logical terms, the question is, What conclusions can we *derive* from them?

Everything is such that *either* it is physical *or* it is mental *and* spiritual; and

everything is such that *either* it is physical *or* it is mental *and not* spiritual.

It may originally seem like these are plausible, *open-ended* alternatives about how reality is divided, about things being either physical or mental, with some additional points about how mental things are related to spiritual things. If that is indeed the intention of these proposals, then this is definitely the *wrong* way to say it, because when they are stated in this way, these proposals logically entail that everything is physical—*contrary* to what was intended. It pays to know some logic, and the rule IP is very handy here.

1. (∀x)[Px ∨ (Mx & Sx)]	Prem	
2. (∀x)[Px ∨ (Mx & ~Sx)]	Prem ∴ (∀x)Px	

3. ~(∀x)Px	Assumption for IP
4. (∃x)~Px	3, QN
5. select name: b	selection for EI
6. ~Pb	4, EI
7. Pb ∨ (Mb & Sb)	1, UI
8. Pb ∨ (Mb & ~Sb)	2, UI

9. Mb & Sb	6,7, Disj Syll
10. Mb & ~Sb	6,8, Disj Syll
11. Sb & ~ Sb	9,10,Simp, Conj
12. (∀x)Px	3-11, IP

The correct way to state the intended philosophical position is:

> everything is such that either (1) it is physical, or (2) it is mental and spiritual, or (3) it is mental and not spiritual
>
> (∀x)[Px ∨ (Mx & Sx) ∨ (Mx & ~Sx)]

and the previous I.P. procedure will not succeed with *this* premiss. Go ahead, try it yourself. (The needed contradiction cannot be generated.) So, the moral of this story is that complicated matters require a knowledge of logic.

Exercise 4.5. A,B,C Deductions with CP and IP

Part A, 1–4. Use the rule I.P. to show that the following arguments are valid. Use the available **Exercise Work Sheet** to submit your work.

1.   ~(∃x)Ux   ∴ ~(∃x)(Mx & Ux)

2.   (∃x)Ux ∨ (Ub ∨ Uc)   ∴ (∃x)Ux

3.   (∀x)(Ax ∨ Bx) , (∀x)(Cx ∨ ~Bx)   ∴ (∀x)(Ax ∨ Cx)

4.   (∀x)Ax ∨ (∀x)Bx   ∴ (∀x)(Ax ∨ Bx)

Part B, 5–8. Use the rule CP to show that the following arguments are valid. Use the available **Exercise Work Sheet** to submit your work.

5.   (∀x)(Ax ⊃ Bx)   ∴ Ae ⊃ (∃x)Bx

6.   (∀x)(Ax ⊃ Bx) , (∀x)Mx   ∴ Ab ⊃ (∃x)(Bx & Mx)

7.   (∃x)(Ax & Bx)   ∴ (∀x)Mx ⊃ (∃x)(Bx & Mx)

8.   (∀x)(Mx ≡ Sx)   ∴ (∀x)~Mx ⊃ (∀x)~Sx

Part C, 9–16. Give deductions for the following arguments. These are more difficult. Use the available **Exercise Work Sheet** to submit your work.

9.   (∀x)[Ax ⊃ (Bx & Cx)] , (∃x)Dx ⊃ (∃x)Ax   ∴ (∃x)(Cx & Dx) ⊃ (∃x)Bx

10. $(\forall x)[(Ax \lor Bx) \supset (Cx \& Dx)]$, $(\forall x)Cx \supset (\forall x)Ex$ $\therefore$ $(\forall x)Ax \supset (\forall x)(Ax \& Ex)$

11. $(\forall x)Ax \lor (\forall x)Bx$, $(\forall x)(Ax \supset Cx)$ $\therefore$ $(\exists x)(Ax \& \sim Bx) \supset (\forall x)Cx$

12. $(\forall x)[Ax \supset (Bx \& Cx)]$, $(\forall x)[(Bx \& Dx) \supset Ex]$ $\therefore$ $(\forall x)\sim Ex \supset [(\forall x)Dx \supset (\forall x)\sim Ax]$

13. $(\forall x)[Fx \supset (Gx \& (\forall y)Hy)]$ $\therefore$ $(\forall x)(\forall y)[Fx \supset (Gx \& Hy)]$

14. $(\forall x)(Ax \supset Cx)$, $(\forall x)[(Cx \& Dx) \supset Ex]$ $\therefore$ $(\exists y)(Ay \& \sim Dy) \lor (\forall x)(Ax \supset Ex)$

15. $(\forall x)(Ax \supset Bx)$, $(\forall x)(Bx \supset \sim Cx)$, $(\exists y)By$ $\therefore$ $\sim(\exists x)(\forall y)[(Ax \& Cx) \lor Cy]$

16. $(\forall x)[(\exists y)(Fx \& Gy) \supset (Hx \& (\forall y)Jy)]$ $\therefore$ $(\forall x)(\forall y)(\forall z)[(Fx \& Gy) \supset (Hx \& Jz)]$

Section 4.6 Demonstrating Invalidity

We can always use the Method of Deduction to show that arguments are valid (when they are), and we have had a lot of practice doing that. But, how do we *show* that arguments are *invalid*? There is a different method for that. We first introduced a method in Chapter 1, when we discussed *deductive validity* and *invalidity*. Then, in Chapter 2, we used the full Truth-table Method to show that certain arguments are invalid, resulting from an invalid *external* connective structure. Now, in Quantificational Logic, some arguments have invalid patterns that involve the *interior* parts of sentences, namely, the "subject sides" and "predicate sides of sentences." (The method we introduce here will also apply to the syllogisms of Traditional Logic.)

Basics

In Chapter 1 we learned what it means for arguments to be valid or invalid, and we gave the following definition:

> An argument is *valid* =def. It is *not logically possible* that all the premisses are true while the conclusion is false. Therefore, if that *is* a logical possibility, then the argument is *invalid*.

This definition gives the outline of a method for demonstrating invalidity. One shows that it is *logically possible* to have *true* premisses and a *false* conclusion. And the way to do this is to *give a description* of *one possible world* in which the premisses are all true and the conclusion is false. What does such a description look like? There are two parts. First, one gives a *list of things that exist* in this possible world. Call this list the *domain* of the possible world, D = { a, b, c, ... }. A rule of thumb here is to keep this list as simple and short as possible (remember, this is only an *imaginary* world). Secondly, one gives a *simple description* of all these things, in terms of all the symbolic predicates, A, B, C, ..., used in the argument at issue. Call this description the *state description* for the domain (again, remember, it's only an *imaginary* world).

Using this description of this possible world, we then need to *demonstrate* that in *this* possible world all the premises have the value **T** and the conclusion has the value **F**. That will prove that the argument is invalid.

Example #1.

		Possible?
Something can sing	$(\exists x)Sx$	$= \mathbf{T}$
Something can dance	$(\exists x)Dx$	$= \mathbf{T}$
So, something can sing and dance	$\therefore (\exists x)(Sx \mathbin{\&} Dx)$	$= \mathbf{F}$

Consider the possible world $\mathbf{W}_{31}$. There are only two things here: a, b. Thing a can sing, but it can't dance. Thing b can dance, but it can't sing. This situation can be summarized in the following matrix:

(1) $D = \{\, a, b \,\}$

| Sa | Da | Sb | Db | [What precision! Impressive!]
| -- | -- | -- | -- |
| T | F | F | T |

Using these initial values, in a world that contains *only* the listed individuals, we must calculate the values of the quantified sentences as follows:

(2)
$$Sa = \mathbf{T} \quad \rightarrow \quad (\exists x)Sx = \mathbf{T}$$
$$Db = \mathbf{T} \quad \rightarrow \quad (\exists x)Dx = \mathbf{T}$$

$$\left.\begin{array}{l} Da = \mathbf{F} \quad \rightarrow \quad Sa \mathbin{\&} Da = \mathbf{F} \\ Sb = \mathbf{F} \quad \rightarrow \quad Sb \mathbin{\&} Db = \mathbf{F} \end{array}\right\} \quad \rightarrow \quad (\exists x)(Sx \mathbin{\&} Dx) = \mathbf{F}$$

(3) So, we have found a possible world in which the premises of the argument are true while the conclusion is false. This proves that the argument is invalid.

Example #2.

		Possible?
Everything is red, or it is not red.	$(\forall x)(Rx \lor \sim Rx)$	$= \mathbf{T}$
So, everything is red, or everything is not red	$\therefore (\forall x)Rx \lor (\forall x)\sim Rx$	$= \mathbf{F}$

Consider the possible world $\mathbf{W}_{57}$. There are only two things here: a, b. Thing a is red, but thing b is not red. This situation can be summarized in the following matrix:

(1) $D = \{\, a, b \,\}$

| Ra | Rb | [Amazingly simple!]
| -- | -- |
| T | F |

Using these initial values, in a world that contains *only* the listed individuals, we must calculate the values of the quantified sentences as follows:

(2)   Ra = T   →   Ra ∨ ~Ra = T ⎫
        Rb = F   →   Rb ∨ ~Rb = T ⎭   →   (∀x)(Rx ∨ ~Rx) = T

        Rb = F   →   (∀x)Rx   = F ⎫
        Ra = T   →   (∀x)~Rx = F ⎭   →   (∀x)Rx ∨ (∀x)~Rx = F

(3)   So, we have found a possible world in which the premisses of the argument are true while the conclusion is false. This proves that the argument is invalid.

Example #3.

		Possible?
All things that are good are good or evil.	(∀x)[Gx ⊃ (Gx ∨ Ex)]	= T
All things that are evil are good or evil.	(∀x)[Ex ⊃ (Gx ∨ Ex)]	= T
So, everything is good or evil.	∴ (∀x)(Gx ∨ Ex)	= F

Consider the possible world **W₁₇**. There are only three things here: a, b, c. Thing a is good and not evil, thing b is evil and not good, and thing c is not good and not evil, (it is a rock). This situation can be summarized in the following matrix:

(1)   D = { a, b, c }

| Ga | Ea | Gb | Eb | Gc | Ec | [Not too hot. Just right!]
|---|---|---|---|---|---|
| T | F | F | T | F | F |

(2)   Only a is G, and so, it is also G or E. So, premiss 1 is T.
      Only b is E, and so, it is also G or E. So, premiss 2 is T.
      But c is not G or E. So, not everything is G or E. So, the conclusion is F.

(3)   So, we have found a possible world in which the premisses of the argument are true while the conclusion is false. This proves that the argument is invalid.

Actually, a domain { c }, with only *one* member, will give the same result. Can you figure this one out?

Exercise 4.6. A,B Demonstrating Invalidity

Part A. Show that the following arguments are invalid. In each case give an appropriate domain and state description. Use the indicated symbolic letters. Your answers should look like the first answer. Use the available **Exercise Work Sheet** to submit your work.

1. Nothing is a red pig. So, some things are not red. (R, P)

    D = { a, b }   Ra Pa Rb Pb This description makes the prems T and concl F.

    $\overline{\text{T F T F}}$

2. George is smart. So, George is a smart person. (g, S, P)

3. George is funny. So, some people are funny. (g, F, P)

4. There are no funny people. So, George is not funny. (F, P, g)

5. Some cats sing. Some cats dance. So, some cats sing and dance. (C, S, D)

6. Some people are not singers. So, some singers are not people. (P, S)

7. All cats have tails. So, all non-cats do not have tails. (C, T)

8. All cats have tails. George has a tail. So, George is a cat. (C, T, g)

9. All cats are smart. Some smarties are funny. So, some cats are funny. (C,S,F)

10. All things are smart. All funny cats are smart. So, all cats are funny. (S, F, C)

Part B. Show that the following arguments are invalid. In each case give an appropriate domain and state description. Use the available **Exercise Work Sheet** to submit your work.

1. (∃x)Ax & (∃x)Bx   ∴ (∃x)(Ax & Bx)

2. (∀x)(Ax ∨ Bx)   ∴ (∀x)Ax ∨ (∀x)Bx

3. (∃x)~(Ax & Bx)   ∴ (∃x)~Ax & (∃x)~Bx

4. (∀x)Ax ⊃ (∃x)Bx ∴ (∃x)Ax ⊃ (∀x)Bx

5. (∀x)Ax ⊃ (∀x)Bx ∴ (∃x)Ax ⊃ (∃x)Bx

6. (∀x)(Ax ⊃ Bx)   ∴ (∀x)[(Ax ∨ Cx) ⊃ Bx]

7. (∀x)(Ax ∨ Bx) , (∀x)(Bx ∨ Cx)   ∴ (∀x)(Ax ∨ Cx)

8. (∀x)(Ax ∨ Cx) , (∃x)(Ax & Bx)   ∴ (∃x)(Ax & Cx)

Section 4.7 Relational Sentences

Our thoughts and reasonings are normally more complicated than the patterns that we have studied so far. This further complexity arises from our use of *relational ideas*, ideas that express *relationships* between things. Relationships are also just called *relations*. Relations are properties that things have, not all by themselves but *in relation to* something to else. Take George, for example. What things are true of George? What properties does the individual George have? Let's say that he is a person, he is a guy, he is six feet tall, he weighs 180 lbs., he has short brown hair, he is somewhat quiet, he is smart. All of the properties in this list are *non*-relational properties. George has these properties *without* reference to other things. George has other properties too, but they are properties that involve a reference to *other things*: George *owns* a sailboat, and George *likes* Liz, and George *lives in* Chicago. These three properties relate George to other things, namely, a sailboat, Liz, and Chicago. So, these three properties are *relations*. And there are many more. Relationships are everywhere. Things enter into all sorts of relationships with other things. What about the tree across the street that you are looking at? Precisely; *you* are in a relationship with *that tree*: you *are looking at* the tree. And what about the person sitting next to you? (This is too easy.) You *are sitting next to* that person.

Symbolization:

We use capital letters A, B, C,. . ., with two or more blanks to represent relations, one blank for each item involved in the relation. Only *name* letters and *variables* are written in those blanks, e.g., xAy, xBy, aAx, eRz.

These relation symbols always represent relations stated in the "active voice" (not "passive"), so that the first item listed is the thing that *performs* the action, and the next things listed are the things *on* which the action is performed.

Here are some examples of how English relational expressions are symbolized.

English expression	*Relation symbol*		*Symbolization*
x sits next to y	_S_	= _ sits next to _	xSy
x likes y	_L_	= _ likes _	xLy
x is liked by y	_L_	= _ likes _	yLx
x was reading y	_R_	= _ reads _	xRy
x owns y	_O_	= _ owns _	xOy
x is taller than y	_T_	= _ is taller than _	xTy
x was looking at y	_L_	= _ looks at _	xLy
x is between y and z	_B_ _	= _ is between_ and _	xByz
x gave y to z	_G_ _	= _ gives _ to _	xGyz
x sold y to z	_S_ _	= _ sells _ to _	xSyz
x introduced y to z	_I_ _	= _ introduces _ to _	xIyz

Many logic books adopt the convention of writing *all the blanks* of a relation on the *right-hand* side of the the relation symbol, whereas we use the convention of writing *one* blank on the left side and the other blank(s) on the right side. So, they write Axy, and Babc, and we write xAy, and aBbc. Actually, we will allow people to use both styles, but we do have a preference for our own convention.

Symbolizing English Sentences

All of the rules for symbolization that we introduced earlier in this chapter must be used with relational sentences as well. Relational sentences will automatically be more complex, but the techniques for symbolizing them will remain the same. We will look at three groups of relational sentences (and there is even some overlap).

English Sentences that State a *Relation* for a *Named* Thing

1. George likes Elizabeth

   gLe   [Use: L = _ likes _]

2. Something likes Elizabeth
   Some thing, it likes Elizabeth

   for some x, x likes Elizabeth
   $(\exists x)(x$ likes $e)$
   $(\exists x)(xLe)$
   incorrect: $(\exists x)Le$

3. Everything likes Elizabeth
   All things, they like Elizabeth

   for all x, x likes Elizabeth
   $(\forall x)(x$ likes $e)$
   $(\forall x)(xLe)$

4. Nothing likes Elizabeth
   All things, they do not like Elizabeth

   for all x, not x likes Elizabeth
   $(\forall x)\sim(x$ likes $e)$
   $(\forall x)\sim(xLe)$
   Equivalent by QN: $\sim(\exists x)(xLe)$

5. George likes something
   Some thing, George likes it

   for some x, George likes x
   $(\exists x)(g$ likes $x)$
   $(\exists x)(gLx)$
   incorrect: $gL(\exists x)$

6. George likes everything
   All things, George likes them

   for all x, George likes x
   $(\forall x)(g$ likes $x)$
   $(\forall x)(gLx)$
   incorrect: $gL(\forall x)$

7. George likes nothing
   All things, George does not likes them

   for all x, not George likes x
   $(\forall x)\sim(g$ likes $x)$
   $(\forall x)\sim(gLx)$
   Equivalent by Q.N.: $\sim(\exists x)(gLx)$

Notice how in the *English* sentences #5, #6, and #7 a quantifier occurs *behind* the verb. But in the symbolic language one is not allowed to write that quantifier behind the relation symbol, because only names and variables may be written in the blanks that accompany the relation symbol. Quantifiers must always be written well in front of the relation symbol and never actually *in* any of the relation-blanks, left or right.

English Sentences With Both a Quantified Subject and a Quantified Predicate

Relational sentences bring with them a new situation that we have not seen before, one in which *each side* of the relation is governed by its *own* quantifier, so that two (or more) quantifiers are both being applied to the *same* relational expression:

(Quant1 x) . . . (Quant2 y) . . . xRy . . .

Clearly, this situation requires that the two quantifiers use *different* variables, because if they both used the same variable, there would be no way of telling which quantifier applied to which side of the relational expression.

(Quant1 x) . . . (Quant2 x) . . . xRx . . .

8. Something likes something	for some x, x likes something
Some thing, it likes something	(∃x)(x likes something)
	(∃x)(for some y, x likes y)
Some thing, some thing, it likes it	(∃x)(∃y)(x likes y)
	(∃x)(∃y)(xLy)
9. Something likes everything	for some x, x likes everything
Some thing, it likes everything	(∃x)(x likes everything)
	(∃x)(for all y, x likes y)
Something, all things, it likes them	(∃x)(∀y)(x likes y)
	(∃x)(∀y)(xLy)
10. Something likes nothing	for some x, x likes nothing
Some thing, it likes nothing	(∃x)(x likes nothing)
	(∃x)(for all y, not x likes y)
Something, all things, not it likes them	(∃x)(∀y)~(x likes y)
	(∃x)(∀y)~(xLy)
11. Everything likes something	for all x, x likes something
All things, they like something	(∀x)(x likes something)
	(∀x)(for some y, x likes y)
All things, some thing, they like it	(∀x)(∃y)(x likes y)
	(∀x)(∃y)(xLy)
12. Everything likes everything	for all x, x likes everything
All things, they like everything	(∀x)(x likes everything)
	(∀x)(for all y, x likes y)

All things, all things, they like them	$(\forall x)(\forall y)(x \text{ likes } y)$
	$(\forall x)(\forall y)(xLy)$

13. Everything likes nothing   for all x, x likes nothing
    All things, they like nothing $(\forall x)(x \text{ likes nothing})$
                                                               $(\forall x)(\text{for all } y, \text{ not } x \text{ likes } y)$
    All things, all things, not they like them $(\forall x)(\forall y){\sim}(x \text{ likes } y)$
                                                               $(\forall x)(\forall y){\sim}(xLy)$
                                                               equivalent by QN: ${\sim}(\exists x)(\exists y)(xLy)$

14. Nothing likes something   for all x, not x likes something
    All things, they do not like something $(\forall x){\sim}(x \text{ likes something})$
                                                               $(\forall x){\sim}(\text{for some } y, x \text{ likes } y)$
    All things, not (some thing, they like it) $(\forall x){\sim}(\exists y)(x \text{ likes } y)$
                                                               $(\forall x){\sim}(\exists y)(xLy)$
                                                               equivalent by QN: ${\sim}(\exists x)(\exists y)(xLy)$

15. Nothing likes everything   for all x, not x likes everything
    All things, they do not like everything $(\forall x){\sim}(x \text{ likes everything})$
                                                               $(\forall x){\sim}(\text{for all } y, x \text{ likes } y)$
    All things, not (all things, they like them) $(\forall x){\sim}(\forall y)(x \text{ likes } y)$
                                                               $(\forall x){\sim}(\forall y)(xLy)$
                                                               equivalent by QN: $(\forall x)(\exists y){\sim}(xLy)$

16. Nothing likes nothing   for all x, not x likes nothing
    All things, they do not like nothing $(\forall x){\sim}(x \text{ likes nothing})$
                                                               $(\forall x){\sim}(\text{for all } y, \text{ not } x \text{ likes } y)$
    All things, not (all things, not they like $(\forall x){\sim}(\forall y){\sim}(x \text{ likes } y)$
    them) $(\forall x){\sim}(\forall y){\sim}(xLy)$
                                                               equivalent by QN: $(\forall x)(\exists y)(xLy)$

English Sentences Whose Predicates are Categorically Quantified

Things are not related to just other *things*, they are related to *special kinds* of things. People don't just eat *something*, they eat some bananas, some candy, some pasta; and they don't just drive something, they drive some car, and so on. Quantifications are normally restricted to certain categories.

Recall the symbolization rules for working with categorical quantifications: After you select the quantifier, you must use a *connective* (either "&" or "⊃") to connect the stated *category* to the stated *predication*, in this case a relation. This can be remembered as the "SOME-AND" rule and the "ALL-THEN" rule.

> some CATEGORY PREDICATE ↔; (∃x)(x is CATEGORY & x is PREDICATE)
>
> all CATEGORY PREDICATE ↔; (∀x)(x is CATEGORY ⊃ x is PREDICATE)

So, we also use these translation rules when the predicate side of the sentence contains a relation with a categorical quantifier, as in "George hates *all insects*."

17. George hates all insects	for all x, x is an insect ⊃ George hates x
All insects, George hates them	(∀x)(Ix ⊃ g hates x)
	(∀x)(Ix ⊃ gHx)
18. All insects hate George	for all x, x is an insect ⊃ x hates George
All insects, they hate George	(∀x)(Ix ⊃ x hates g)
	(∀x)(Ix ⊃ xHg)
19. Every dog chews on some bone	for all x, x is a dog ⊃ x chews on some bone
All dogs, they chew on some bones	(∀x)(Dx ⊃ x chews on some bone)
All dogs, some bones, they chew	(∀x)[Dx ⊃ (∃y)(y is a bone & x chews on y)]
on them	(∀x)[Dx ⊃ (∃y)(By & xCy)]
20. Some bird ate all the frogs	for some x, x is a bird & x ate all the frogs
Some bird, it ate all frogs	(∃x)(Bx & x ate all the frogs)
Some bird, all frogs, it ate them	(∃x)[Bx & (∀y)(y is a frog ⊃ x ate y)]
	(∃x)[Bx & (∀y)(Fy ⊃ xAy)]

Arguments with Relational Sentences

It goes without saying that the kinds of relational sentences we have been analyzing here form the premises and conclusions of many, if not most, of our everyday arguments. Consider,

Every elephant is bigger than every mouse.	1. (∀x)[Ex ⊃ (∀y)(My ⊃ xBy)]
Dumbo is an elephant, and Mickey is a mouse.	2. Ed & Mm
————	————
So, Dumbo is definitely bigger than Mickey.	∴ dBm

Here is another.

George bought a mean and nasty kangaroo.	1. (∃x)[(Mx & Nx & Kx) & gBx]
You own what you have bought.	2. (∀x)(∀y)(xBy ⊃ xOy)
————	————
So, George owns a kangaroo.	∴ (∃x)(Kx & gOx)

In the next section we will show how to give deductions for these relational arguments as well as others more complicated.

Exercise 4.7. A,B Symbolizing Relations

Part A. Symbolize the following sentences, using the indicated predicate letters, relation letters, and name letters. Use the available **Exercise Work Sheet** to submit your work.

P = person ,   R = _ has read _ ,   s = Shakespeare ,
B = book ,   W = _ wrote _ ,   r = *Romeo and Juliet*

1.   Shakespeare wrote *Romeo and Juliet*.
2.   *Romeo and Juliet* is a book, written by Shakespeare.
3.   Shakespeare wrote some books.
4.   Some person wrote *Romeo and Juliet*.
5.   *Romeo and Juliet* is a book, written by some person.
6.   *Romeo and Juliet* has been read by every person.
7.   Some people have not read *Romeo and Juliet*, a book written by Shakespeare.
8.   *Romeo and Juliet* is a book that has been read by every person.
9.   Something has written something.
10.   Some person has written nothing.
11.   Some person wrote some book.
12.   Some person has read all books.
13.   No person has read all books.
14.   Not any person wrote any book.
15.   Some books have been read by every person.
16.   Some books have been read by no person.
17.   Some people have read whatever Shakespeare wrote.
18.   Whatever a person has writen, he has also read.

Part B. Symbolize the following arguments, using the indicated predicate letters, relation letters, and name letters. Use the available **Exercise Work Sheet** to submit your work.

1.   There is something that caused everything. So, something has caused itself. (C)
2.   Dumbo is bigger than any mouse. Mickey is a mouse. So, Dumbo is bigger than some mouse. (d, m, B)

3.   Nothing can cause itself. So, nothing can cause everything. (C)

4.   Bill the Barber shaves only those who pay him. Whoever pays someone has money. George has no money. So, Bill does not shave George. (b, P, S, M, g)

5.   Everything affects something important, but some things are not important. So, some important things are affected by some unimportant things. (A, I)

6.   Nancy is a girl who loves all boys. Frank is a boy who hates all girls. So, some girl likes some boy who hates her. (n, G, L, B, f, H)

7.   God can stop any event that is about to happen, provided he knows of it. God knows all events that are about to happen. So, God can stop all bad events that are about to happen. (g, E, A, K, S, B)

8.   Whatever. So, red things that have blue things are things that have things. (R, B, H)

9.   Whatever is alive has some non-physical component. Whatever is non-physical is outside of time. Whatever is outside of time is eternal. So, whatever is alive has some eternal component. (A, P, C, O, E)

10.   All spiritual things in the actual situation are spiritual in all possible situations. In all possible situations, all spiritual things are outside of time. So, all spiritual things in the actual situation are outside of time in all possible situations. (Px = x is a possible situation, a = actuality, xSy = x is spiritual in situation y, xOy = x is outside of time in situation y)

Section 4.8 Deductions with Relational Sentences

The good news is that deductions for arguments with quantified relational sentences are exactly the same as deductions for regular quantificational sentences. And the bad news— there is none. So, let's just go through a few deductions to see how things are done. We can start with Dumbo and Mickey Mouse. Who is bigger?

Every elephant is bigger than every mouse. Dumbo is an elephant.

Mickey is a mouse. So, Dumbo is definitely bigger than Mickey.

1. $(\forall x)[Ex \supset (\forall y)(My \supset xBy)]$ Prem
2. Ed   Prem
3. Mm   Prem   ∴ dBm

_____

4. $Ed \supset (\forall y)(My \supset dBy)$ 1, UI   d/x

Since Premiss 1 is a universal sentence, UI was applied in the usual way: every occurrence of the variable x, including the x that occurred behind the second quantifier, was replaced by any name of our choosing, and we picked the name d. The second quantifier is not not yet in play, since it buried inside a larger sentence. But, an easy MP makes the second quantifier accessible.

5. (∀y)(My ⊃ dBy)   2,4, MP
6. Mm ⊃ dBm   5, UI   m/y
7. dBm   3, 6, MP

Again, line 5 is a universal sentence, and UI was applied: every occurrence of the variable y was replaced by any name of our choosing, and this time we picked the name m. Notice, of course, that the name d occurring in line 5, already became fixed in line 4, so that it cannot be affected by the present use of UI.

Let's try another one. This time we will try to derive an existential conclusion (∃x)(. . .) from an existential premiss (∃x)(. . .) together with a universal premiss (∀x)(. . .). This is a typical situation, and the strategy is the same as it was earlier in the chapter. We must use the rule EI, and that always begins with a selection step.

> George bought a mean and nasty kangaroo. You own what you have bought. So, George owns a kangaroo.

1. (∃x)[(Mx & Nx & Kx) & gBx]   Prem
2. (∀x)(∀y)(xBy ⊃ xOy)   Prem   ∴ (∃x)(Kx & gOx)

───────────

3. select name: b   Selection [name is correct]
4. (Mb & Nb & Kb) & gBb   1, EI b/x
5. Kb   4, Simp
6. gBb   4, Simp
7. . . .

Done with Premiss 1. We have milked it for all it is worth. We turn to Premiss 2. There are two universal quantifiers at the front of the sentence, but only the first one, (∀x), is accessible to us, since the second one, (∀y), is at this point buried *deep inside* that whole line. We will use UI on the first quantifier, making sure that the name we pick matches the name in line 6 above. That means we pick the name g. All that creates a new universal sentence, with the quantifier (∀y). Again we use UI, and this time we pick b, again matching the name given in line 6. Then we put the pieces back together again and add an existential quantifier (∃x) with the rule EG.

7. (∀y)(gBy ⊃ gOy)   2, UI g/x
8. gBb ⊃ gOb   7, UI b/y

9. gOb	6,8, MP
10. Kb & gOb	5,9, Conj
11. (∃x)(Kx & gOx)	10, EG x/b

Let's try another argument, this time one that requires the rule UG. It's an easy problem. The rule UG requires that we use a UG-box that begins with a selection step and that ends with a representative line. (Do check the definition for that).

George hates vegetables. Carrots are vegetables. So, George hates carrots.

1. (∀x)(Vx ⊃ gHx)	Prem
2. (∀x)(Cx ⊃ Vx)	Prem ∴ (∀x)(Cx ⊃ gHx)

3. select name: a	Selection for UG [name is correct]
4. Va ⊃ gHa	1, UI a/x
5. Ca ⊃ Va	2, UI a/x
6. Ca ⊃ gHa	4,5, Hyp Syll

7. (∀x)(Cx ⊃ gHx)	6, UG x/a [ln. 6 is representative]

After we selected the name a, we derived line 6, and that line does not violate the representativity restriction described earlier in Section 4.4. So, we may generalize the instance of line 6 into the universal assertion of line 7.

One danger of having a lot of quantifiers hanging around is that it increases the likelihood that one will violate the instantiation and generalization restrictions on the quantificational rules. For example, the rule EI. has a restriction on the included selection step, and the rule UG not only has a restriction on the included selection step but it also has a restriction on when one may terminate the UG-box. Let's see how these things might go. Consider the following incorrect argument:

Everything is such that something causes it.   [Yeah. That's good.]

So, there is something that causes everything.   [Whoa! Wait a minute!]

1. (∀x)(∃y)(yCx)	Prem ∴ (∃y)(∀x)(yCx)

2. ?

The conclusion is (∃y)[. . .y. . .] , and that has to come by the rule EG from a corresponding instance [. . .b. . .], for some or other name b. Specifically, that instance must be (∀x)(bCx). So, the problem requires that, starting in step 2, we begin to derive the universal sentence (∀x)(bCx). We begin with a UG-box and a selection step.

1. $(\forall x)(\exists y)(yCx)$	Prem $\therefore$ $(\exists y)(\forall x)(yCx)$	

2. select name: a	Selection for UG	[required, and correct]
3. $(\exists y)(yCa)$	1, UI a/x	[required, and correct]
4. select name: b	Selection for EI	[required, and correct]
5. bCa	3, EI b/y	[required, and correct]

6. ~~$(\forall x)(bCx)$~~	5, UG?? ERROR. Ln. 5 is un-representative
7. ~~$(\exists y)(\forall x)(yCx)$~~	BLOCKED

So, the inference to line 6 is *illegal*, and the inference to line 7 is blocked, because the move from line 5 to 6 is blocked. On the one hand, line 5 is exactly what is needed to get line 6, but on the other hand, line 5 will always contain an EI'd name, so that line 5 is always unrepresentative, and the required UG cannot be performed. So, this argument does *not* work. But the next argument *does* work. (It's about Superman.)

There is a hero that everyone knows. So, everyone knows some hero or other.

1. $(\exists x)[Hx \,\&\, (\forall y)(Py \supset yKx)]$	Prem $\therefore$ $(\forall y)[Py \supset (\exists x)(Hx \,\&\, yKx)]$

2. select name: s	Selection for EI [name is correct]
3. $Hs \,\&\, (\forall y)(Py \supset yKs)$	1, EI s/x
4. Hs	3, Simp
5. $(\forall y)(Py \supset yKs)]$	3, Simp

6. select name: b	Selection for UG [name is correct]

7. Pb	Assumption for CP
8. $Pb \supset bKs$	5, UI b/y
9. bKs	7,8, MP
10. $Hs \,\&\, bKs$	4,9, Conj
11. $(\exists x)(Hx \,\&\, bKx)$	10, EG x/s

12. $Pb \supset (\exists x)(HX \,\&\, bKx)$	7—11, CP

13. $(\forall y)[Py \supset (\exists x)(Hx \,\&\, yKx)]$	12, UG y/b [ln. 12 is representative]

Truths about Relations

Many relations are *special* in the sense that there are *general truths* specifically about them. This situation is not so unusual, because most of our ideas do have connections to other ideas, and these connections create general truths about such ideas. Consider the relation of being *greater than* something. There is a hidden truth here: if one thing, George, is greater than another thing, Sally, and Sally in turn is greater than some thing, Harry, then George must be greater than Harry, or, more generally,

$$(\forall x)(\forall y)(\forall z)[\ (xGy\ \&\ yGz) \supset xGz]$$

The same rule would be true for other comparative relations as well, such as *smaller than*, *later than*, *richer than*, *more educated than*, and many more. Many of these relations are *mathematical* comparisons of quantities, and the truths about these relations are actually basic mathematical (and necessary) truths. Another example of such a mathematical truth is that the relation *greater than* is anti-symmetric:

$$(\forall x)(\forall y)\ (xGy \supset \sim(yGx))$$

How is this situation related to the process of reasoning? Clearly, these general truths are in fact always being used by us when we reason things out, but we almost never make an explicit acknowledgement of these facts. They are part of a *hidden background*. So, when we do our logic, we must formally acknowledge that such general truths are being used, as we illustrate in the next example:

All such general truths, when they are being used, must be first be stated as *premisses* for the argment, alongside the other premisses.

George, Sally, and Harry, for this photo, the taller ones must stand behind the others. George, you are taller than Sally, and Sally, you are taller than Harry. So, George, you must stand behind Harry.

This is clear and effective reasoning, but it secretly uses a *general truth* about the tallness relation. To present this formally, we first *add* this general truth as Premiss 3, and we then derive that George is taller than Harry and stands behind him.

1. $(\forall x)(\forall y)(xTy \supset xBy)$	Premiss	
2. $gTs\ \&\ sTh$	Premiss	
3. $(\forall x)(\forall y)(\forall z)[\ (xTy\ \&\ yTz) \supset xTz\ ]$	*Missing Premiss*	$\therefore$ gBh
4. $(\forall y)(\forall z)[\ (gTy\ \&\ yTz) \supset gTz]$	3, UI g/x	
5. $(\forall z)[\ (gTs\ \&\ sTz) \supset gTz]$	4, UI s/y	
6. $(gTs\ \&\ sTh) \supset gTh$	5, UI h/z	
7. gTh	2,6, MP	
8. $(\forall y)(gTy \supset gBy)$	1, UI g/x	
9. $gTh \supset gBh$	8, UI h/y	
10. gBh	7,9, MP	

Exercise 4.8. A,B Deductions with Relations

Part A. These arguments have the English meanings given in Exercise 4.7.B. Give deductions for these arguments. Some are more difficult, and some require use of the rule CP. Use the available **Exercise Work Sheet** to submit your work.

1. (∃x)(∀y)(xCy)   ∴ (∃x)(xCx)

2. (∀x)(Mx ⊃ dBx) , Mm   ∴ (∃x)(Mx & dBx)

3. (∀x)~(xCx)   ∴ (∀x)~(∀y)(xCy)

4. (∀x)(~xPb ⊃ ~bSx) , (∀x)[(∃y)(xPy) ⊃ Mx] , ~Mg   ∴ ~bSg

5. (∀x)(∃y)(Iy & xAy) , (∃x)~Ix   ∴ (∃y)[Iy & (∃x)(~Ix & xAy)]

6. Gn & (∀x)(Bx ⊃ nLx) , Bf & (∀x)(Gx ⊃ fHx)   ∴ (∃x){Gx & (∃y)[(By & yHx) & xLy]}

7. (∀x)[(Ex & Ax & gKx) ⊃ gSx] , (∀x)[(Ex & Ax) ⊃ gKx]   ∴ (∀x)[(Ex & Bx & Ax) ⊃ gSx]

8. p   ∴ (∀x){ [Rx & (∃y)(By & xHy)] ⊃ (∃y)(xHy) }

9. (∀x)[Ax ⊃ (∃y)(~Py & yCx)] , (∀x)(~Px ⊃ Ox) , (∀x)(Ox ⊃ Ex)

      ∴ (∀x)[Ax ⊃ (∃y)(Ey & yCx)]

10. (∀x)[(xSa & Pa) ⊃ (∀y)(Py ⊃ xSy)] , (∀y)[Py ⊃ (∀x)(xSy ⊃ xOy)]

       ∴ (∀x)[(xSa & Pa) ⊃ (∀y)(Py ⊃ xOy)]

Part B. Symbolize and give deductions for the following arguments. These problems are difficult. Check the symbolization answers given below. Use the available **Exercise Work Sheet** to submit your work.

1. People like to do what they are good at. People are also good at something if and only if they practice it. So, people like to do what they practice. (P = person, G = x is good at y, L = x likes to do y, R = x practices y)

2. *L'amour.* Everybody loves a lover. Well, George and Barb, and Cindy and Mike, are really nice people, but Barb just doesn't love George. So, that's how one figures out that Cindy does not love Mike. (P = person, N = really nice, L = x loves y, g = George, b = Barb, c = Cindy, m = Mike)

3. People do think with whatever heads they have, if they can. People can think with whatever heads they have, if those heads are not full. Many people have heads that are not full. So, many people have heads that they do think with. (P = person, H = head, H = x has y, T = x thinks with y, C = x can think with y, F = is full)

4. There are things that everybody wants to have. All those kinds of things are very hard to get. Whatever is very hard to get is very expensive. People who don't have a lot of money can't afford very expensive things. People who want things that they can't afford are always miserable. You

are a person who does not have a lot of money, but you think you are content. People who think they are content but are actually miserable are deluding themselves. So, you are deluding yourself. (a = you, P = person, H = very hard to get, E = very expensive, L = has lots of money, M = miserable, W = x wants to have y, A = x can afford y, C = x thinks y is content, D = x deludes y)

Symbolization answers. Here are the symbolization answers for Part B, but do try to figure these out for yourself first, really.

1. (∀x)[Px ⊃ (∀y)(xGy ⊃ xLy)] , (∀x)[Px ⊃ (∀y)(xGy ≡ xPy)]

    ∴ (∀x)[Px ⊃ (∀y)(xPy ⊃ xLy)]

2. (∀x){Px ⊃ (∀y)[(Py & (∃z)(Pz & yLz)) ⊃ xLy]} ,

    Pg & Ng & Pb & Nb & Pc & Nc & Pm & Nm , ~(bLg) ∴ ~(cLm)

3. (∀x){Px ⊃ (∀y)[(Hy & xHy) ⊃ (xCy ⊃ xTy)]},

    (∀x)[Px ⊃ (∀y)((Hy & xHy & ~Fy) ⊃ xCy)] , (∃x)[Px & (∃y)(Hy & xHy & ~Fy)]

    ∴ (∃x)[Px & (∃y)(Hy & xHy & xTy)]

4. (∃y)(∀x)(Px ⊃ xWy) , (∀y)[(∀x)(Px ⊃ xWy) ⊃ Hy] , (∀y)(Hy ⊃ Ey) ,

    (∀x)[(Px & ~Lx) ⊃ (∀y)(Ey ⊃ ~xAy)] , (∀x){[Px & (∃y)(xWy & ~xAy)] ⊃ Mx} ,

    Pa & ~La & aCa , (∀x)[(Px & xCx & Mx) ⊃ xDx] ∴ aDa

Section 4.9 Working with Identities

The Identity Relation

One of the most important relations is the *identity relation*, as it is called. This is a relation that arises from the fact that a single thing can be uniquely described in different ways, especially when the descriptions are made by different people or in different contexts. We can refer to someone by *name*, for example, "Neil Armstrong," and we can also refer to the *same* person by the *description* "the first person to walk on the Moon." This leads to the identity statement, "Neil Armstrong *is identical to* the first person to walk on the Moon." In logic it is customary to use the mathematical equal sign, "x = y," to represent the identity relation, rather than some capital letter, "xIy," as one would use for all the other relations.

A *singular term* is any expression that represents a *single* thing, as opposed to a group of things. Regular proper names, such as "George," are singular terms, and so are *definite descriptions*, such as "the first prime number." We may use the name letter symbols, a, b, c, d, . . . , to symbolize all singular terms.

Neil Armstrong is the first person to walk on the Moon: $a = w$
Clark Kent is Superman: $c = s$
The Sun is the center of our solar system: $s = c$
Shakespeare is not the Archangel Michael: $\sim(s = m)$
2 is the first prime number: $2 = f$

There are some common *quantity* expressions in our ordinary language that do not explicitly mention the identity relation, but they nevertheless employ the identity relation in their *meaning*. We list eight of these common English patterns.

1. **At least two** people will win. (Also: **more than one**)

   $(\exists x)(Px \& Wx) \& (\exists y)(Py \& Wy)$ NO. WRONG!

Wrong, because this only says the same thing two times in a row, "some person x will win, and some person y will win." There is no guarantee that two separate things are involved: maybe x and y are different, and maybe not. What we need is:

   $(\exists x)(\exists y)[\,(Px \& Px) \& (Py \& Py) \& \sim(x = y)\,]$ YES. RIGHT.

Some person x will win, and some person y will win, and x and y are *not equal*.

2. **At most one** person will win.

   (Also; **not more than one**, also: **not at least two**, also: **less than two**)
   $\sim(\exists x)(\exists y)[\,(Px \& Wx) \& (Py \& Wy) \& \sim(x = y)\,]$ (this is the negation of type #1)
   also: $(\forall x)(\forall y)[\,((Px \& Wx) \& (Py \& Wy)) \supset x = y\,]$ (by using the Q.N. Law)

3. **Only one** person will win.

   (Also: **exactly one**, also: **just one**, also: *one*, with emphasis)

This means, at least one person will win, plus no more than one will win. This means the existential quantifier "at least one" is combined with the quantifier "at most one."

   (**At least one** person will win) & (**at most one** person will win)
   $(\exists x)(Px \& Wx) \;\&\; (\forall x)(\forall y)[\,((Px \& Wx) \& (Py \& Wy)) \supset x = y\,]$
   also: $(\exists x)[\,(Px \& Wx) \;\&\; (\forall y)((Py \& Wy) \supset x = y)\,]$

4. **Only George** in group F is happy.

   $Fg \& (\forall x)[\,(Fx \& \sim(x = g)) \supset \sim Hx\,] \& Hg$

There are three elements in this kind of sentence. First of all, an "only George" sentence always refers to some group F to which the named thing, here George, belongs. Perhaps, the group is the people at the party, and George is one of those. Secondly, George is the only one in that group that has the property in question, in this case, being happy. This means, just as with any use of the word "only," that there is an *exclusion*: all in the group who are *not* George, are *not* happy. And thirdly, it is claimed that George *does* have the property in question: he is happy.

5. **No one except George** in group F is happy.

This says *exactly* the same thing as #4 above, and it has the same symbolization.

Fg & (∀x)[(Fx & ~(x = g)) ⊃ ~Hx] & Hg

Again, there are three elements. First, there is a reference to some group F, to which George belongs. Secondly, the entire group F, except for George, does *not* have the property in question, they are all unhappy. And thirdly, George *does* have the property in question, he is happy.

6. **All except George** in group F are happy.

Fg & (∀x)[(Fx & ~(x = g)) ⊃ Hx] & ~Hg

This is similar to #5, except that it is the *affirmative* version. Again, there are three elements. There is a reference to some group F, to which George belongs. Secondly, the entire group F, except for George, has the property in question: here, being happy. And thirdly, George does *not* have the property in question, he is not happy.

7. **George is the R-est** in group F.

Fg & (∀x)[(Fx & ~(x = g)) ⊃ gRx]

George is the smart*est* in his class. This means that he is smart*er* than everyone in his class. Wait. He can't be smarter than himself. So, *all* in the class, except for George, are such that George is smarter than them. This sounds familiar. Yes, this is similar to type #6 above, but not the same. The sentence, "Mount Everest is the tallest mountain in the world," is also like this, where group F is all the mountains.

8. **The one and only** person that did win **is** happy.

Exactly one person did win, **and he is** happy
Some person did win, **and** he is happy, **and at most one** person did win

(∃x)[(Px & Wx) & Hx] & (∀x)(∀y)[((Px & Wx) & (Py & Wy)) ⊃ x = y]

also: (∃x)[(Px & Wx) & Hx & (∀y)((Py & Wy) ⊃ x = y)]

The Laws of Identity

The identity relation is governed by some important logical truths (rules) that must be employed when this relation is used in an argument. One method for using these important truths is to simply list these truths among the premises for an argument, as we did with the *greater than* relation, discussed at the end of Section 4.8. This would be an entirely adequate method. However, in logic and mathematics, it is customary to introduce special *rules* of logic, called the *Laws of Identity*, which are to be used in the same way that all the other rules are used: they are simply applied to the various lines in a deduction. In stating these laws, we will use a new kind of notation. We use the Greek letters α, β, and γ as *variables* to represent all *name* expressions, and we use the notation "(. . .α. . .)" to represent any simple or complex expression containing the name α. There are five identity laws. Ident1 is also a tautology. These are all very intuitive rules, so there is not much to learn here.

Ident1. (Reflexivity)	Ident2. (Symmetry)	Ident3. (Transitivity)	Ident4. (Substitution)	Ident5. (Difference)
	$\alpha = \beta$	$\alpha = \beta$ $\beta = \gamma$	$\alpha = \beta$ $(\ldots \alpha \ldots)$	$(\ldots \alpha \ldots)$ $\sim(\ldots \beta \ldots)$
∴ $\alpha = \alpha$	∴ $\beta = \alpha$	∴ $\alpha = \gamma$	∴ $(\ldots \beta \ldots)$	∴ $\sim(\alpha = \beta)$

The Laws of Reflexivity, Symmetry, and Transitivity do not require much comment. They state some *extremely* obvious truths about identity, and yet, they show how special the identity relation is, since *non-identity* relations do not satisfy all three of these laws. For example, the *love* relation does not satisfy any of the identity laws, and neither does the *see* relation, nor does the *hit* relation, and so forth. So, these special facts need to be explicitly stated.

The Laws of Substitution and Difference are more substantial. *Substitution*: If two named things are one and the same thing, **a = b**, then whatever is true of the first named thing must also be true of the second named thing, **Fa** ∴ **Fb**, because it's only *one* thing. *Difference*: If two named things are different *in some way*, **Fa & ~Fb**, then those named things must be two different things, **~(a = b)**.

Let's put some of these rules to work.

#1. George is a mathematician and a philosopher. Hilda is a mathematician and not a philosopher. So, at least two different mathematicians exist.

1. Mg & Pg	Prem
2. Mh & ~Ph	Prem ∴ (∃x)(∃y)[Mx & My & ~(x = y)]
3. Pg	1, Simp
4. ~Ph	2, Simp
5. ~(g = h)	3,4, **Difference**
6. Mg & Mh & ~(g = h)	1,Simp,2,Simp,5,Conj
7. (∃y)[Mg & My & ~(g = y)]	6, EG y/h
8. (∃x)(∃y)[Mx & My & ~(x = y)]	7, EG x/g

#2. George is a psychologist who will talk only to Sally. However, Sally is not a psychologist. So, George will not talk to any psychologists, not even himself.

1. Pg	Prem
2. (∀x)(gTx ⊃ x = s)	Prem
3. ~Ps	Prem ∴ (∀x)(Px ⊃ ~gTx) & ~gTg
4. select name: a	Selection for UG
5. Pa	Assumption for CP
6. ~(a = s)	3,5, **Difference**
7. gTa ⊃ a = s	2, UI a/x
8. ~gTa	6,7, MT
9. Pa ⊃ ~gTa	5—8, CP
10. (∀x)(Px ⊃ ~gTx)	9, UG x/a
11. Pg ⊃ ~gTg	10, UI g/x
12. ~gTg	1,11, MP
13. (∀x)(Px ⊃ ~gTx) & ~gTg	10,12, Conj

#3. At the party, George was the only one who danced. At some point some drunks at the party started to dance, and they were arrested, and they had to spend the night in jail. So, George was arrested too and had to spend the night in jail.

1. (∀x)[(Px & Dx) ⊃ x = g]	Prem
2. (∃x)(Ux & Px & Dx & Ax & Sx)	Prem ∴ Ag & Sg
3. select name: a	Selection
4. Ua & Pa & Da & Aa & Sa	2, EI a/x

5. Pa & Da	4, Simp
6. (Pa & Da) ⊃ a = g	1, UI a/x
7. a = g	5,6, MP
8. Aa & Sa	4, Simp
9. Ag & Sg	7,8, **Substitution** g/a

Exercise 4.9. A,B,C Working with Identities

Part A. Symbolize the following sentences, using the indicated predicate letters, relation letters, and name letters. Use the available **Exercise Work Sheet** to submit your work.

S = skyscraper	I = _ is in _	s = The Sears Tower
E = expensive to live in	T = _ is taller than _	c = Chicago
B = very big	L = _ lives in _	n = New York

1. There is at least one skyscraper in Chicago, and it is very big.

2. There are at least two skyscrapers in Chicago.

3. There is at most one skyscraper in Chicago.

4. There is exactly one skyscraper in Chicago.

5. The Sears Tower is the only skyscraper in Chicago.

6. Every skyscraper except the Sears Tower is in Chicago.

7. The one and only skyscraper in Chicago is expensive to live in.

8. The Sears Tower is one of at least two skyscrapers in Chicago.

9. Some skyscraper in Chicago is taller than another skyscraper in New York.

10   No skyscraper in Chicago can be identical to some skyscraper in New York.

11   The Sears Tower is the tallest skyscraper there is.

12   Some skyscraper in Chicago has at least two occupants (they live there).

Part B. Symbolize the following arguments, using the indicated predicate letters, relation letters, and name letters. Use the available **Exercise Work Sheet** to submit your work.

L = likes to dance	D = Dutchman	F = _ is a friend of _
H = hairdresser		A = _ admires _
P = person	g = George	T = _ talks to _
E = exhausted	s = Sally	K = _ knows _ (active voice)
T = is in town	h = Harry	F = _ is faster than _
S = skater	n = Sally's neighbor	outskated = some skater is faster

1. George is a friend of Sally and also of Harry. Sally likes to dance, but Harry does not. So, George has at least two different friends.

2. Sally is a friend of all hairdressers but not of George, who is her neighbor. So, her neighbor is not a hairdresser.

3. Sally doesn't admire anything except herself. Sally sometimes talks to herself, but she has never talked to George. So, Sally does not admire George.

4. Only Sally is known by Harry, and only Harry is known by Sally. Some people are known by both Harry and by Sally. Sally is exhausted. So, Harry is exhausted.

5. Some people in town know Sally. At most one person knows Sally. So, no one outside of town knows Sally.

6. The fastest skater is a Dutchman. So, any skater who is not a Dutchman can be outskated.

Part C. Give deductions for the following arguments. Use the available **Exercise Work Sheet** to submit your work.

1. gFs & gFh,   Ds & ~Dh   ∴   (∃x)(∃y)[gFx & gFy & ~(x = y)]

2. (∀x)(Hx ⊃ sFx) & ~sFg & g = n   ∴   ~Hn

3. (∀x)[~(x = s) ⊃ ~sAx] & sAs,   sTs & ~sTg   ∴   ~sAg

4. (∀x)[~(x = s) ⊃ ~hKx] & hKs,   (∀x)[~(x = h) ⊃ ~sKx] & sKh,
    (∃x)(Px & hKx & sKx),   Es   ∴   Eh

5. (∃x)(Px & Tx & xKs),   (∀x)(∀y)[(Px & Py & xKs & yKs) ⊃ x = y]
    ∴   (∀x)[(Px & ~Tx) ⊃ ~xKs]

6. (∃x){ Dx & Sx & (∀y)[(Sy & ~(y = x)) ⊃ xFy)] }
    ∴   (∀y)[(Sy & ~Dy) ⊃ (∃x)(Sx & xFy)]

CHAPTER 5

LOGICAL FALLACIES

Section 5.1 Introduction

- Logical fallacy: A type of argument that is unsound but is often accepted as sound.

When people reason they do make mistakes: they make logical mistakes in their inferences and factual mistakes in their premisses. Some of these mistakes are more common than others. It is these *common* mistakes that are known as *logical fallacies*. Careful reflection, study, and observation help people avoid these common mistakes.

A note about our procedure in this chapter. When people are careful and considerate in their thinking, they do not fall prey to logical fallacies. But, people are not always careful, and they do not always consider matters fully. So, for the present discussion, we will suppose *the worst case scenario*: a case in which both the giver of the argument (the arguer) and the audience of the argument (the listener) are careless and inconsiderate thinkers, and are unaware of the criticisms that await them. From this perspective one can better appreciate the extent to which logical fallacies are a serious threat to rational thinking. We will focus on the following 24 fallacies:

Fallacies of Irrelevance

1. Argumentum ad Baculum
2. Argumentum ad Hominem
3. Argumentum ad Populum
4. Argumentum ad Verecundiam
5. Argumentum ad Misericordiam
6. Argumentum ad Ignorantiam
7. Tu Quoque Fallacy
8. Guilt by Association Fallacy
9. Red Herring Fallacy

Fallacies of Misconstrual	10. Straw Man Fallacy
	11. Post Hoc Ergo Propter Hoc Fallacy
	12. Fallacy of Special Pleading
	13. Fallacy of Improper (Hasty) Generalization
	14. Fallacy of Improper Instance
	15. Complex Question Fallacy
	16. Fallacy of Syntactic Ambiguity
	17. Fallacy of Semantic Equivocation
	18. Fallacy of Division
	19. Fallacy of Composition
Fallacies of Presumption	20. False Dichotomy Fallacy
	21. Slippery Slope Fallacy
	22. Fallacy of Ad Hoc Reasoning
	23. Petitio Principii Fallacy
	24. Fallacy of Inconsistent Premisses

Formal Fallacies

Some fallacies are *formal* fallacies. These inferences use *invalid argument patterns*, but because of their similarity to certain valid patterns, they are often *mistaken* for valid ones. We list here the main formal fallacies, but since we have discussed these earlier, we will not discuss them further here.

(1) **Illicit modus ponens**, or, **fallacy of affirming the consequent**:

If p is so, then q is so.	$p \supset q$,	If Sam went, there was trouble.
And, q *is* so.	q	And, there was trouble.
Therefore, p is also so.	so, p	So, Sam was there.

(2) **Illicit modus tollens**, or **fallacy of denying the antecedent**:

If p is so, then q is so.	$p \supset q$,	If Sam goes, there will be trouble
But, p is *not* so.	$\sim p$	But, Sam won't go.
Therefore, q is also not so.	so, $\sim q$	So, there won't be any trouble.

(3) **Illicit conditional contraposition**:

If p is so, then q is so.	$p \supset q$,	If Sam goes, there will be trouble
So, if not p, then not q.	so, $\sim p \supset \sim q$	So, if Sam doesn't, there won't be.

(4) **Illicit universal contraposition:**

| all S are P | All capitalists desire to become rich. |
| So, all non-S are non-P | So, all who are not capitalists do not desire to become rich. |

(5) **Illicit negative conjunction:**

| Not both p and q | That actor is not rich and famous. |
| So, not p and not q | So, that actor is not rich and not famous. |

(6) **Illicit categorical syllogism:**

all S are M	All capitalists desire to become rich.
all P are M	All bank robbers desire to become rich.
So, all S are P	So, all capitalists are bank robbers.

Informal Fallacies

The remaining fallacies are called *informal* fallacies. The difference between formal and informal fallacies is the following: with formal fallacies, people mistake an invalid pattern for a valid one: they think that certain patterns are *rules* when they are *not rules*. With informal fallacies, on the other hand, *that* mistake does not happen. Rather, there is a different kind of a mistake, and it concerns the premises.

Informal Fallacies that are Invalid

Now, as it turns out, most informal fallacies are, in fact, *invalid* inferences, because the premises are not sufficient reasons to establish the conclusion. But, because of the *special content* of the premises, the premises are nevertheless *persuasive*, that is, they have the psychological power to fool the audience into accepting the conclusion anyway. Since these inferences are invalid, each of these inferences is referred to as a **non sequitur**, which is Latin for "it does not follow." Non sequiturs fall into two main groups: Types (1)—(9) below form a group called *fallacies of irrelevance*, and types (10)—(19) below form a group called *fallacies of misconstrual*.

Informal Fallacies that are Valid

Some informal fallacies, however, make a valid inference. Their mistake is not the inference; their mistake is a special kind of *defect* of the premises. We call these *fallacies of presumption*. Types (20) and (21) below use special kinds of premises that are *empirically false*; types (22)—(23) use premises that are completely *unsupported*; and type (24) uses premises that are *inconsistent*, and whose simultaneous assertion forms a conjunction that is necessarily false.

FORMAL FALLACIES	INFORMAL FALLACIES		
Invalid Arguments	Invalid Arguments		Valid Arguments
Non-rules Taken as Rules	Fallacies of Irrelevance	Fallacies of Misconstrual	Fallacies of Presumption

A Note about the Classification of Fallacies

There is significant disagreement in the logic literature about how logical fallacies are to be *classified*. While there is a reasonable agreement about how individual fallacies are named and analyzed, there is not the same kind of agreement about how they are to be grouped into *families*. One problem is to determine what characteristics of fallacies should be used to create classifications, and a related problem is what characteristics will neatly divide all fallacies into a small number of distinct groups.

One important characteristic, on which there is agreement, is the condition of whether the premisses are *relevant* to producing the conclusion. This creates the family of *Fallacies of Irrelevance*. Fallacies in which the premisses are totally irrelevant to the conclusion belong to this family. And what about the other fallacies? Some authors propose the characteristic of having premisses that are *ambiguous* in meaning, and this creates a family of *Fallacies of Ambiguity*, and a number of fallacies fit very nicely in this group. Also, some authors propose a rather vague characteristic of using *poor assumptions* to generate the conclusion, and this creates the family of *Fallacies of Presumption*. One difficulty with these three families, as defined, is that there are a number of fallacies that are *left over*, and these authors have to stretch their criteria in unacceptable ways in order to accommodate these left-over fallacies. Examples are the Straw Man fallacy, the fallacy of Improper Generalization, the fallacy of Improper Instance, the fallacy of Special Pleading, the Post Hoc Ergo Propter Hoc fallacy, and the fallacy of Inconsistent Premisses. These fallacies really fit into *none* of these families (as defined). We propose a solution.

The classification scheme that we use is a revision of the previously mentioned conditions, and it accommodates all the logical fallacies:

1. *Fallacies of Irrelevance.* These are fallacies in which the premisses are *not relevant* to the conclusion (and so, the inference is invalid).

Where the premisses are relevant, the following obtain:

2. *Fallacies of Misconstrual [Misconstruction].* These are fallacies in which the premisses are *misconstrued* in order to produce the conclusion (and so, the inference is invalid).

3. *Fallacies of Presumption.* These are fallacies in which the premisses are *not established* facts, although the inference is valid.

These three families are represented in the diagram displayed above. (By the way, these families could also usefully be called Fallacies of Irrelevant Premisses, Fallacies of Misconstrued Premisses, and Fallacies of Unestablished Premisses.)

Section 5.2 Fallacies of Irrelevance

The Fallacies of Irrelevance form one main division of informal fallacies. In these types of arguments, the premisses are *totally irrelevant* to the conclusion, but the premisses are nevertheless persuasive. Obviously, with such a lack of connection, these arguments would have to be invalid. These types of fallacies are also called *Fallacies of Relevance.*

1. Argumentum ad Baculum

The Latin name of this fallacy means "argument from the stick (club)." In this type of argument the arguer is making an *appeal to force*, that is, the arguer in some way is using a *threat* (or sometimes, a promise of *reward*) to get the listener to agree with the conclusion. As a practical, but not logical, matter, the listener may have to acquiesce, but regardless of that, the conclusion does not follow from the premisses. The argument is a non sequitur.

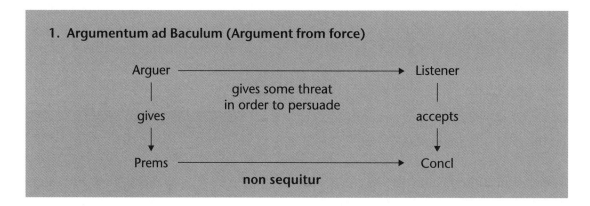

An example of this fallacy is the following:

"I urge you to accept Management's moderate proposal. It is the best course of action for the company and its employees. Those of you who don't agree will probably be more comfortable in another job."

This argument has the structure:

1. If you do not consent to X, then Y will happen.
2. But you do not want Y to happen.
3. So, you consent to X.
4. So, X is correct.

This argument is doubly erroneous. First of all, causal events (such as punishment or reward) are irrational reasons for giving consent. Consent should be based on *evidence* for the correctness of what is being consented to. Secondly, even if consent is given, that *also* is not evidence for the correctness of what is being consented to. Mere consent is evidence for nothing, since consent can be given for the worst of reasons, for example, force, or favor.

Translation note. Several fallacies have Latin names that begin with "argumentum ad . . . ." These can be translated equally well in two different ways, either as "appeal to . . .," as in "Appeal to Pity," or as "argument from [based on] . . .," as in "Argument from Pity." This book favors the second version.

2. Argumentum ad Hominem

The Latin name of this fallacy means "argument against the person." In this type of argument the arguer is making *a personal attack* on the opponent in order to persuade the listener to reject the opponent's thesis. The personal attack can take the form of an *abusive* attack on the character of the opponent, such as that he can't control his emotions or desires (an abusive ad hominem), or an attack that presents some negative *circumstances* regarding the opponent, such as that he did not attend the best law school (a circumstantial ad hominem). Since such matters are usually completely irrelevant to the conclusion, the argument is a non sequitur.

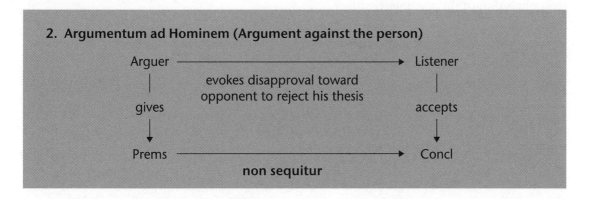

An example of this fallacy is the following:

"The senator would have us all believe that cigarette smoking is a social evil that can only be eliminated by imposing a $10 tax on each package of cigarettes sold. But why should we believe him? Everybody who knows him thoroughly dislikes him. I've never met as rude and egotistical a person as him."

This argument has the structure:

1.   Person A proposes X.

2.   Person A has some characteristics F.

3.   The audience does not approve of F.

[This causes the audience to have a general negative attitude towards person A, including A's proposal X.]

4.   So, proposal X is not correct.

Here too, the argument is doubly erroneous. First of all, disapproval of some characteristic F of a person is not a rational reason to have a general negative attitude towards that person. Secondly, even when there is a general negative attitude towards a person, that fact has no connection to the correctness of a given view, even if that view happens to be proposed by that person.

3. Argumentum ad Populum

The Latin name of this fallacy means "argument from the people." In this type of popular argument the arguer makes an *appeal to popular sentiments* in an attempt to persuade the listener that the conclusion is correct. Such sentiments are usually completely irrelevant to the conclusion of the argument.

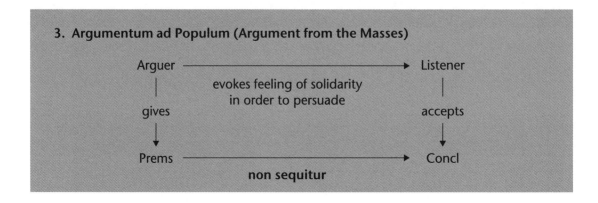

An example of this fallacy is the following:

> "The senator has proposed a bill that will allow oil exploration in federal parks. We all know him to be a man of great personal strength. He served this great country of ours with honor during the War; he has spent most of his life in public office on behalf of plain folk like you and me; he has always followed the simple rule that if you want to get something done right, then you have got to get in there and do it yourself. He is a man you can trust, and he deserves our support on this bill."

This argument has the following structure (here person A can be the arguer himself or some person advocated by the arguer):

1. Person A proposes X.
2. Person A has some characteristics F.
3. The audience approves of F.

[This causes the audience to have a general positive attitude towards person A, including A's proposal X.]

4. So, proposal X is correct.

There are clear similarities between this type of argument and the preceding type. We could say that this argument is the affirmative counterpart to the negative *ad hominem* fallacy. Once again, the argument is doubly erroneous. First of all, approval of some characteristic F of a person is not a rational reason to have a general positive attitude towards that person. Secondly, even when there is a general positive attitude towards a person, that fact has no connection to the correctness of a given view, even if that view happens to be proposed by that person.

4. Argumentum ad Verecundiam

The Latin of this fallacy means "argument from reverence." In this type of argument the arguer cites some sort of authoritative source to support the conclusion, using the highly favorable status of the source as a means to persuade the listener that the conclusion is correct. The problem here becomes apparent when the source cited is *irrelevant* to the particular case at hand, as is the case when the source is an expert in a different area only. This fallacy is often called an *appeal to an unqualified authority*.

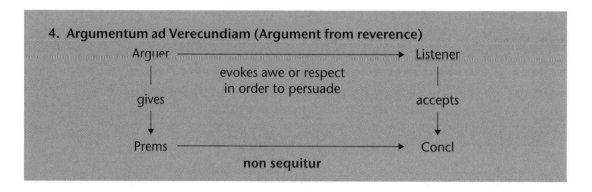

Consider the following example:

> "The view by various religious groups that we should not waste our money or time on gambling is actually correct. Even Albert Einstein, who is the greatest scientific genius of all time, gave as a reason for rejecting quantum level indeterminacy that God does not play dice with the universe."

This argument has the structure:

1. Person A is an authority in matters of area S.
2. Person A supports position X, which is outside of area S.
3. So, position X is correct.

When someone *is* an authority in a certain area, then that person's expert opinion is good evidence for matters pertaining to that area. A dentist's opinion is good evidence for dental issues, good evidence in the sense that whatever a dentist says within the area of his or her expertise is likely to be true. Arguments based in this way on expert opinions are inductively strong arguments.

In the same way, when someone is *not* an authority in a certain area, then that person's opinion is not good evidence for matters pertaining to that area. A dentist's opinion is not good evidence for legal issues, and it is not true that whatever a dentist says about legal issues is likely to be true. Arguments based on people's opinions outside their areas of expertise are without merit; they are non sequiturs. (But notice that an argument like this is a fallacy when the *only* reason given for the conclusion is that an unqualified authority said so. The argument is *not* a fallacy when it *also* gives *other* reasons, for example, the reasons that the unqualified authority had for making the proposal in the first place. Then the argument would be evaluated using those other reasons as well.)

5. Argumentum ad Misericordiam

The Latin name of this fallacy means "argument from pity." In this type of argument the arguer tries to persuade the listener of the correctness of the conclusion by an *appeal to pity*. The arguer presents various facts that have the effect of arousing feelings of *sympathy*, hoping thereby to gain the agreement of the listener. While such tactics often have their desired effect, the reasoning used is fallacious, because the factors that are cited are completely irrelevant to the conclusion.

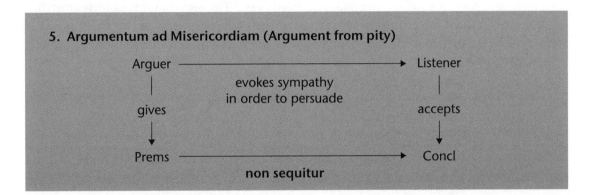

An example of this fallacy is the following:

> "I know that you expected us to study hard and come to class regularly, and I didn't do that. But you have to understand that I have little money, and so I must have a job. I have to work very long hours to pay for all my costs, including this really high tuition fee. You know how difficult it is when you go to school and work at the same time. Life is really hard for me. I think that all that counts, and I should get a passing grade for the course."

This argument has the structure (here, person A can be the arguer himself or some person advocated by the arguer):

1. Some proposal X favorable to some person A is proposed.
2. The audience is led to pity person A.

[This causes the audience to have a general attitude of sympathy towards person A, including the proposal X about A.]

3. So, proposal X is correct.

This argument is doubly erroneous. First of all, specific areas of pity are not rational reasons for extending that sympathy to other areas. Secondly, even when there is sympathy for a person regarding any matter, that has no connection to the correctness of any view, even when that view concerns that person.

6. Argumentum ad Ignorantiam

The Latin name of this fallacy means "argument from ignorance." In this type of argument the arguer claims that the conclusion is correct because no one has proved that it is wrong. This is an *appeal to ignorance*, that is, to lack of knowledge. The weakness of this type of reasoning becomes clear when one adds the word "yet." The fact that it is not the case that someone has proved it wrong, yet, is relevant only to what we know at *this* point of time. Tomorrow the matter may change; someone may prove it wrong tomorrow. The argument is therefore a non sequitur.

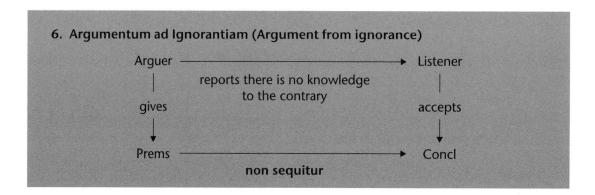

An example of this fallacy is the following:

"My view is that there is definitely a spiritual side to things. A lot of people don't believe this, but there is one fact that decides the matter for me: No one has ever proved that this is not so. You see, this view must be right."

This argument has the structure:

1. No one has proved that proposal X is wrong.
2. So, proposal X is correct.

This argument is clearly erroneous. Consider that no one has proved that George Washington did not have a headache on his 20th birthday. But that is not evidence that he *did* have a headache then. And so it is in general with this kind of argument. (But note that *some* arguments of this type might *not* be fallacies, if the premises *also* included a strong investigation of a testable issue, such as: Was there bacterial life on the Moon? Such arguments could be strong inductive arguments.)

7. Tu Quoque Fallacy

The Latin name for this fallacy means "And you [do it] too!" In this type of argument the arguer discredits his opponent by pointing out that his opponent does not even believe his own position. So, why should anyone else believe it? The weakness of this kind of reasoning is obvious when one considers that we all do things that we should not do, and inversely, fail to do things that we should do. (This fallacy could also be considered to be another form of the *ad hominem* fallacy, along with the abusive and circumstantial form.)

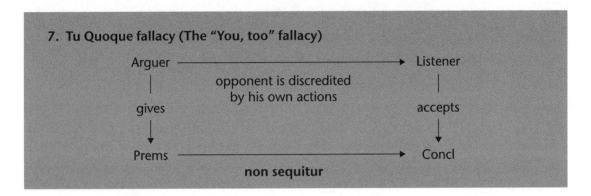

An example of this fallacy is the following:

> "The senator would have us all believe that cigarette smoking is a social evil that can only be eliminated by imposing a $10 tax on each package of cigarettes sold. But you cannot trust what he says. Everybody knows that even he himself is a smoker!"

This argument has the structure:

1. Person A proposes X.   [The arguer wants to discredit person A.]
2. Person A acts contrary to X.   ["And you do it too!"]
3. So, person A does not believe X.
4. So, proposal X is not correct.

This pattern is doubly erroneous. First of all, a person's actions are not reliable indicators of what a person believes. Secondly, even if the opponent did not believe his own position, the position could still be correct. Such irony is certainly possible.

8. Guilt by Association Fallacy

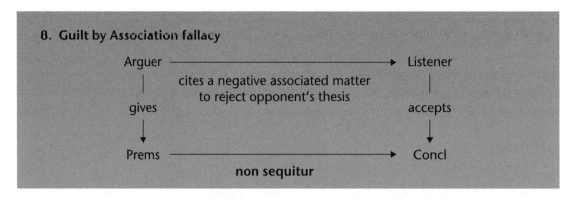

In this type of argument the arguer aims to reject a proposal by using certain negative facts that are in some concrete way *associated* with the proposal. These negative facts could be about the origin of the proposal or about some other historical matters that involve the proposal in some way. Because of this, the fallacy is also called the *Genetic Fallacy*. (When the negative facts refer to the arguer's opponent, this type of argument may also be considered to be an instance of the *ad hominem* fallacy.) The associated matters are typically quite tangential, and are in no way evidence regarding the correctness of the proposal at issue. So, these arguments are non sequiturs. Still, they can be quite persuasive. An example of this fallacy is the following:

> "When Mr. Jones argued that the tax he proposed was fair to all the residents of the township, he conveniently forgot to mention that the idea of that tax originally came from the Township Clerk, who, as we all know, was convicted last year of embezzlement. So what do you think of this tax proposal now!"

This argument has the following structure:

1. Proposal X is concretely associated in some manner with matter F.
2. The audience rejects or disapproves of F.
3. So, proposal X is wrong.

The structure of this type of argument makes it clear that the inference is invalid. Matters merely *associated* with a proposal cannot be evidence regarding its correctness. The fact that Adolf Hitler once favored a certain proposal is irrelevant to its correctness. (Still, because of that matter, a lot of people would reject such a proposal outright.)

It is interesting to note that there is a *positive version* of the Guilt by Association Fallacy, and we could call it the *Favor by Association Fallacy*. But that kind of argument form is very similar to the Argumentum ad Populum fallacy discussed above, and so it needs no special category of its own. It has the structure:

1. Proposal X is concretely associated in some manner with matter F.
2. The audience accepts or approves of F.
3. So, proposal X is correct.

9. Red Herring Fallacy

The name of this type of fallacy refers to the old practice of training bloodhounds to track missing persons by dragging stinky red herrings across the paths of the hounds to try to throw them off the scent. In this type of argument the arguer sneakily introduces an irrelevant matter to side-track the main point of the opponent. This transition is made possible by somehow relating in the digression to something that the opponent has said, which produces the illusion that the digressed matter is what the argument is all about.

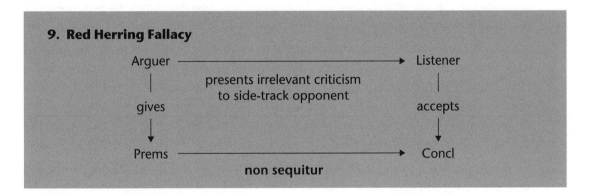

An example of this fallacy is the following:

> "The administration has argued strongly for a much larger budget for the military. But the admininstration also spent a lot of money on tax cuts for special interest groups, which was totally unnecessary and only shows how special interest groups can manipulate the political system. We need finance reform. We do not need larger budgets for the military."

This argument has the structure:

1. Person A presents proposal X.
2. Person B substitutes proposal Y for X.
    [X and Y have some point of slight similarity, but they are different matters.]

3.   Proposal Y is unacceptable [acceptable] for reasons P, Q, R.

4.   So, proposal X is wrong [right].

Notice that there are actually two versions of this type of argument, one negative and the other affirmative. In each case it is rather obvious why this type of reasoning is erroneous. Since the two proposals X and Y are different matters, the reasons given against, or for, the one proposal, are not reasons given against, or for, the other proposal.

Exercise 5.2. Fallacies of Irrelevance

Instructions. Identify the fallacies that are committed in the following passages. It is possible that some passages contain more than one fallacy. Use the available **Exercise Work Sheet** to submit your work.

1.   The alarmists have not been able to show that hormone-enhanced foods are detrimental to our health, so we should take advantage of this new techology to produce large quantities of necessary foods.

2.   This guy knows what he is talking about. He received his J.D. degree from Harvard Law School, he has written a dozen books on international law, and makes tons of money on his international lecture tours. I predict his views on the effects of electric shock therapy will be widely accepted.

3.   If the Senator will not support my bill, he should be reminded that no other group has opposed my bill except for the Democratic Anarchists Union.

4.   We should not listen to music composed by Richard Wagner. After all, Wagner was Adolf Hitler's favorite composer.

5.   These poor children have no shoes, have no food, have no roofs over their heads, no one to care for them. Your contribution to our organization can help these needy children. Please open your hearts.

6.   Our product is very special, and it has received a lot of attention lately. Many Hollywood celebrities have tried and liked it. Our product costs more than some people can afford, but it is worth every penny.

7.   It is in no way important that countries like France and Russia strongly objected to our military action in Iraq. After all, these countries acted only out of their own self-interest in this matter.

8.   It is false that capitalism is an unjust institution. It was Lenin who claimed that it was unjust, but he was a Red Communist.

9.   You want us to ban billboards on state land along public tollroads. You probably want to eliminate the tolls as well! But road tolls are a proper way for states to collect taxes.

States have a constitutional right to collect money, and your proposal is completely wrong.

10. You say this bill illegally favors large, rich corporations and violates federal anti-trust laws, and that we should vote against it. You realize, of course, the implications of what you are saying. If we don't pass this bill, these corporations will move to another state, and we will lose millions of tax dollars; and many proposals, including your own proposal to support local community businesses, will have to be scrapped.

Section 5.3 Fallacies of Misconstrual

The Fallacies of Misconstrual form a second main division of informal fallacies. In these types of arguments, the arguer begins with some information in the premises that is then *misconstrued* into some unwarranted conclusion. These kinds of fallacies are different from the Fallacies of Irrelevance because the premises in these cases are not totally irrelevant. They are relevant, but they are misconstrued into something unwarranted.

10. Straw Man Fallacy

With this type of argument the arguer presents a *distorted* or *exaggerated* version of his opponent's position. He then proceeds to criticize the *distorted* version, and concludes that the *original* position of the opponent has been refuted. Of course, the distorted position is not at all what the opponent wanted to assert, and often, no one else does either. The distorted position is truly a *straw man*, having no substance and nothing, and no one, to recommend it.

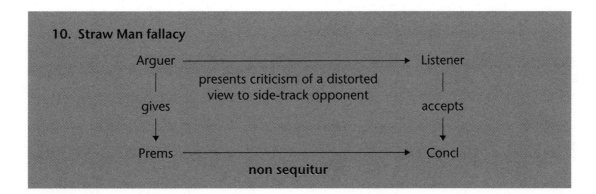

It is always easy to distort a view. The simplest truisms can be turned into absurdities: someone says, "Eating fruit is good for you," and someone replies, "So, you mean then that eating fruit with enormous helpings of whipped cream and sweet sauces is good for you, too, right?" Exaggerations can be funny, but they are generally worthless.

A more typical example of the *Straw Man* fallacy is the following:

> "You say wealthy people should give more money to the poor. I disagree. Someone could spend his entire savings of $500,000 that way, by giving out dollar bills to the poor he meets on the streets, and that, you must agree, accomplishes absolutely nothing."

This argument has the structure:

1. Proposal Y is a distorted version of proposal X.
2. Proposal Y is unacceptable, for reasons A, B, C.
3. So, Proposal X is wrong.

It is clear why this kind of reasoning is erroneous. The distorted version and the original version are two different positions. Therefore, the reasons given for or against the one are not reasons given for or against the other.

The Straw Man fallacy has some similarities to the Red Herring fallacy. In each case a new position is substituted for the original position, but there is this difference: In the Red Herring fallacy, the new view is an unrelated position that shifts the focus of discussion to a substantially different matter. In the Straw Man fallacy, the general topic stays the same, and the distorted view is not so easily distinguished from the original view.

11. Post Hoc Ergo Propter Hoc Fallacy

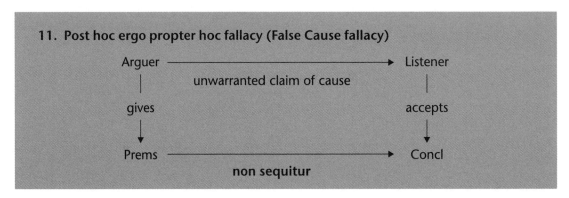

The Latin name of this fallacy means "After this, therefore, because of this." In this type of argument, the arguer notes that one situation *came after* another situation, and that, therefore, it *was caused by* the other one. The argument then continues with further recommendations based on the noted causal relationship.

It must be mentioned right away that there is nothing wrong with causal reasoning. In fact, to make conclusions based on causal relationships is an important and correct method of reasoning about what actions people should or should not take. Rather, the fallacy here is claiming the existence of a causal relationship when in fact there is none. One thing may *come after* another thing, but that is not a good reason to conclude that the one thing *was caused by* the other thing. The *post hoc ergo propter hoc* fallacy is also called the *false cause* fallacy, and also the *post hoc* fallacy (not to be confused with the *ad hoc* fallacy discussed below).

An example of *post hoc ergo propter hoc* reasoning is the following:

> "Everyone has heard of the large increases in student enrollments at all colleges and universities all across the country these last two years. And especially at our own university the increase has been quite dramatic. But that is no accident. Our enrollments were low, and the admissions office knew they had to come through. So this dedicated staff worked extra hard to achieve better enrollments, and they will tell you how much extra that effort was compared to all the previous years. And you can see it worked! After that effort, the applications came pouring in. This university owes its enrollment success to the heroic efforts of the admissions office staff, and ultimately to the leadership of the Administration. Applause, please."

This argument claims that the increased enrollments were caused by the efforts of the admissions staff and the administration, and that, because increased enrollments are so important, these efforts are to be greatly praised. This argument ignores the fact the increased enrollments were most likely caused by the demographic surge in eligible college-aged students evident all over the country. The staff and administration efforts probably had only little to do with the enrollments, in which case, no special praise is warranted. *After* the efforts, yes; *because* of the efforts, no.

The Post Hoc Fallacy has two forms, and our example used the first:

Positive version	*Negative version*
1. F occurred after X.	1. F occurred after X.
2. So, F was caused by X.	2. So, F was caused by X.
3. Moreover, F is good.	3. Moreover, F is bad.
4. So, X is good.	4. So, X is bad.

12. Fallacy of Special Pleading

In this type of argument, the desired conclusion is something that should be based on weighing the various pros and cons that are relevant to the case, but the arguer presents only some reasons that *favor his point of view*, and all evidence to the contrary is just ignored. Such selectivity can never be the basis for making a correct inference. The following is an example of this fallacy:

"But surely, letting me skydive from the Sears Tower will be good P.R. for the city. You could make a poster of it, with the caption: *Chicago—the place of soaring opportunity*."

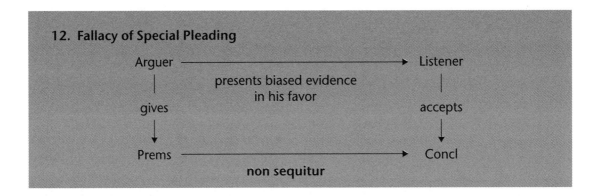

12. Fallacy of Special Pleading

Arguer ———————————————→ Listener
| |
gives   presents biased evidence   accepts
| in his favor |
↓   ↓
Prems ———————————————→ Concl
non sequitur

Is that the reason? Some questionable public relations poster? The arguer is ignoring all the reasons why the permission should *not* be granted, and that list is actually quite long. (You can supply the reasons.) Special pleading is unacceptable reasoning.

Special pleading arguments do not have any common form. Their distinguishing feature is that the relevant facts are ignored, and only some reasons that favor the position of the arguer are selected as premisses.

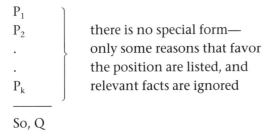

P_1
P_2 there is no special form—
.   only some reasons that favor
.   the position are listed, and
P_k relevant facts are ignored
———
So, Q

13. Fallacy of Improper Generalization

In these arguments, the premises present some individual facts, and the conclusion involves a *generalization* based on these facts. The fallacy occurs when the available facts cited do not justify a generalization of such a range. This fallacy is also called *Hasty Generalization*. An example is the following:

"No, Mr. Smith, we cannot give you a permit to skydive from the Sears Tower. If we give some people permits for this, then the entire city of Chicago will be eligible for these permits, and what chaos there would be. The answer is, 'Absolutely not.'"

The denial of the skydiving permit is warranted, but *not* for the reason given. The proposed generalization is altogether implausible. A *different* reason for the rejection should have been provided.

Such improper, hasty generalizations must be distinguished from *correct generalizations*, in which the concluded level of generality is in fact justified by the premisses. For example, when a wide selection of students at a school are asked whether they are satisfied with the selection of food available at the cafeteria, and 60 percent respond that they are not satisfied, then one may correctly infer the conclusion, "Most of the student body is dissatisfied with the selection of food." But it would be improper to generalize that conclusion still further to, "Most people at the school, including administrators, are dissatisfied with the selection of food." When we compare improper generalizations to correct generalizations, we can see that the improper ones all share the same defect:

	correct generalizations		*improper generalizations*
P_1	In many cases, Q_1 is	P_1	In the fallacy cases, Q_2 is
P_2	a general conclusion	P_2	*more* general than what is
P_3	correctly inferred	P_3	justified by the premisses.
———	from the premisses.	———	But the less general Q_1
So, Q_1		So, Q_2	would have been correct.

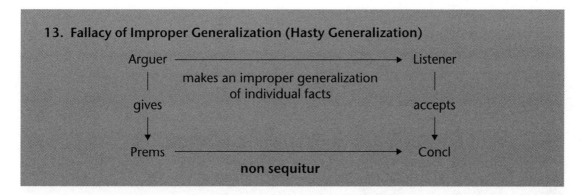

13. Fallacy of Improper Generalization (Hasty Generalization)

Arguer ——————————————————→ Listener

| makes an improper generalization of individual facts |

gives   accepts

Prems ——————————————————→ Concl

non sequitur

14. Fallacy of Improper Instance

In this type of argument, the arguer begins with a (correct) general premiss and then infers a particular case. The fallacy occurs when the inferred particular case is not a proper instance of the original general premiss. Here is an example of this fallacy:

"You say that my client is guilty of tax evasion. But my client is exercising his right to private property, which the founding fathers of our great country took such great pains to establish. No one has the right to take away what is yours. You claim the evasion is a violation of the law, but he is merely acting on a founding principle of our great democracy."

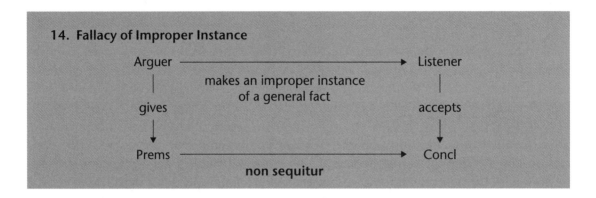

What the arguer has done is to erroneously expand the range of the original general premiss P_1 to an unacceptable level of generalilty, P_2, in this case, from the right to private property to some right of absolute and unalterable possession of anything one has once owned. The instance is not an instance of the original premiss P_1 but rather of the unacceptable premiss P_2.

	correct instantiations		*improper instantiations*
P_1	the generality of the	P_1	the generality of premiss P_1 is
————	premiss P_1 is correct,	————	correct, but the conclusion Q_2 is
So, Q_1	and the conclusion Q_1	So, Q_2	not an instance of P_1 but of a more
	is an instance of P_1		general but incorrect P_2

15. Complex Question Fallacy

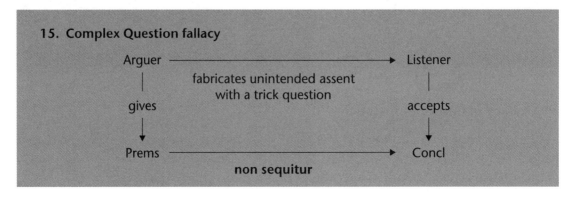

In this type of argument the arguer asks *two questions*, **Q1** and **Q2**, but because of the wording, they are confused as a single question **Q**. (Sometimes, instead of asking a double question, the arguer makes a double proposal as though it were one.) The listener fails to notice the duplicity and gives a simple response to question **Q2**, but the arguer uses the response as an answer to both questions **Q1** and **Q2**. Of course, that means the *arguer* has made an intentional mistake, but the listener is to blame as well, for not noticing the arguer's mistake. Examples of complex questions are:

> "Have you stopped beating your wife?" "Of course not! Oops, I mean, yes, I have. Oops, uhm . . ."

> "Who was your accomplice in this crime?" "I had no accomplice!" "So, you acted alone." "Oops. No, I did not act alone." "So, you admit you had an accomplice." "Oops, uhm . . ."

> "Are you always this late for your appointments?" "No, sir." "So, this time is special?" "Oops, no, this time is not special. Oops . . ."

> "Was George Washington King of France for only a short time?" "No, not for a short time at all." "Ah, you mean, for a long time, then?" "Oops, no, not for a long time." "So, for a short time, after all." "Oops, no, uhm . . ."

In all cases of arguments involving complex questions, if the conclusion is not based on the premiss that was *intended*, the argument is a non sequitur. (Also, since such arguments involve ambiguity, they may also be classified as a special case of the Fallacy of Syntactic Ambiguity.)

An example of the Complex Question Fallacy is the following:

> "When you were asked whether you would work much harder if we paid you $1,000 per hour, you said yes. So, you admit that you have not been working so hard, which we always suspected. We are going to have to increase your work load."

Here **Q1** is "You are not working hard, right?," and **Q2** is "If we paid you $1,000 per hour, will you work harder?" The person answered "yes" to **Q2**, and the arguer uses that answer as an answer to **Q1** and **Q2**. But, the person never intended to answer "yes" to question **Q1**, and in fact he never did. The arguer *invented* that answer, *he* has made a mistake, and *his* inference is a non sequitur.

16. Fallacy of Syntactic Ambiguity

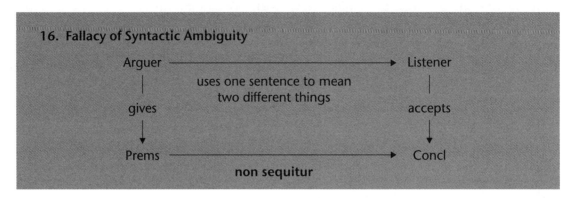

This fallacy occurs when the argument contain a *grammatical ambiguity* that permits two *conflicting interpretations*. Both interpretations are needed in the argument, the one interpretation being needed to make the premisses true, and the other being needed to make the conclusion follow from the premisses. Consider the following example involving the provisions of a last will and testament:

> The will stated, "The estate is to be divided equally between the two sisters, Lisa and Mandy. The distribution is to be as follows: To Lisa will go the art collection, to Mandy, the family jewels, and the three houses, to Lisa, also, all the company stocks." The executor of the estate concluded that Lisa was to receive the art collection, the three houses, and all the company stocks, and Mandy was to receive the family jewels. (Mandy then sued the executor for violating the provisions of the will.)

The two conflicting interpretations derive from the ambiguously written provision regarding the "three houses." The wording can be taken to say that (1) to Mandy will go "the family jewels, and the three houses," or that (2) "the three houses" are to go to Lisa. Interpretation (1) agrees with the equal distribution required by premiss 1, and interpretation (2) allows the executor to draw the conclusion that he did.

We can now summarize the fallacy in the following way. The arguer presents an original argument, say with the two premisses A, B and the conclusion Q. But, one premiss, say B, is *syntactically ambiguous* in that it can mean B_1 or B_2. So, the original argument must be evaluated as two different arguments. The fallacy occurs because the argument appears to be sound, but it is not. Version B_1 is required to make the premisses true, but then the conclusion Q does not follow. On the other hand, version B_2 is required to make the conclusion follow, but then the premisses are not true. Either way, the argument is *unsound*.

ambiguous argument

prem. B is ambiguous	*version #1*	*version #2*
A	A	A
B	B_1	B_2
———	———	———
So, Q	So, Q	So, Q
prems. A, B, seem true,	premiss B_1 is true,	premiss B_2 is false,
argument seems valid,	argument is invalid,	argument is valid,
argument seems sound.	argument is unsound.	argument is unsound.

17. Fallacy of Semantic Equivocation

Equivocation occurs when one word is used with two different meanings at the same time. This situation easily occurs because most of our words have *several* different meanings. This means that when a word is used, it can represent any one of several ideas, the selection depending on the intention of the speaker and of the listener. So, when equivocation occurs, different ideas with different consequences are mixed together, as though they were one, and errors are likely to occur.

A serious example of this fallacy is the following argument that derives from the notable philosopher David Hume:

> "It is commonly thought that the events of nature occur of necessity. But this is a mistake. For if something is necessary then the contrary is not possible. But any event may be imagined not to occur, which means that the contrary is indeed possible. Therefore, there is no necessity in nature."

Here, Hume aims to show that the commonsense view—that the events of nature occur with causal necessity—is a mistaken view. That is an *astonishing* claim, and if it were correct, it would turn much of our ordinary thinking into nonsense. So, this is definitely a *very important* argument. The argument may be reorganized as follows (and it is amazingly simple):

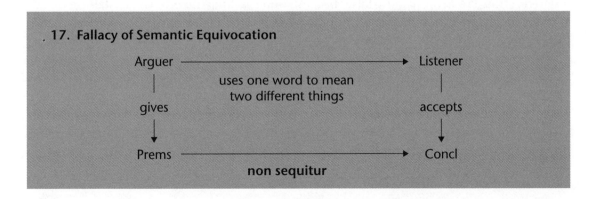

original (ambiguous) argument

1. For any natural event, the event may be imagined not to occur.

2. If an event may be imagined not to occur, then it is not necessary that it occurs.

3. So, for any natural event, it is not necessary that the event occurs.

The word "necessary" is ambiguous, and this gives the argument the *appearance* of being a good argument, because it fails to distinguish between the two meanings of this one word. The word can mean *causally necessary*, or it can mean *logically necessary*, with quite different results. So, the argument needs to be restated with this distinction in mind, resulting in two different versions of the argument. Since the conclusion is intended to deny that there is *causal* necessity in nature, each restated version of the argument will state the conclusion in that intended way. It is only Premiss 2 that will be restated with the two different meanings. As it turns out, in each case, the resulting argument is unsound.

Version #1

1. For any natural event, the event may be imagined not to occur.

2. If an event may be imagined not to occur, then it is *not logically necessary* that it occurs.

3. So, for any natural event, it is *not causally necessary* that the event occurs.

Version #2

1. For any natural event, the event may be imagined not to occur.

2. If an event may be imagined not to occur, then it is *not causally necessary* that it occurs.

3. So, for any natural event, it is *not causally necessary* that the event occurs.

These reconstructions make the matter clear. In the first version, the two premisses are true. But the argument is not valid. The argument makes an *invalid* inference, since Premiss 2 and the conclusion are talking about different senses of necessity. The connection is missing, and so the argument is unsound. In the second version, there is a clear connection between the premisses and the conclusion, so that the argument is valid. But this time, there is a different error: Premiss 2 is now false, because one *can* imagine oneself not falling down, and hovering instead, but it is *not* causally possible not to fall down, that is, to hover. Again, the argument is unsound.

In general, the pattern of the Fallacy of Equivocation is very similar to the pattern of the Fallacy of Syntactical Ambiguity. The arguer presents an original argument, say with some premisses A, B, and the conclusion Q. But, some premiss, say the second premiss B, has an *ambiguous word*, so that this premiss can mean either B_1 or B_2. So, the original argument must be evaluated as two different arguments. The fallacy occurs when the original argument appears to be sound, but the two reconstructed arguments are unsound.

ambiguous argument

prem. B is ambiguous	*version #1*	*version #2*
A	A	A
B	B_1	B_2
———————	———	———
So, Q	So, Q	So, Q
prems. A, B, seem true,	premiss B_1 is true,	premiss B_2 is false,
argument seems valid,	argument is invalid,	argument is valid,
argument seems sound.	argument is unsound.	argument is unsound.

18. Fallacy of Division

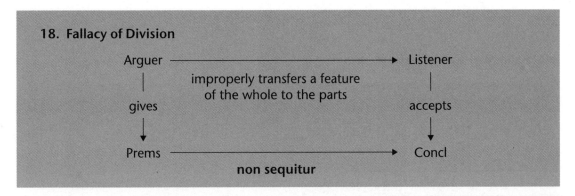

In this type of argument, the premisses introduce a characteristic that applies to something considered *as a whole*, and the conclusion asserts that this characteristic, therefore, applies to the *individual parts* of that whole. The fallacy occurs when the characteristic in question does not have this dual application. An example of this fallacy is the following:

> "Faculty and students, we will be changing our Core Curriculum in a fundamental way. As you know, our Core Curriculum contains well over 100 different courses, of which each student must select 15. And as you also know, we have been mandated by the Board of Trustees to make sure that our Core Curriculum will promote values in the areas of social justice, human diversity, faith traditions, and civic leadership. In compliance with this mandate we will now require that all courses included in the Core Curriculum must incorporate into their design the promotion of those listed values. This is a large undertaking, but this is what we must do."

The reasoning here is clearly in error. The Core Curriculum *as a whole* is required to promote the stated values. But it does not follow that *all the individual courses* in the Core Curriculum are required to promote those values. For example, one possible way to satisfy the requirement is to have just *one* required course in the Core Curriculum, a Super-Saturated Value

Course, that promotes all the values listed. And there are also other ways to implement the original requirement.

Again, a note of caution. *Not all* cases of applying a characteristic of the whole to the parts are fallacies. Sometimes it is very appropriate to make such an application. Here is an easy one: Our entire body is located on Earth. So, each part of our body is located on Earth. There is nothing wrong with that inference. This one is correct as well: This book is made (entirely) of matter. So, each part of the book is made of matter.

in some cases, division is correct	in some cases, division is incorrect
1. X as a whole has property F	1. X as a whole has property F
2. So, all parts of X have property F	2. So, all parts of X have property F

19. Fallacy of Composition

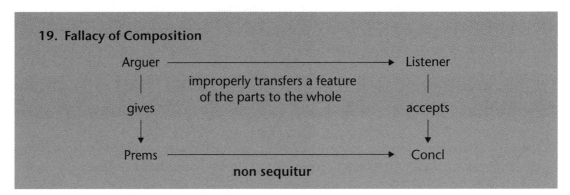

In this type of argument, the premisses introduce a characteristic that applies to the *individual parts* of some considered thing, and the conclusion asserts that this characteristic, therefore, applies to that considered thing *as a whole*. The fallacy occurs when the characteristic in question does not have this dual application. An example of this fallacy is the following:

> "Some of you are wondering whether the Perk Company is financially sound enough to co-operate with us in this new venture. Let me put your minds at ease on this point. We know that all of the Perk's top management people have incredibly huge salaries. Money is just not an issue for them. So, we may safely conclude that the Perk Company has strong cash reserves and will not be a risky partner."

The error is obvious. The financial solvency of the individuals who manage Perk is also attributed to the Perk Company as a whole. We have seen especially in recent years that things don't work like that. A lot of money may go to management, and there may be little for the rest of the company. There are also many other examples where such composition is incorrect. Parts may be cheap, but the whole thing is expensive. Again, the parts may weigh less than a pound, but the whole thing weighs 100 pounds. But again, a word of caution. Sometimes the composition is correct, as for example, when the parts are multi-colored, and the whole is therefore multi-colored. Also, the parts can be made of recycled material, so that the whole is therefore made of recycled material.

in some cases, composition is correct	in some cases, composition is incorrect
1. All parts of X have property F	1. All parts of X have property F
2. So, X as a whole has property F	2. So, X as a whole has property F

Exercise 5.3. Fallacies of Misconstrual

Instructions. Identify the fallacies that are committed in the following passages. It is possible that some passages contain more than one fallacy. Use the available **Exercise Work Sheet** to submit your work.

1. Everyone, including myself, has a right to speak freely, to express his opinions, without restrictions imposed by governmental rules. So, as presiding judge in this case, I can tell you that what the defendant has done is a great evil and violates God's moral law. I urge you to keep this in mind as you begin your jury deliberations.

2. Studies have shown that students who are philosophy majors score significantly higher on LSAT tests than other majors. You would do well to become a philosophy major.

3. If we had a National Health Insurance in this country, then the overall quality of health care in this country would be lowered. So, it is better not to have a National Health Insurance.

4. Peace negotiations always cause an increase in violence, because we have observed that each time when peace negotiations start, the violence on both sides increases dramatically.

5. You say that these records contain sensitive information, and that they should therefore be kept confidential. But when people are sensitive in their dealings with others they should be commended for those actions; and so, we should make these records public.

6. Three out of four doctors recommend the healing ingredient in Moladilin. Use what most doctors recommend. Use Moladilin.

7. This war must stop. Our boys are getting killed every day. We cannot let such an evil situation continue any longer.

8. This war must continue until we win. Many of our brave soldiers have died for this cause. We must not let their deaths be in vain.

9. We have recently learned an important fact: Most people in this country are strongly opposed to the policies of this administration. We base this conclusion on the fact that almost all the people who answered this question on our political organization's website were opposed to the policies.

10. And we should stop saying that *all people are created equal*. It just isn't true. Some people are richer than others, some are smarter than others, some are stronger than others, some are more talented than others, some are more successful than others, and on and on. It's a fact: We are definitely *not* equal.

Section 5.4 Fallacies of Presumption

The Fallacies of Presumption form the third main division of informal fallacies. One thing that sets these fallacies apart is that they are *deductively valid*. So, with these, the problem is not the inference to the conclusion. Rather, the problem lies with the premisses. The premisses are presented as if they were established truths, but they are, in fact, not established truths at all. Unless the listeners are especially careful, they will be led by the arguer to accept the premisses and also the conclusion that validly follows.

20. False Dichotomy Fallacy

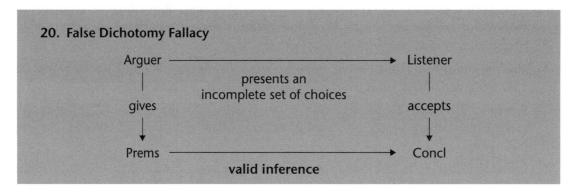

What is characteristic of this fallacy is that it makes crucial use of a premiss that asserts a *false set of choices*. The choices have their consequences, and so a conclusion does follow, but the assertion of choices is wrong. This typically involves the situation where *the choices leave out other possibilities*.

An example of this fallacy is the following:

"I know that Capitalism is a view rejected by some social thinkers, but that should not deter us from accepting Capitalism as the best economic system. Remember what a dismal failure Communism was in the former Soviet Union."

This argument has the structure:

1. X or Y [this premiss falsely omits other choices]
2. not Y
3. So, X

The choice presented is Capitalism or Communism in the Soviet Union. But these are not logical opposites. There are *several* different economic systems, and these two choices do not exhaust all the possible alternatives. The premiss is a *false dichotomy*. So, while the argument is valid, it is not sound. And that means that the conclusion has not been established.

21. Slippery Slope Fallacy

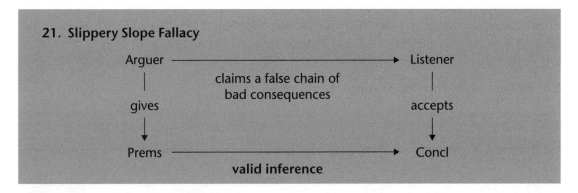

In this kind of argument the premisses claim that a certain matter X has a long *string* of consequences Y_1, Y_2, Y_3, Y_4, etc. The consequences follow one another much like when one slides down some *slippery slope*: there is an inevitable sequence leading to an inevitable final state. The audience recognizes that these consequences are a *disaster*, in one of the following two ways: either the consequences are mild at the outset and disastrous at the end, or the totality of all the consequences is a disaster. The conclusion then follows by a *modus tollens*. The problem here is that the premisses are false. The chain of conseqences just does not exist; the real world does not produce such a causal sequence of events. The arguer is lying, or exaggerating, or is himself deceived. Unfortunately, the audience accepts the wild claims of the arguer, and is led to accept the conclusion as well.

An example of this fallacy is the next passage (a reconstruction of an actual event):

"This nation owes Larry Flint, the long-time editor of *Hustler* Magazine, a great debt. Some people are highly offended by the kind of pornography that Mr. Flint produces.

But Mr. Flint is actually a champion of the most important of our liberties—Freedom of Speech. Mr. Flint repeatedly fought the legal campaigns brought against him, and he won. And what a victory that was. Had he not won the legal battle to produce such pornography, the censorship of other popular magazines would have been inevitable, and next, the censorship of books, and next, newspapers, art, and all forms of free speech. But he did win, and in this way he helped secure our freedom. For this effort, Mr. Flint will be honored tonight with this special award."

This argument has the following structure (here, X = "Offensive pornography ought to be legally prohibited"):

1. If X then Y_1, Y_2, Y_3, Y_4, etc.
2. Those results Y_1, Y_2, Y_3, Y_4, etc., are terrible things.
3. So, X is wrong.

This argument pattern is valid, but the slippery slope described in the first premiss just doesn't exist. This first premiss is false, and the argument is unsound.

22. Fallacy of Ad Hoc Reasoning

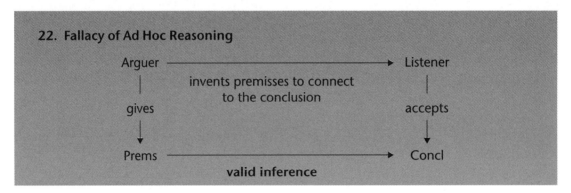

The Latin phrase literally means "[made] for this [matter]." This fallacy concerns a proposed explanation of why, or how, some matter came about. The proposed explanation seems to do the job, in that the matter at issue is indeed explained by the proposal, except for one little problem—instead of using known facts to explain the matter at issue, the arguer has simply *invented* an explanation, by using *mere possibilities* without any additional support.

An example of this fallacy is the following:

"We know that somehow the money in the account went from one million dollars to one thousand dollars. So, we need to explain that. The way I see it is that one of the computer maintenance programs probably malfunctioned and sent $999,000 into some other account somewhere. You see, if that happened, that would explain how the money disappeared. Yes, that's what must have happened."

This argument has the following structure:

Purpose: Q has happened. To explain why Q has happened.

1. If theory T is true, then Q happens.
2. Theory T is true.
3. Theory T has no sources of support. ← Incredible!!
4. So, Q happened.

When stated in this form, it is clear that this kind of thinking can never constitute an acceptable explanation of why something has happened. What if someone invented another theory T2, some crazy story about the cleaning staff tidying up the office and, well, you fill in the story. These are just made-up stories, and there is *no reason whatsoever* for thinking that these theories are really true. But the made-up stories *happen* to explain the event in question. Such is the nature of *ad hoc* reasoning.

It must be pointed out that *ad hoc* reasoning is similar in some respects to another type of reasoning, one that employs a *correct inductive inference pattern* and that is used on a regular basis by scientists in every area of science, and, we may add, by detectives, such as Detective Columbo. This other type of reasoning is known as *inference to the best explanation*. There are some important differences.

Purpose: Q has happened. To explain why Q has happened.

1. If theory T is true, then Q happens.
2. There is at least some (independent) evidence for theory T being true.
3. There is no other theory available for Q that is better than theory T.
4. So, theory T is true. [correct inductive inference]
5. So, Q happened. [valid deductive inference]

There are two differences between this correct pattern and the previous fallacious pattern. First of all, the correct pattern includes an extra premiss that says that the theory was not merely invented: there are some specific reasons (A, B, C, etc.) for thinking that the theory is true. (These are not foolproof reasons, for otherwise those reasons themselves would establish that the theory is true, and this inference pattern would then be pointless.) What is important here is that a theory that is supported by evidence (A, B, C) becomes a *stronger* theory when it succeeds in also explaining other real events. The second difference between the correct pattern and the fallacy is a second extra premiss that says that there is no other theory available that is better than the present one and that also explains the occurrence of the matter Q. Clearly, if there are alternative theories available, with similar levels of plausibility, then nothing can be concluded.

So, when a theory meets these conditions, we may conclude that the theory is true—with this qualification: the inference is inductively correct only; it is not a logically valid inference. Given the available evidence, the theory is probably true, but it has not been conclusively established.

23. Petitio Principii Fallacy

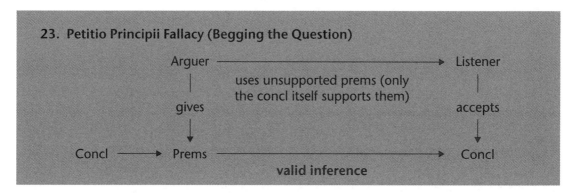

The Latin name of this fallacy means "a petition to the very principle at issue," and the fallacy is usually called "Begging the Question." In this kind of argument, the arguer presents premises that validly produce a conclusion, even though there is *no further evidence* for the premises themselves. But there is something else that happens in this type of argument. The purpose of this argument is to establish (prove) a proposal X regarding some controversial matter. The proposal X has been *challenged*, and the listener expects an argument that will settle the matter once and for all. Now, what is unique here is that the arguer presents premises that are completely unsupported—except that the proposal X itself is secretly or explicitly made a reason to support the premises. But *that*, of course, is the very question that was supposed to be proved. The premises are assuming for their *own* support the very conclusion that they are supposed to be supporting. The argument goes around in a *vicious circle*, and ultimately, the proposal X remains unsupported.

An example of this fallacy is the following:

"I know you question whether God exists. But, have you considered that the Bible itself says that God exists, and whatever the Bible says must be true?"

1. The Bible says that God exists.

2. Whatever the Bible says is true.

3. So, God most assuredly exists.

The arguer does not explicitly say *why* he asserts Premiss 2 to be true, but the *background* argument is certainly something like:

1. God exists.

2. God is infallible.

3. God is the author of the Bible.

So, What the Bible says is true.

People who believe that what the Bible says must be true believe that because they believe that God exists. So, the argument originally proposed does indeed *Beg the Question*. This argument and all cases of Question Begging have the general form:

Main argument *for proposal X*	*Background argument* *for premiss P_2*
1. P_1 premiss	1. X premiss = orig. concl.
2. P_2 premiss	2. Q_1 premiss
3. P_3 premiss	3. Q_2 premiss
4. etc.	4. etc.
So, X conclusion	So, P_2

This pattern makes it clear that the reasoning *goes around in a circle*. The proposal X always remain unsupported, and so, as conclusion, proposal X is never established.

24. Fallacy of Inconsistent Premisses

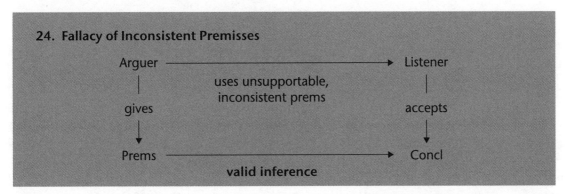

Sometimes when we reason about certain matters we are caught up in a debate of conflicting opinions. That is not unusual. People disagree with each other quite a bit. What is unusual is the situation when people agree on the basic premisses, and yet they end up with deep disagreement. How does that happen? Actually, the same thing happens even just with ourselves. We start with some basic premisses and we end up with conflicting results.

This situation will certainly arise when, unknown to the participants, the premisses that form the starting point are an *inconsistent set*. Such premisses are self-contradictory: what some of them assert, others of them deny. Clearly, if people start with an inconsistent set of premisses, then conflicts must eventually emerge as the discussion develops. To use a simplistic example, suppose Smith and Jones are having a discussion and they agree to start with the following six premisses:

1. $A \supset B$	4. $D \supset E$	premisses that
2. $B \supset C$	5. A	both Smith and
3. $C \supset D$	6. $\sim E$	Jones use here

7. Smith: Jonesy, my friend, I think that:	B	1,5, MP	
8. Jones: Of course, Smithy, and I think:	~D	4,6, MT	
9. Smith: Then, I have to conclude that:	C	2,7, MP	
10. Jones: Wait you idiot, I conclude that:	~C	3,8, MT	KAPOW!!!

You can see that people could start with a set of premisses, and because they are not careful enough, they could *initially* fail to notice a latent inconsistency, and *later*, in the course of further discussions, be caught up in a contradiction.

But, let's consider a more plausible case. One easy way to get caught up in a contradiction is to make some *unrestricted claims*, that is, claims that are not properly qualified as to exceptions. *That* can get you into trouble.

"You are such a jerk, Bill! You *never* tell me the truth."

"I'm sorry, Liz. You're so right about that."

Whoops! Liz just got trapped in a *contradiction*: In the act of making the assertion, Liz is claiming that she is right; but because of the content of her assertion, she is claiming that Bill is wrong when he says that she is right, so that she is actually saying that she is wrong! She is claiming to be both right and wrong at the same time. And poor Bill, he contradicted himself, too! He said she was right, which means then that he lied about Liz being right, which means that she was not right. So, according to Bill, Liz is both right and wrong. The moral of this story is: *Be careful with unrestricted claims.* Here is another, very much more serious example, about the situation of September 11:

"Our constitutional liberties must be safeguarded at all costs. We will therefore detain, search, and coerce various people to discover whether they intend to destroy our liberties, and if so, to stop them from doing so."

1. Our constitutional liberties may not be violated.
2. If our constitutional liberties may not be violated, then we must do everything we can to preserve our constitutional liberties.
3. So, we must do everything we can to preserve our constitutional liberties.
4. So, we must detain, search, and coerce various people to discover whether they intend to destroy our liberties, and if so, to stop them from doing so.

The further conclusion that also follows has been conveniently suppressed:

5. So, we must sometimes violate our constitutional liberties.

Clearly, we have arrived at an *explicit contradiction* by lines 1 and 5. This means that the original premisses, lines 1 and 2, form a set of inconsistent premisses, and therefore, no one is allowed to accept *both* premisses.

The arguments at issue here have the following structure:

P_1
P_2
.
P_k

} The premisses do not have any typical pattern.

_____

.
Q
.
.
$\sim Q$

} However, an explicit contradiction can be derived from them.

In cases such as this, *no one* is permitted to assert *all* of the premisses $P_1, \ldots, P_k$, because at least one of those premisses *must* be false. So? So, don't ever do it.

Exercise 5.4.A Fallacies of Presumption

Part A. Identify the fallacies that are committed in the following passages. It is possible that some passages contain more than one fallacy. Use the available **Exercise Work Sheet** to submit your work.

1. Abundant nuclear energy is not an acceptable goal, because that would require thousands of nuclear facilities all over the country, which in turn would lead to many radiation disasters, and hundreds of thousands of deaths.

2. People necessarily act in accordance with what they desire, and what they desire is necessarily beyond their control. So, this proves that people are never free in their actions.

3. An atheist should believe that there is no distinction between right and wrong. This follows from the fact that either there is a God and what is right and wrong follows from divine laws, or there is no God and there is no possibility of a basis for any moral distinction.

4. Many colleges and universities have experienced large increases in student enrollments in recent years. And especially at our own university the increase has been quite dramatic— double the usual number. We were surprised by this increase because we had all been assuming that our admissions office had not been able to make additional efforts due to cutbacks in their staff. But that assumption was clearly wrong given the increased enroll-ments. We conclude that the admissions staff members must have doubled their efforts, and that they must have secretly worked many hours of overtime. What dedication! They all deserve a big merit raise.

5. In this war, you are either with us or against us. Your objections to our strenuous efforts in waging this war show that you are not with us. So, you are against us in this war.

6. You say that a divine being created the universe. That's impossible, because no individual being can create something like the universe.

7. We urge you to agree with our assessment that traditional methods of instruction need a complete overhaul. Pointless accumulation of facts, mind-numbing exercises, and excessive adherence to older views have no place in a correct educational curriculum.

8. We must save the species of Yellowbacked Grand Valley Minnows at all costs. Violations of ecological conservation measures such as this one will one day lead to disastrous global ecological consequences. We have to hold the line.

Exercise 5.4.B All Fallacies Considered

Part B. Identify the fallacies that are committed in the following passages. These fallacies include any of the fallacies of Relevance, of Misconstrual, or Presumption. It is possible that some passages contain more than one fallacy. Use the available **Exercise Work Sheet** to submit your work.

1. The project proposed by this scholar promises to be an analytical *tour de force*, a project that analytically defines and substantially inter-relates all the major concepts that comprise this field, which for years people have been incapable of doing. This project will establish this field as a science in its own right. In a previous book, the same scholar was very

successful in analyzing one of those concepts. So, some of the analysis has already been done, and we can expect success for the overal project.

2. We should definitely contribute money to the senator's campaign. She is, we know, a great Country singer, and the *National Enquirer* said that the senator had almost no money left, and that she had to sell the memorabilia of her dear grandmother, herself a great Hollywood actress, just to keep the campaign alive.

3. My opponent said that we should provide state funds for new treatment programs for mental illness, even if that means that we need to levy new taxes for that. I suppose that means we should create new taxes to fund all sorts of programs, for example, contemporary music appreciation. But a new tax for that is inexcusable. We cannot go down that road. My opponent is wrong.

4. Our candidate is unknown to you all, and that is why we want to introduce him to the people of this state. The first thing to notice is that no one has ever publicly said anything negative about our candidate. That is very important, because he is the only one in this whole primary of whom you can say this. Everyone else is being attacked on all sides—but not our candidate. He is a real winner.

5. I don't know how he does it, but the President obviously controls the entire oil industry. The price per barrel of oil was going through the roof, so he anounced that he was lifting the presidential embargo on off-shore oil drilling, and within a few days the price of oil fell 25 percent. That is amazing.

6. We must not provide public funds to Public Television stations that show programs with sexual content. People don't want their children to see repulsive, degrading, offensive, pornographic depictions on regular TV channels during family hours. So, why should we spend their tax dollars to fund such programs?

7. Please pay attention to what is happening. This candidate is not who you think he is. Just look at the people that he deals with. All of them are radicals. Those people are against everything that you and I stand for and believe in. If you support this candidate, you are supporting them too. You must reconsider.

8. All human beings have an absolute, inalienable right to life. But, one cannot have it both ways. One cannot say, on the one hand, that all human beings have an absolute, inalienable right to life, and on the other hand, that elected or appointed officials have the right and obligation to kill people in certain cases. Therefore, the death penalty must be abolished in this country.

9. Religion should be abolished. One need only consider the many horrors of the wars fought in the name of religion that have occurred throughout history. That is what religion brings about. Humanity can do much better without it.

10. The following is a sound model regarding the relationship of morality and legal rights. In short, personal moral views cannot infringe on public, legal rights. That is to say, while many people personally believe that abortion is morally wrong, such personal conviction

may not infringe on the rights of other people. Therefore, according to law, people have the right to have an abortion. The moral convictions of others may not infringe on this right.

11. The Mayor is concerned about your disagreement with the rest of the Planning Commission regarding the upcoming proposal. The Mayor has always stressed the importance of being a team player, and now it looks like you are not a team player. But I think you understand how important it is for you not to look like you're not a team player. Well, I am glad we cleared that up.

12. Commentators argue that the extreme violence in movies and television has caused a great increase in murders in our society. But that is ridiculous. Movies don't kill people—people kill people.

13. Well, of course, there is a purpose for our existence. Look around you: there is a purpose for birds to have wings, for pens to have ink, for ships to have sails, for cars to have wheels, for flowers to smell, for the sun to shine. There is a purpose for everything.

14. The Green movement is irresponsible. Consider the matter of global warming. The Green advocates claim that the increased carbon dioxide emissions produced by our present technology and industry are causing the global temperature to rise. But it is a known fact that the Earth's temperature has risen in past ages through only natural, geological causes, and these advocates cannot prove that the present rise in temperature is not due to such natural geological causes.

GLOSSARY AND INDEX OF TERMS

argument. An argument is a group of given sentences such that some of these sentences are being offered as *reasons* for one other sentence in the group. For example, "Many people have great happiness. After all, many people have loved ones, and such love gives people great happiness." 8, 10.

argument, cogent An inductive argument is cogent, if (1) all the premisses are known to be true, and (2) the conclusion has a *strong* degree of probability (51% or greater) relative to the premisses. Otherwise, the argument is uncogent. 48–49.

argument, deductive An argument is deductive, if the connection of the premisses to the conclusion is based on the *laws of logic*. If the connection is based on *empirical relationships of probabilities* then the argument is an *inductive* argument. 14.

argument, erroneous. An argument is erroneous, if it is known to be unsound; that is, if either the argument is known to be invalid, or some premiss is known to be false. Arguments that are inconclusive at one point in time can become erroneous arguments as we learn information that shows the premisses to be false. 37–38.

argument, formally stated. An argument is formally stated, if (1) all its sentences are *statements*, (2) all the *intended* parts of the argument are explicitly stated, and (3) the argument has the *format* in which all the premisses are listed first, and the (final) conclusion is listed last. A formally stated argument may, or may not, also be accompanied by a full or partial *deduction* that provides a number of intermediate conclusions. 10, 16.

argument, inconclusive. An argument is inconclusive, if it is valid, but there is a *questionable* premiss, whose status is *unknown*, that is, we do not know whether this premiss is true, or false. 37–38.

argument, inductive strength of. An argument has an inductive strength corresponding to *the degree of probability* of the conclusion relative to the premisses. An argument is *inductively strong* if this probability is high, and an argument is *inductively weak* if this probability is low. If the probability is 100%, the argument is inductively valid. 14, 47–49.

argument, inductively valid. An argument is inductively valid, if the conclusive connection at issue is based not on conceptual necessity but instead on *empirical relationships* that are *known to have no exceptions*, such as the laws of science. 48.

argument, informally stated. An argument is informally stated, if it does not meet the criteria of a *formally stated* argument. 10, 16.

argument, proof. An argument is a proof, if (1) the argument is *known* to be valid, and (2) all the premisses are *known* to be true. (This is the same as saying: A proof is an argument that is *known to* *be sound*.) Examples are often complicated ones, but this one is easy: "All people are born. I am a person. So, I was born." 37–38.

argument, sound. An argument is sound, if it satisfies two criteria: (1) the *connection criterion*, that there is a conclusive connection, and (2) the *truth criterion*, that all the premisses are in fact true. (Bonus! If an argument is sound, then the conclusion will *automatically* be true as well.) If an argument fails either of these two criteria, then the argument is *unsound*. 24–26.

argument, valid (the preliminary version). An argument is valid, if it satisfies the *connection criterion*, that is, if there is a *conclusive connection* leading from the premisses to the conclusion. If an argument is not valid, it is *invalid*. 22.

argument, logically valid (conceptual version). An argument is logically valid, if the conclusive connection at issue is a matter of *conceptual necessity* in the following sense: It is not logically possible that all the premisses be true while at the same time the conclusion is false; concretely, that kind of disagreement is not even *imaginable*. If an argument is not logically valid, it is *logically invalid*. [Logical validity is also called *deductive validity*, and it is also called *logical implication*.] 44–46.

Aristotelian Logic. See: Traditional Logic. 203.

categorical sentence. See: sentence, categorical. 150, 201.

categorical syllogism. See: syllogism, categorical. 195.

conclusion. The conclusion of an argument is that sentence in the argument for which the other sentences of the argument are given as *reasons*. The conclusion is often introduced by the word "so" or "therefore." 8.

conditions, necessary; requirements. When a conditional sentence is used to state that a situation p *requires* a situation q, the English conditional sentence typically uses one of the following special grammatical constructions: p *only if* q; *not* p *without* q; *not* p *unless* q; p *requires* q; q *is required for* p; q *is a required condition for* p; if p then q *must also* obtain; p *necessitates* q; q *is necessary for* p; q *is a necessary condition for* p. All of these constructions are represented as: if p then q, or equivalently, if not q then not p. 71–73.

conditions, sufficient. When a conditional sentence is used to state that a situation p *is sufficient for* a situation q, the English conditional sentence typically uses one of the following special grammatical constructions: *if* p *then* q; *if* p, q; q, *if* p; *given that* p, q; *in the event that* p, q; p *is sufficient for* q; and sometimes, *provided that* p, q. All of these constructions are represented as: if p then q. [Note that it is the same thing to say that p is sufficient for q as it is to say that q is necessary for p.] 71–73.

conditions, necessary and sufficient. A biconditional sentence "p if and only if q" asserts the conjunction "p if q, *and* p only if q." The left side "if q then p" expresses that q is sufficient for p, and the right side "p only if q" expresses that q is necessary for p. Thus, a biconditional sentence always expresses that one situation is both a *necessary and sufficient condition* for another situation (and vice versa). 69, 74, 77.

connective. See: sentence operator. 53, 58.

consistency and inconsistency, semantical version. A set of sentences is *inconsistent* if there is no possible *interpretation* of all the basic components of all these sentences that makes all these sentences have the resultant value **T** together. The set is *consistent* if there is such an interpretation that makes all these sentences have the resultant value **T** together. *Truth-functionally* inconsistent sets are inconsistent in virtue of the structure of the *sentence connectives* involved. This distinction means that some sets are *truth-functionally consistent*, but they are nevertheless inconsistent in the general sense, in virtue of the more detailed structures involving their quantifiers and terms. For example, the three sentences "All pets are dogs; All dogs are singers; Some pets are not singers" form an inconsistent set, but this set is truth-functionally consistent. 99, 145.

contingent sentence. A sentence is contingent if it is not necessarily true and it is not necessarily false. This is the same as saying that a contingent sentence is one that is either true and possibly false or false and possibly true, which in turn is the same as saying that a contingent sentence is the same as an empirical sentence. 33–35.

contingently false. A sentence is contingently false if it is a contingent sentence that is false in the real world. See: contingent. 33–35.

contingently true. A sentence is contingently true if it is a contingent sentence that is true in the real world. See: contingent. 33–35.

contradiction (logical falsehood), semantical version. A sentence is a *logical falsehood* if for every possible *interpretation* of all the basic components of that sentence, that sentence always has the resultant value **F**. A logical falsehood is also called a contradiction. For example, "Some talking animals are not animals." [Truth-functional logical falsehoods form a smaller subgroup within the group of logical falsehoods.] 96–97, 145.

contradiction. A sentence is a logical falsehood, also called a contradiction, if it results in asserting two contradictory parts, p and not-p. Since these parts cannot both be true, any sentence that incorporates them cannot be true, and will thus be a necessary falsehood. For example, "Yesterday Tom found a perfectly cubical sphere," and "Some red apples in Chicago are not red." 31–32, 96–97.

contradiction, explicit. A sentence is an explicit contradiction, if it has the grammatical form "p and not p." For example, "Tom is married, but Tom is not married." 31–32, 96.

contradiction, implicit. A sentence is an implicit contradiction, if it is a contradiction but not an explicit contradiction. For example, "Tom is a married bachelor." 31–32, 97.

copula. The copula of a categorical sentence is the expression that links the subject terms to the predicate term. Our main treatment permits only the expression "are." Augmented Traditional Logic includes *singular* categorical sentences that use the singular copula "is." 150, 153, 201.

deduction, for an argument. A deduction for an argument is a (vertical) sequence of sentences (1) beginning with the premisses of the argument, and (2) ending with the conclusion of the argument, and (3) all the sentences in the sequence that come after the premisses (the intermediate conclusions and the final conclusion) are derived from previous sentences in the sequence by the *rules of inference*. 117–118.

deduction, for syllogisms and extended syllogisms. There is a deductive system for Traditional Logic that is never introduced to students (except in this course). This system consists of the four usual equivalences rules (QN, Conv, Contrap, Obv) and the two basic syllogisms (Univ Syll, Part Syll). This deductive system provides easy deductions for all valid categorical syllogisms and for all valid extended syllogisms (sorites). 194–196.

deduction, proper annotations of. Deductions are to be properly annotated. Such annotations consist of three vertically aligned and coordinated columns: (1) a column that numbers all the lines of the deduction, (2) a column of the sentences that make up the deduction, and (3) a column of the reasons for each step. These reasons list (a) the line-numbers of the previously listed lines involved in the step, and (b) a short label that identifies the rule being used. For example, "12. not M and not S   2,10, Conj." 117.

definite description. An expression that designates a single thing, symbolized either by a name symbol or a special quantified expression involving identity, for example, "the cat that chased you." 279.

empirical sentence. A sentence is empirical, if it is either empirically true or empirically false. An empirical sentence is one that can be imagined to be true and can also be imagined to be false. For example, "Some people can dance," "Some elephants can fly." 33–35.

empirically false. A sentence is empirically false, if it is false in the real world, but one can imagine it to be true. Hence, it is in fact false, but possibly true. For example, "Some elephants can fly." 33–35.

empirically true. A sentence is empirically true, if it is true in the real world, but one can imagine it to be false. Hence, it is in fact true, but possibly false. For example, "Some people can dance." 33–35.

equivalence (the conceptual version). Two sentences are equivalent if they *mean* exactly the same thing. This gives the following criterion: it is not logically possible (imaginable) that either one of the two sentences is true while the other one is false. For example, "Some women are astronauts" and "some astronauts are women." 93–94.

equivalence, semantical version. Two sentences are *equivalent* if for every possible interpretation of all the basic components of the two sentences, the resultant value of the one sentence is always the same as the resultant value of the other sentence. For example, the sentence "Not all dogs sing" is equivalent to the sentence "Some dogs do not sing" (not all D are S; some D are not S). [Truth-functionally equivalent sentence-pairs form a smaller subgroup within the set of equivalent sentences-pairs.] 93–94, 145.

fallacies. A logical fallacy is a type of argument that is in fact *unsound* but yet is often *accepted* to be sound. Fallacies make a *typical* mistake in the nature of the inference or in the truth of the premises. Nevertheless, they succeed in *persuading* the listener that the conclusion is correct. Fallacies are classified as *formal* fallacies or *informal* fallacies, and most fallacies are of the informal type. 286–289.

fallacies, formal. Formal fallacies are arguments that employ invalid patterns, but people mistake them for valid ones. People think these patterns are rules of logic when in fact they are not rules at all; e.g., the fallacy of denying the antecedent. 287.

fallacies, informal. Informal fallacies are types of arguments that have *defective premisses* that nevertheless *persuade* the listener that the conclusion is correct; e.g., the argumentum ad baculum fallacy. 288.

fallacies, of irrelevance (relevance). A main classification of informal fallacies. A general group of informal fallacies in which the premisses are *totally irrelevant* to the conclusion, but the premisses are nevertheless persuasive. Obviously, with such a lack of connection, these arguments would have to be invalid. 290.

fallacies, of misconstrual. A main classification of informal fallacies. A general group of informal fallacies in which the arguer begins with some information in the premisses that is then *misconstrued* into some unwarranted conclusion. These kinds of fallacies are different from the fallacies of irrelevance because the premisses in these cases are not totally irrelevant. They are relevant, but they are misconstrued into something unwarranted. 301.

fallacies, non sequitur. Latin for "it does not follow." Any kind of inference in which the conclusion *does not follow* from the premisses, regardless of the status of the premisses. 288.

fallacies, of presumption. A main classification of informal fallacies. A general group of informal fallacies in which the premisses are presented as if they were established truths, but they are, in fact, not established truths at all. The inference to the conclusion, on the other hand, is valid, and unless the listener is especially careful, he will be led by the arguer to accept the premisses and also the conclusion that validly follows. 314.

fallacy, ad hoc reasoning, fallacy of. Latin for "[something made] for this [matter]." A fallacy of presumption. *Ad hoc* reasoning concerns a proposed explanation of why, or how, some matter came about. The proposed explanation seems to do the job, in that the matter at issue is indeed explained by the proposed premises, except that, instead of using known facts as premises to explain the matter at issue, the arguer has simply *invented* an explanation, by using premises that are *mere possibilities*, and that have no other support. 316.

fallacy, affirming the consequent. A formal fallacy. The mistaken inference, confused with the rule of modus ponens, that from a conditional sentence and from its consequent part, one may infer its antecedent part. "If Tom went then Sue went. And we also know that Sue went. So, Tom must have gone as well." *pattern*: p ⊃ q , q ∴ p. 103, 287.

fallacy, ambiguity (syntactic), fallacy of. A fallacy of misconstrual. In this type of argument, one of the premises has an ambiguous grammatical form that allows the sentence to be understood in two different ways. The fallacy occurs when the argument has a *shift in meaning*, when the premises start with the one meaning, and the conclusion ends with the other meaning. So, the argument is a non sequitur. 308.

fallacy, argumentum ad baculum. A fallacy of irrelevance. Latin for "argument from the club [stick]." In this type of argument the arguer is making an appeal to *force* (or even some *reward*) to get the listener to agree with the conclusion. 290.

fallacy, argumentum ad hominem. A fallacy of irrelevance. Latin for "argument against the person." In this type of argument the arguer is making a *personal attack* on some opponent in order to persuade the listener to reject that opponent's thesis. 291.

fallacy, argumentum ad ignorantiam. A fallacy of irrelevance. Latin for "argument from ignorance." In this type of argument the arguer claims that the conclusion is correct because no one has proved that it is wrong. This is an *appeal to ignorance*, to a lack of knowledge. The error in this reasoning becomes clear when one adds the one word "yet": the fact that no one has proved the conclusion wrong *yet* is irrelevant to the conclusion. 296.

fallacy, argumentum ad misericordiam. A fallacy of irrelevance. Latin for "argument from pity." In this type of argument the arguer makes an *appeal to the listener's pity* to persuade the listener of the correctness of the conclusion. The arguer arouses feelings of *sympathy* and, through that, agreement. 295.

fallacy, argumentum ad populum. A fallacy of irrelevance. Latin for "argument from the people." In this type of popular argument the arguer makes an *appeal to popular sentiments* in an attempt to persuade the listener that the conclusion is correct. 292.

fallacy, argumentum ad verecundiam. A fallacy of irrelevance. Latin for "argument from reverence." In this type of argument the arguer cites a source that is "revered" in an attempt to persuade the listener that the conclusion is correct. The fallacy occurs when the source cited is *irrelevant* to the particular case at hand, e.g., when the source is an expert in a different area only. This fallacy is often called an *appeal to an unqualified authority*. 293.

fallacy, complex question fallacy. A fallacy of misconstrual. In this type of argument, the arguer asks two questions that are disguised as a single question. The fallacy occurs when the listener fails to notice the duplicity and gives an answer that is then taken as an answer to the unsuspected question. 306.

fallacy, composition, fallacy of. A fallacy of misconstrual. In this type of argument, the premises introduce a characteristic that applies to the *individual parts* of some considered thing, and the conclusion asserts that this characteristic, therefore, applies to that considered thing *as a whole*. The fallacy occurs when the characteristic in question does not have this dual application. 312.

fallacy, denying the antecedent. A formal fallacy. The mistaken inference, confused with the rule of modus tollens, that from a conditional sentence and from the denial of its antecedent part, one may infer the denial of its consequent part. "If Tom went then Sue went. But, not Tom went. Therefore, not Sue went." *pattern*: p ⊃ q , ~p ∴ ~q. 104, 287.

fallacy, division, fallacy of. A fallacy of misconstrual. In this type of argument, the premisses introduce a characteristic that applies to something considered *as a whole*, and the conclusion asserts that this characteristic, therefore, applies to the *individual parts* of that whole. The fallacy occurs when the characteristic in question does not have this dual application. 311.

fallacy, equivocation (semantic), fallacy of. A fallacy of misconstrual. Equivocation can readily occur, because many of our words have more than one meaning. In this type of argument, the premisses begin with using one meaning of a word, and the conclusion ends with using another meaning of that same word. So, the argument is a non sequitur. 309.

fallacy, false dichotomy fallacy. A fallacy of presumption. What is characteristic of this fallacy is that it makes crucial use of a premiss that asserts a *false set of choices*. The choices have their consequences, and so a conclusion does follow, but the assertion of choices is wrong. This typically occurs when the arguer leaves out *other possible choices*. 314.

fallacy, guilt by association fallacy. A fallacy of irrelevance. In this type of argument the arguer rejects some proposal on the basis of certain *negative facts* that are in some concrete way *associated* with the proposal. The fallacy occurs when the associated matters are quite tangential and irrelevant to the conclusion. This fallacy is also called the *Genetic Fallacy*, because the negative facts may be about the origin of the proposal or about some other historical matters regarding the proposal. When the negative facts refer to the arguer's opponent, this type of argument is also an *ad hominem* fallacy. 298.

fallacy, improper (hasty) generalization, fallacy of. A fallacy of misconstrual. In this type of argument, the premisses present some individual facts, and the conclusion involves a *generalization* based on these facts. The fallacy occurs when the available, individual facts cited do not support the proposed generalization. Also called the fallacy of *hasty generalization*. 304.

fallacy, improper instance, fallacy of. A fallacy of misconstrual. In this type of argument, the arguer begins with a (correct) general premiss and then infers a particular case. The fallacy occurs when the inferred particular case is not a proper instance of the general premiss. 305.

fallacy, inconsistent premisses, fallacy of. A fallacy of presumption. In this type of argument, the premisses, at first glance, do not seem to be problematic, and they validly produce the conclusion. But on closer inspection it becomes clear that the premisses actually form a *contradiction*. Clearly, such premisses are unsupportable. 319.

fallacy, petitio principii fallacy. Latin for "petition to the principle [at issue]." A fallacy of presumption. This fallacy is usually called *Begging the Question*. In this type of argument, the arguer presents premisses that have *no evidence* to support them, although they do validly produce the conclusion. Moreover, further attention to the premisses reveals that the proposed conclusion is secretly or explicitly made a reason to support the premisses. So, the premisses are assuming for their *own* support the very conclusion that they are supposed to be supporting. The argument goes around in a *vicious circle*; and so, the proposed conclusion remains unsupported. 318.

fallacy, post hoc ergo propter hoc fallacy. Latin for "After this, therefore, because of this." A fallacy of misconstrual. In this type of argument, the arguer notes that one situation *came after* another situation, and therefore was *caused* by it. The argument continues with further assertions involving the noted causal relationship. The fallacy occurs when there is no evidence that such a causal relationship exists. One thing may happen after another thing, but that does not require causation. The *post hoc ergo propter hoc* fallacy is also called the *false cause* fallacy, and also the *post hoc* fallacy. 302.

fallacy, red herring fallacy. A fallacy of irrelevance. The name of this type of fallacy refers to the old practice of training bloodhounds to track missing persons by dragging smelly red herrings across the paths of the hounds to try to throw them off the scent. In this type of argument the arguer sneakily introduces some other, irrelevant, issue as a substitute for the proposal of the opponent. The faults of the irrelevant side issue are then illicitly transferred to the main proposal. 299.

fallacy, slippery slope fallacy. A fallacy of presumption. In this type of argument the premisses claim that a certain matter X has a long *string* of consequences Y1, Y2, Y3, Y4, etc. with an inevitable disastrous final state. The fallacy occurs when the alleged chain of conseqences in fact does not exist; the premisses are false. 315.

fallacy, special pleading, fallacy of. A fallacy of misconstrual. In this type of argument, the sought-after conclusion is something that should be based on a weighing of the various pros and cons that are relevant to the case, but the arguer presents only reasons that *favor his point of view*. Such selectivity cannot be the basis for making a correct inference. 303.

fallacy, straw man fallacy. A fallacy of misconstrual. With this type of argument the arguer presents a *distorted* or *exaggerated* version of his opponent's position. He then proceeds to criticize the *distorted* version, and concludes that the *original* position of the opponent has been refuted. Of course, the distorted position is not at all what the opponent wanted to assert, and often, no one else does either. The distorted position is truly a *straw man*, having no substance and nothing, and no one, to recommend it. 301.

fallacy, tu quoque fallacy. Fallacy of irrelevance. Latin for "And you [do it] too!" In this type of argument the arguer discredits some opponent by pointing out that this opponent acts contrary to his own position, and that therefore we do not have to believe what the opponent is saying. The error in this reasoning becomes clear when one considers that *truth* and *practice* are two different things. We *all* do things that we should not do, and inversely, fail to do things that we should do. (This fallacy is a variety of the *ad hominem* fallacy.) 297.

falsehood, logical; contradiction. See: contradiction. 31–32, 96–97.

falsehood, necessary. A sentence is necessarily false, if the sentence is false in every logically possible (imaginable) circumstance, including the real world. Necessary falsehoods consist of mathematical falsehoods, falsehoods of logic, and definitional falsehoods [and some other special falsehoods known as synthetic apriori falsehoods]. 31–32.

falsehood, possible. A sentence is possibly false, if the sentence is false in at least one logically possible (imaginable) circumstance. [The real world counts as a possible circumstance.] Thus, possible falsehoods are ones that are not necessary truths. For example, "Some people can dance." 28–30.

identity, laws of. Laws of logic that are true regarding the identity relation. See rules, below. 282.

identity relation. The special relational predicate "__is identical to__," as for example, "Clark Kent is identical to Superman," or, c = s. 279.

identity, restricted quantifiers. Quantifiers that are limited by means of an identity restriction, for example, "something *other than* the Moon is round." 281.

implication. Some sentences (one or more) together *imply* another sentence if the corresponding inference from those sentences to that other sentence is a valid argument. 44, 85.

impossible sentence. A sentence is impossible if it is not possibly true, and hence, it is a sentence that is necessarily false. See: possible. 31–32.

individual constant, proper name, singular term. A singular term is a word or expression that represents (or purports to represent) exactly *one* thing. *Proper names* are also called *individual constants*, and they are a type of singular terms. Examples are "Abraham Lincoln," "Chicago," "the Earth," "the Statue of Liberty," "God," "5," "the Solar System," etc. Singular terms are not properly represented within Traditional Logic. In Quantificational Logic, singular terms are represented by *lower-case* letters: a, b, c, . . . , u, v, w. (The letters x, y, and z have a different function.) 201, 217, 279.

inference indicator. An inference indicator is a word, or phrase, that indicates that an inference is being made. Some inference indicators introduce a premiss ("since" or "because"), and some introduce the conclusion ("so" or "therefore"). Formally stated arguments always require the latter kind. 13.

logic. Logic is the study of correct reasoning. This study includes an introduction to a variety of special methods as well as a large number of principles known as the laws of logic. This study also includes some important cases of incorrect reasoning. 2, 5–7.

logic, formal. Formal logic is the study of correct reasoning with a special emphasis on representing correct reasoning as part of a comprehensive formal system consisting of well-defined terms, rigorously drafted techniques, and precisely stated universal laws. Concrete application to everyday affairs receives a lesser emphasis than does the study of the formal techniques. 5–7.

logic, informal. Informal logic is the study of correct and incorrect reasoning with a special emphasis on concrete application to everyday affairs. The study includes some laws of logic and a variety of logical fallacies, but a comprehensive formal system with universal laws and formal techniques is not introduced. 5–7.

logical truth (tautology), semantical version. A sentence is a *logical truth* if for every possible interpretation of all the basic components of that sentence, that sentence always has the resultant value **T**. A logical truth is also called a *tautology*. For example, "All talking animals are animals." [Truth-functional logical truths form a smaller subgroup within the group of logical truths.] 95, 145.

method of direct proof in deduction. When the special rules of Conditional Proof and Indirect Proof are *not* used in a deduction, the deduction is said to employ the method of *direct proof*. 135, 138.

necessary conditions. See: conditions. 71–73.

parentheses, punctuation. In natural language, punctuation marks are used to indicate how the parts of our sentences and larger passages are grouped into units. In logic there are no punctuation marks whatsoever, except the left and right parentheses, and their function is precisely to make a *unit* out of whatever is enclosed by them. For example, (A & B) ∨ (~C & ~D). Sometimes commas are used as a *practical visual aid* to separate two or more symbolic formulas, For example, "(A & B)⊃C , B , ~C," but these commas are completely unnecessary, because, even without the commas, the *lack* of operators and the lack of parentheses on the right-hand side of the sequence *forces* the sequence to *break* at the two places indicated. 56, 60.

pattern (form), argument. An argument pattern is a small list of sentence patterns (the premisses), followed by an inference indicator ("therefore"), followed by one other sentence pattern (the conclusion). An argument pattern has an infinite number of specific arguments as instances. 53, 58, 119.

pattern (form), sentence. All grammars make a distinction between *content* (or *descriptive*) words, such as "red," "dance," "person," "smart," on the one hand, and *formal* (or *non-descriptive*) words, such as "not," "only," "and," "every," on the other hand. A *sentence pattern* is an arrangement of *formal* words and *blanks* that act as place-holders for certain kinds of *content* words. Blanks are usually represented by specially selected letters. For example, "some X are Y" and "if not p then not q" are sentence patterns. A sentence pattern has an infinite number of specific sentences as instances. 53, 58, 119.

possible falsehood. See: falsehood, possible. 28–30.

possible truth. See: truth, possible. 28–30.

predicate term. See: term. 150, 152.

predicates, relational, relations. An expression that describes an individual thing by relating it to some other thing, for example, "__lives on__," as in "George *lives on* the Moon," or, gLm. 267.

predicates, simple. A *predicate* is an expression that characterizes individual things. A *simple* predicate is a predicate that is not grammatically built from other predicate expressions. Simple predicates are represented by capital letters A, B, C,. . ., and complex predicates must be represented in terms of these. For example, "George is smart" is symbolized as "Sg," and "George is a smart person" is symbolized as "Sg & Pg." 217, 222.

premiss. A premiss of an argument is a sentence that is offered in the argument as a *reason* for the conclusion. Premisses are often introduced by the word "since" or "because." 8.

Propositional Logic (Sentential Logic). Propositional Logic is the study of the structure (form, pattern, arrangement) that *sentences* and *arguments* have in virtue of only the following components: *simple sentences* and *sentential operators*. The internal structure of simple sentences themselves is ignored in this study. For example, the sentence "George is funny, but not all people are funny" has the propositional form: p and not q. Propositional Logic is also called *Sentential Logic*. 52.

Quantificational Logic (Modern Logic). Quantificational Logic is a comprehensive study of the detailed elements that make up the various structures of simple sentences. All our reasonings, both ordinary and advanced, involve minutely structured patterns. We need a correspondingly detailed formal language to study these patterns and to assess their validity. Traditional Logic was an incomplete introduction to this study. [Quantificational Logic is also called *Modern Logic*, as well as *Predicate Logic*.] 216.

quantifier. A quantifier is a word that indicates the *quantity* of things under discussion. In Traditional Logic, there are exactly three quantifiers words: "all," "some," "no." 150, 219, 220.

quantifier, alternative variations. In Traditional Logic only three quantifiers are allowed. So, all other English quantifier expressions are considered to be *variations* on these three. For example, "all" = "every" = "each" = "whatever," "some" = "there are" = "a few," "no" = "not any" = "there are no" = "all. . .are not," and others as described below. 156.

quantifier, "a." English sentences often use the quantifier "a," as in "A tiger is dangerous," or "A car smashed into the tree." The "a" quantifier must be replaced by "all" or "some" in accordance with the predicate space-time restriction criterion. 160.

quantifier, "any." English sentences often use the quantifier "any." This quantifier is always translated as "all," *but* the so translated sentence must always *begin* with the word "all." "Not any person heard the music" becomes "*all* persons did *not* hear the music." 161.

quantifier, combined. An English sentence whose quantifier is a *combination* must be restated as two separate sentences with separate quantifiers. E.g. "Some but not all dogs are mean" must be restated as the conjunction "Some dogs are mean; and not all dogs are mean." (some D are M) & ~(all D are M). 166.

quantifier, conditional. The sentence scheme "all S are P" has several *conditional* variations in English: "If it's an S then it's P," "if you're an S then you're P," "if something is S then it is P," "if anything is S then it is P." [But not: "if everything is an S then it is P." The latter is ungrammatical and has a confused meaning.] 156.

quantifier, existential. An existential quantifier is an expression that makes reference to *some unspecified*members of the universe of discourse. The quantifier contains a variable *tag* to indicate what individual variable will be used to continue its reference. The existential quantifiers are the

#

constructions "for some thing x," "for some thing y," "for some thing z," and are further symbolized as "(∃x)," "(∃y)," "(∃z)." For example, "Some things are physical and not eternal" is represented as "for some thing x, x is physical and x is not eternal," that is, "(∃x)(Px & ~Ex)." 219.

quantifier, missing. Many English sentences *suppress* their quantifiers. The missing quantifier must be reintroduced according to the predicate space-time restriction criterion: If the action of the verb is *not* restricted in space or time, then the missing quantifier is "all"; if action of the verb *is* restricted in space or time, then the missing quantifer is "some." E.g, "people like ice cream" means "all people like ice cream," and "people were dancing all night" means "some people were dancing all night." 160.

quantifier, "only." The "only" quantifier can be interpreted in two distinct, but logically equivalent ways. "Only Seniors will graduate in June" means (1) "All who will graduate in June are Seniors," or equivalently, (2) "all who are not Seniors will not graduate in June." (only S are G = all G are S = all non-S are non-G). 162.

quantifier, places. Some English sentences employ dedicated *place quantifiers*, such as "everywhere," "wherever," "nowhere," "somewhere." They must be put into categorical form. For example, "Everywhere George went, people shouted" must be reworded as "All places-where-George-went are places-where-people-shouted." (all W are S). 167.

quantifier, restricted by identity,. Quantifiers that are limited by means of an identity restriction, for example, "something *other than* the Moon is round." 281.

quantifier, scope of. The scope of a quantifier tagged with a variable **x** is the expression written after the quantifier that is governed by the quantifier. From a practical point of view, this expression extends as far as there are occurrences of the variable **x**, or further if parentheses group the expression into a yet larger unit. For example, "Something is mental, and if it is eternal then it is not physical" is represented as "for some x, x is mental and if x is eternal then x is not physical," that is, "(∃x)[Mx & (Ex ⊃ ~Px)]." Here, the scope of the quantifier "(∃x)" is the expression "[Mx & (Ex ⊃ ~Px)]." 222–223.

quantifier, times. Some English sentences employ dedicated *time quantifiers*, such as "always," "whenever," "never," "sometimes." They must be put into categorical form. For example, "Whenever George is angry, he turns red" must be reworded as "All times-when-George-is-angry are times-when-George-is-red." (all A are R). 167.

quantifier, universal. A universal quantifier is an expression that makes reference to *all* the members of the Universe of discourse. The quantifier contains a variable *tag* to indicate what individual variable will be used to continue its reference. The universal quantifiers are the constructions "for every thing x," "for every thing y," "for every thing z," and are further symbolized as "(∀x)," "(∀y)" , "(∀z)." For example, "All things are physical and not eternal" is represented as "for every thing x, x is physical and x is not eternal," that is, "(∀x)(Px & ~Ex)" . 220.

questionable premiss. A questionable premiss is one whose truth-value status is *unknown*, that is, we do not know whether this premiss is true or false. For example, "There once was life on Mars." Arguments using this as a premiss would be inconclusive arguments. 38.

reason, for a conclusion. A sentence is a reason for a conclusion, if that sentence, if true, makes it reasonable to think that the conclusion is true. For example, the sentence "George likes Meg; and whenever George likes someone, he gives that person some flowers" is a reason for the conclusion "George gives Meg some flowers." Whether or not the reason is a *conclusive* reason is another matter. (For example, it was not stated that Meg is a person.) 8.

relation, identity. The special relational predicate "__is identical to__," as for example, "Clark Kent is identical to Superman," or, c = s. 279.

relational general truths. Some relations are characterized by necessary relationships, for example, "for all x, for all y, for all z, if x is taller than y, and y is taller than z, then x is taller than z." 277.

relational predicate term, relation. An expression that describes an individual thing by relating it to some other thing, for example, "_lives on_," as in "George *lives on* the Moon," or, gLm. 267.

relational sentence. A sentence containing a relational predicate that relates individual things that are referred to explicitly by name or indefinitely by quantifiers, for example, "something hit George," $(\exists x)(xHg)$. 267.

rule, all forms, rules of inference. The rules of deduction for logic are a set of *selected* rules, already known to be valid, by means of which one is permitted to derive certain sentences from already given sentences if those sentences satify the conditions specified in the rules. There is an important division of these rules into the rules that are *basic argument forms* and the rules that are *basic equivalence forms.* 120–121.

rule, basic argument forms, rules of inference. These rules permit one to infer a certain conclusion from some given premises. These rules specify the pattern that the premises must have and the pattern that the conclusion must have; e.g., *Modus Ponens,* 120–121.

rule, basic equivalence forms, rules of inferences. These rules permit one to infer a certain conclusion from a given premiss. These rules specify that some part of the premiss may be changed into an alternative form while the remainder stays fixed; e.g., the rule *Double Negation,* $\sim(\sim p) = p$. 120–121.

rule, association. A conjunction with multiple conjuncts that are grouped in one way is equivalent to that conjunction when its conjuncts are grouped in some other way. "Tom went, and Sue and Mary went" **equals** "Tom and Sue went, and Mary went." Similarly, a disjunction with multiple disjuncts that are grouped in one way is equivalent to that disjunction when its disjuncts are grouped in some other way. "Tom went, or Sue or Mary went" **equals** "Tom or Sue went, or Mary went." Such items are interchangeable. **Assoc.** $p \& (q \& r) = (p \& q) \& r$; also, $p \lor (q \lor r) = (p \lor q) \lor r$. 111.

rule, bicondition. A biconditional sentence is equivalent to the conjunction of the *two* conditional sentences formed from its two sides. These sentences are interchangeable. "Tom went if and only if Sue went" **equals** "If Tom went then Sue went, and if Sue went then Tom went." **Bicond.** $p \equiv q = (p \supset q) \& (q \supset p)$. 108.

rule, commutation. A conjunction is equivalent to that conjunction when its conjuncts are switched. "Tom and Sue went" **equals** "Sue and Tom went." Similarly, a disjunction is equivalent to that disjunction when its disjuncts are switched. "Tom or Sue went" **equals** "Sue or Tom went." Such items are interchangeable. **Comm.** $p \& q = q \& p$; also, $p \lor q = q \lor p$. 111.

rule, conditional proof. One may reserve a portion of a deduction for a special procedure that begins with an extra *assumption*, p, and that uses the rules of inference to derive some result, q. This reserved portion of the deduction becomes de-activated and is replaced by a conclusion that is the conditional sentence: "if p then q." **CP.** When a deduction for an argument makes use of the rule of Conditional Proof, the deduction is said to employ the method of Conditional Proof. 136.

rule, conditional relation. A *conditional* sentence is equivalent to a *disjunctive* sentence whose two choices are, one, the opposite of that antecedent part and, two, that same consequent part. These equivalent sentences are interchangeable. "If Tom went then Sue went" **equals** "either not Tom went or [in case he did, then] Sue went." **Cond.** $p \supset q = \sim p \lor q$. 109.

rule, conjunction. From two sentences, one may infer a sentence that is the conjunction of those two sentences. **From** "Tom went" **and from** "Sue went" **infer** "Both Tom and Sue went." **Conj.** p , q ∴ p & q. 106.

rule, contraposition, categorical version. The rule of Traditional Logic, restricted to *universal-affirmative* sentences, whereby one may *switch* the *subject* and the *predicate* terms if at the same time one takes the *opposite* of each. "All cats are non-humans" **equals** "All humans are non-cats." **Contrap.** All **S** are **P** = all non-**P** are non-**S**. 190.

rule, contraposition, propositional version. A conditional sentence is equivalent to the conditional sentence that results by switching the two sides *and* taking the opposite of each. These equivalent items are interchangeable. "If Tom went then Sue went" **equals** "if not Sue went then not Tom went." **Contrap.** p ⊃ q = ~q ⊃ ~p . 169.

rule, conversion. The rule of Traditional Logic, permitted for *particular-affirmative* sentences, and consequently also for *universal-negative* sentences, whereby one may simply *switch* the subject term and the predicate term. "Some squirrels are well-trained animals" **equals** "some well-trained animals are squirrels." **Conv.** some **S** are **P** = some **P** are **S** ; no **S** are **P** = no **P** are **S**. 189.

rule, De Morgan's Laws. The opposite of the *conjunction* of two sentences is equivalent to the *disjunction* of the opposites of the two sentences. "Not both Tom and Sue went" **equals** "Either not Tom went or not Sue went." Likewise, the opposite of the *disjunction* of two sentences is equivalent to the *conjunction* of the opposites of the two sentences. "Not either Tom or Sue went" **equals** "both not Tom went and not Sue went." Such equivalent items are interchangeable. **DeMorg.** ~(p & q) = ~p ∨ ~q ; also, ~(p ∨ q) = ~p & ~q. 108.

rule, dilemma. From a disjunctive sentence with two choices, and from two conditional sentences that assert the respective results of those choices, one may infer the disjunctive sentence whose two choices are those results. **From** "Either Tom or Sue went" **and from** "If Tom went then Liz went" **and from** "If Sue went then Matt went" **infer** "Either Liz or Matt went." **Dilemma.** p ∨ q , p ⊃ r , q ⊃ s ∴ r ∨ s. 105.

rule, disjunctive addition. From a given sentence, one may infer the *weaker* disjunctive sentence in which the given sentence is one choice and *any* sentence is the other choice. **From** "Tom went" **infer** "Tom or Sue went." **Disj Add,** or **Add.** p ∴ p ∨ q. 106.

rule, disjunctive syllogism. From a disjunctive sentence with two choices, and from a sentence that is the opposite of one of the choices, one may infer the sentence that is the remaining choice. **From** "Tom or Sue went" **and from** "Not Tom went" **infer** "Sue went." **Disj. Syll** or **D.S.** p ∨ q , ~p ∴ q. 106.

rule, distribution. A *conjunctive* sentence, one of whose components is a disjunction, is equivalent to the *disjunctive* sentence that results when the one conjunct is conjunctively distributed over the two disjuncts. "Tom went, and either Sue or Mary went" **equals** "Tom and Sue went, or else Tom and Mary went." Likewise, a *disjunctive* sentence, one of whose components is a conjuction, is equivalent to the *conjunctive* sentence that results when the one disjunct is disjunctively distributed over the two conjuncts. "Tom went, or both Sue and Mary went" **equals** "Tom or Sue went, and also, Tom or Mary went." Such items are interchangeable. **Distr.** p & (q ∨ r) = (p & q) ∨ (p & r) ; also, p ∨ (q & r) = (p ∨ q) & (p ∨ r). 111.

rule, double ifs (exportation). A conditional sentence whose one antecedent is a *double condition* is equivalent to the *single*, complex conditional sentence in which the two conditions are stated as separate antecedent parts. "If both Tom and Sue went then Mary went" **equals** "If Tom went, then, further, if Sue went, then Mary went" **equals** "If Tom went, and if Sue went, then Mary went." Such equivalent complex sentences are interchangeable. **D.Ifs** (also, **Exp.**) (p & q) ⊃ r = p ⊃ (q ⊃ r). 110.

rule, double negation. The *denial* of a *denial* of a sentence is equivalent to just that sentence. These equivalent items are interchangeable. "It is not the case Tom didn't go" **equals** "Tom did go." **D.N.** ~(~p) = p. 108.

rule, double thens. From a conditional sentence stating a *double result*, one may infer a corresponding conditional sentence stating only *one* of those two results. **From** "If Tom went then both Sue and Mary went" **infer** "If Tom went then Sue went," and also, "If Tom went then Mary went." This inference also works in the reverse. **D.Thens.** p ⊃ (q & r) ∴ p ⊃ q, p ⊃ r. 107.

rule, duplication. A conjunction consisting of a sentence conjoined with itself is equivalent to that sentence by itself. "Tom went, and moreover, Tom went" **equals** "Tom went." Similarly, a disjunction consisting of a sentence disjoined with itself is equivalent to that sentence by itself. "Tom went, or else Tom went" **equals** "Tom went." Such equivalent items are interchangeable. **Dupl.** p & p = p ; also, p ∨ p = p. 110.

rule, existential generalization, EG. From a sentence about any named individual (no restriction), one may infer the existentially quantified generalization of that sentence. **From** "Chicago is not a bird and Chicago is not a mountain" **infer** "for some thing x, x is not a bird and x is not a mountain." **EG.** F*a* ∴ (∃x) Fx , where *a* is any proper name, no restriction. 246.

rule, existential instantiation, E.I. From an existential sentence, one may infer a sentence that is an *instance* of that sentence, provided the name selected has no prior use and no prior significance of any kind. **From** "Something caused the universe" **infer** "unspecified thing A caused the universe." **E.I.** (∃x) Fx ∴ (**select name**: *a*) , ∴ F*a* , where *a* is a name introduced here by a separate *selection step*. 243.

rule, hypothetical syllogism. From a conditional sentence and from another conditional sentence that is the *continuation* of the first, one may infer the conditional sentence whose condition is the condition of the first one, and whose result is the result of the second one. **From** "If Tom went then Sue went" **and from** "If Sue went then Mary went" **infer** "If Tom went then Mary went." **Hyp. Syll**, or **H.S.** p ⊃ q , q ⊃ r ∴ p ⊃ r. 104.

rule, identity, law of reflexivity. The law that anything is identical to itself. ∴ *a* = a. 282.

rule, identity, law of symmetry. The law that an identity relation is reversible. *a* = b ∴ *b* = a. 282.

rule, identity, law of transitivity. The law that the relationship of being identical is transferred among its participants. *a* = b , *b* = c ∴ *a* = c . 282.

rule, identity, law of substitution of equals. The law that when two things are identical, they have the same properties. *a* = *b* , F*a* ∴ F*b* . 282.

rule, identity, law of difference of non-equals. The law that when two things have different properties, they are non-identical. F*a* , ~F*b* ∴ ~(*a* = *b*). 282.

rule, indirect proof. One may reserve a portion of a deduction for a special procedure that begins with an extra *assumption* and that uses the rules of inference to derive an explicit contradiction. This reserved portion of the deduction becomes de-activated and is replaced by a conclusion that is the negation-opposite of the assumption in question. **IP.** When a deduction for an argument makes use of the rule of Indirect Proof, the deduction is said to employ the method of Indirect Proof. 139.

rule, modus ponens. From a conditional sentence and from the sentence that is its antecedent part, one may infer the sentence that is its consequent part. **From** "If Tom went then Sue went" **and from** "Tom went" **infer** "Sue went." **MP.** p ⊃ q , p ∴ q. 103.

rule, modus tollens. From a conditional sentence and from the sentence that is the opposite of its consequent part, one may infer the sentence that is the opposite of its antecedent part. **From**

"If Tom went then Sue went" **and from** "not Sue went" **infer** "Not Tom went." **MT.** p ⊃ q , ~q ∴ ~p. 104.

rule, name-negation law A rule for named things, by which an external negation is equated with a negative predicate, for example, "not (Alex is hungry)" *equals* "Alex is non-hungry." **Name-Neg.** 202.

rule, the particular syllogism. One of the two basic categorical syllogisms used in deductions in Traditional Logic. This rule is the following: **Part Syll.** Some **S** are **M**. All **M** are **P**. So, some **S** are **P**. The second premiss provides the *universal continuation* that is always required for syllogistic inferences. This rule is also known as the **AII-1**, **Darii**, syllogism. 195.

rule, predicate-double-negation. A special version of the rule of Traditional Logic known as Obversion. When the predicate side of a sentence is doubly negated, one may simply reduce the predicate to the affirmative form, and vice versa. "Some people are not uneducated" **equals** "Some people are educated." **Pred-DN.** . . . . are (not non-**P**) = ... are **P** . 187.

rule, the primary categorical syllogisms. These are the two basic argument forms in Traditional Logic that we call *the Universal Syllogism*, **Univ Syll**, and *the Particular Syllogism*, **Part Syll.** 195.

rule, quantifier-negation laws, categorical. The rule that changes the *denial* of a quantified sentence into a modified quantified sentence with a negated predicate, and vice versa. "Not all cats are docile" **equals** "Some cats are non-docile"; also, "Not some dogs are red" **equals** "All dogs are non-red." **QN** not all **S** are **P** = some **S** are non-**P**; also, not some **S** are **P** = all **S** are non-**P** = no **S** are **P**. Also known as the *square of opposition* relations. 188.

rule, quantifier-negation laws, QN. The rule that changes the negation of an absolute quantified sentence into a modified absolute quantified sentence with a negated predicate, and vice versa. "Not everything is mental" **equals** "Something is not mental." Also, "Not something is physical" **equals** "Everything is not physical." **QN** ~(∀x) Fx = (∃x) ~Fx ; also, ~(∃x) Fx = (∀x) ~Fx. There are corresponding versions for restricted quantified sentences. 251.

rule, reductio ad absurdum. If a hypothesis (a condition) leads both to one result and also to its denial, then one may infer that the hypothesis is false and that its opposite is true. **From** "If Tom went then Sue went" **and from** "if Tom went then not Sue went" **infer** "It can't be that Tom went." **RAA** p ⊃ q , p ⊃ ~q ∴ ~p. 107.

rule, simplification. From a conjunctive sentence that asserts two parts, one may infer a sentence that is one of those two parts. **From** "Both Tom and Sue went" **infer** "Tom went." **Simp.** p & q ∴ p. 105.

rule, the singular particular syllogism. A rule that infers a general categorical sentence from a pair of singular sentences. For example: **From** "Soxtrox is an ant" **and** "Soxtrox is noisy," **infer** "some ants are noisy." **Sing Part Syll.** 202.

rule, the singular universal syllogism. A rule that applies a universal categorical sentence to a named thing. For example: **From** "all animals are active" **and** "Soxtrox is an animal," **infer** "Soxtrox is active." **Sing Univ Syll.** 202.

rule, the super syllogisms. These are extensions of the universal syllogism and the particular syllogism by means of additional universal premisses to continue the connection. 197.

rule, syllogism categorical. See: rule, universal syllogism, particular syllogism. 195.

rule, tautology, logical truth. At any point in a deduction one may assert any sentence that is one of the allowed logical truths (tautologies). **Assert** "either Tom went or not Tom went." **Taut.** p ∨ ~p. 122.

rule, universal generalization, UG. From a sentence about a named individual (with strong restrictions), one may infer the universally quantified generalization of that sentence. **From** "George is not a synthetic astronomer" **infer** "for all things x, x is not a synthetic astronomer."

UG (**select name**: *a*) , . . . , F*a* ∴ (∀x) Fx , where *a* is a name introduced by a separate *selection step*. 248.

rule, universal instantiation, UI. From a universal sentence, one may infer a sentence that is an *instance* of that sentence, without regard to what instance name is selected. **From** "Everything is an eternal mental thing" **infer** "Chicago is an eternal mental thing." **UI** (∀x) Fx ∴ F*a* , where *a* is any proper name, no restriction. 241.

rule, the universal syllogism. One of the two basic categorical syllogisms used in deductions in Traditional Logic. This rule is the following: **Univ Syll.** All **S** are **M**. All **M** are **P**. So, all **S** are **P**. The second premiss provides the *universal continuation* that is always required for syllogistic inferences. This rule is also known as the **AAA-1**, **Barbara**, syllogism. 195.

sentence, biconditional. A biconditional sentence is a sentence that asserts that two sentences are *reciprocal* conditions for each other, so that they have the same truth-status. A biconditional sentence is also called a *biconditional*. In regular English, biconditional sentences can take various forms, but in Propositional Logic one uses the complex operator expression "if and only if," and the latter is always placed between the two *sides*. For example, "Dogs can think if and only if cats can think" (p if and only if q). 55.

sentence, categorical. A categorical sentence is a simple sentence that has the form: *quantifier + term + copula + term*, where these elements are of a required type. For example, "All snails are very-slow-movers," where "all" is a quantifier, "snails" and "very-slow-movers" are terms, and "are" is a copula. Traditional Logic can be *augmented* to include *singular* categorical sentences, such as "Earth is a planet," and "Chicago is a non-planet." 150, 201.

sentence, compound. A compound sentence is a sentence that is grammatically constructed out of other sentences by means of sentential operators, such as "or." For example, "George saw Liz, or the party was cancelled" (p or q). 52.

sentence, conditional. A conditional sentence is a sentence that asserts that if one situation obtains (called the *condition* or the *antecedent*), then another situation also obtains (called the *result*, or the *consequent*). A conditional sententce is also called a *conditional*. In regular English, conditional sentences can take a wide variety of forms, but in Propositional Logic they take the standard form: "if condition then result." A conditional sentence is always represented with the condition listed on the left-hand side. For example, "If Liz goes to at the party, then George will be happy" (if p then q). 55.

sentence, conjunctive. A conjunctive sentence is a sentence that makes a *double assertion*. Such a sentence is formed by applying a conjunctive operator to the two sentences being asserted. A conjunctive sentence is also called a *conjunction*, and the two component sentences are called the *conjuncts* of the conjunction. In regular English there are many different conjunctive operator expressions. In Propositional Logic these are all represented by the one operator "and," and the latter is always placed between the two sentences being asserted. For example, "Dogs bark, and cats meow" (p and q). 54.

sentence, disjunctive. A disjunctive sentence is a sentence that asserts two *alternatives* (choices). Such a sentence is formed by applying a disjunctive operator to the two sentences at issue. A disjunctive sentence is also called a *disjunction*, and the two component sentences are called the *disjuncts* of the disjunction. In regular English there are several different disjunctive operator expressions. In Propositional Logic these are all represented by the one operator "or," and the latter is always placed between the two sentences being asserted. For example, "Dogs bark, or cats meow" (p or q). 54.

sentence, elementary. The smallest grammatical sentence structure by which other sentence structures are generated. This notion is relative to the level of logic being studied. In Propositional

Logic an elementary sentence is a simple sentence, in Traditional Logic it is a categorical sentence, and in Quantificational Logic it is a singular sentence (but not a quantified sentence). 52, 150, 222.

sentence, negative. A negative sentence is a sentence that is the explicit *denial* of another sentence. Such a sentence is formed by applying a negative operator to the sentence that is being denied. In regular English there are many different negative operator expressions. In Propositional Logic these are all represented by the one operator "not" that is always placed in front of the sentence being denied. For example, "Not the Sun will shine tomorrow" (not p). 54.

sentence, operator. A sentential operator is a grammatical operator that is applied to *sentences* to form more complex *sentences*. These are divided into the following types: the negative operator "not," the conjunctive operator "and," the disjunctive operator "or," and the conditional operator "if." Additional sentential operators may also be studied in Propositional Logic, such as the *modal* operators "necessary" and "possible." Sentential operators are also called *connectives*. 53.

sentence, quantified, absolute. A classification of a sentence with respect to its English grammatical structure. This English structure is: *quantifier* + *subject* + *predicate*, where the *quantifier* is one of the words "all," "some," "no," and where the *subject* is the *one* word "things." For example, "all *things* are eternal mental stuff," "some *things* can fly." Absolute sentences have a subject *range* that is the entire universe and have a mandatory symbolization of "$(\forall x)Px$," "$(\exists x)Px$," or "$(\forall x)\sim Px$," where "Px" is the symbolization of whatever was the original English *predicate*. Note that "nothing" becomes "$(\forall x)\sim$." 225.

sentence, quantified, categorical. A classification of a sentence with respect to its English grammatical structure. This English structure is: *quantifier* + *subject* + *predicate*, where the *quantifier* is one of the words "all," "some," "no," and where the *subject* is an expression that is *not* the word "things." For example, "All *spirits* are eternal," "some *old cars* are expensive." Categorical sentences have a subject *range* that is some smaller subset of the entire universe, and they have a required symbolization "$(\forall x)(Sx \supset Px)$," "$(\exists x) (Sx \ \& \ Px)$," or "$(\forall x)(Sx \supset \sim Px)$," where "Sx" and "Px" are the symbolizations of whatever are the original English *subject* and *predicate*. 225.

sentence, quantified, instance of. An instance with respect to the name *a* of a quantified sentence is the result of deleting the quantifier of the sentence and at the same time replacing all the occurrences of the individual variable in question throughout the sentence by occurrences of the selected name *a*. For example, an instance of the quantified sentence "$(\forall x)[(Fx \ \& \ Gx) \lor \sim Sx]$" to the name "g" is: "$[(Fg \ \& \ Gg) \lor \sim Sg]$." 241, 247.

sentence, relational. A sentence containing a relational predicate that relates individual things that are referred to explicitly by name or indefinitely by quantifiers, for example, "something hit George," $(\exists x)(xHg)$. 266.

sentence, singular (name sentence). A simple singular sentence is a sentence consisting of a simple predicate term applied to a singular term. Singular sentences therefore never contain any quantifiers. For example, "George is smart" is symbolized as "Sg." The compound sentence "George is a smart person," or "Sg & Pg," is a conjunction of two simple singular sentences. 225.

sentence, simple. A simple sentence is a sentence that is not grammatically constructed out of other sentences by means of sentential operators. For example, "Some people walked on the Moon." 52.

singular terms, proper names. A singular term is a word or expression that represents (or purports to represent) exactly *one* thing. All *proper names* are singular terms. For example, "Abraham Lincoln," "Chicago," "the Earth," "the Statue of Liberty," "God," "5," "the Solar System," etc. Traditional treatments of Traditional Logic do not include singular terms, with the result that many arguments about specific individuals cannot be properly evaluated. When Traditional Logic is *augmented* to included singular terms in its grammar and deduction method, this deficiency is rectified. 201, 217, 279.

singular categorical sentence. An additional sentence type that can be added to the grammar of Traditional Logic, having the form: **n** is **S**, where **n** is a singular term. For example, "The Moon is a non-planet." 201.

singular universal syllogism. An additional rule that can be added to the deduction method of Traditional Logic, having the form: **Sing Univ Syll**. all **S** are **P**. **n** is **S**. So, **n** is **P**, where **n** is a singular term. "All planets are sun-orbiters. Earth is a planet. So, Earth is a sun-orbiter." 202.

singular particular syllogism. An additional rule that can be added to the deduction method of Traditional Logic, having the form: **Part.Univ.Syll**. **n** is **S**. **n** is **P**. So, some **S** is **P**, where **n** is a singular term. "Earth is a planet. Earth is with life. So, some planet is with life." 202.

square of opposition. When the four main types of categorical sentences are arranged as a square, some important logical relationships are displayed, namely, that *opposite* corners are *negation opposites*, that is, contradictory sentences. (Left upper corner: all **S** are **P**; right upper corner: no **S** are **P**; left lower corner: some **S** are **P**; right lower corner: some **S** are non-**P**.) Now known as the *Quantifier-Negation Laws*. 188.

statements. A statement is a sentence that is *true or false*. This rules out questions, commands, and interjections of feelings. For example, the sentence "The earth is round" is a (true) statement, and the sentence "Bill Clinton ate an elephant for breakfast today" is a (false) statement. The truth or falsity of such simple, basic statements is determined by the situation of *the real world*. In ordinary logic one considers only sentences that are statements, and so, in ordinary logic the terms "sentence" and "statement" are used interchangeably. 10.

subject term. See: term. 150.

sufficient conditions. See: conditions. 71–73.

syllogism. "Syllogism" means "argument" in Greek. Hence, this term is used for a number of argument patterns in Propositional Logic ("hypothetical syllogism," "disjunctive syllogism") "conjunctive syllogism," and is regularly used in Traditional Logic. 195.

syllogism, categorical. A type of argument important in Traditional Logic. A categorical syllogism is an argument with two premises and a conclusion. All the sentences are categorical sentences, and have a total of three terms, each of which is used (twice) in two different sentences. For example, "Some persons are singers. All singers are musicians. So, some persons are musicians." 195.

syllogism, extended, sorites. When syllogisms (consisting of only categorical sentences) have more than two premises, they have more than a total of three terms. Such syllogisms, when they are valid, can be demonstrated to be valid by treating them as a linked series of valid categorical syllogisms. Such extended syllogisms are also called *sorites* (so-ri'-tes). For example, "Some A are B. All B are C. All C are D. All D are E. No E are F. So, some A are (not F)." 193.

tautology. See: logical truth. 95.

term, general term. A general term is a word or group of words that represents some *group of things* in the universe. If the term occurs on the "subject side" of a categorical sentence, then it is also called the *subject term* of that sentence, and if it occurs on the "predicate side," it is called the *predicate term*. Examples of terms are: "person," "book," "smart cat," "wild dancer," "watcher of the sky." Affirmative terms are represented by capital letters A, B, C, etc. 150.

term, negative. For every *affirmative* term that represents one group of things, there is another corresponding *negative term* that represents the group of things that is the *rest* of the universe. Negative terms are constructed by attaching the negative operator "non-" to the affirmative term.

Examples of negative terms are: "non-person," "non-book," "non-smart-cat" (non-P, non-B, non-S). 152.

term, two combined subjects. An English sentence whose subject is a *combination* must be restated as two separate sentences with separate subjects. For example, "Dogs and cats have tails" must be restated as the conjunction "All dogs have tails; and all cats have tails." (all D are T) & (all C are T). 163.

Traditional Logic (Aristotelian Logic). Traditional Logic is the study of certain simple sentences, called *categorical sentences*, together with certain kinds of arguments involving them, called *categorical syllogisms*. E.g, "Some pets are lizards. No lizards are warmblooded. So, some pets are not warmblooded," is a valid categorical syllogism, and is represented as "some P are L, no L are W. So, some P are (not W)." Traditional Logic is also known as *Aristotelian Logic, Syllogistic Logic*, and *The Logic of Terms*. From a modern perspective, Traditional Logic may be considered to be a more comprehensive system that also includes the laws of Propositional Logic. 149.

Traditional Logic, augmented. The system that results when *singular* categorical sentences ("Earth is a planet") are added to the grammar and deduction method of Traditional Logic. 203.

truth, apriori. A sentence is an apriori truth, if the sentence is true in every *imaginable* circumstance. Such sentences do not depend for their truth on any observations of sensory experience, and hence are said to be knowable "prior to" experience. 31.

truth, correspondence theory of. The correspondence theory of truth is the view that the *truth-value* of simple, basic sentences is determined solely by the situation of the real world. The truth-value of complex sentences then depends in a *functional* way on the *truth-value* of the relevant simple, basic sentences. [We restrict the real world correspondence to just basic sentences, since it is not correct to say that *grammatical* complexity, such as "if. . .then," or "either. . .or," or "not," somehow has a correspondence with the real world.] Thus, "The Earth is round" is **T**, because that sentence corresponds to the real world, and "The Moon is a cube" is **F**, because that sentence does not correspond to the real world. Based on those values, the sentence "*Some* thing is round, *and* The Moon is *not* a cube" acquires the value T. 11.

truth, definitional. A sentence is a definitional truth if the sentence is true in virtue of the definitions of the words in the sentence. For example, "All equilateral triangles have three equal sides." Since nothing here depends on specific conditions of the real world, a definitional truth will be true in every logically possible (imaginable) circumstance, and hence, necessarily true. 31.

truth, known. A sentence is *known* to be true, if (1) it is *accepted* or *believed* to be true, (2) this belief is based on *adequate evidence*, and (3) the sentence is also *in fact true*. For example, "The Earth is many millions of years old" is a known truth. 36–38, 81.

truth, necessary. A sentence is necessarily true, if the sentence is true in every logically possible (imaginable) circumstance, including the real world. Necessary truths consist of mathematical truths, truths of logic, and definitional truths [and some other special truths known as synthetic apriori truths]. 31.

truth, of logic. A sentence is a truth of logic, if the sentence is true in virtue of the logical form of the sentence. For example, "It rains, or it doesn't." Since nothing here depends on specific conditions of the real world, a truth of logic will be true in every logically possible (imaginable) circumstance, and hence, necessarily true. 31, 95, 142.

truth, of mathematics. A sentence is a truth of mathematics, if the sentence is true in virtue of the mathematical relationships expressed in the sentence. For example, "3 is greater than 1+1." Since nothing here depends on specific conditions of the real world, a truth of mathematics will be true in every logically possible (imaginable) circumstance, and hence, necessarily true. 31.

truth, possible. A sentence is possibly true, if the sentence is true in at least one logically possible (imaginable) circumstance. [The real world also counts as one logically possible (imaginable) circumstance.] Thus, possible truths are ones that are not necessary falsehoods. For example, "Some horses can fly." 28–30.

truth-functional consistency and inconsistency. A set of sentences is *truth-functionally inconsistent* if there is *no* possible assignment of truth-values **T** and **F** to all the simple components of all these sentences that makes all these sentences have the resultant value **T** together. The set is *truth-functionally consistent* if there is such an assignment of values that makes all these sentences have the resultant value **T** together. For example, the three sentences "If cats sing, then dogs sing; Cats don't sing; Dogs do sing" form a truth-functionally consistent set. 99, 145.

truth-functional equivalence. Two sentences are *truth-functionally equivalent* if for every possible assignment of truth-values **T** and **F** to all the simple components of the two sentences, the resultant value of the one sentence is *always the same as* the resultant value of the other sentence. For example, the sentence "Not both dogs sing and cats sing" is truth-functionally equivalent to the sentence "Either not dogs do sing or not cats do sing" (not both p and q; either not p or not q). 93, 145.

truth-functional implication. Some sentences (one or more) together truth-functionally *imply* another sentence if the corresponding inference from those sentences to that other sentence is a truth-functionally valid argument. 85, 145.

truth-functional logical falsehood (contradiction). A sentence is a *truth-functional logical falsehood* if for every possible assignment of truth-values **T** and **F** to all the simple components of that sentence, that sentence *always* has the resultant value **F**. A truth-functional logical falsehood is also called a truth-functional *contradiction*. For example, "If cats sing, then dogs sing; but cats sing and dogs don't." (if p then q; and p and not q). 96, 145.

truth-functional logical truth (tautology). A sentence is a *truth-functional tautology* if for every possible assignment of truth-values **T** and **F** to all the simple components of that sentence, that sentence *always* has the resultant value **T**. A truth-functional logical truth is also called a truth-functional *tautology*. Example, "If both dogs and cats sing then dogs sing" (if p and q then p). 95, 145.

truth-functional validity. An argument is *truth-functionally valid* if for every possible assignment of truth-values **T** and **F** to all the simple components of all the sentences of the argument, it is *never* the case that all the premises have the resultant value **T** while the conclusion has the resultant value **F**. 85, 145.

truth-table for a group of sentences. A truth-table for a group of sentences is a table with columns and rows that lists the resultant truth-values of the given sentences for each of the possible combinations of truth-values to the simple sentences out of which the given sentences are constructed. The vertical columns are headed by the given sentences, and each of the horizontal rows begins with one of the possible combinations of truth-values to the simple components. Auxiliary columns are introduced to contain the intermediate resultant values of the subparts leading up to the resultant values of the given sentences. This kind of tabular display permits one to investigate the logical characteristics of the given sentences by an examination of their possible truth-value behavior. 86–90.

truth-values. In logic, one refers to sentences *being true*, or *being false*, as sentences *having the truth-value* true (**T**), or *having the truth-value* false (**F**). 10–11.

truth-value conditions, rules for calculating truth-values. There are specific *rules*(with no exceptions) for calculating the truth-value of negations, conjunctions, disjunctions, conditionals, and biconditionals, based on the truth-values of their component sentences. For example, "Some dogs sing, or some cats sing" is false, because "Some dogs sing" is false, and "Some cats sing" is false. 82.

validity, semantical version. An argument is *valid* in the semantical sense if for every possible *interpretation* of all the basic components of all the sentences of the argument, it is *never* the case that all the premises have the resultant value **T** while the conclusion has the resultant value **F**. [Semantical validity is the formal version of the conceptual criterion of validity. Truth-functionally valid arguments form a smaller subgroup within the group of (semantically) valid arguments.] 85.

variable, bound. A *bound* occurrence of a variable is one that occurs within the scope of a matching quantifier. For example, all occurrences of the variable x in the sentence "$(\exists x)(Px\ \&\ Ex)\ \vee\ (\exists x)[(\sim Px\ \&\ Ex)\ \vee\ \sim Ex]$" are bound by a matching quantifier. Also see: free variable. 222–223.

variable, free. A *free* occurrence of a variable is one that does not occur within the scope of a matching quantifier. For example, "$[(\exists x)(Px\ \&\ \sim Ex)]\ \vee\ Mx$" has the last occurrence of the variable x as free, because the brackets around the left-hand side of the expression force the scope to end with "$\sim Ex$." This expression is *nonsense* from both a formal and an application point of view, since a free variable has *no reference* whatsoever. By moving the brackets, the expression becomes a meaningful assertion, "$(\exists x)[(Px\ \&\ \sim Ex)\ \vee\ Mx]$." The brackets may be *dropped* altogether under a *special convention*, namely, that the scope extends at least as far as the last occurrence of the variable at issue, "$(\exists x)\ (Px\ \&\ \sim Ex)\ \vee\ Mx$." Under such a convention, all three occurrences of the variable x are *bound* by the quantifier, but such a convention requires further conditions for more complicated cases. 222–223.

variable, individual. An individual variable functions in logic in the way that a *pronoun* functions in English: it *continues* a reference to a previously introduced subject. In logic, an individual variable refers back only to a subject that was introduced by a *quantifier*, and subjects introduced by a proper name continue to be referenced only by that proper name. Individual variables are represented by the three lower-case letters x, y, z, and if additional variables are needed by u, v, w as well. For example, "Something is mental, and it is eternal" is represented as "for some thing x, x is mental and x is eternal," and is symbolized as "$(\exists x)(Mx\ \&\ Ex)$." 219, 222.

universe of discourse, domain of discouse. The Universe (of discourse) is the set of everything that is real, everything that exists in the world. The Universe thus includes many things, including physical things and non-physical things (mental, or spiritual, or abstract). Logic presupposes that there is a Universe of discourse, but logic per se is indifferent as to what is actually real. 217, 220.

SYMBOLS AND ABBREVIATIONS

Chapter 2. Propositional Logic

A, B, C, . . .	Capital letters symbolize concrete English simple sentences.	
p, q, r, s	These lower case letters are variables that represent all sentences.	
~	Sentence negation operator.	"~p" means "not p."
&	Sentence conjunction operator.	"p & q" means "p and q."
∨	Sentence disjunction operator.	"p ∨ q" means "p or q."
⊃	Sentence implication operator.	"p ⊃ q" means "if p then q."
≡	Sentence equivalence operator.	"p ≡ q" means "p if and only if q."
∴	Argument inference operator.	"p, q ∴ r" means "p, q, so, r."
( ), [ ], { }	Parentheses, brackets, braces group complex items into units.	
T, F	Truth-values of sentences: true, false.	

Chapter 3. Traditional Logic

A, B, C, . . .	Capital letters symbolize general terms representing sets of things.
non-A, . . .	Negative general terms, "non-apple," "non-bottle," etc.
(not A), . . .	Alternative notation for negative terms.
all, some, no	Quantifiers, with terms and copula generate categorical sentences.
are	Copula, English negative copulas become negative general terms.
a, b, c, . . ., w	Lower case letters symbolize proper names of single objects.
is	Singular copula, used only with proper names.

Chapter 4. Modern Quantificational Logic

a, b, c, . . ., w	Lower case letters symbolize proper names of single objects.
x, y, z	Variables, refer to unspecifed objects introduced by a quantifier.

Ax, Bx, Cx,. . .	Capital letters symbolize characteristics of things.
$(\forall x),(\forall y),(\forall z)$	Universal quantifiers, symbolize "for all things x,. . .," etc.
$(\exists x),(\exists y),(\exists z)$	Existential quantifiers, symbolize "for some things x,. . .," etc.

Chapter 4. Advanced Topics: Relations and Identity

xAy, xBy, . . .	Capital letters symbolize relations between things.
$x = y$	The equal sign symbolizes the relation "x is the same thing as y."

Abbreviations of Rule Names

Assoc	Association
Bicond	Bicondition
Comm	Commutation
CP	Conditional Proof
Cond	Conditional Relation
Conj	Conjunction
Contrap	Contraposition
Conv	Conversion
DeMorg	De Morgan's Laws
Dilem	Dilemma
DP	Direct Proof
Disj Add	Disjunctive Addition (Add)
Disj Syll	Disjunctive Syllogism (DS)
Dist	Distribution
Dbl Ifs	Double Ifs (Exportation, Exp)
Dbl Neg	Double Negation (DN)
Dbl Thens	Double Thens
Dupl	Duplication
EG	Existential Generalization
EI	Existential Instantiation
Hyp Syll	Hypothetical Syllogism (HS)
Ident	Identity Laws
IP	Indirect Proof
MP	Modus Ponens
MT	Modus Tollens
Name-Neg	Name Negation Law
Part Syll	Particular Syllogism
Pred-DN	Predicate Double Negation
QN	Quantifier Negation
RAA	Reductio Ad Absurdum

Simp	Simplication
Sing Part Syll	Singular Particular Syllogism
Sing Univ Syll	Singular Universal Syllogism
Sup Part Syll	Super Particular Syllogism
Sup Univ Syll	Super Universal Syllogism
Taut	Tautology
UG	Universal Generalization
UI	Universal Instantiation
Univ Syll	Universal Syllogism